Treasures of the World's Religions
Series

World Wisdom
The Library of Perennial Philosophy

The Library of Perennial Philosophy is dedicated to the exposition of the timeless Truth underlying the diverse religions. This Truth, often referred to as the *Sophia Perennis*—or Perennial Wisdom—finds its expression in the revealed Scriptures as well as the writings of the great sages and the artistic creations of the traditional worlds.

The Perennial Philosophy provides the intellectual principles capable of explaining both the formal contradictions and the transcendent unity of the great religions.

Ranging from the writings of the great sages of the past, to the perennialist authors of our time, each series of our Library has a different focus. As a whole, they express the inner unanimity, transforming radiance, and irreplaceable values of the great spiritual traditions.

The Golden Chain: An Anthology of Pythagorean and Platonic Philosophy appears as one of our selections in the Treasures of the World's Religions series.

Treasures of the World's Religions series

This series of anthologies presents scriptures and the writings of the great spiritual authorities of the past on fundamental themes. Some titles are devoted to a single spiritual tradition, while others have a unifying topic that touches upon tradition from both the East and West, such as prayer and virtue. Some titles have a companion volume within the Perennial Philosophy series.

Cover: The Acropolis, Athens

The Golden Chain
An Anthology of Pythagorean and Platonic Philosophy

Selected and edited by
Algis Uždavinys

Foreword by
John F. Finamore

World Wisdom

Library of Congress Cataloging-in-Publication Data

The golden chain : an anthology of Pythagorean and Platonic philosophy /
selected and edited by Algis Uždavinys ; foreword by John F. Finamore.
    p. cm. – (Treasures of the world's religions)
Includes bibliographical references and index.
ISBN 0-941532-61-5 (pbk. : alk. paper)
1. Philosophy, Ancient. I. Uždavinys, Algis. II. Series.
B171.G65 2004
182'.2–dc22

                                                                    2004018009

Printed on acid-free paper in Canada

For information address World Wisdom, Inc.
P.O. Box 2682, Bloomington, Indiana 47402-2682

www.worldwisdom.com

Table of Contents

FOREWORD

Plato compares philosophy with preparing for death (*Phaedo* 67cd) and its goal with becoming like god (*Theaetetus* 176b). This view of philosophy implies two doctrines central to the Platonic tradition: the immortality of the soul and the community (*koinonia*) of the human and divine. These ideas were not new with Plato nor did they die with him. It is the nature of the philosophical endeavor to borrow and transform the ideas of others and to pass these ideas on for others to use and adapt. Plato is arguably the single most important ancient Greek thinker, although his strength lies not merely in his innovation but also, and perhaps especially, in his critical understanding of the philosophical tradition.

The Golden Chain provides important texts in the history of Platonism. It begins, perhaps startlingly but certainly correctly, with excerpts about Pythagoras, moves through the Pythagorean tradition, then comes to Plato himself, and continues with excerpts from the major Neoplatonist writers. What unfolds is an evolution of a philosophy, a Platonic philosophy, one that starts before Plato is born and continues to grow after his death—and indeed well beyond the times and writings of the pagan Neoplatonists presented here.

We do not know much about Pythagoras. Given his fame and large numbers of followers, that may seem strange. We know of multiple biographies of him (four of which are excerpted in Part I, below), but they are all late and suspect. As is the case with all famous individuals, the history of Pythagoras took on a life of its own. Stories of miracles, of divine genealogy, and of superhuman wisdom became associated with the philosopher. Making the matter murkier, others began writing treatises under his name. (See the works collected in Part II, below.) It is therefore very difficult to separate truth from fiction, Pythagoras' doctrine from later additions.

This wealth of information, however, is not so troubling. All philosophy evolves over time, but there are kernels of original doctrines present. We may not know precisely what Pythagoras taught his students, but we can be sure that his teachings included the soul's immortality, the cycle of birth, and the existence and beneficence of the gods.

Plato traveled to Sicily and southern Italy and studied with Pythagoreans. He had already imbibed philosophy from Socrates and was devoting himself to the major ethical questions to which Socrates had introduced him. We do not know what impelled Plato to study with Pythagoreans, but we can certainly make some educated guesses. Plato was concerned with ethics and politics, to be sure, but also with their relation to the human life, to the soul. His own beliefs in immortality and perhaps already in transmigration would have been piqued by what he had read and heard about Pythagorean philosophy. Philosophers are by nature curious and eager to learn. Plato would have been no different.

The later Pythagoreans and the later Platonists ("Neopythagoreans," "Middle Platonists," and "Neoplatonists," we call them) came to believe that Plato was a Pythagorean. We need not be so naïve. Plato studied Pythagorean texts and held discussions with Pythagorean philosophers, but he was far too independent a thinker to adopt their philosophy wholesale. He was clearly taken with their ideas of the soul's immortality, for example, but his initial beliefs certainly pre-dated his encounter with Pythagoreans. Their doctrines shaped his to some degree, but he also would have reworked theirs to fit his own grand view. Here I am thinking especially of Plato's evolving doctrine of the Forms, which is certainly not Pythagorean but was probably fine-tuned in accordance with their doctrines of rebirth. Moreover, I would argue that their doctrine of transmigration is not the same as Plato's. The Platonic version stresses philosophical wisdom in a way that I see as foreign to the more religious thinking of the Pythagoreans. For Plato it is the rational soul that serves the individual in the time between its taking on human bodies. In the Myth of Er, it is the soul's philosophical aptitude that allows it to make a wise choice of life. In the *Phaedrus*, it is the rational part of the soul that makes possible a clear vision of the Forms and an eventual escape from the cycle of rebirth. We thus see Plato adopting and adapting the Pythagorean doctrines and fitting them into his own larger philosophical structure.

The Middle Platonists and Neoplatonists continued to expand Plato's philosophy. (See Part IV, below.) The crucial thinker in this ever-evolving melting pot of Platonism is Iamblichus, who lived during a time of major crisis in ancient philosophy. The world was changing. Christianity was coming to the fore, presenting what to pagan philosophers seemed like new and impious doctrines. (Porphyry, an older contemporary of Iamblichus, wrote a detailed attack of the new religion. Christian religious authorities deemed it so dangerous that it was publicly burned in later years and exists now only in fragments.) Iamblichus presented a unified theory of paganism. He not only saw Plato as a Pythagorean, but he saw both philosophers (and indeed all pagan Greek philosophers, with the exception of the materialists) as part of a continuing source of true knowledge. His unified theory included not only Greek philosophers and poets, but also Egyptians, Chaldeans, and other non-Greek pagans. All were teaching the same Truth, which the upstart Christians had abandoned.

The later pagan Neoplatonists (Hierocles, Proclus, Damascius, and others) embraced Iamblichus' vision, while of course tinkering with some of his philosophical doctrines. (Philosophers cannot help themselves from making such revisions.) Whether or not Iamblichus ever used the phrase, it is certain that Proclus adapted the Homeric "Golden Chain" to the Neoplatonic heritage of wisdom. Platonism now stood in the proper relation to thousands of years of human thought. It was part of the Golden Chain of knowledge, ultimately secured from the highest realms of the universe, from the gods and the One itself. Pythagoras, Plato, and the ancients had tapped this source of wisdom, kept it alive, and passed it on to the Neoplatonists, who continued to keep the flame of truth burning.

John F. Finamore
University of Iowa

INTRODUCTION

The present anthology of the Pythagorean and Platonic tradition disagrees in certain important respects with the modern understanding of philosophy in general and of Platonism and Pythagoreanism in particular. Following the valuable insights of Pierre Hadot (supported by the witness of countless traditional sages throughout the world) we regard ancient philosophy as essentially a way of life: not only inseparable from "spiritual exercises," but also in perfect accord with cosmogonical myths and sacred rites. In the broader traditional sense, philosophy consists not simply of a conceptual edifice (be it of the order of reason or myth), but of a lived concrete existence conducted by initiates, or by the whole theocentric community, treated as a properly organized and well-guided political and theurgical "body" attended to the principle of *maat*—"truth" and "justice" in the ancient Egyptian sense of the word.

In Plato's definition of philosophy as a training for death (*Phaedo* 67cd) an implicit distinction was made between philosophy and philosophical discourse. Modern Western philosophy (a rather monstrous and corrupted creature, initially shaped by late Christian theology and post-Descartesian logic) has been systematically reduced to a philosophical discourse of a single dogmatic kind, through the fatal one-sidedness of its professed secular humanistic mentality, and a crucial misunderstanding of traditional wisdom. The task of the ancient philosophers was in fact to contemplate the cosmic order and its beauty; to live in harmony with it and to transcend the limitations imposed by sense experience and discursive reasoning. In a word, it was through philosophy (understood as a kind of *askesis*) that the cultivation of the natural, ethical, civic, purificatory, theoretic, paradigmatic, and hieratic virtues (*aretai*) were to be practiced; and it was through this noetic vision (*noesis*) that the ancient philosophers tried to awaken the divine light within, and to touch the divine Intellect in the cosmos. For them, to reach *apotheosis* was the ultimate human end (*telos*). Christos Evangeliou correctly observes that, "Neither Aristotle nor any other Platonic, or genuinely Hellenic philosopher, would have approved of what the modern European man, in his greedy desire for profit, and demonic will to power, has made out of Hellenic *philosophia.*"[1]

The purpose of our highly selective anthology is to glimpse the Pythagorean and Platonic tradition from the traditional Hellenic and especially Neoplatonic perspective. However, one ought to remember that the term "Neoplatonism" itself was an artificial invention of the 18th century Protestant scholars and preachers of the Enlightenment era, who rejected the claim that Plato's philosophy was propounded in unwritten doctrines and oral teachings, and the "Neoplatonic presumption" of harmony between Plato and Aristotle. These founders of modern philosophical hermeneutics pretended to understand Plato better than the latter understood himself. Looking down upon Plato, Plotinus, and Proclus from the tower of their so-called "Enlightenment," they claimed to have discovered "the real Plato"—one who had to be thoroughly cleansed from the filth of Neoplatonic interpretations. Thus, Neoplatonism was pictured as the root and source of all evils. This highly prejudiced opinion prevailed as unquestioned dogma despite the heroic resistance of such Platonic scholars as Thomas Taylor, and is still prevalent among the contemporary "priests" of current scientistic ideologies. According to the narrow Protestant mentality of the 19th century, and even that of modern secular scholarship, the ancient Hellenic Neoplatonists were madmen, liars and foolish forgers, who preferred illusions and imaginations to sound reason. They were regarded as "men inflated by metaphysical dreams, who always opposed Plato to Christ," trying "to find a new way of impeding the progress of Christianity."[2] It is little wonder, then, that in reading certain texts of classical scholarship (even those that are quite sympathetic), and thereafter proceeding to the ancient authors themselves, one cannot escape an impression of hearing two different stories and following two different paths that never really meet, despite certain appearances to the contrary.

The essential aspect of the ancient philosophical tradition was its oral transmission and living praxis. Theory, therefore, was never

1. Christos C. Evangeliou, *The Hellenic Philosophy: Between Europe, Asia, and Africa* (New York: Binghamton University, 1997), p.71.
2. E.N. Tigerstedt, *The Decline and Fall of the Neoplatonic Interpretation of Plato* (Helsinki: Societas Scientiarum Fennica, 1974), p.55.

regarded as an end in itself, but was put in the service of practice, often understood in terms of an "alchemical" transformation and an elevation of the soul through the rites of purification and the cultivation of the virtues. In most cases this cultivation was so all-encompassing as to make the philosopher—as a "lover of wisdom"—strange to the world of mortals and close to the immortal gods, or archetypal principles (*archai*) of cosmic manifestation. Since putting oneself in accord with the divine principles allowed one to experience the eternal irradiation of the Good, Platonic and Neoplatonic philosophy was not simply a discourse about the gods and the world, but an anagogic path leading the soul to a concrete union with the divine Intellect and the ineffable One. All complementary sciences and arts served as the direct or indirect means to this goal and provided meaningful symbols and icons for contemplation. In a sense, there was a lived logic, a lived hermeneutics, physics, and ethics. Hence, as Pierre Hadot has pointed out, the practice of philosophy did not ultimately consist in "producing the theory of logic, that is the theory of speaking well and thinking well, nor in producing the theory of physics, that is of the cosmos, nor in producing the theory of acting well, but it concerned actually speaking well, thinking well, acting well, being truly conscious of one's place in the cosmos."[3]

Most narrow-minded modernists—for whom philosophy as such is tantamount to an abstract philosophical discourse based on the rationalistic scientific method and its methodically obtained "truths"—believe that Thales of Miletus must have been the first to use a rational method to investigate the interrelationship of visible things and their inner causes. In a highly presumptuous and uncritical manner, they assert that Thales made a deliberate break with the mythology of the past and was seeking a new, rational account of the cosmos. They therefore installed him as the founder of *philosophia* as such and pictured him as a distant forerunner of modern Western thought, without, however, presenting any evident and reliable support for this view. As S.H. Nasr has remarked:

---

3. Pierre Hadot, *Philosophy as a Way of Life: Spiritual Exercises from Socrates to Foucault*, ed. with an intro. by Arnold I. Davidson (Oxford and Cambridge, Mass.: Blackwell, 1995), p.24.

The perspective within which the origin of modern philosophy is conceived and the choice of which philosophers to include and which to exclude in the account of the history of philosophy all reflect a particular "ideology" and conception of philosophy and are related to modern man's view of himself.[4]

In this respect the Safavid Persian *hakim*s were perhaps closer to the truth when they identified the water of Thales with the Breath of the Compassionate (*nafas al-Rahman*) of the Sufis, and considered the so-called Presocratic philosophers to have used a symbolic language in order to reveal the unity of Being. Indeed, "when one reads the Presocratics with an open mind and sensitive ear, one cannot help being struck by the religious note in much of what they say. Few words occur more frequently in their fragments than the term 'god.'"[5] To conventionally assume that Thales simply opposed myth to "rational account" (*logos*) is to misunderstand the Greek word *logos* and follow the modern reductionist tendency to render it exclusively as "reason" or "discursive reasoning" (*dianoia*). But even Plato himself, who finally recognized that the only thing worth being serious about was God, made no clear distinction between attitude to myth and philosophical reasoning. If practiced with real wisdom, he maintained, both myth-telling and dialectic could lead towards truth; but otherwise they would misguide. Since the ultimate God was beyond human speech, "Plato repeatedly tends to set up the two apparently opposing categories of myth and logic only to end up merging and demolishing them."[6] But the Greek word *logos* can also mean divine speech (the demiurgic word of Ra rendered into operative wisdom by Thoth, to use the Egyptian theological terms) as well as noetic apprehension of the first indemonstrable and sacred principles, archetypes, or gods (Gr. *Theoi*; Eg. *neteru*), which are transcendent and immanent at the same time. In addition, *logos* can mean analogy and proportion.

4. Zailan Moris, "The Essential Relation between Revelation and Philosophy in Islam and its Importance in Understanding the Nature and History of Islamic Philosophy" in *The Philosophy of Seyyed Hossein Nasr*, ed. Lewis Edwin Hahn, Randall E. Auxier, and Lucian W. Stone, Jr. (Chicago and La Salle: Open Court, 2001), p.634.

5. Gregory Vlastos, "Theology and Philosophy in Early Greek Thought" in *Studies in Presocratic Philosophy*, vol. 1, ed. D.J. Furley and R.E. Allen (New York: Humanities Press, 1970), p.92.

6. Peter Kingsley, *Ancient Philosophy, Mystery, and Magic: Empedocles and Pythagorean Tradition* (Oxford: Clarendon Press, 1995), p.166.

Introduction

In the original Orphico-Pythagorean sense, philosophy meant wisdom (*sophia*) and love (*eros*) combined in a moral and intellectual purification in order to reach the "likeness to God" (*homoiosis theo*, [Plato, *Theaet.* 176b]). This likeness was to be attained by *gnosis*, knowledge. The same Greek word *nous* ("intellect," understood in a macrocosmic and microcosmic sense) covers all that is meant both by "spirit" (*spiritus, ruh*) and "intellect" (*intellectus, 'aql*) in the Medieval Christian and Islamic lexicon. Thus Platonic philosophy (and especially Neoplatonism) was a spiritual and contemplative way of life leading to enlightenment; a way which was properly and intrinsically intellectual; a way that was ultimately based on intellection or noetic vision (*noesis*), which transcends the realm of sense perception and discursive reasoning. Through an immediate grasp of first principles, the non-discursive intelligence lead to a union (*henosis*) with the divine Forms. "Knowledge of the gods," says Iamblichus, "is virtue and wisdom and perfect happiness, and makes us like to the gods" (*Protr.* 3). Even for Aristotle, who seems to be a much more earthly-minded rationalist, the highest and eternally active Intellect, or God, as the ultimate metaphysical *telos* of any true philosopher, erotically attracts and harmoniously moves everything in the multi-dimensional cosmos:

> It is the great Beauty with which the entire Cosmos seems to be in Love. It is the Great Light and cause of enlightenment for the mind of the true philosopher in the triple Socratic manifestation: as lover of Hellenic *mousike* (that is, practitioner of the art of poetic rhythm, harmonious sound, and all audibly appreciated beauty); as lover of Hellenic *eidike* (that is, practitioner of the art of visible patterns, symmetrical forms, and all optically appreciated beauty); and as lover of Hellenic *dialektike* (that is, practitioner of the art of logic, ordered form, principled life, rational discourse, intuitive grasp of principles, and noetically appreciated truth).[7]

Of course, Hellenic philosophy in general differed from the earlier traditions of wisdom precisely by its developed set of formal logic and dialectic, along with its abstract technical vocabulary, as well as a new type of rationality of a more or less "scientific" character. But this additional edifice was built on the ancient metaphysical superstructure itself—supported by certain divine revelations, cos-

7. Christos C. Evangeliou, *The Hellenic Philosophy: Between Europe, Asia, and Africa*, p.55.

mogonical myths, and rituals aimed at the establishment of cosmic order and justice, as well as the transformation and elevation of the soul by a restoration of her true identity. By the time of Plato the soul was no longer regarded as the phantom (*eidolon*) of the body. On the contrary, the body had become a simple appearance and transitory image of the soul, which, by reminiscence (*anamnesis*), purification, concentration, separation and philosophical *askesis* was able to restore the memory of her divine abode. Thus, to be a philosopher in this sense was to turn away from the realm of seeming and to transcend the simulacrum-like body, thereby elevating the soul to the intelligible world of the stars. This reawakened soul, regarded as an image of the divine Intellect, is actually the same as the winged Egyptian *ba* which was to be turned into the spiritual light, *akh*, in the same way as Osiris was transformed into Ra. It meant that finally the soul was assimilated to that God who is the All.

In some respects a one-sided philosophical discourse, instead of being a love of wisdom, was indeed turned into the passion for merely speaking *about* wisdom, and in some cases developed into skepticism. However, in most cases the goal of ancient philosophy remained the same. Thus, by "philosophizing" was meant both noetic activity and spiritual practice; and this was attributed not only to various Hellenic philosophers who belonged to different *haireseis* (schools or theoretically founded ways of life), but also to the Egyptian priests, Chaldeans, and Indian Gymnosophists. As to the sources of truth and wisdom, many *haireseis* and traditions were agreed in tracing their origins back to the gods themselves.

According to Isocrates, the Egyptians, who were famous for their piety and practical wisdom (*eusebeia kai phronesis*), introduced for the soul the practice (*askesis*) of philosophy as a means to strengthen the laws and to investigate the nature of the cosmos. Pythagoras was the first to have brought to Hellas the philosophy of the Egyptians (*Busiris* 21–22). Parmenides, Plato, and Aristotle developed theories of the world in the light of the distinctions between opinion (*doxa*) and knowledge (*episteme*), which repeat the distinction between the outer surface of myths, rites, and statues, and their inner meaning—the shining power of spiritual archetypes, *akhu*—revealed by the anagogical hermeneutics practiced already by the Egyptian priests of the 18th dynasty (1551–1292 B.C.E.) and earlier.

Both Plato and Aristotle traced the origin of philosophy to wonder; by "philosophy" they meant the contemplation (*theoria*) of the manifested cosmic order, or of the truth and beauty of the divine principles (be they visible stars or invisible noetic archetypes). Therefore Aristotle asserts:

> That philosophy is not a science of production is clear even from the history of the earliest philosophers. For it is owing to their wonder that men both now begin and at first began to philosophize .... And a man who is puzzled and wonders thinks himself ignorant (whence even the lover of myth is in a sense a lover of wisdom, for the myth is composed of wonders) (*Metaph.* 982b, 11–19).

But if human wonder is the true origin of philosophy, then Christos Evangeliou is correct in his claim that the beginnings of philosophical speculation go back as far as the appearance of *Anthropos.*[8] In fact, Adam himself was the first prophet, according to the Islamic tradition. To put the matter in other terms: the Egyptian Thoth (regarded as both the Intellect and the creative Word of Ra), or Hermes (who became identified with the mythical prophet Idris, called "the Father of philosophers" [*Abu'l-hukama*]), was the first philosopher in the archetypal sense. This primordial philosophy was originally a form of revealed truth and intellectual hymns sung by those who kept an image of Hermes in their hearts and belonged to the "Hermaic chain" (*Hermaike seira*). This chain symbolized irradiations from the divine Intellect. Thus, the true philosopher was *theios aner*, the divine man, who contemplated the light of the noetic gods and tried to live philosophically, i.e., in accord with the divine wisdom. At the highest grade of philosophy, learning, instruction, and purification came to an end, and the pure vision—analogous to the *epopteia* of the mysteries—was granted to the sage. Finally, he was able to return to his "starry Heaven"—the original inner abode of the unbearable glory reached through recollection and spiritual exercises, including intellectual training (dialectics) and theurgy.

Contrary to the prevalent view of modern historians of science and philosophy, the ancient Hellenes considered themselves to be students of the much older Oriental civilizations. It seems that Plato was substantially indebted to the so-called Orphic tradition (*Orpheos*

8. Christos C. Evangeliou, *The Hellenic Philosophy: Between Europe, Asia, and Africa*, p.105.

paradosis, partly based on Indian and Egyptian influences) and the Pythagorean oral teaching. Though the strong Neoplatonic conviction that the philosophy of Plato was a prolongation of the Orphic theology is disregarded by some modern scholars, Olympiodorus may be partly correct in asserting that "Plato paraphrases Orpheus everywhere" ("*pantachou gar ho Platon paroidei ta Orpheos,*" [Olympiodorus, *In Phaed.* 10.3.13]). To summarize the matter briefly: Platonists believed in a revelation given to the ancient sages and theologians, i.e., to divinely inspired poets and hierophants. This primordial revelation was viewed as unchangeable; there could be nothing "new" regarding metaphysics and divine truths. According to Celsus, Plato never claimed to have discovered anything new. Plotinus, too, plainly rejected the idea that he taught anything new—though changing historical conditions, the personal characteristics of philosophers and their audiences, as well as concrete philosophical problems to be solved, inevitably determined certain logical forms and the style of any particular philosophical discourse. One ought also to remember that the curious figure who since the time of Pythagoras was called a *philosophos* (though the equivalent ancient Egyptian term *mer reh* was already attested) was practically analogous to the figure of the specialized expert in purificatory rites and words of power; this figure was an initiate craftsman, magician, and healer, as well as legislator, poet, and inspired interpreter (*hermeneus*) of divine tokens, signs, and symbols. The *philosophos* wandered across the Mediterranean Sea, Assyria, and Egypt, and their practical wisdom (*sophia* or *hikmah*)— applied at every level of existence—was based on the ancient cosmological, theurgical, medical, and mythological traditions of the Near East. They were true forerunners of the later Pythagorean brotherhoods.

Various branches of the Egyptian *scientia sacra* (including the science of an alchemical transformation and theurgical ascent to the realm of the divine light; a theory of hieratic symbols and hermeneutics; as well as the principles of mathematics, music, medicine and politics) contributed to the purifying of the entire state, regarded as tantamount to the temple; in addition to transforming different levels of the statue-like human being. By establishing cosmic equilibrium and keeping to the truth (*maat*) they led the soul (*ba* and other vital principles) back to the stars, or spiritual archetypes. The same goal of "philosophizing" was attested within the later Hellenic traditions. The schools of Pythagoreanism and Platonism founded the chain of transmission which was partly rooted in ancient Egyptian wisdom. According to Porphyry, such doctrines as that the soul is immortal; that it changes into other kinds of living beings; that all living things are akin; that events recur in certain cycles, Pythagoras imported from the Egyptian and Mesopotamian sources. The Pythagorean number theory and the Platonic theory of Ideas, as well as the Orphic and Socratic conception of the immortal soul, and the image of the philosopher as a semi-divine figure, or as an ideal ruler in the theocratic body-like state, also have their deep Egyptian and Mesopotamian roots.

Due to this ancient metaphysical and cultic legacy, followers of Orpheus, Pythagoras, Empedocles, and Plato regarded their philosophical tradition as a mystery into which one might be initiated. Thus, the mathematician Theon of Smyrna, who belonged to the so-called Middle Platonic period, distinguished five stages of this initiation: (1) purification; (2) communication of the ritual; (3) vision (*epopteia*); (4) "adornment with garlands"; (5) "the joy that comes from unity and converse with the gods." In the context of such philosophical mystagogy, Plato himself can be viewed as a hierophant of the truest rites (*teletai*).

By now it should be clear that the Neoplatonic promotion of theurgy as both the transcendent and immanent background of "philosophizing," and the very summit of philosophy itself, was simply an attempt to revitalize the ancient transformative wisdom ("the Assyrian dogmas," as Proclus was wont to say) against the degenerated form of one-sided rationalism, sentimental hedonism and the Academic skepticism of Arcesilaus and Carneades.

Antiochus of Ascalon broke away from the skeptical tradition, and Numenius of Apamea, the Pythagorean and Middle Platonic forerunner of Plotinus, urged the rediscovery of the sacred paths of Platonism and early Pythagoreanism, which he traced back to the doctrines and rituals of the ancient Near East. Through a Pythagoreanizing allegorical exegesis he tried to reestablish a sort of primordial *philosophia perennis*, regarded as the common wisdom of the Chaldean, Egyptian, Phoenician, Jewish, and Indian sages. The semi-mythical Pythagoras himself, to whom the origin of the Greek term *philosophia* is credited by some traditional Hellenic authors, was eager to build up a great philosophical and scientific synthesis of various ancient metaphysical doctrines, mythical accounts and practices. He undoubtedly used mathematical and astrological materials from Babylonia and practiced an incubation rite related to the esoteric conception of the immortal soul. The Pythagorean table of opposites was close to the Akkadian and Babylonian rules for interpreting auspices and tokens in divination. Even the imagery of Parmenides, who is counted among the fathers of Western philosophy, was rooted in the Assyrian and Babylonian cosmic mythology and related religious cults.

Since the time of Plato, genuine lovers of wisdom and truth considered the tree of the Orphic (Apollonian and Dionysiac) tradition, and Hellenic philosophy in general, to have grown out of Oriental seeds. So, for Porphyry, the famous student of Plotinus, the entire Hellenic philosophy is a relatively modern and in many respects corrupted version of the divinely inspired Egyptian and Chaldean wisdoms. Searching for the universal way of salvation, Porphyry understood that only a few were capable of following the way of philosophy and escaping from the cycle of existences. In thus dismissing philosophy as a universal means of salvation, he looked towards the Chaldean theurgy and Indian *disciplina*, regarding the Indian Gymnosophists (the Brahmans and Samanaeans) as true philosophers concerned with divine wisdom who lived a life of righteousness, with "the whole day and greater part of the night set apart for hymns and prayers to the gods" (*De abst.* IV.16–18). According to such a universalist and perennialist perspective, the teachings of Neoplatonism were not a sort of regrettable innovation (as modern classicists would have it), but the faithful perpetuation of pre-Platonic metaphysics put into a new dress. Plato himself was merely a link (albeit crucial) in the Golden Chain of the Pythagorean, Orphic and different Oriental traditions.

Another crafty fable invented by modern historians of philosophy, along with the label "Neoplatonism," is the artificial division between early (and therefore "true") Pythagoreanism and later (hence "false") Neopythagoreanism, despite the undoubted similarity and underlying continuity between them. But, as Peter Kingsley has pointed out:

> To portray the Platonizing reinterpretation of Pythagoreanism as an aberrant departure from the "true," "pure" pre-Platonic

Pythagoreanism is to overlook the essential fact that—before Plato's time as well—Pythagoreanism was perpetually changing, reformulating itself, consciously adapting to incorporate new developments.[9]

There was no rigidly established "orthodoxy" or official certification in the realm of Platonic tradition, which maintained itself by a process of oral transmission from master to pupil. Thus, philosophers might provide quite different solutions to a common set of problems whilst, nevertheless, belonging to the same Golden Chain. They might, for example, differ on such questions as the basic tenets of cosmology and the creation of the world, or the definition of virtue and the best system of logic; however, all would agree as regards the transcendence of God, the theory of Platonic Ideas, or eternal divine archetypes, and the immortality of the soul, which required that it be purified, elevated and reestablished in its original union (*henosis*) with the divine source.

In the Athenian school of Syrianus and Proclus, the Homeric image of the Golden Chain (*seire chruseie, Iliad* VIII.18), stretching from Heaven to Earth, was used to describe both the unbroken vertical connection with the first principles (noetic sources of the demiurgic descent, as well as paradigms of the revealed wisdom), and the horizontal, or historical, succession of the qualified masters and interpreters—a succession which was not always based exclusively on direct physical relations. In fact, the Golden Chain is the same as the Hermaic Chain. This chain was both the chain of theophany, manifestation, or descent (*demiourgike seira*), and the ladder of ascent. This imagery of the Golden Chain was inseparable from the metaphysics of light and solar symbolism. Socrates also regarded the Homeric Golden Rope as referring to the Sun. It signified that "so long as the Heavens and the Sun continue to move round, all things in Heaven and Earth are kept going, whereas if they were bound down and brought to a stand, all things would be destroyed and the world, as they say, turned upside down" (Plato, *Theaet.* 153c8–d5). Thus, the Emperor Julian's claimed descent from the Sun (Helios) meant his vertical (or inner) relationship with the divine Intellect which was the source of illumination and manifestation of the *logos*, or *logismos*—including the power of reasoning in

9. Peter Kingsley, *Ancient Philosophy, Mystery, and Magic: Empedocles and Pythagorean Tradition*, p.328.

general. According to Marinus' testimony, Proclus was convinced that he belonged to the Hermaic tradition: he believed, following a dream he once had, that he possessed the soul of the Pythagorean philosopher Nichomachus of Gerasa. And so he used to say that the philosopher must be the hierophant of the entire cosmos (*"koine hierophantes tou holou kosmou,"* [*Vita Procli* 19.28]). Marinus also attests that the young Hegias, an attendant of the Athenian school, "showed clear signs from childhood of possessing all the virtues of his ancestors and of belonging to the Golden Chain of philosophers that started with Solon" (*ibid.*, 26).

Since the Golden Age was the Age of Kronos, and the rule of Kronos, as a blissful time, meant the rule of Intellect (*nous*), the Golden Race of Platonic philosophers can be understood as an idealized succession of god-like sages. Their mythical status in the hierarchy of being and knowledge is akin to that of the Egyptian Horus—the golden philosopher-king, who was son of Ra (Sun, or Intellect) and the manifested wisdom of Thoth—the Hindu *avatara* and the Sufi *qutb* or *al-insan al-kamil* (the axial and perfect man). In Egypt, gold was a symbol of the perfect god-like state. The same was true for the Orphic and Pythagorean tradition. According to Empedocles, exiled gods had to wander for thrice ten thousand seasons far from the company of the blessed (fr. 115). At last they were able to restore their original perfection through purificatory rites (*teletai*), regained virtues and a knowledge that implied the recollection of their own god-like-nature. Thus for Proclus, Platonism was the divine philosophy which shone forth through the grace of the gods. The philosophers who belonged to the Golden Chain were "true priests and hierophants of the divine Plato" (*Plat. Theol.* 1.1). They (e.g. Plotinus the Egyptian and his pupils) were regarded as the exegetes of the Platonic vision and the promoters of the true interpretation of the divine mysteries.

Philosophy, as understood by Proclus and other Neoplatonists, was not just a rational training and a sport of mind merged in doubts. To put the matter in later Islamic terms, the Platonic philosophy was tantamount to *hikmah* (wisdom) derived from "the niche of prophecy" (*mishkat al-nubuwwah*). It combined discursive philosophy and spiritual practice in order to attain illumination, direct vision (*epopteia*) of truth, and union (*henosis*) with the divine principles. In his Gifford Lectures, S.H. Nasr significantly remarked that:

The rediscovery of the sacred character of knowledge today would lead, almost before anything else, to a rediscovery of Greek wisdom, of Plato, Plotinus, and other Graeco-Alexandrian sages and writings such as Hermeticism, not as simply human philosophy but as sacred doctrines of divine inspiration to be compared much more with the Hindu *darsana*s than with philosophical schools as they are currently understood.[10]

Plato's "Orphic" conception of the philosopher seeking release from the wheel of cyclical time and return to his native Star is analogous to the Hindu doctrine of the path of escape developed by the Ajivika teacher Gosala, the Jain master Mahavira and the Upanishadic philosophers Yajnavalkya and Uddalaka, who promoted the so-called Tripartite Doctrine[11] of philosophical monism, itself perhaps influenced by the Egyptian Osiris cult at some early stages of formation. Alain Daniélou has suggested (though at first sight his claim sounds unlikely) that even Orphism was derived from the influence of Jainism;[12] and according to Giovanni Reale,[13] "without Orphism we cannot explain Pythagoras, nor Heraclitus, nor Empedocles and naturally not Plato and whatever was derived from him." Thomas McEvilley goes much further in his statement that:

In Greece, the word philosophy—*philosophia*, "love of knowledge," or desire for the knowledge that frees the soul from the wheel (which is what this word, coined, they say, by Pythagoras, must have meant to him)—is the closest equivalent of yoga; *sadhana* finds a very close equivalent in *bios*, meaning a specially adopted lifestyle, such as the Orphic *bios*, the Pythagorean *bios*, and so on.[14]

---

10. Seyyed Hossein Nasr, *Knowledge and the Sacred* (Albany, New York: SUNY, 1980), p.35.

11. The Tripartite Doctrine claims that (1) the world is *samsara*, (2) it is governed by *karma*, and (3) the goal of escape is *moksha*, liberation, release. *Samsara* refers to the cyclic process of transmigration (gr. *metempsuchosis*).

12. Alain Danièlou, *Siva and Dionysus*, trans. K.F. Hurry (London and the Hague: East-West Publications, 1982), p.28.

13. Giovanni Reale, *A History of Ancient Philosophy, vol. 1, From the Origins to Socrates*, trans. John R. Catan (Albany, New York: SUNY, 1987), p.15.

14. Thomas McEvilley, *The Shape of Ancient Thought: Comparative Studies in Greek and Indian Philosophies* (New York: Allworth Press, 2002), p.100.

According to Hermetic doctrine, there were four kinds of men who received human bodies with the task of being transformed into divinity: just kings, true philosophers, genuine prophets, and root-cutters, or magical healers (*Kore kosmou* 41–42). An image and function of the "philosopher" partly depended on the archetype of the divine ruler and priest who was a son of Ra, or the divine Intellect, in the terms of Egyptian solar theology. Thus one can say that true *philosophia* was an inspired task aimed at a transformation of the soul—an intellectual search for the meaning of forms and ideas, symbols and images, metaphysical and natural causes. The Pythagoreans considered philosophy in terms of medicine and therapeutics and regarded themselves as adherents of a tradition greater than their own personalities, in most cases preserving anonymity and attributing their achievements to the archetypal figure of Pythagoras or to other semi-legendary sages.

For Iamblichus and his successors, who were concerned about the gradual corruption and distortion of knowledge in their time, the origins of Hellenic philosophy were to be traced back to ancient revelations. As the Egyptians and Chaldeans were original revelatory sources for all mankind, so Pythagoras was for Hellenic philosophy.[15] Hence, the science of the divine established by Plato, including the famous theory of Ideas, was thought of as being derived and developed from the Pythagorean sources which, in turn, depended on certain "perennial" patterns drawn from the various civilizations of the ancient East. For the late Neoplatonists, the true Hellenic "love of wisdom" could be supported and illustrated not only by the inspired poetry of Orpheus, Homer, and Hesiod, but also by the Egyptian, Phoenician, and Assyrian myths and "theological dogmas," including the so-called *Chaldean Oracles* (*ta logia*). Endeavoring to show the close relationship between Pythagoras and Plato, Proclus gave Pythagoras a central role and asserted that his teaching was

> … in harmony with the first principles of Plato and with the secret revelations of the theologians. For all Greek theology derives from Orphic mystagogy, Pythagoras first learning from Aglaophemus the secrets concerning the gods, Plato after him receiving the com-

---

15. Dominic J. O'Meara, *Pythagoras Revived: Mathematics and Philosophy in Late Antiquity* (Oxford: Clarendon Press, 1997), p.103.

plete science of the gods from Pythagorean and Orphic writings (*Plat. Theol.* 1.5.25).

Accordingly, both in metaphysics and physics, Platonism can be reduced to Pythagoreanism and subordinated to the revealed wisdom of the ancient East. What distinguishes the theology of Plato from that of the Egyptian, Babylonian, and Assyrian initiates as well as the Homeric, Orphic, and Pythagorean sages, is its scientific and demonstrative character. The proper objects of the Platonic science of dialectic are higher realities, or metaphysical "things" (*ta pragmata*), not passing phenomena. But in Neoplatonism this science itself was finally surpassed and transcended by the supra-rational "vision" and theurgic union conducted by the gods themselves.

Proclus described the Orphic and Pythagorean approach as inspired, symbolic, anagogic, and revelatory in contrast to the Socratic approach which was rational, ethical, and demonstrative. He thought that Plato was able to combine both these methods. Thus, just as Iamblichus tried to prove that Pythagoras provided scientific form to revelations of the Egyptian and Chaldean wisdom, so Syrianus and Proclus granted to Plato the role of the first strictly scientific thinker, who put the ancient revelations into scientific and dialectical terms. But Orphism and Pythagoreanism still belonged to the revelatory realm of anagogic symbolism. In short, philosophy was a tradition of divinely revealed truth which might be more or less successfully rendered into the auxiliary set of abstract logic and strictly rational categories that were "philosophical" in the narrow sense of the word. But this revealed truth—revealed and then rationalized (i.e., adapted to the rules of human logic)—was conveyed to fallen souls for their salvation by the superior daemonic souls of those hermeneutists who belonged to the Golden Chain and were directly connected with the divine realm.

The fall in philosophical insight, as well as the mission of the superior souls sent down to recall corrupted souls to the divine abode, was exemplified in the *Phaedrus* of Plato. Thus even Socrates, who described philosophy as a kind of divinely inspired madness (*mania*), was referred to as a savior by Hermeias of Alexandria. According to him, Socrates had been sent down to the world of becoming as a benefit to mankind and to turn souls—each in a different way—to philosophy. Not only Pythagoras, Archytas, Socrates, and Plato, but also later philosophers such as Ammonius Saccas,

Plotinus, Porphyry, Iamblichus and Syrianus were "companions of the gods" (*apadous theon andras*) and belonged to the revelatory and soteriological tradition of philosophy, the main principles of which were received from daemons and angels. Such men were ranked with divine beings and called "daemonic" by the Pythagoreans. They were members of the divine choir, free from subjection to the body and "instructed by the divine" (*theodidaktos*). Thus philosophy was "sent down" along with those who preserved intact their pure vision of the gods in the heavenly procession (or the solar boat of Osiris-Ra, to express the matter in Egyptian terms), who were the providential agents of Eros and the inspired interpreters of the noetic realities. They were the keepers of anagogic power, because dialectic and discursive thought were regarded as necessary aspects of the ascent. According to Hermeias, true philosophers were divine-like souls who derived their wisdom from the immaterial realm and then translated it to fallen souls—those who ought to regrow their wings through the complete course of purification and recollection of their archetypal origins.

The ultimate goal of Pythagorean and Platonic philosophy was assimilation to god through the cultivation of virtue and truth. It meant a return to the first principles reached through philosophical education (*paideia*) and recollection (*anamnesis*), scientific investigation, contemplation, and liturgy (or theurgic ascent), based on the ineffable symbols and sacramental rites. By this philosophical practice the initiate student was transformed into a saintly and divine man (*theios aner*). As Hermeias says, Socrates

> ... thought it right to call the divine men gods in the *Sophist*, for the wise and divine men are as gods in relation to men. And so he was wont often to credit his works to the divine men, in the *Phaedrus* to Pythagoras, in the *Charmidas* to Zalmoxis, a wise man, and the story of Atlantis in the *Timaeus* to the Egyptians (*In Phaedr.* 253.18–25).

*　　*　　*

The present anthology consists of four unequal parts, starting with accounts on the life of Pythagoras as attested by comparatively late Hellenic and even Byzantine writers, who strictly obey the rules of the particular genre. We are thus not too preoccupied with the historical precision of these accounts; we wish, rather, to present an archetypal and sometimes idealized mythological background, along with the important hermeneutical contents of the Pythagorean and Platonic tradition. Even if frequent references to the Eastern sources cannot be proved as valid in a strictly historical sense, they serve as the important icons and symbols of a consciously constructed Pythagorean-Platonic self-image, and mark the frame of certain metaphysical horizons.

Some Pythagorean excerpts presented in the second part are regarded as "spurious" by many modern scholars simply because their real authors or editors belong to times later than claimed. The majority of scholars too easily forget that in the ancient world an "author" could be regarded as *auctoritas*: sometimes the whole tradition (or school, *hairesis*) was concealed under such archetypal names as Hermes, Solomon, or Pythagoras. The ideas were not their personal belongings and so those who searched for a sacred meaning paid attention to the inner contents, not the outer personal identities. As 'Allamah Tabataba'i has remarked: "for us the person who wrote the *Nahj al-balaghah* is 'Ali even if he lived a century ago."[16]

The excerpts selected from Plato's *Symposium, Phaedrus, Timaeus* and other dialogues are pivotal for the understanding of what sense is conveyed by the word "philosophy" and how Plato used cosmological and philosophical myths in order to build an integral and meaningful world picture.

The fourth and largest part of the anthology is devoted to Hellenic Neoplatonism, from Plotinus and Porphyry to Damascius. The main emphasis is laid on various hermeneutical aspects of late Platonic metaphysics and sacred mythology, as well as philosophical ethics and theurgy. The close relationship between the Platonic and Pythagorean perspectives is revealed, while referring to the Egyptian and Near Eastern parallels attested by the Neoplatonists themselves. This is a view "from the inside" of the Neoplatonic tradition (*paradosis*).

Despite the minor shortcomings and anachronistic renderings of the Hellenic divinities by Roman names, we have used some texts translated from the Greek into English by Thomas Taylor, the

---

16. Seyyed Hossein Nasr, "Reply to Zailan Moris" in *The Philosophy of Seyyed Hossein Nasr*, p.635.

famous Platonist who has been systematically neglected by the narrow-minded scholars of the 19th and 20th centuries. The first reason for including these texts is that Thomas Taylor had a deep understanding of Hellenic philosophy and his renderings are in principle quite correct. The second reason is very simple: there are no other English translations at all. Because of the prevailing negative attitude toward late Neoplatonism by modern historians of philosophy (with Plotinus as a rare exception), certain works by Proclus, Hermeias and Damascius are to this day only available in the Greek originals. What seems most important to a student of metaphysics, hieratic imagination, and theurgy is regarded as a worthless fable by the positivist heirs of the Enlightenment.

The rediscovery of this ancient Hellenic wisdom allows us to see the crucial importance of the Neoplatonic doctrines for the formation of traditional Christian, Jewish and Islamic thought. If freed from modern misreadings—which, unfortunately, even had an effect on some contemporary Traditionalist writers—the ancient Pythagorean and Platonic tradition can be regarded as one of the main intellectual pillars of the *sophia perennis*.

Algis Uždavinys

PART I

TRADITIONAL ACCOUNTS
ON THE LIFE AND TEACHINGS OF PYTHAGORAS

Though Pythagoras (born c.570 B.C.E.) did not invent philosophy as such, his role as a spiritual guide who reinterpreted and synthesized all available religious and philosophic knowledge (including the mysteries of Egypt and the science of Babylonia, inherited from Sumer) was crucial to the rise of the Hellenic intellectual tradition and the establishment of the so-called esoteric "house of mysteries." In a sense, Pythagoras exemplified Heracles (Melqart of the Phoenicians), i.e., as being an archetype of the spiritual hero who practiced the rites of incubation, oracular dreams, and was immortalized through the theurgic (or alchemical) fire. He joins the company of the gods in Heaven, thus following certain Phoenician and Hittitian cultic patterns. By emphasizing the sacred (both cosmogonical and soteriological) aspect of Number as reflecting the One and its irradiations, Pythagoras maintained the presence of Truth, Goodness, and Beauty in the orderly hierarchical cosmos. While asserting that unity was the principle of all things, he set up Limit (*peras*) and the Unlimited (*apeiron*) as the two most basic archetypes of theophany.

Several comparatively late accounts devoted to the life and teachings of Pythagoras have survived. They are based on much earlier sources and reflect, at the very least, the universally accepted and partly idealized views regarding this legendary hero, who not only "established science" (i.e., brought it from the East), but promoted the distinctive Pythagorean way of life (*bios Puthagorikos*).[1] According to the Hellenic tradition, Pythagoras restricted the use of the word wisdom (*sophia*) so as to make it refer only to the science of immaterial realities treated as true Being, against the fluid mate-

---

1. We transcribe *Puthagorikos* instead of *Pythagorikos*, thus following J.O. Urmson's *The Greek Philosophical Vocabulary* (Duckworth, 1990). The same principle is followed in transcribing other terms in the text such as *psuche* (instead of *psyche*), *dunamis* (instead of *dynamis*), and *huparxis* (instead of *hyparxis*).

rial world of becoming whose very flow imitates the archetypes of true Being and derives from them. Before him wise men in Greece called themselves sages (*sophoi*, tantamount to those "exceeding in wisdom" who bear the attributes of the god Ea in Mesopotamia), but Pythagoras was the first among the Greeks to call himself a lover of wisdom, *philosophos*. He regarded *philosophia* as a form of purification, a way of life aimed at assimilation to God and the gaining of immortality.

This metaphysical attitude was established on the ground of Oriental arts and sciences and certain esoteric practices of Orphism. For example, Pythagoras envisaged the mathematical sciences as preparing the human soul for a higher pursuit, thereby acting as a bridge from the material world to the immaterial divine Intellect. The school of Pythagoras was thus a religious society centered around the Muses and their leader Apollo, the solar Intellect. Following the lead of Apollo and Pythagoras, one thereby became aware of the divine order and unity. But to know the cosmos was to seek and know the divine and archetypal structure within the soul, since the soul, according to Orphism, was a divine spark of Dionysus (who himself is tantamount to the Egyptian Osiris) bound in the mortal body as to a tomb, which also served as an alchemical vessel. By means of contemplation, the universal principles were perceived and through spiritual exercises the soul was transformed and harmonized.

The Pythagorean strain survived in Neoplatonism. For Porphyry and other Neoplatonists, Pythagoras was a member of a great chain of ancient prophets, theologians, and sages, essentially a Platonic philosopher whose many doctrines could be traced to their Eastern prototypes.

Presented below are selected excerpts from the anonymous biography preserved by Photius (c.820–891, or 897 C.E.), a Byzantine patriarch and teacher of philosophy at the Imperial Academy in Constantinople. Some scholars surmise that this unknown author may in fact preserve some parts of Aristotle's lost treatise *On the Pythagoreans*. Diogenes Laertius (3rd century C.E.) compiled his *Lives of the Eminent Philosophers*, drawn from a great many sources, amongst which are some testimonies on Pythagoras. The works on Pythagoras produced by Porphyry (c.232–c.305 C.E.) and Iamblichus (c.245–c.325 C.E.) partly reflect Neoplatonic and

Neopythagorean approaches, which in many respects faithfully follow that of ancient Pythagoreanism. The opinion of some modern scholars that Pythagoreanism only later developed as a religious philosophy based on ritual activities is rather bizarre and entirely false.

1. Anonymous
The Life of Pythagoras

The excerpts here reproduced from the anonymous *Life of Pythagoras* are taken from the writings of the Byzantine patriarch Photius, a politician, literary critic, and tutor of philosophy at the Imperial Academy in Constantinople. In his search for "sobriety," Photius took the side of Aristotle and criticized Plato. The author of the *Life of Pythagoras*, as preserved by Photius, cannot be identified; but it is clear that he tries to connect Pythagoras and Aristotle when he says: "Plato was the pupil of Archytas, and thus the ninth in succession from Pythagoras; the tenth was Aristotle." This treatise is important as a source of Pythagorean cosmology, especially as regards the ancient idea that man is a microcosm who reflects the entire universe.

The texts were rendered into English by Kenneth Sylvan Guthrie, *Pythagoras Source Book and Library* (Platonist Press, 1919).

1. Plato was the pupil of Archytas, and thus the ninth in succession from Pythagoras; the tenth was Aristotle. Those of Pythagoras' disciples that were devoted to contemplation were called *sebastici*, the reverend, while those who were engaged in business were called politicians (*politikoi*). Those who cultivated the disciplines of geometry and astronomy were called students (*mathematikoi*). Those who associated personally with Pythagoras were called Pythagoreans (*Puthagorikoi*), while those who merely imitated his teachings were called Pythagoristians (*Puthagoristai*). All these generally abstained from the flesh of animals; at a certain time they tasted the flesh of sacrificial animals only....

3. The Pythagoreans preach a difference between the Monad, and the One; the Monad dwells in the intelligible realm, while the One dwells among numbers. Likewise, the Two exists among numerable things, while the Dyad is indeterminate.

4. The Monad expresses equality and measure, the Dyad expresses excess and defect. Mean and measure cannot admit of more or less, while excess and defect, which proceed to infinity, admit it; that is why the Dyad is called indeterminate. Since, because of the all-inclusion of the Monad and Dyad, all things refer to number, they call all things numbers; and the number is perfected in the decad. Ten is reached by adding in order the first four figures; that is why the Ten is called the Quaternary [or Tetraktys].

5. They affirm that man may improve in three ways: first, by conversation with the Gods, for to them none can approach unless he abstain from all evil, imitating the divinity, even unto assimilation; second, by well-doing, which is a characteristic of the divinity; third by dying, for if the slight soul-separation from the body resulting from discipline improves the soul so that she begins to divine, in dreams—and if the deliria of illness produces visions—then the soul must surely improve far more when entirely separated from the body by death....

7. The Pythagoreans considered the Monad as the origin (*arche*) of all things, just as a point is the beginning of a line, a line of a surface, and a surface of a solid, which constitutes a body. A point implies a preceding Monad, so that it is really the principle of bodies, and all of them arise from the Monad.

8. The Pythagoreans are said to have predicted many things, and Pythagoras' predictions always came true.

9. Plato is said to have learned his speculative and physical doctrines from the Italian Pythagoreans, his ethics from Socrates, and his logic from Zeno, Parmenides and the Eleatics. But all of these teachings descended from Pythagoras....

15. It was Pythagoras who first called heaven *kosmos*, because it is perfect, and "adorned" with infinite beauty and living beings.

With Pythagoras agreed Plato and Aristotle that the soul is immortal, although some who did not understand Aristotle claimed he thought the soul was mortal.

Pythagoras said that man was a *microcosm*, which means a compendium of the universe; not because, like other animals, even the least, he is constituted by the four elements, but because he contains all the powers of the cosmos. For the universe contains Gods, the four elements, animals and plants. All of these powers are contained in man. He has reason, which is a divine power; he has the nature of the elements, and the powers of moving, growing, and reproduction. However, in each of these he is inferior to the others. For example, an athlete who practices five kinds of sports, diverting his powers into five channels, is inferior to the athlete who practices a single sport well; so man, having all of the powers, is inferior in each. We have less reasoning powers than the Gods, and less of each of the elements than the elements themselves. Our anger and desire are inferior to those passions in the irrational animals, while our powers of nutrition and growth are inferior to those in plants. Constituted therefore of different powers, we have a difficult life to lead.

16. While all other things are ruled by one nature only, we are drawn by different powers; as for instance, when by God we are drawn to better things, or when we are drawn to evil courses by the prevailing of the lower powers. He who, like a vigilant and expert charioteer,[2] within himself cultivates the divine element, will be able to utilize the other powers by a mingling of the elements, by anger, desire and habit, just as far as may be necessary. Though it seems easy to *know yourself*, this is the most difficult of all things. This is said to derive from the Pythian Apollo, though it is also attributed to Chilo, one of the Seven Sages. Its message is, in any event, to discover our own power, which amounts to learning the nature of the whole extant world which, as God advises us, is impossible without philosophy.

17. There are eight organs of knowledge: sense, imagination, art, opinion, deliberation, science, wisdom and mind. Art, prudence, science and mind we share with the Gods; sense and imagination, with the irrational animals; while opinion alone is our characteristic. Sense is a fallacious knowledge derived through the body; imagination is a notion in the soul; art is a habit of cooperating with reason. The words "with reason" are here added, for even a spider operates, but it lacks reason. Deliberation is a habit selective of the rightness of planning deeds; science is a habit of those things which remain ever the same, with Sameness; wisdom is a knowledge of the first causes; while Mind is the principle and fountain of all good things.

2. Cf. Plato's *Phaedrus* 246ff for the myth of the charioteer.

2. Diogenes Laertius
The Life of Pythagoras

The few excerpts here reproduced are taken from the renowned *Lives of the Eminent Philosophers*, compiled by the author Diogenes Laertius, which he composed from quotations of diverse unknown sources now lost to posterity.

The texts were translated into English by Kenneth Sylvan Guthrie, *Pythagoras Source Book and Library* (Platonist Press, 1919). For a translation of the entire work see Diogenes Laertius, *Lives of the Eminent Philosophers*, 2 vols., trans. R.D. Hicks (Harvard University Press, 1925).

VIII.2–5

He (Pythagoras, the son of Mnesarchus, a gem-engraver) was a pupil, as I have already mentioned, of Pherecydes the Syrian, and after his death he came to Samos, and became a pupil of Hermodamas, the descendant of Creophylus, who was already an old man now.

As he was a youth devoted to learning, he left his country, and had himself initiated into the Grecian and barbarian sacred mysteries. Accordingly he went to Egypt, on which occasion Polycrates gave him a letter of introduction to Amasis; and he learned the Egyptians' language as Antiphon tell us, in his treatise *On Those Men Who Have Become Conspicuous for Virtues*, and he also associated with the Chaldeans and Magi.

Afterwards he went to Crete, and in company with Epimenides, he descended into the Idaean cave—and in Egypt too he had entered into the holiest parts of their temples, and learned all the most secret mysteries that relate to their Gods. Then he returned again to Samos, and finding his country under the absolute dominion of Polycrates, he set sail, and fled to Croton in Italy. Having given laws to the Italians, he there gained a very high reputation, together with his followers, who were about three hundred in number, and governed the republic in a most excellent manner, so that the constitution was very nearly an aristocracy.

Heracleides of Pontus says that he was accustomed to speak of himself in this manner: that he had formerly been Aethalides, and had been accounted to be the son of Hermes, and that Hermes had desired him to select any gift he pleased except immortality.

Accordingly, he had requested that, whether living or dead, he might preserve the memory of what had happened to him. While, therefore, he was alive, he recalled everything, and when he was dead he retained the same memory. At a subsequent period he passed into Euphorbus, and was wounded by Menelaus. While he was Euphorbus, he used to say that he had formerly been Aethalides; and that he had received as a gift from Hermes the perpetual transmigration of his soul, so that it was constantly transmigrating and passing into whatever plants or animals it pleased, and he had also received the gift of knowing and recollecting all that his soul had suffered in Hades, and what sufferings too are endured by the rest of the souls.

But after Euphorbus died, he said that his soul had passed into Hermotimus, and when he wished to convince people of this, he went into the territory of the Branchidae, and going into the temple of Apollo, he showed his shield which Menelaus had dedicated there as an offering. For he said that he, when he sailed from Troy, had offered up his shield which was already getting worn out, to Apollo, and that nothing remained but the ivory face which was on it. He said that when Hermotimus died he had become Pyrrhus, a fisherman of Delos, and that he still recollected everything, how he had formerly been Aethalides, then Euphorbus, then Hermotimus, and then Pyrrhus. When Pyrrhus died, he became Pythagoras, and still recollected all the circumstances I have been mentioning.

VIII.8

Sosicrates, in his *Successions of Philosophers*, relates that when asked who he was by Leon, the tyrant of the Phliasians, Pythagoras replied, "A philosopher." He adds that Pythagoras used to compare life to the Greater Games where some people come to contend for the prizes, and others for the purposes of traffic, but the best as spectators. So also in life the men of slavish dispositions are born hunters after glory and covetousness, but philosophers are seekers after the truth. Thus he spoke on this subject.

VIII.11

He is said to have been a man of the most dignified appearance, and his disciples adopted an opinion that he was Apollo who had come from the Hyperboreans. It is also said that once when he was stripped naked he was seen to have a golden thigh, and many people affirmed that when he was crossing the river Nessus it addressed him by name.

VIII.13

The only altar at which he worshiped was that of Apollo the Giver of Life, at Delos, which is at the back of the Altar of Horns, because wheat and barley, and cheese cakes are the only offerings laid upon it, as it is not dressed by fire, and no victim is ever slain there, as Aristotle tells us, in his *Constitution of the Delians*. It is also said that he was the first person who asserted that the soul, revolving around the circle of necessity, is transformed and confined at different times in different bodies.

3. Porphyry
The Life of Pythagoras

The excerpts here reproduced are from the *Life of Pythagoras* by Porphyry, the disciple of Plotinus. Porphyry the Phoenician regarded Pythagoras as essentially a Platonic philosopher whose views could be corroborated by reference to the divinely revealed teachings of the Egyptian priesthood. The *Life of Pythagoras* was initially part of the first book of a *Philosophical History* in four books. This history, now lost, covered Hellenic philosophy from Homer to Plato. The *Life of Pythagoras* is a learned compilation of source materials. According to Porphyry, Pythagoras' philosophy was based on Egyptian, Chaldean, Phoenician, Arabic, Jewish, and Persian wisdom. However, this philosophy emerges as a kind of Platonism aimed at liberation from the body, and knowledge of immaterial realities.

The texts were rendered into English by Kenneth Sylvan Guthrie, *Pythagoras Source Book and Library* (Platonist Press, 1919).

6. As to his knowledge, it is said that he learned the mathematical sciences from the Egyptians, Chaldeans, and Phoenicians; for of old the Egyptians excelled in geometry, the Phoenicians in numbers and proportions, and the Chaldeans in astronomical theorems, divine rites, and worship of the Gods; other secrets concerning the course of life he received and learned from the Magi.

7. These accomplishments are the more generally known, but the rest are less celebrated. Moreover, Eudoxus, in the second book of his *Description of the Earth,* writes that Pythagoras practiced the greatest purity, and was shocked at all blood-shedding and killing; that he not only abstained from animal food, but never in any way approached butchers or hunters. Antiphon, in his book *On Illustrious Virtuous Men,* praises his perseverance while he was in Egypt, saying that Pythagoras, desiring to become acquainted with the institutions of the Egyptian priests, and diligently endeavoring to participate therein, requested the Tyrant Polycrates [of Samos] to write to Amasis, the King of Egypt, his friend and former host, to procure him initiation. Coming to Amasis, he was given letters to the priests, but the priests of Heliopolis sent him on to those at Memphis, on the pretense that they were the more ancient. On the same pretense, he was sent on from Memphis to Diospolis [or ancient Thebes].

8. From fear of the King, the latter priests dared not make excuses [to initiate Pythagoras], but thinking that he would desist from his purpose as a result of great difficulties, they enjoined on him very hard precepts, entirely different from the institutions of the Greeks. These he performed so readily that he won their admiration, and they permitted him to sacrifice to the Gods, and to acquaint himself with all their sciences, a favor never previously granted to a foreigner.

9. Returning to Ionia, he opened in his own country a school which is even now called Pythagoras' Semicircle, and in which the Samians meet to deliberate about matters of common interest. Outside the city he adapted a cave to the study of his philosophy, in which he lived day and night, discoursing with a few of his associates. He was now forty years old, says Aristoxenus. Seeing that Polycrates' government was becoming so violent that soon a free man would become a victim of his tyranny, he journeyed towards Italy....

11. He (Mnesarchus) sent the boy (Pythagoras) to a lyre player, a gymnast and a painter. Later he sent him to Anaximander at Miletus, to learn geometry and astronomy. Then Pythagoras visited the Egyptians, the Arabians, the Chaldeans and the Hebrews, from whom he acquired expertise in the interpretation of dreams, and acquired the use of frankincense in the worship of divinities.

12. In Egypt he lived with the priests, and learned the language and wisdom of the Egyptians, and their three kinds of letters, the epistolographic, the hieroglyphic, and symbolic, whereof one imitates the common way of speaking, while the others express the sense of allegory and parable. In Arabia he conferred with the king. In Babylon he associated with the other Chaldeans, especially attaching himself to Zaratus [= Zoroaster], by whom he was purified from the pollutions of his past life, and taught the things from which a virtuous man ought to be free. Likewise he heard lectures about Nature, and the principles of wholes. It was from his stay among these foreigners that Pythagoras acquired the greater part of his wisdom....

17. Going to Crete, Pythagoras besought initiation from the priests of Morgos, one of the Idaean Dactyls, by whom he was purified with the meteoric thunderstone, during which he lay, at dawn, stretched upon his face by the seaside, and at night, beside a river, crowned with a black lamb's woolen wreath. Descending into the Idaean cave, wrapped in black wool, he stayed there twenty-seven days, according to the custom; he sacrificed to Zeus, and saw the couch which there is yearly made for him. On Zeus' tomb Pythagoras inscribed an epigram, "Pythagoras to Zeus," which begins: "Zan deceased here lies, whom men call Zeus"....

34. As to food, his breakfast was chiefly of honey; at dinner he used bread made of millet, barley or herbs, raw and boiled. Only rarely did he eat the flesh of sacrificial victims, nor did he take this from every part of the anatomy. When he intended to sojourn in the sanctuaries of the divinities, he would eat no more than was necessary to still hunger and thirst. To quiet hunger he made a mixture of poppy seed and sesame, the skin of a sea-onion, well washed until entirely drained of the outward juices, of the flowers of the daffodil, and the leaves of mallows, of paste of barley and chick peas, taking an equal weight of which, and chopping it small, with honey of Hymettus he made it into a mass. Against thirst he took the seed of cucumbers, and the best dried raisins, extracting the seeds, and coriander flowers, and the seeds of mallows, purslane, scraped cheese, wheat meal and cream, all of which he mixed up with wild honey.

35. He claimed that this diet had, by Demeter, been taught to Hercules, when he was sent into the Libyan deserts. This preserved

his body in an unchanging condition, not at one time well, and at another time sick, nor at one time fat, and at another lean. Pythagoras' countenance showed the same constancy that was also in his soul. For he was neither more elated by pleasure, nor dejected by grief, and no one ever saw him either rejoicing or mourning....

37. His utterances were of two kinds, plain or symbolical. His teaching was twofold: of his disciples some were called Students (*mathematikoi*), and others Hearers (*akousmatikoi*). The Students learned the fuller and more exactly elaborate reasons of science, while the Hearers heard only the summarized instructions of learning, without more detailed explanations.

38. He ordained that his disciples should speak well and think reverently of the Gods, daemons, and heroes, and likewise of parents and benefactors; that they should obey the laws; that they should not relegate the worship of the Gods to a secondary position, but should perform it eagerly, even at home; that to the celestial divinities they should sacrifice uncommon offerings, and ordinary ones to the inferior deities. [The world he divided into] opposite powers: the better is the Monad, light, right, equal, stable and straight; while the worse is an inferior Dyad, darkness, left, unequal, unstable and curved....

41. Such things taught he, though advising above all things to speak the truth, for this alone deifies men. For as he had learned from the Magi, who call God Horomazda, God's body is like light, and his soul is like truth. He taught much else, which he claimed to have learned from Aristokleia at Delphi. Certain things he declared mystically, symbolically, most of which were collected by Aristotle, as when he called the sea a tear of Kronos, the Great and Little Bear the hands of Rhea, the Pleiades the lyre of the Muses, and the planets the dogs of Persephone. He called the sound caused by striking on brass the voice of a daemon enclosed in the brass....

46. He cultivated philosophy, the scope of which is to free the mind implanted within us from the impediments and fetters within which it is confined, without whose freedom none can learn anything sound or true, or perceive the unsoundness in the operation of sense. Pythagoras thought that mind alone sees and hears, while all the rest are blind and deaf. The purified mind should be applied to the discovery of beneficial things, which can be effected by certain arts, which by degrees induce it to the contemplation of eter-

nal and incorporeal things which never vary. This orderliness of perception should begin from consideration of the most minute things, lest by any change the mind should be jarred and withdraw itself, through the failure of continuousness in its subject-matter.

47. That is the reason he made so much use of the mathematical disciplines and speculations, which are intermediate between the physical and the incorporeal realm, for the reason that, like bodies, they have a three-fold dimension, and yet share the impassibility of incorporeals. [These disciplines he used] as degrees of preparation to the contemplation of the really existent things, by an artistic principle diverting the eyes of the mind from corporeal things, whose manner and state never remain in the same condition, to a desire for true [spiritual] food. By means of these mathematical sciences therefore, Pythagoras rendered men truly happy, by this artistic introduction of truly existent things.

48. Among others, Moderatus of Gades, who learnedly treated of the qualities of numbers in eleven books, states that the Pythagoreans specialized in the study of numbers to explain their teachings symbolically, as do geometricians, inasmuch as the primary forms and principles are hard to understand and express otherwise in plain discourse. A similar case is the representation of sounds by letters, which are known by marks, which are called the first elements of learning; later, they inform us these are not the true elements, which they only signify.

49. As the geometricians cannot express incorporeal forms in words, and have recourse to the drawings of figures, saying "This is a triangle," and yet do not mean that the actually seen lines are *the* triangle, but only what they represent, the knowledge in the mind, so the Pythagoreans used the same objective method in respect to first reasons and forms. As these incorporeal forms and first principles could not be expressed in words, they had recourse to demonstration by numbers. Number One denoted to them the reason of Unity, Identity, Equality, the purpose of friendship, sympathy, and conservation of the Universe, which results from persistence in Sameness. For unity in the details harmonizes all the parts of a whole, as by the participation of the First Cause.

50. Number Two, or Dyad, signified the dual reason of diversity and inequality, of everything that is divisible, or mutable, existing at one time in one way, and at another time in another way. After all, these methods were not confined to the Pythagoreans, being used

by other philosophers to denote unitive powers, which contain all things in the universe, among which are certain reasons of equality, dissimilitude and diversity. These reasons are what they meant by the terms Monad and Dyad, or by the words uniform, biform, or diversiform.

51. The same reasons apply to their use of other numbers, which were ranked according to certain powers. Things that had a beginning, middle and end they denoted by the number Three, saying that anything that has a middle is triform, which was applied to every perfect thing. They said that if anything was perfect it would make use of this principle, and be adorned according to it; and as they had no other name for it, they invented the form, Triad, and whenever they tried to bring us to the knowledge of what is perfect they led us to that by the form of this Triad. So also with the other numbers, where were ranked according to the same reasons.

52. All other things were comprehended under a single form and power, which they called Decad, explaining it by a pun, as *decha-da* ("receptacle"), meaning comprehension. That is why they call Ten a perfect number, the most perfect of all, as comprehending all difference of numbers, reasons, species and proportions. For if the nature of the universe be defined according to the reasons (*logoi*) and proportions of numbers, and if that which is produced, increased and perfected, proceed according to the reason of numbers and since the Decad comprehends every reason [or ratio] of numbers, every proportion, and every species—why should Nature herself not be denoted by the most perfect number, Ten? Such was the use of numbers among the Pythagoreans.

4. Iamblichus
On the Pythagorean Life

Iamblichus was one of the most eminent among the Neoplatonists. His native residence was at Chalcis in Syria. It is not firmly established whether Iamblichus was an actual disciple of Porphyry, although according to Eunapius, "As a pupil of Anatolius, who ranks next after Porphyry, he made great progress and attained to the highest distinction in philosophy. Then leaving Anatolius he attached himself to Porphyry, and in no respect was he inferior to Porphyry except in harmonious structure and force of style" (*Lives of the Philosophers and Sophists* 457–458). Iamblichus founded his school in Apamea (Syria), and Libanius speaks "of a choir of philosophers of Apamea, of whom the chorus-leader (Iamblichus) resembled the gods" (*Or.* 52.21).

Iamblichus thought of himself as both a Pythagorean and Platonic philosopher. At the same time, he belonged to the Chaldean tradition of "sacred art" (*hieratike techne*), or theurgy. The treatise *On the Pythagorean Life* (*Peri tou Puthagorikou biou*) is the first book of his large work *On Pythagoreanism*, made up of nine or perhaps ten books. Though Iamblichus endeavored to produce a rather Neoplatonic interpretation of the Pythagorean teachings, he often quoted verbatim very ancient sources which are not presently available. According to Iamblichus, the philosophy named after Pythagoras was revealed by the gods. It therefore transcends mere human capacities and can only be grasped through divine guidance. Pythagoras himself was regarded as the divine guide.

Iamblichus' biography of Pythagoras adheres closely to the guidelines prescribed by the ancient rhetoricians. Contemporary scholars surmise that the wondrous stories of Pythagoras' birth, education, and travels constitute not a biographical narrative, but a symbolical account which serves to emphasize Pythagoras' unique relation to the divine and his soteriological mission. But that a measure of historical background exists in such stories cannot be doubted, though Pythagoras is indeed praised as a hero, and his biography is represented as an archetypal pattern for spiritual practice. For this reason Pythagoras' spiritual rather than bodily genealogy is emphasized.

The excerpts reproduced here were translated by Thomas Taylor, *Iamblichus' Life of Pythagoras and Fragments of the Ethical Writings of Certain Pythagoreans in the Doric Dialect* (1818).

1. Since wise people are in the habit of invoking the divinities at the beginning of any philosophic consideration, this is all the more necessary on studying that one which is justly named after the divine Pythagoras. Inasmuch as it emanated from the divinities it cannot be apprehended without their inspiration and assistance. Besides, its beauty and majesty so surpasses human capacity that it cannot be comprehended all in one glance. Only gradually can some details of it be mastered when, under divine guidance, we approach the subject with a quiet mind. Having therefore invoked the divine guidance, and adapted ourselves and our style to the divine circumstances, we shall acquiesce in all the suggestions that come to us. Therefore we shall not begin with any excuses for the long neglect of this sect, or with any explanations about its having

been concealed by foreign disciplines, or by mystic symbols, nor insist that it has been obscured by false and spurious writings, nor make apologies for any special hindrances to its progress. For us it is sufficient that this is the will of the Gods, which will enable us to undertake tasks even more arduous than these. Having thus acknowledged our primary submission to the divinities, our secondary devotion shall be to the prince and father of this philosophy as a leader....

2.... That Pythagoras was the son of Apollo is a legend due to a certain Samian poet, who thus described the popular recognition of his noble birth. Sang he,

> Pythais, the fairest of the Samian race
> From the embraces of the God Apollo
> Bore Pythagoras, the friend of Zeus.

It might be worthwhile to relate the circumstances of this prevalent report. Mnesarchus had gone to Delphi on a business trip, leaving his wife without any signs of pregnancy. He enquired of the oracle about the event of his return voyage to Syria, and he was informed that his trip would be lucrative, and most conformable to his wishes, but that his wife was new with child, and would present him with a son who would surpass all others who had ever lived in beauty and wisdom, and that he would be of the greatest benefit to the human race in everything pertaining to human achievements. But when Mnesarchus realized that the God, without waiting for any question about a son, had by an oracle informed him that he would possess an illustrious prerogative, and a truly divine gift, he immediately changed his wife's former name Parthenis to one reminiscent of the Delphic prophet and her son, naming her Pythais, and the infant, who was soon after born at Sidon in Phoenicia, Pythagoras, by this name commemorating that such an offspring had been promised him by the Pythian Apollo. The assertions of Epimenides, Eudoxus and Xenocrates, that Apollo having at that time already had actual connection with Parthenis, causing her pregnancy, had regularized that fact by predicting the birth of Pythagoras, are by no means to be admitted. However, no one will deny that the soul of Pythagoras was sent to mankind from Apollo's domain, having either been one of his attendants, or more intimate associates, which may be inferred both from his birth and his versatile wisdom....

When he had attained his eighteenth year, there arose the tyranny of Polycrates; and Pythagoras foresaw that under such a government his studies might be impeded, as they engrossed the whole of his attention. So by night he privately departed with one Hermodamas—who was surnamed Creophilus, and was the grandson of the host, friend and general preceptor of the poet Homer—going to Pherecydes, to Anaximander the natural philosopher, and to Thales at Miletus. He successively associated with each of these philosophers in a manner such that they all loved him, admired his natural endowments, and admitted him to the best of their doctrines. Thales especially, on gladly admitting him to the intimacies of his confidence, admired the great difference between him and other young men, who were in every accomplishment surpassed by Pythagoras. After increasing the reputation Pythagoras had already acquired, by communicating to him the utmost he was able to impart to him, Thales, laying stress on his advanced age and the infirmities of his body, advised him to go to Egypt, to get in touch with the priests of Memphis and Zeus. Thales confessed that the instruction of these priests was the source of his own reputation for wisdom, while neither his own endowments nor achievements equaled those which were so evident in Pythagoras. Thales insisted that, in view of all this, if Pythagoras should study with those priests, he was certain of becoming the wisest and most divine of men.

3. Pythagoras had benefited by the instruction of Thales in many respects, but his greatest lesson had been to learn the value of saving time, which led him to abstain entirely from wine and animal food, avoiding greediness, confining himself to nutriments of easy preparation and digestion. As a result, his sleep was short, his soul pure and vigilant, and the general health of his body was invariable.

Enjoying such advantages, therefore, he sailed to Sidon, both because it was his native country, and because it was on his way to Egypt. In Phoenicia he conversed with the prophets who were the descendents of Moschus the physiologist, and with many others, as well as with the local hierophants. He was also initiated into all the mysteries of Byblos and Tyre, and in the sacred function performed in many parts of Syria. He was led to all this not from any hankering after superstition, as might easily be supposed, but rather from a desire and love for contemplation, and from an anxiety to miss nothing of the mysteries of the divinities which deserved to be learned.

After gaining all he could from the Phoenician mysteries, he found that they had originated from the sacred rites of Egypt, forming as it were an Egyptian colony. This led him to hope that in Egypt itself he might find monuments of erudition still more genuine, beautiful and divine. Therefore following the advice of his teacher Thales, he left, as soon as possible, through the agency of some Egyptian sailors, who very opportunely happened to land on the Phoenician coast under Mount Carmel where, in the temple on the peak, Pythagoras for the most part had dwelt in solitude. He was gladly received by the sailors, who intended to make a great profit by selling him into slavery. But they changed their mind in his favor during the voyage, when they perceived the chastened venerability of the mode of life he had undertaken. They began to reflect that there was something supernatural in the youth's modesty, and in the manner in which he had unexpectedly appeared to them on their landing, when, from the summit of Mount Carmel, which they knew to be more sacred than other mountains, and quite inaccessible to the vulgar, he had leisurely descended without looking back, avoiding all delay from precipices or difficult rocks; and that when he came to the boat, he said nothing more than, "Are you bound for Egypt?" What is more, on their answering affirmatively he had gone aboard and had, during the whole trip, sat silent where he would be least likely to inconvenience them at their tasks.

For two nights and three days Pythagoras had remained in the same unmoved position, without food, drink, or sleep, except that, unnoticed by the sailors, he might have dozed while sitting upright. Moreover, the sailors considered that contrary to their expectations, their voyage had proceeded without interruptions, as if some deity had been on board. From all these circumstances they concluded that a veritable divinity had passed over with them from Syria into Egypt. Addressing Pythagoras and each other with a gentleness and propriety that was uncommon, they completed the remainder of their voyage through a halcyon sea, and at length happily landed on the Egyptian coast. Reverently the sailors here assisted him to disembark; and after they had seen him safe onto a firm beach, they raised before him a temporary altar, heaped on it the now abundant fruits of trees, as if these were the first fruits of their freight, presented them to him and departed hastily to their destination. Pythagoras, however, whose body had become emaciated through the severity of so long a fast, did not refuse the sailors' help on landing, and as soon as they had left partook as much of the fruits as was requisite to restore his physical vigor. Then he went inland, in entire safety, preserving his usual tranquility and modesty.

4. Here in Egypt he frequented all the temples with the greatest diligence, and most studious research, during which time he won the esteem and admiration of all the priests and prophets with whom he associated. Having most solicitously familiarized himself with every detail, he did not, nevertheless, neglect any contemporary celebrity, whether a sage renowned for wisdom, or a peculiarly performed mystery. He did not fail to visit any place where he thought he might discover something worthwhile. That is how he visited all of the Egyptian priests, acquiring all the wisdom each possessed. He thus passed twenty-two years in the sanctuaries of temples, studying astronomy and geometry, and being initiated in no casual or superficial manner in all the mysteries of the Gods. At length, however, he was taken captive by the soldiers of Cambyses, and carried off to Babylon. Here he was overjoyed to be associated with the Magi, who instructed him in their venerable knowledge, and in the most perfect worship of the Gods. Through their assistance, likewise, he studied and completed arithmetic, music and all the other sciences. After twelve years, about the fifty-sixth year of his age, he returned to Samos....

6. The Cenobites[3] were students that philosophized; but the greater part of his followers were called Hearers (*akousmatikoi*) of whom, according to Nicomachus, there were two thousand that had been captivated by a single oration on his arrival in Italy. These, with their wives and children, gathered into one immense auditory, called the Auditorium (*Homacoion*), which was so great as to resemble a city, thus founding a place universally called Greater Greece (*Magna Graecia*). This great multitude of people, receiving from Pythagoras laws and mandates as so many divine precepts, without which they declined to engage in any occupation, dwelt together in the greatest general concord, estimated and celebrated by their neighbors as among the number of the blessed, who, as was already observed, shared all their possessions.

Such was their reverence for Pythagoras that they ranked him with the Gods, as a genial beneficent divinity. While some celebrated him as the Pythian, others called him the Hyperborean Apollo.

3. Cenobites: those who lived a communal, as opposed to a solitary life.

18

Others considered him Paeon,[4] others, one of the divinities that inhabit the moon; yet others considered that he was one of the Olympian Gods, who, in order to correct and improve terrestrial existence, appeared to their contemporaries in human form, to extend to them the salutary light of philosophy and felicity. Never indeed came, nor, for the matter of that, ever will come to mankind a greater good than that which was imparted to the Greeks through this Pythagoras. Hence, even now, the nickname of "long-haired Samian" is still applied to the most venerable among men....

12. Pythagoras is said to have been the first to call himself a philosopher, a word which heretofore had not been an appellation, but a description. He likened the entrance of men into the present life to the progression of a crowd to some public spectacle. There assemble men of all descriptions and views. One hastens to sell his wares for money and gain; another exhibits his bodily strength for renown; but the most liberal assemble to observe the landscape, the beautiful works of art, the specimens of valor, and the customary literary productions. So also in the present life men of manifold pursuits are assembled. Some are influenced by the desire of riches and luxury; others, by the love of power and dominion, or by insane ambition for glory. But the purest and most genuine character is that of the man who devotes himself to the contemplation of the most beautiful things, and he may properly be called a philosopher.

Pythagoras adds that the survey of the whole heaven, and of the stars that revolve therein, is indeed beautiful, when we consider their order, which is derived from participation in the first and intelligible essence. But that first essence is the nature of Number and "reasons" (*logoi*, productive principles) which pervades everything, and according to which all those [celestial] bodies are arranged elegantly, and adorned fittingly. Now veritable wisdom is a science conversant with the first beautiful objects which subsist in invariable sameness, being undecaying and divine, by the participation in which other things also may well be called beautiful. The desire for something like this is philosophy. Similarly beautiful is devotion to erudition, and this notion Pythagoras extended, in order to effect the improvement of the human race.

4. Paeon: a form of Apollo as the physician of the gods.

13. According to credible historians, his words possessed an admonitory quality that prevailed even with animals, which confirms that in intelligent men learning tames even wild or irrational beasts. The Daunian bear, who had severely injured the inhabitants, was by Pythagoras detained. After long stroking it gently, feeding it on maize and acorns, and compelling it by an oath to leave alone living beings, he sent it away. It hid itself in the mountains and forest, and was never since known to injure any irrational animal.

At Tarentum he saw an ox feeding in a pasture, where he ate green beans. He advised the herdsman to tell the ox to abstain from this food. The herdsman laughed at him, remarking he did not know the language of oxen; but that if Pythagoras did, he had better tell him so himself. Pythagoras approached the ox's ear and whispered into it for a long time, whereafter the ox not only refrained from them, but never even tasted them. This ox lived a long while at Tarentum, near the temple of Hera, and was fed on human food by visitors till very old, being considered sacred.

Once happening to be talking to his intimates about birds, symbols and prodigies, and observing that all these are messengers of the Gods, sent by them to men truly dear to them, he brought down an eagle flying over Olympia, which he gently stroked, and dismissed.

Through such and similar occurrences, Pythagoras demonstrated that he possessed the same dominion as Orpheus over savage animals, and that he allured and detained them by the power of his voice....

15. Pythagoras conceived that the first attention that should be given to men should be addressed to the senses, as when one perceives beautiful figures and forms, or hears beautiful rhythms and melodies. Consequently he laid down that the first erudition was that which subsists through music's melodies and rhythms, and from these he obtained remedies of human manners and passions, and restored the pristine harmony of the faculties of the soul. Moreover, he devised medicines calculated to repress and cure the diseases of both bodies and souls. Here is also, by Zeus, something which deserves to be mentioned above all: namely, that for his disciples he arranged and adjusted what might be called "preparations" and "touchings," divinely contriving mingling of certain diatonic, chromatic and enharmonic melodies, through which he

easily switched and circulated the passions of the soul in a contrary direction, whenever they had accumulated recently, irrationally, or clandestinely—such as sorrow, rage, pity, over-emulation, fear, manifold desires, angers, appetites, pride, collapse or spasms. Each of these he corrected by the rule of virtue, attempering them through appropriate melodies, as through some salutary medicine.

In the evening, likewise, when his disciples were retiring to sleep, he would thus liberate them from the day's perturbations and tumults, purifying their intellective powers from the influxive and effluxive waves of corporeal nature, quieting their sleep, and rendering their dreams pleasing and prophetic. But when they arose again in the morning, he would free them from the night's heaviness, coma and torpor through certain peculiar chords and modulations, produced by either simply striking the lyre, or adapting the voice. Not through instruments or physical voice-organs did Pythagoras effect this; but by the employment of a certain indescribable divinity, difficult of apprehension, through which he extended his powers of hearing, fixing his intellect on the sublime symphonies of the world, he alone apparently hearing and grasping the universal harmony and consonance of the spheres, and the stars that are moved through them, producing a melody fuller and more intense than anything effected by mortal sounds.

This melody was also the result of dissimilar and varying sounds, speeds, magnitudes and intervals arranged with reference to each other in a certain musical ratio, producing a convoluted motion most musical and gentle. Irrigated therefore with this melody, his intellect ordered and exercised thereby, he would, to the best of his ability exhibit certain symbols of these things to his disciples, especially through imitations thereof through instruments or the physical organs of voice. For he conceived that, of all the inhabitants of earth, by him alone were these celestial sounds understood and heard, as if coming from the central spring and root of nature. He therefore thought himself worthy to be taught, and to learn something about the celestial orbs, and to be assimilated to them by desire and imitation, inasmuch as his body alone had been well enough conformed thereto by the divinity who had given birth to him. As to other men, he thought they should be satisfied with looking to him and the gifts he possessed, and in being benefited and corrected through images and examples, in consequence of their inability truly to comprehend the first and genuine archetypes of things. Just as to those who are unable to look intently at the sun, we contrive to show its eclipses in either the reflections of some still water, or in melted pitch, or some smoked glass, or well brazen mirror, so we spare the weakness of their eyes devising a method of representing light that is reflective, though less intense than its archetype, to those who are interested in this sort of thing.

This peculiar organization of Pythagoras' body, far finer than that of any other man, seems to be what Empedocles was obscurely driving at in his enigmatical verses:

> Among the Pythagoreans was a man transcendent in knowledge;
> Who possessed the most ample stores of intellectual wealth,
> And in the most eminent degree assisted in the works of the wise.
> When he extended all the powers of his intellect,
> He easily beheld everything,
> As far as ten or twenty ages of the human race!

These words "transcendent," "he beheld every detail of all beings," and "the wealth of intellect," and so on, describe as accurately as possible his peculiar and exceptionally accurate method of hearing, seeing and understanding.

16. Music therefore performed this Pythagorean soul-adjustment. But another kind of purification of the discursive reason, and also of the whole soul, through various studies, was effected [by asceticism]. He had a general notion that disciplines and studies should imply some form of labor; and therefore, like a legislator, he decreed trials of the most varied nature, punishments, and restraints by fire and sword for innate intemperance, or an ineradicable desire for possessions, which the depraved should neither suffer nor sustain. Moreover, his intimates were ordered to abstain from all animal food, and any others that are hostile to the reasoning power by impeding its genuine energies. On them he likewise enjoined suppression of speech, and perfect silence, exercising them for years at a time in the subjugation of the tongue, while strenuously and assiduously investigating and ruminating over the most difficult theorems. Hence also he ordered them to abstain from wine, to be sparing in their food, to sleep little, and to cultivate an unstudied contempt of and hostility to fame, wealth, and the like; unfeignedly to reverence those to whom reverence is due, genuinely to exercise democratic assimilation and benevolence towards their fellows in age, and towards their juniors courtesy and encouragement without envy.

Moreover, Pythagoras is generally acknowledged to have been the inventor and legislator of friendship, under its many various forms, such as universal amity of all towards all, of God towards men through their piety and scientific theories, or of the mutual inter-relation of teachings, or universally of the soul towards the body, and of the rational to the irrational part, through philosophy and its underlying theories; or whether it be that of men towards each other, of citizens indeed through sound legislation, but of strangers through a correct physiology; or of the husband to the wife, or of brothers and kindred, through unperverted communion; or whether, in short, it be of all things towards all, and still farther, of certain irrational animals through justice, and a physical connec-tion and association; or whether it be the pacification and concilia-tion of the body which of itself is mortal, and of its latent conflicting powers, through health, and a temperate diet conformable to this, in imitation of the salubrious condition of the mundane elements.

In short, Pythagoras procured his disciples the most appropriate converse with the Gods, both waking and sleeping—something which never occurs in a soul disturbed by anger, pain, or pleasure, and surely all the more by any base desire, or defiled by ignorance, which is the most noxious and unholy of all the rest. By all these inventions, therefore, he divinely purified and healed the soul, resuscitating and saving its divine part, and directing to the intelli-gible its divine eye, which, as Plato says (*Rep.* 527e) is more worth saving than ten thousand corporeal eyes, for when it is strength-ened and clarified by appropriate aids, when we look through this, we perceive the truth about all being. In this particular respect, therefore, Pythagoras purified the discursive power of the soul. This is the [practical] form that erudition took with him, and such were the objects of his interest.

17. As he therefore thus prepared his disciples for culture, he did not immediately receive as an associate any who came to him for that purpose until he had tested them and examined them judi-ciously. To begin with he inquired about their relation to their par-ents and kinsfolk. Next he surveyed their laughter, speech or silence, as to whether it was unseasonable; further, about their desires, their associates, their conversation, how they employed their leisure, and what were the subjects of their joy or grief. He observed their form, their gait, and the whole motions of their body. He considered their frame's natural indications physiognom-

ically, rating them as visible exponents of the invisible tendencies of the soul.

After subjecting a candidate to such trials, he allowed him to be neglected for three years, still covertly observing his disposition towards stability, and genuine studiousness, and whether he was sufficiently averse to glory, and ready to despise popular honors.

After this the candidate was compelled to observe silence for five years, so as to have made definite experiments in continence of speech, inasmuch as the subjugation of the tongue is the most difficult of all victories, as has indeed been unfolded by those who have instituted the mysteries.

During this probation, however, the property of each was disposed of in common, being committed to trustees, who were called politicians, economizers, or legislators. Of these probationers, after the five-year silence, those who by modest dignity had won his approval as worthy to share in his doctrines, then became *esoterics*, and within the veil both heard and saw Pythagoras. Prior to this they participated in his words through the hearing alone, without seeing him who remained within the veil, and themselves offering to him a specimen of their manners.

If rejected, they were given the double of the wealth they had brought, but the *homacoi* raised to them a tomb, as if they were dead, the disciples being generally called Hearers. Should these later happen to meet the rejected candidate, they would treat him as a stranger, declaring that he whom they had by education modeled had died, inasmuch as the object of these disciplines had been to turn out good and honest men.

Those who were slow in the acquisition of knowledge were considered to be badly organized, or, we may say, deficient and sterile.

If, however, after Pythagoras had studied them physiognomically, their gait, motions and state of health, he conceived good hopes of them; and if, after the five years' silence, and the emotions and initiations from so many disciplines together with the ablutions of the soul, and so many and so great purifications produced by such various theorems, through which sagacity and sanctity is ingrained into the soul—if, after all this even, some one was found to be still sluggish and dull, they would raise to such a candidate within the school a pillar or monument, such as was said to have been done to Perialus the Thurian, and Cylon the prince of the Sybarites, who were rejected. They expelled them from the auditorium, loading them down with silver and gold. This wealth had by them been deposited in common, in the care of certain custodians, aptly called Economics. Should any of the Pythagoreans later meet with the reject, they did not recognize him who they accounted dead. Hence, also Lysis, blaming a certain Hipparchus for having revealed the Pythagorean doctrines to the profane, and to such as accepted them without disciplines or theory, said, "It is reported that you philosophize indiscriminately and publicly, which is opposed to the customs of Pythagoras. With assiduity you did indeed learn them, O Hipparchus; but you have not preserved them. My dear fellow, you have tasted Sicilian tidbits, which you should not have repeated. If you give them up, I shall be delighted; but if you do not, you will to me be dead. For it would be pious to recall the human and divine precepts of Pythagoras, and not to communicate the treasures of wisdom to those who have not purified their souls, even in a dream. It is unlawful to give away things obtained with labors so great, and with assiduity so diligent to the first person you meet, quite as much as to divulge the mysteries of the Eleusinian goddesses to the profane. Either thing would be unjust and impious. We should consider how long a time was needed to efface the stains that had insinuated themselves in our breasts, before we became worthy to receive the doctrines of Pythagoras. Unless the dyers previously purified the garments in which the desired colors were to be fixed, the dye would either fade, or be washed away entirely. Similarly, that divine man prepared the souls of lovers of philosophy, so that they might not disappoint him in any of these beautiful qualities which he hoped they would possess. He did not impart spurious doctrines, nor stratagems, in which most of the Sophists, who are at leisure for no good purpose, entangle young men; but his knowledge of things human and divine was scientific. These Sophists, however, use his doctrines as a mere pretext to commit dreadful atrocities, sweeping the youths away as in a dragnet most disgracefully, making their auditors become rash nuisances. They infuse theorems and divine doctrines into hearts whose manners are confused and agitated, just as if pure, clear water should be poured into a deep well full of mud, which would stir up the sediment and destroy the clearness of the water. Such a mutual misfortune occurs between such teachers and disciples. The intellect and heart of those whose initiation has not proceeded by disciplines, are surrounded by thickets dense and thorny, which obscure the mild, tranquil and reasoning power of the soul, and impede the development and elevation of the intellective part. These thickets are produced by intemperance and avarice, both of which are prolific...."

23. Pythagoras considered most necessary the use of symbols in instruction. Most of the Greeks had adopted it, as the most ancient, and it had been both preferentially and in principle employed by the Egyptians, who had developed it in the most varied manner. In harmony with this it will be found that Pythagoras attended to it sedulously, if from the Pythagoric symbols we unfold their significance and arcane intentions, developing their content of rectitude and truth, liberating them from their enigmatic form. When, according to straightforward and uniform tradition, they are accommodated to the sublime intelligence of these philosophers, they deify beyond human conception.

Those who came from this school, not only the most ancient Pythagoreans, but also those who during his old age were still young, such as Philolaus, and Eurytus, Charondas and Zaleucus, Brysson and the elder Archytas, Aristaeus, Lysis and Empedocles, Zalmoxis and Epimenides, Milo and Leucippus, Alcmaeon and Hippasus, and Thymaridas were all of that age, a multitude of savants, incomparably excellent—all these adopted this mode of teaching, both in their conversations, commentaries and annotations. Their writings also, and all the books which they published, most of which have been preserved to our times, were not composed in popular or vulgar diction, or in a manner usual to all other writers, so as to be immediately understood, but in a way not to be easily apprehended by their readers. For they adopted Pythagoras' law of reserve, in an arcane manner concealing divine mysteries from the uninitiated, obscuring their writings and mutual conversations.

The result is that they who present these symbols without unfolding their meaning by a suitable exposition, run the danger of exposing them to the charge of being ridiculous and inane, trifling and garrulous. When, however, the meanings are expounded according to these symbols, and made clear and obvious even to the crowds, then they will be found analogous to prophetic sayings, such as the oracles of the Pythian Apollo. Their admirable meaning will inspire those who unite intellect and scholarliness.

It might be well to mention a few of them in order to explain this mode of discipline: Do not negligently enter into a temple, nor adore carelessly, even if only at the doors. Sacrifice and adore unshod. Shunning public roads, walk in unfrequented paths. Do not without light speak about Pythagoric affairs.

Such is a sketch of the symbolic mode of teaching adopted by Pythagoras....

29. The Pythagoreans' commentaries best express his wisdom, being accurate, concise, savoring of the ancient elegance of style, and deducing the conclusions exquisitely. They contain the most condensed conceptions, and are diversified in form and matter. They are both accurate and eloquent, full of clear and indubitable arguments, accompanied by scientific demonstration, in syllogistic form, as indeed will be discovered by any careful reader.

In his writings, Pythagoras, from a supernal source, delivers the science of intelligible natures and the Gods. Afterwards, he teaches the whole of physics, completely unfolding ethics and logic. Then come various disciplines and other excellent sciences. There is nothing pertaining to human knowledge which is not discussed in these encyclopedic writings. If therefore it is acknowledged that of the [Pythagorean] writings which are now in circulation, some were written by Pythagoras himself, while others consist of what he was heard to say, and on this account are anonymous, though of Pythagoric origin—if all this be so, it is evident that he was abundantly skilled in all wisdom.

It is said that while he was in Egypt he very much applied himself to geometry. For Egyptian life bristles with geometrical problems since, from remote periods, when the Gods were fabulously said to have reigned in Egypt, on account of the rising and falling of the Nile, the skillful have been compelled to measure all the Egyptian land which they cultivated, wherefrom indeed the science's name, geometry (i.e., "earth measure"), was derived. Besides, the Egyptians studied the theories of the celestial orbs, in which Pythagoras also was skilled. All theorems about lines also seem to have been derived from that country.

All that relates to numbers and computation is said to have been discovered in Phoenicia. The theorems about the heavenly bodies have by some been referred to the Egyptians and Chaldeans in common. Whatever Pythagoras received, however, he developed further, he arranged them for learners, and personally demonstrated them with perspicuity and elegance. He was the first to give a name to philosophy, describing it as a desire for and love of wisdom, which later he defined as the science of objectified truth. Beings he defined as immaterial and eternal natures, alone possessing a power that is efficacious, as are incorporeal essences. The rest of things are beings only figuratively, and considered such only through the participation of real beings; such are corporeal and material forms, which arise and decay without ever truly existing. Now wisdom is the science of things which are truly existing beings, but not of the mere figurative entities. Corporeal natures are neither the objects of science, nor admit of a stable knowledge, since they are indefinite, and by science incomprehensible; and when compared with universals resemble non-beings, and are in a genuine sense indeterminate. Indeed it is impossible to conceive that there should be a science of things not naturally the objects of science; nor could a science of non-existent things prove attractive to any one. Far more desirable will be things which are genuine beings, existing in invariable permanency, and always answering to their description. For the perception of objects existing only figuratively, never truly being what they seem to be, follows the apprehension of real beings, just as the knowledge of particulars is posterior to the science of universals. For, as said Archytas, he who properly knows universals will also have a clear perception of the nature of particulars. That is why beings are not alone, only-begotten, nor simple, but various and multiform. For those genuine beings are intelligible and incorporeal natures, while others are corporeal, falling under the perception of sense, communicating with that which is really existent only by participation. Concerning all these Pythagoras formed the most appropriate sciences, leaving nothing uninvestigated. Besides, he developed the master sciences of method, common to all of them, such as logic, definitions, and analysis, as may be gathered from the Pythagorean commentaries.

To his intimates he was wont to utter symbolically oracular sentences, wherein the smallest number of words were pregnant with the most multifarious significance, not unlike certain oracles of the Pythian Apollo, or like Nature herself in tiny seeds, the former exhibiting conceptions, and the latter effects innumerable in multitude, and difficult to understand. Such was Pythagoras' own maxim, "The beginning is the half of the whole." In this and similar utterances the most divine Pythagoras concealed the sparks of truth, as in a treasury, for those capable of being kindled thereby. In this brevity of diction he deposited an extension of theory most ample and difficult to grasp, as in the maxim, "All things accord in number," which he frequently repeated to his disciples. Another one was, "Friendship is equality; equality is friendship." He even used single words, such as *kosmos* or "adorned world"; or, by Zeus, *philosophia*, or further, *Tetraktys!*

All these and many other similar inventions were by Pythagoras devised for the benefit and amendment of his associates; and by those that understood them, they were considered to be so worthy of veneration, and so divinely inspired, that those who dwelt in the common auditorium adopted this oath:

> I swear by the discoverer of the Tetraktys,
> Which is the spring of all our wisdom,
> The perennial root of Nature's fount.

This was the form of his so admirable wisdom.

Of the sciences honored by the Pythagoreans not the least were music, medicine and divination.

Of medicine, the most emphasized part was dietetics, and they were most scrupulous in its exercise. First they sought to understand the physical symptoms of symmetry, labor, eating and repose. They were nearly the first to make a business of the preparation of food, and to describe its methods. More frequently than their predecessors the Pythagoreans used poultices, disapproving more of medicated ointments, which they chiefly limited to the cure of ulcerations. Most of all they disapproved of cuts and cauterizations. Some diseases they cured by incantations. Music, if used in a proper manner, was by Pythagoras supposed to contribute greatly to health. The Pythagoreans likewise employed select sentences of Homer and Hesiod for the amendment of souls.

The Pythagoreans were habitually silent and prompt to hear, and he won praise who listened [most effectively]. But that which they had learned and heard was supposed to be retained and preserved in memory. Indeed this ability of learning and remembering determined the amount of disciplines and lectures, inasmuch as learning is the power by which knowledge is obtained, and remembering that by which it is preserved. Hence memory was greatly honored, abundantly exercised, and given much attention. In learning also it was understood that they were not to dismiss what they were taught, till its first rudiments had been entirely mastered. This was their method of recalling what they daily heard. No Pythagorean rose from his bed till he had first recollected the transactions of the day before; and he accomplished this by endeavoring to remember what he first said, or heard, or ordered done by his domestics before rising, or what was the second or third thing he had said, heard or commanded. The same method was employed for the remainder of the day. He would try to remember the identity of the first person he had met on leaving home, and who was the second, and with whom he had discoursed first, second or third. So also he did with everything else, endeavoring to resume in his memory all the events of the whole day, and in the very same order in which each of them had occurred. If, however, after rising there was enough leisure to do so, the Pythagorean reminisced about the day before yesterday. Thus they made it a point to exercise their memories systematically, considering that the ability of remembering was most important for experience, science and wisdom.

This Pythagorean school filled Italy with philosophers; and this place which before was unknown, was later, on account of Pythagoras, called Greater Greece, which became famous for its philosophers, poets and legislators. Indeed the rhetorical arts, demonstrative reasonings and legislation was entirely transferred from Greece. As to physics, we might mention the principal natural philosophers, Empedocles and Parmenides of Elea. As to ethical maxims, there is Epicharmus, whose conceptions are used by almost all philosophers.

Thus much concerning the wisdom of Pythagoras, how in a certain respect he very much impelled all his hearers to its pursuit, so far as they were adapted to its participation, and how perfectly he delivered it.

PART II

TESTIMONIES OF PYTHAGOREAN
AND NEOPYTHAGOREAN TRADITION

———————— ✑◎◉◎✑ ————————

There is underlying continuity—which cuts across the recognized boundaries—and similarity between early Pythagoreanism and so-called "Neopythagoreanism." The latter term was invented by modern scholarship both for reasons of classification and for the rather sinister wish to dismiss the clear analogies between early Pythagoreanism (which already regarded the philosopher as a healer of souls) and later Pythagoreanism, ostensibly "transformed into revelation" and blended with Greco-Egyptian alchemy.

Philolaus of Tarentum (born c.474 B.C.E.) belongs to early Pythagoreanism. He was the first member of the school to record Pythagorean teachings in writing; these considerably influenced Plato and the Old Academy, especially Spcusippus. Philolaus reinterpreted Homeric mythology and transposed it into his own cosmology, which was also shaped by Babylonian influences.

Archytas of Tarentum (first half of the 4th century B.C.E.) was a student of Philolaus and a personal friend of Plato. Timaeus of Locri was also related to Plato, and the famous dialogue *Timaeus* bears his very name. The extant treatise attributed to Timaeus, however, was perhaps a summary made by a student at a later date and reflects some doctrines of Middle Platonism.

A great many Pythagorean works were composed around the 3rd century B.C.E., probably as philosophical textbooks for the uninitiated, since the main teaching was transmitted orally. These writings were traditionally attributed to original members of the early Pythagorean school, which, however, should not be understood in a strictly literal or historical sense. The exact dates of the texts attributed (or perhaps really composed?) by Theages, Euryphamus, and Crito are presently beyond historical verification; but the Sentences of Sextus the Pythagorean were possibly compiled in Alexandria around the 1st century C.E.

In approaching these texts, one should refrain from calling them "forgeries," in the modern pejorative sense of the word, in that it was a widespread practice in ancient times to publish writings—important for the entire depersonalized hieratic tradition—and to attribute them to the revered masters of the past; or rather, certain archetypal masks, which may be compared to the divine Names in Islamic theology. Thus, some Pythagoreans published writings and attributed them to Pythagoras himself, who was regarded as a veritable noetic icon and an ever-living "spiritual substance" for the community. According to some testimonies, Pythagoras himself attributed certain of his poems to Orpheus. Modern scholars surmise that a large portion of the *Golden Verses* may indeed go back to the *Sacred Discourse* (*Hieros Logos*) of Pythagoras, a renowned poem in which he set out the principles of his philosophy as well as a rule of life for members of his school.

1. The *Golden Verses* of Pythagoras

There are different opinions regarding the authorship of the *Golden Verses,* which was attributed to Pythagoras by the Neoplatonists. As the French scholar Armand Delatte has pointed out, a large portion of the poem may indeed go back to the *Sacred Discourse* of Pythagoras. The *Golden Verses* may have been composed by later followers of the Pythagorean tradition during the Hellenistic age. In fact, the poem outlines the principles of daily conduct aimed at the divinization of the soul, and these principles (at first transmitted orally) are the same as those set out in the school of Pythagoras as the main rules of life.

The *Golden Verses* were used by Iamblichus in the introductory part of his *On Pythagoreanism,* and by Hierocles, who composed the *Commentary on the Golden Verses.* According to Hierocles, the *Golden Verses* and other similar Pythagorean texts were exhortations (*parangelmata*) which contained basic rules and starting-points in philosophy. These commands and exhortations were conferred on men for their edification and guidance by superior, or daemonic, souls who were free from subjection to the body and were to be honored with divine beings carried around with the divine choir. The *Golden Verses* contain the basic principles of philosophy and serve as initial marks on the way, aimed at the final assimilation to god (or rather God, since the particular gods are the masks of the supreme Divinity) through the practice of virtue and contemplation of truth. There are Arabic versions of two commentaries on the *Golden Verses,* one attributed to Iamblichus, the other to Proclus.

The *Golden Verses* have been edited and translated several times. An excellent English version by John Norris, a Platonic thinker, was published already in 1682. Here is reproduced a translation of the *Golden Verses* from Kenneth Sylvan Guthrie, *Pythagoras Source Book and Library* (Platonist Press, 1919). According to Guthrie, it has been taken from André Dacier (see Hierocles, *Commentary of Hierocles on the Golden Verses of Pythagoras,* trans. N. Rowe [from the French version of André Dacier], [1907]).

First honor the immortal gods, as the law demands;
Then reverence thy oath, and then the illustrious heroes;
Then venerate the divinities under the earth, due rites performing;
Then honor your parents, and all of your kindred.
Among others make the most virtuous thy friend!
Love to make use of his soft speeches, and learn from his deeds that are useful;
But alienate not the beloved comrade for trifling offences,
Bear all you can, what you can, for power is bound to necessity.
Take this well to heart: you must gain control of your habits;
First over stomach, then sleep, and then luxury, and anger.
What brings you shame, do not unto others, nor by yourself.
The highest of duties is honor of self.
Let justice be practiced in words as in deeds;
Then make the habit, never inconsiderately to act;
Neither forget that death is appointed to all;
That possessions here gladly gathered, here must be left;
Whatever sorrow the fate of the Gods may here send us
Dear, whatever may strike you, with patience unmurmuring;
To relieve it, so far as you can, is permitted,
But reflect that not much misfortune has Fate given to the good.
The speech of the people is various, now good, and now evil;
So let them not frighten you, nor keep you from your purpose.
If false calumnies come to your ears, support it in patience;
Yet that which I now am declaring, fulfill it faithfully:
Let no one with speech or with deeds e'er deceive you

To do or to say what is not the best.
Think, before you act, that nothing stupid results;
To act inconsiderately is part of a fool;
Yet whatever later will not bring you repentance, that you
    should carry through.
Do nothing beyond what you know,
Yet learn what you may need: thus shall your life grow happy.
Do not neglect the health of the body;
Keep measure in eating and drinking, and every exercise of
    the body.
By measure, I mean what later will not induce pain.
Follow clean habits of life, but not the luxurious;
Avoid all things which will arouse envy.
At the wrong time, never be a prodigal, as if you did not know
    what was proper,
Nor show yourself stingy, for a due measure is ever the best.
Do only those things which will not harm thee, and deliber-
    ate before you act.
Never let slumber approach thy wearied eyelids,
Ere thrice you review what this day you did:
Wherein have I sinned? What did I? What duty is neglected?
All, from the first to the last, review; and if you have erred
    grieve in your spirit, rejoicing for all that was good.
With zeal and with industry, this, then, repeat; and learn to
    repeat it with joy.
Thus wilt thou tread on the paths of heavenly virtue.
Surely, I swear it by him who into our souls has transmitted
    the Sacred Quaternary,
The spring of eternal Nature.
Never start on your task until you have implored the blessing
    of the Gods.
If this you hold fast, soon will you recognize of Gods and
    mortal men
The true nature of existence, how everything passes and
    returns.
Then will you see what is true, how Nature in all is most
    equal,
So that you hope not for what has no hope, nor that anything
    should escape you.

Men shall you find whose sorrows they themselves have cre-
ated,
Wretches who see not the Good that is too near, nothing they
hear;
Few know how to help themselves in misfortune.
That is the Fate that blinds humanity; in circles,
Hither and yon they run in endless sorrows;
For they are followed by a grim companion, disunion within
themselves;
Unnoticed, ne'er rouse him, and fly from before him!
Father Zeus, O free them all from sufferings so great,
Or show unto each the Genius, who is their guide!
Yet, do not fear, for the mortals are divine by race,
To whom holy Nature everything will reveal and demon-
strate;
Whereof if you have received, so keep what I teach you;
Healing your soul, you shall remain insured from manifold
evil.
Avoid foods forbidden; reflect that this contributes to the
cleanliness
And redemption of your soul. Consider all things well:
Let reason, the gift divine, be thy highest guide;
Then should you be separated from the body, and soar in the
ether,
You will be imperishable, a divinity, a mortal no more.

2. Pythagorean Sentences

The Pythagorean Sentences of Sextus and those collected by Iamblichus
and Stobaeus in some respects stand close to the genre of so-called wisdom
literature current in the ancient Near East and Egypt. The tradition of wise
"sentences" (*gnomai*) was, however, also prevalent in the Hellenic world.
But while the Pythagorean "symbols" (*sumbola*) resemble ancient esoteric
riddles, the Pythagorean maxims, or sentences, are pithy sayings of metaphysical and ethical doctrine, which serve as instruction, advice, and
exhortation—particularly suitable for usage in a school context. A maxim
or aphorism is, strictly speaking, a definition, or an axiomatic expression,
which functions as a wise instruction within the cross-cultural genre of gno-
mic literature. But the Pythagorean maxims have their own distinctive fla-

vor and character; they belong to the same rank as the Hermetic philosophical maxims such as the *Sayings of Agathos Daimon.*

The Sentences of Sextus the Pythagorean were popular among the Neopythagoreans, Middle Platonists, and even some early Christians (witness the case of Origen). Scholars surmise that they were composed in 2nd century C.E. Alexandria, but this is merely speculation. A more insightful view is simply to regard these sentences as the voice of a consistent and unified Neopythagorean tradition. Some of these Pythagorean sentences were collected by Iamblichus in his *Protreptic* (*Exhortation to Philosophy*), which constitutes the second book of his *On Pythagoreanism*; others were preserved by Joannes Stobaeus, a Byzantine writer, who at some date not far from 500 C.E., compiled a large collection of extracts from various Hellenic philosophers; whilst two sentences were preserved by Clement of Alexandria (c.150–c.215 C.E.), head of the famous Catechetical School of Alexandria, in his *Stromateis* or "Miscellaneous Studies."

All these Pythagorean maxims were rendered by Thomas Taylor in *Fragments of the Ethical Writings of Certain Pythagoreans in the Doric Dialect, and a Collection of Pythagoric Sentences from Stobaeus and others* (1818).

i. The Sentences of Sextus the Pythagorean

1. To neglect things of the smallest consequence is not the least thing in human life.

2. The sage and the despiser of wealth most resemble God.

3. Do not investigate the name of God because you will not find it. For everything called by a name receives its appellation from that which is more worthy than itself, so that it is one person that calls and another that hears. Who is it, therefore, who has given a name to God? The word "God" is not a name of his, but an indication of what we conceive of him.

4. God is a light incapable of receiving its opposite.

5. You have in yourself something similar to God, and therefore use yourself as the temple of God, on account of that which in you resembles God.

6. Honor God above all things that he may rule over you.

7. Whatever you honor above all things, that which you so honor will have dominion over you.

8. The greatest honor which can be paid to God is to know and imitate him.

9. There is not anything, indeed, which wholly resembles God; nevertheless, the imitation of him as much as possible by an inferior nature is grateful to him.

10. God, indeed, is not in want of anything, but the wise man is in want of God alone. He, therefore, who is in want of but few things, and those necessary, emulates him who is in want of nothing.

11. Endeavor to be great in the estimation of divinity, but among men avoid envy.

12. The sage whose estimation with men was but small while he was living will be renowned when he is dead.

13. Consider lost all the time in which you do not think of divinity.

14. A good intellect is the choir of divinity.

15. A bad intellect is the choir of evil spirits.

16. Honor that which is just on this very account that it is just.

17. You will not be concealed from divinity when you act unjustly, nor even when you think of acting so.

18. The foundation of piety is continence, but the summit of piety is to love God.

19. Wish that what is expedient and not what is pleasing may happen to you.

20. Such as you wish your neighbor to be to you, such also be to your neighbors.

21. That which God gives you none can take away.

22. Neither do nor even think of that which you are unwilling God should know.

23. Before you do anything think of God, that his light may precede your energies.

24. The soul is illuminated by the recollection of God.

25. The use of animal food is indifferent, but it is more rational to abstain from it.

26. God is not the author of any evil.

27. You should not possess more than the use of the body requires.

28. Possess those things that no one can take away from you.

29. Bear that which is necessary, as it is necessary.

30. Ask God of things such as it is worthy of God to bestow.

31. The reason that is in you is the light of your life.

32. Ask from God those things that you cannot receive from man.

33. Wish that those things which labor ought to precede may be possessed by you after labor.

34. Be not anxious to please the multitude.

35. It is not proper to despise those things of which we shall be in want after the dissolution of the body.

36. Do not ask of divinity that which, when you have obtained, you cannot perpetually possess.

37. Accustom your soul after [it has conceived all that is great of] divinity, to conceive something great of itself.

38. Esteem precious nothing which a bad man can take from you.

39. He is dear to divinity who considers those things alone precious which are esteemed to be so by divinity.

40. Everything superfluous is hostile.

41. He who loves that which is not expedient will not love that which is expedient.

42. The intellect of the sage is always with divinity.

43. God dwells in the intellect of the wise man.

44. The wise man is always similar to himself.

45. Every desire is insatiable and therefore is always in want.

46. The knowledge and imitation of divinity are alone sufficient to beatitude.

47. Use lying as poison.

48. Nothing is so peculiar to wisdom as truth.

49. When you preside over men remember that divinity presides over you also.

50. Be persuaded that the end of life is to live conformably to divinity.

51. Depraved affections are the beginnings of sorrows.

52. An evil disposition is the disease of the soul, but injustice and impiety is the death of it.

53. Use all men in a way such as if, after God, you were the common curator of all things.

54. He who uses mankind badly uses himself badly.

55. Wish that you may be able to benefit your enemies.

56. Endure all things in order that you may live conformably to God.

57. By honoring a wise man you will honor yourself.

58. In all your actions keep God before your eyes.

59. You may refuse matrimony in order to live in incessant pres-

ence with God. If, however, you know how to fight and are willing to, take a wife and beget children.

60. To live, indeed, is not in our power; but to live rightly is.

61. Be unwilling to entertain accusations against a man studious of wisdom.

62. If you wish to live successfully, you will have to avoid much in which you will come out only second-best.

63. Sweet to you should be any cup that quenches thirst.

64. Fly from intoxication as you would from insanity.

65. No good originates from the body.

66. Estimate that you are suffering a great punishment when you obtain the object of corporeal desire; for desire will never be satisfied with the attainments of any such objects.

67. Invoke God as a witness to whatever you do.

68. The bad man does not think that there is a Providence.

69. Assert that the true man is he in you who possesses wisdom.

70. The wise man participates in God.

71. Wherever that which in you is wise resides, there also is your true good.

72. That which is not harmful to the soul does not harm the man.

73. He who unjustly expels from his body a wise man, by his iniquity confers a benefit on his victim; for he is thus liberated from his bonds.

74. Only through ignorance of his soul is a man saddened by fear of death.

75. You will not possess intellect till you understand that you have it.

76. Realize that your body is the garment of your soul and then you will preserve it pure.

77. Impure daemons let not the impure soul escape them.

78. Not to every man speak of God.

79. There is danger, and no negligible one, to speak of God even the things that are true.

80. A true assertion about God is an assertion of God.

81. You should not dare to speak of God to the multitude.

82. He who does not worship God does not know him.

83. He who is worthy of God is also a God among men.

84. It is better to have nothing than to possess much and impart it to no one.

85. He who thinks that there is a God, and that he protects nothing, is no better than he who does not believe that there is a God.

86. He best honors God who makes his intellect as like God as possible.

87. He who injures none has none to fear.

88. No one who looks down to the earth is wise.

89. To lie is to deceive, and be deceived.

90. Recognize what God is, and that in you which recognizes God.

91. It is not death, but a bad life, which destroys the soul.

92. If you know him by whom you were made, you would know yourself.

93. It is not possible for a man to live conformably to divinity unless he acts modestly, well and justly.

94. Divine wisdom is true science.

95. You should not dare to speak of God to an impure soul.

96. The wise man follows God, and God follows the soul of the wise man.

97. A king rejoices in those he governs, and therefore God rejoices in the wise man. He who governs likewise is inseparable from those he governs; and therefore God is inseparable from the soul of the wise man, which he defends and governs.

98. The wise man is governed by God, and on this account is blessed.

99. A scientific knowledge of God causes a man to use but few words.

100. To use many words in speaking of God obscures the subject.

101. The man who possesses a knowledge of God will not be very ambitious.

102. The erudite, chaste and wise soul is the prophet of the truth of God.

103. Accustom yourself always to look to the Divinity.

104. A wise intellect is the mirror of God.

ii. Pythagorean Sentences from the *Exhortation to Philosophy* of Iamblichus

105. As we live through soul, it must be said that by the virtue of

this we do live well; just as because we see through the eyes, we see well through their virtues.

106. It must not be thought that gold can be injured by rust, or virtue by baseness.

107. We should betake ourselves to virtue as to an inviolable temple, so that we may not be exposed to any ignoble insolence of soul with respect to our communion with, and continuance in, life.

108. We should confide in virtue as in a chaste wife, but trust to fortune as an inconstant mistress.

109. It is better that virtue should be received accompanied by poverty, than wealth with violence; and frugality with health, than voracity with disease.

110. An overabundance of food is harmful to the body, but the body is preserved when the soul is disposed in a becoming manner.

111. It is as dangerous to give power to a depraved man as it is to give a sword to a madman.

112. As it is better for a part of the body that contains purulent decay to be burned than to continue as it is, thus also is it better for a depraved man to die than to continue to live.

113. The theorems of philosophy are to be enjoyed as much as possible, as if they were ambrosia and nectar. For the resultant pleasure is genuine, incorruptible and divine. They are also capable of producing magnanimity, and though they cannot make us eternal, yet they enable us to obtain a scientific knowledge of eternal natures.

114. If vigor of sensation is, as it is, considered to be desirable, so much more strenuously should we endeavor to obtain prudence; for it is, as it were, the sensitive vigor of the practical intellect, which we contain. And as through the former we are not deceived in sensible perceptions, so through the latter we avoid false reasonings in practical affairs.

115. We shall properly venerate Divinity if we purify our intellect from vice as from a stain.

116. A temple should, indeed, be adorned with gifts, but the soul with disciplines.

117. As the lesser mysteries are to be delivered before the greater, thus also discipline must precede philosophy.

118. The fruits of the earth, indeed, appear annually, but the fruits of philosophy ripen at all seasons.

119. As he who wishes the best fruit must pay most attention to the land, so must the greatest attention be paid to the soul if it is to produce fruits worthy of its nature.

iii. Pythagorean Sentences from Stobaeus

120. Do not even think of doing what ought not to be done.

121. Choose rather to be strong in soul than in body.

122. Be sure that laborious things contribute to virtue more than do pleasurable things.

123. Every passion of the soul is most hostile to its salvation.

124. Pythagoras said that it is most difficult simultaneously to walk in many paths of life.

125. Pythagoras said that we must choose the best life, for custom will make it pleasant. Wealth is a weak anchor, glory still weaker, and similarly with the body, dominion, and honor. Which anchors are strong? Prudence, magnanimity and fortitude; these can be shaken by no tempest. This is the law of God: that virtue is the only thing strong, all else is a trifle.

126. All the parts of human life, just as those of a statue, should be beautiful.

127. As a statue stands immovable on its pedestal, so should stand a man on his deliberate choice, if he is worthy.

128. Incense is for the Gods, but praise for good men.

129. Men unfairly accused of acting unjustly should be defended, while those who excel should be praised.

130. It is not the sumptuous adornment of the horse that earns him praise, but rather the nature of the horse himself; nor is the man worthy merely because he owns great wealth, but rather because his soul is generous.

131. When the wise man opens his mouth the beauties of his soul present themselves to view as the statues in a temple.

132. Remind yourself that all men assert wisdom is the greatest good, but that there are few who strenuously endeavor to obtain this greatest good (Pythagoras).

133. Be sober, and remember to be disposed to believe, for these are the nerves of wisdom (Epicharmus).

134. It is better to live lying on the grass, confiding in divinity and yourself, than to lie on a golden bed with perturbation.

135. You will not be in want of anything, which is in the power of Fortune to give or take away (Pythagoras).

136. Despise all those things which you will not want when liberated from the body; and exercising yourself in those things of which you will be in want when liberated from the body, be sure to invoke the Gods to become your helpers (Pythagoras).

137. It is as impossible to conceal fire in a garment as a base deviation from rectitude in time (Demophilus, rather than Socrates).

138. Wind increases fire, but custom increases love (Demophilus, rather than Socrates).

139. Only those are dear to divinity who are hostile to injustice (Democritus or Demophilus).

140. Bodily necessities are easily procured by anybody without labor or molestation; but those things whose attainment demands effort and trouble are objects of desire not to the body, but to depraved opinion (Aristoxenus the Pythagorean).

141. Thus spoke Pythagoras of desire: This passion is various, laborious and very multiform. Of desires, however, some are acquired and artificial, while others are inborn. Desire is a certain tendency and impulse of the soul, and an appetite of fullness, or presence of sense, or of an emptiness and absence of it, and of non-perception. The three best known kinds of depraved desire are the improper, the unproportionate, and the unseasonable. For desire is either immediately indecorous, troublesome or illiberal; or if not absolutely so, it is improperly vehement and persistent. Or, in the third place, it is impelled at an improper time, or towards improper objects (Aristoxenus).

142. Pythagoras said: Endeavor not to conceal your errors by words, but to remedy them by reproofs.

143. Pythagoras said: It is not so difficult to err, as not to reprove him who errs.

144. As a bodily disease cannot be healed, if it is concealed or praised, thus also can neither a remedy be applied to a diseased soul which is badly guarded and protected (Pythagoras).

145. The grace of freedom of speech, like beauty in season, is productive of great delight.

146. To have a blunt sword is as improper as to use ineffectual freedom of speech.

147. Neither is the sun to be taken from the world, nor freedom of speech from erudition.

148. As one who is clothed with a cheap robe may have a good habit of body, thus also may he whose life is poor possess freedom of speech.

149. Pythagoras said: Prefer those that reprove to those that flatter; but avoid flatterers as much as enemies.

150. The life of the avaricious resembles a funeral banquet. For though it has all desirable elements no one rejoices.

151. Pythagoras said: Acquire continence as the greatest strength and wealth.

152. "Not frequently man from man," is one of the exhortations of Pythagoras, by which obscurely he signifies that it is not proper frequently to engage sexual connections.

153. Pythagoras said: A slave to his passions cannot possibly be free.

154. Pythagoras said that intoxication is the preparation for insanity.

155. On being asked how a wine-lover might be cured of intoxication Pythagoras said, "If he frequently considers what were his actions during intoxication."

156. Pythagoras said that unless you had something better than silence to say, you had better keep silence.

157. Pythagoras said that rather than utter an idle word you had better throw a stone in vain.

158. Pythagoras said: Say not few things in many words, but much in few words.

159. Epicharmus said: To men genius is a divinity, either good or evil.

160. On being asked how a man ought to behave towards his country when it had acted unjustly towards him, Pythagoras said, "As to a mother."

161. Traveling teaches a man frugality and self-sufficiency. The sweetest remedies for hunger and weariness are bread made of milk and flour, on a bed of grass (Attributed to Democritus, but probably Democrates or Demophilus).

162. Every land is equally suitable as a residence for the wise man; the worthy soul's fatherland is the whole world.

163. Pythagoras said that into cities enter first, luxury; then being glutted; then lascivious insolence; and last, destruction.

164. Pythagoras said that the best city was that which contained the worthiest man.

165. "You should do those things that you judge to be beautiful, though in doing them you should lack renown, for the rabble is a bad judge of a good thing. Wherefore despise the reprehension of those whose praise you despise" (Pythagoras).

166. Pythagoras said that "Those who do not punish bad men are really wishing that good men be injured."

167. Pythagoras said: Not without a bridle can a horse be governed, and no less riches without prudence.

168. The prosperous man who is vain is no better than the driver of a race on a slippery road (Attributed to Socrates, but probably Democrates or Demophilus).

169. There is not any gate of wealth so secure which the opportunity of Fortune may not open (Attributed to Democritus, but probably Democrates or Demophilus).

170. The unrestrained grief of a torpid soul may be expelled by reasoning (Democrates, not Democritus).

171. Poverty should be born with equanimity by a wise man (Democrates, not Democritus).

172. Pythagoras said: Spare your life, lest you consume it with sorrow and care.

173. Favorinus, in speaking of old age, said, "Nor will I be silent as to this particular, that both to Plato and Pythagoras it appeared that old age was not to be considered with reference to an egress from the present life, but to the beginning of a blessed one."

iv. Pythagorean Sentences from the *Stromateis* (Book 3) of Clement of Alexandria

174. Philolaus said that the ancient theologians and priests testified that the soul is united to the body as through a certain punishment, and that it is buried in this body as a sepulcher.

175. Pythagoras said that "Whatever we see when awake is death, and when asleep is a dream."

3. Fragments of Philolaus

Philolaus of Tarentum was the first member of the Pythagorean school to record Pythagorean teachings in writing. Iamblichus argues for Philolaus as coming from Heraclea; but Aristoxenus' list, which he reproduces, mentions Philolaus among the Pythagoreans from the region of Tarentum (present-day south Italy).

The Philolaic fragments are recognized as being authentic and provide the earliest testimony of the original Pythagorean teachings. With the name of Philolaus is associated the idea of the central fire, or a fiery hearth, as the center of the universe. The closest body to the central fire is the counter-earth (*antichton*). For his astronomical and astrological knowledge Philolaus was indebted to Babylonia. He influenced the thought of Plato and his immediate successor Speusippus, who had direct contact with Pythagoreans and wrote on Pythagorean metaphysics. Thus, Speusippus stands in a line of tradition which closely links Philolaus and the Old Academy in her attempts to modernize Pythagorean doctrine and harmonize it with current Platonism.

The selected fragments here reproduced were rendered into English by Kenneth Sylvan Guthrie, *Pythagoras Source Book and Library* (Platonist Press, 1919). He took them from A.E. Chaignet, *Pythagore et la philosophie pythagoricienne*, 2 vols. (Paris: Librairie Academique, 1874), vol. 1, pp.226-254.

11A. (Stobaeus, *Eclog. Physic.* 1.22.1, p.488). Philolaus has located the fire in the middle, the center; he calls it Hestia, of the All, the Guardpost of Zeus, the Mother of the Gods, the Altar, the Link, and the Measure of Nature. Besides, he locates a second fire, quite at the top, surrounding the world. The center, says he, is by its nature the first; around it, the ten different bodies carry out their choral dance. These are: the heaven, the planets, lower the sun, and below it the moon; lower the earth, and beneath this, the counter-earth, then beneath these bodies the fire of Hestia, in the center, where it maintains order. The highest part of the Covering, in which he asserts that the elements exist in a perfectly pure condition, is called Olympus; the space beneath the revolution-circle of Olympus, and where in order are disposed the five planets, the sun and moon, forms the Cosmos; finally, beneath the latter is the sublunar region, which surrounds the earth, where are the generative things, susceptible to change. All that is the heaven. The order which manifests in the celestial phenomena is the object of science;

the disorder which manifests in the things of becoming, is the object of virtue; the former is perfect, the latter is imperfect....

17. (Iamblichus, *In. Nicom.* 11). Philolaus says that Number is the sovereign and autogenic force which maintains the eternal permanence of cosmic things.

18A. (Stobaeus, 1.3.8). The power, efficacy and essence of Number is seen in the Decad; it is great, it realizes all its purposes, and it is the cause of all effects. The power of the Decad is the principle and guide of all life, divine, celestial, or human into which it is insinuated; without it everything is unlimited, obscure, and furtive. Indeed, it is the nature of Number which teaches us comprehension, which serves us as guide, and teaches us all things which would otherwise remain impenetrable and unknown to every man. For there is nobody who could get a clear notion about things in themselves, nor in their relations, if there was no Number or Number-essence. By means of sensation, Number instills a certain proportion, and thereby establishes among all things harmonic relations, analogous to the nature of the geometric figure called the gnomon; it incorporates intelligible reasons of things, separates them, individualizes them, both in limited and unlimited things. And it is not only in matters pertaining to daemons or Gods that you may see the force manifested by the nature and power of Number, but it is in all its works, in all human thoughts, everywhere indeed, and even in the productions of arts and music. The nature of Number and Harmony is numberless, for what is false has no part in their essence and the principle of error and envy is thoughtless, irrational, indefinite nature. Never could error slip into Number, for its nature is hostile thereto. Truth is the proper, innate character of Number.

18B. (Iamblichus, *Theol. Arith.* 61). The Decad is also named Faith, because, according to Philolaus, it is by the Decad and its elements, if utilized energetically and without negligence, that we arrive at a solidly grounded faith about beings. It is also the source of memory, and that is why the Monad has been called Mnemosyne.

19A. (Theon of Smyrna, *Plat. Math.* 4). Archytas and Philolaus use the terms Monad and Unity interchangeably.

19B. (Syrianus, *Comment. in Arist. Met.* 1.14). You must not suppose that the philosophers begin by principles supposed to be opposite; they know the principle above these two elements, as Philolaus acknowledges when saying that it is God who hypostasizes the Limited and Unlimited. He shows that it is by Limit that every coordinate series of things further approaches Unity, and that it is by the Unlimited that the lower series is produced. Thus even above these two principles they posited the unique and separate cause distinguished by all of its excellence. This is the cause which Archinetus called the cause before the cause, and which Philolaus vehemently insists is the principle of all, and of which Brontinus says that in power and dignity it surpasses all reason and essence.

20. (Proclus, *In. Eucl.* 130; 166–167; 173). Even among the Pythagoreans we find different angles consecrated to the different divinities, as did Philolaus, who attributed to some the angle of the triangle, to others the angle of the rectangle, to others other angles, and sometimes the same to several.

The Pythagoreans say that the triangle is the absolute principle of generation of begotten things, and of their form; that is why Timaeus says that the reasons of physical being, and of the regular formation of the elements are triangular; indeed, they have the three dimensions, in unity they gather the elements which in themselves are absolutely divided and changing; they are filled with the infinity characteristic of matter, and above the material beings they form bonds that indeed are frail. That is why triangles are bounded by straight lines, and have angles which unite the lines, and are their bonds. Philolaus was therefore right in devoting the angle of the triangle to four divinities, Kronos, Hades, Ares, and Bacchus, under these four names combining the fourfold disposition of the elements, which refers to the superior part of the universe, starting from the sky, or sections of the zodiac. Indeed, Kronos presides over everything humid and cold in essence; Ares, over everything fiery; Hades contains everything terrestrial, and Dionysus directs the generation of wet and warm things, represented by wine, which is liquid and warm. These four divinities divide their secondary operations, but they remain united; that is why Philolaus, by attributing to them one angle only, wished to express this power of unification.

The Pythagoreans also claim that, in preference to the quadrilateral, the tetragon bears the divine impress, and by it they express perfect order. For the property of being straight imitates the power of immutability, and equality represents that of permanence; for motion is the result of inequality, and rest, that of equality. Those are the causes of the organization of the being that is solid in its totality, and of its pure and immovable essences. They were therefore right to express it symbolically by the figure of the tetragon. Besides, Philolaus, with another stroke of genius, calls the angle of the tetragon that of Rhea, of Demeter, and of Hestia. For considering the earth as a tetragon, and noting that this element possesses the property of continuousness, as we learned from Timaeus, and that the earth receives all that drips from the divinities, and also the generative powers that they contain, he was right in consecrating the angle of the tetragon to these divinities which procreate life. Indeed, some of them call the earth Hestia and Demeter, and claim that it partakes of Rhea, in its entirety, and that Rhea contains all the begotten cause. That is why, in obscure language, he says that the angle of the tetragon contains the single power which produces the unity of these divine creations.

And we must not forget that Philolaus assigns the angle of the triangle to four divinities, and the angle of the tetragon to three, thereby indicating their penetrative faculty, whereby they influence each other mutually, and showing how all things participate in all things, the odd things in the even and the even in the odd. The triad and the tetrad, participating in the generative and creative beings, contain the whole regular organization of begotten things. Their product is the dodecad, which ends in the single monad, the sovereign principle of Zeus, for Philolaus says that the angle of the dodecagon belongs to Zeus, because in unity Zeus contains the entire number of the dodecad.

4. Pythagorean Pseudepigrapha

Around the 3rd century B.C.E. and later, a number of Pythagorean writings were composed—some of them as philosophical textbooks for laymen. Many of these writings were attributed to original members of the old Pythagorean school, though, as mentioned, they cannot be regarded as "forgeries" in the modern sense of the word. For the most part they were composed in a Doric literary dialect and included much Platonic and Aristotelian doctrine. Of these writings only some works attributed to the 4th century B.C.E. Pythagoreans Philolaus and Archytas have any real chance of being genuine. We do not know by whom or when they were really written. As John Dillon has pointed out:

We may guess from the contents of the works that their purpose was to reveal Pythagoras, or at least some Pythagorean, as the originator of various Platonic and Aristotelian doctrines, and perhaps to satisfy the demand in Hellenistic libraries for "genuine" Pythagorean works. (King Juba of Mauritania, for instance, was a great enthusiast for *Pythagorica*). The fact of their having been composed at all does testify to a continuing interest in some quarters in the Pythagorean tradition. It is in this period also, presumably, that the myth of Pythagoras' life took the shape which we find reflected later in the Lives of Pythagoras by Diogenes Laertius, Porphyry and Iamblichus, since this image of Pythagoras serves as an inspiration to Apollonius of Tyana in the first part of the first century C.E., and indeed as a stimulus to Philo in composing his portrait of Moses.[1]

Archytas of Tarentum was a disciple of Philolaus and knew Plato personally. He was elected chief magistrate of Tarentum seven times, and made some contribution to harmonic theory and Pythagorean mathematics. Iamblichus used a logical work incorrectly attributed to Archytas and, as a consequence, believed that Aristotle was inspired by Archytas.

Timaeus of Locri is the main character of Plato's dialogue *Timaeus* which presents the Pythagorean cosmology. We know nothing about Timaeus as a person. The Neoplatonists thought that the writings by Timaeus inspired Plato, but it seems that the treatise surviving under his name was only an epitome of the cosmology espoused by Plato and consists of reduced statements along with some later additions. It thus seems to be a summary made by a student of Hellenistic times (3rd–1st century B.C.E.).

Nothing can be said about Theages, Euryphamus and Crito, except that the texts under their names are deeply imbued with Pythagorean ideas and undoubtedly belong to the Pythagorean tradition. It is also possible that they were produced before the so-called Neopythagorean revival which took place at the beginning of the 1st century C.E.

The excerpts of Timaeus and Archytas were rendered by Kenneth Sylvan Guthrie in *Pythagoras Source Book and Library* (Platonist Press, 1919). He took Archytas from A.E. Chaignet, *Pythagore et la philosophie pythagoricienne*, 2 vols. (Paris: Librairie Academique, 1874), vol. 1, pp.256–331.

The texts of Theages, Euryphamus and Crito were translated by Thomas Taylor, *Fragments of the Ethical Writings of Certain Pythagoreans in the Doric Dialect* (1818).

---

1. John Dillon *The Middle Platonists. A Study of Platonism 80 B.C. to A.D.220*, (London: Duckworth, 1996), p.119.

i. The Fragments of Archytas

1. There are necessarily two principles of beings: the one contains the series of beings organized, and finished; the other, contains unordered and unfinished beings. That one which is susceptible of being expressed, by speech, and which can be explained, embraces both beings, and determines and organizes the non-being.

For every time that it approaches the things of becoming, it orders them, and measures them, and makes them participate in the essence and form of the universal. On the contrary, the series of beings which escapes speech and reason, injures ordered things, and destroys those which aspire to essence and being; whenever it approaches them, it assimilates them to its own nature.

But since there are two principles of things of an opposite character, the one the principle of good, and the other the principle of evil, there are therefore also two reasons, the one of beneficent nature, the other of maleficent nature.

That is why the things that owe their existence to art, and also those which owe it to nature, must above all participate in these two principles: form and substance.

The form is the cause of essence; substance is the substrate which receives the form. Neither can substance alone participate in form, by itself; nor can form by itself apply itself to substance; there must therefore exist another cause which moves the substance of things, and forms them. This cause is primary, as regards substance, and the most excellent of all. Its most suitable name is God.

There are therefore three principles: God, the substance of things, and form. God is the artist, the mover; the substance is the matter, the moved; the essence is what you might call the art, and that to which the substance is brought by the mover. But since the mover contains forces which are self-contrary, those of simple bodies, and as the contraries are in need of a principle harmonizing and unifying them, it must necessarily receive its efficacious virtues and proportions from numbers, and all that is manifested in numbers and geometric forms, virtues and proportions capable of binding and uniting into form the contraries that exist in the substance of things. For, by itself, substance is formless; only after having been moved towards form does it become formed and receive the rational relations of order. Likewise, if movement exists, besides the thing moved, there must exist a prime mover; there must therefore be three principles: the substance of things, the form, and the principle that moves itself, and which by its power is the first; not only must this principle be an intelligence, it must be above intelligence, and we call it God.

Evidently the relation of equality applies to the being which can be defined by language and reason. The relation of inequality applies to the irrational being, and cannot be fixed by language; it is substance, and that is why all begetting and destruction take place in substance and do not occur without it.

2. In short, the philosophers began only by so to speak contrary principles; but above these elements they knew another superior one, as is testified to by Philolaus, who says that God has produced, and realized the Limited and Unlimited, and shown that at the Limit is attached the whole series which has a greater affinity with the One, and to the Unlimited, the series that is below. Thus, above these two principles they have posited a unifying cause, superior to everything; which, according to Archenetus, is the cause before the cause, and, according to Philolaus, the universal principle.

ii. Timaeus of Locri
On the World and the Soul

1. Timaeus of Locri said the following:

Of all the things in the universe there are two causes: Mind, of things existing according to reason; and Necessity, of things [existing] by force, according to the power of bodies. The former of these causes is the nature of the good, and is called God, and the principle of things that are best, but what accessory causes follow are referred to Necessity. Regarding the things in the universe, there exist Form, Matter and the Perceptible which is, as it were, an offspring of the two others. Form is unproduced, unmoved, stationary, of the nature of the Same, perceptible by the mind, and a pattern of such things produced as exist by a state of change: that is what Form is said to be.

Matter, however, is a recipient of impressions, is a mother and a nurse, and is procreative of the third kind of being; for receiving upon itself the resemblances of form, and as it were remolding them, it perfects these productions. He asserted moreover that matter, though eternal, is not unmoved; and though of itself it is formless and shapeless, yet it receives every kind of form; and that which is around bodies is divisible and partakes of the nature of the Different; and that matter is called by the twin names of Place and Space.

These two principles then are opposite to each other, of which Form is analogous to a male power and a father, while matter is analogous to a female power and a mother. The third thing is their offspring. Being three, they are recognizable by three marks: Form, by mind, according to knowledge; Matter by a spurious kind of reasoning, because it cannot be mentally perceived directly, but by analogy; and their production by sensation and opinion.

2. Before the heavens, then, there existed through reason Form and Matter, and the God who develops the best. But since the older surpasses the younger, and the ordered surpasses the orderless, the deity, being good—on seeing that Matter receives Form, and is altered in every way, but without order—found the necessity of organizing it, altering the undefined to the defined, so that the differences between bodies might be proportionately related, not receiving various alterations at random. He therefore made this world out of the whole of Matter, laying it down as a limit to the nature of being, through its containing in itself the rest of things, being one, only-begotten, perfect, endowed with soul and reason—for these qualities are superior to the soulless and the irrational—and of a sphere-like body, for this is more perfect than the rest of forms.

Desirous then of making a very good production he made it a divinity, created and never to be destroyed by any cause other than the God who had put it in order, if indeed he should ever wish to dissolve it. But on the part of the good there is no rushing forward to the destruction of a very beautiful production. Such therefore being the world, it continues without corruption and destruction, being blessed. It is the best of things created, since it has been produced by the best cause, which looked not to patterns made by hand but to Form in the abstract, and to Existence, perceiving by the mind to which the created thing, having been carefully adjusted, has become the most beautiful. It is even perfect in the realm of sense because its pattern, containing in itself all the living things perceived by mind, left out nothing, being the limit of the things perceived by mind, as this world is of those perceived by sense.

Being solid and perceptible by touch and sight, the world has a share of earth and fire, and of the things between them, air and water; and it is composed of all perfect bodies, which are in it as wholes, so that no part might ever be left out, in order that the body of the Universe might be altogether self-sufficient, uninjured by corruption from without or within; for apart from these there is nothing else, and hence the things combined according to the best proportions and with equal powers, neither rule over, nor are ruled by each other in turn, so that some receive an increase, others a decrease, remaining indissolubly united according to the very best proportions.

3. Whenever there are any three terms with mutually equal intervals that are proportionate, we then perceive that, after the matter of an extended string, the middle is to the first, as is the third to it, and this holds true inversely and alternately, interchanging places and order, so that it is impossible to arrange them numerically without producing an equivalence of results. Likewise the world's shape and movement are well arranged; the shape is a sphere, self-similar on all sides, able to contain all shapes that are similar, and the movement endlessly exhibits the change dependent on a circle. Now as the sphere is on every side equidistant from the center, it is able to retain its poise whether in movement or at rest, neither losing its poise nor assuming another. Its external appearance being exactly smooth, it needs no mortal organs such as are fitted to and present in all other living beings because of their wants. The world soul's element of divinity radiates out from the center entirely penetrating the whole world, forming a single mixture of divided substance with undivided form; and this mixture of two forces, the Same and the Different, became the origin of motion, which indeed was not accomplished in the easiest way, being extremely difficult.

Now all these proportions are combined harmonically according to numbers, which proportions were scientifically divided according to a scale which reveals the elements and the means of the soul's combination. Now seeing that the earlier is more powerful in power and time than the later, the deity did not rank the soul after the substance of the body, but made it older by taking the first of unities, 384. Knowing this first, we can easily reckon the double (square) and the triple (cube); and all the terms together, with the complements and eights, there must be 36 divisions, and the total amounts to 114,695....

5. The Earth, fixed at the center, becomes the hearth of the Gods and the boundary of darkness and day, producing settings and risings according to the occultation produced by the things that form the boundary, just as we improve our sight by making a tube with our closed hand, to exclude refraction. Earth is the oldest body in the heavens. Water was not produced without earth, nor air without moisture, nor could fire continue without moisture and the materials that are inflammable, so that earth is fixed upon its balance at the root and base of all other substances.

Of produced things, the substratum is Matter, while the reason of each shape is abstract Form; of these two the offspring is Earth and Water, Air and Fire.

This is how they were created. Every body is composed of surfaces, whose elements are triangles, of which one is right-angled, and the other has all unequal sides, with the square of the longer side being thrice the size of the lesser, while its least angle is the third of a right angle. The middle one is the double of the least, for it is two-thirds of a right angle. The greatest is a right angle, being one-and-a-half times greater than the middle one, and the triple of the least. Now this unequal sided triangle is half of an equilateral triangle, cut into two equal parts by a line let down from the apex to the base. In each of these triangles there is a right angle; but in the one, the two sides about the right angle are equal, and in the other all the sides are unequal. Now let this be called a scalene triangle; while the other, the half of the square, is the principle of the constitution of Earth. For the square produced from this scalene triangle is composed of four half-squares and from such a square is produced the cube, the most stationary and steady form in every way, having six sides and eight angles. On this account Earth is the heaviest and most difficult elemental body to move, and its substance is inconvertible, because it has no affinity with the other type of triangle. Only Earth has a peculiar element of the square, while the other triangle is the element of the three other substances, Fire, Air and Water. For when the half triangle is put together six times it produces the solid equilateral triangle, the exemplar of the tetrahedron, which has four faces with equal angles, which is the form of Fire, as the easiest to be moved, and composed of the finest particles. After this ranks the octahedron, with eight faces and six angles, being the element of Air; and the third is the icosahedron, with twenty faces and twelve angles, being the element of Water, composed of the most numerous and heaviest particles.

These then, as being composed of the same element, are transmuted into one another. But the deity made the dodecahedron the image of the Universe, as being the nearest to the sphere. Fire then, by the fineness of its particles, passes through all things; and Air through the rest of things, with the exception of Fire; and Water through the Earth. All things are therefore full, and have no vacuum. They cohere by the revolving movement of the Universe, and are pressed against and rubbed by each other in turn, and produce the never-failing change from generation to destruction.

6. By making use of these the deity put together this world, sensible to touch through the particles of Earth, and to sight through those of Fire, which two are the extremes. Through the particles of Air and Water he had conjoined the world by the strongest chain, namely proportion, which restrains not only itself but all its subjects. Now if the conjoined object is a plane surface one middle term is sufficient, but if a solid there will be need of two mean terms. With two middle terms, therefore, he combined two extremes, so that as Fire is to Air, Air is to Water; and as Air is to Water, so is Water to Earth; and by alternation, as Fire is to Water, Air might be to Earth. Now since all are equal in power, their ratios are in a state of equilibrium. This world then is one, through the bond of the deity, made according to proportion.

Now each of these substances possesses many forms. Fire has those of flame, burning and luminousness, through the inequality of the triangles in each of them. In the same manner Air is partly clear and dry, and partly turbid and foggy. Water can be partly flowing and partly congealed, as it is in snow, frost, hail or ice. That which is moist is in one respect flowing as honey and oil, but in another is compact as pitch and wax. Concerning solids some are fusible, as gold, silver, copper, tin, lead and copper, and some brittle as sulfur, asphalt, niter, salt, alum, and similar materials.

7. After putting together the world, the deity planned the creation of mortal beings so that, himself being perfect, he might perfectly complete the world. Therefore he mixed up the soul of man out of the same proportions and powers, and after taking the particles and distributing them, he delivered them over to Nature, whose office is to effect change. She then took up the task of working out

mortal and ephemeral living beings, whose souls were drawn in from different sources, some from the moon, others from the sun, and others from various planets, [from] that cycle within the Difference, with the exception of one single power which was derived from Sameness, which she mixed up in the rational portion of the soul, as the image of wisdom in those of a happy fate.

Now in the soul of man one portion is rational and intellectual, and another irrational and unintellectual. Of the logical part the best portion is derived from Sameness, while the worst comes from Difference, and each is situated around the head so that the other parts of the soul and body may minister to it, as the supreme part of the whole body. Of the irrational portion, that which represents passion hovers around the heart, while desire inhabits the liver. The principle of the body and root of the marrow is the brain, wherein resides the ruling power; and from this, like an effusion, through the back-bone flows what is left over from the brain, from which are separated the particles of semen and seed. The marrow's surrounding defenses are the bones, of which the flesh is the covering and concealment. To the nerves he united joints by tendons, suitable for their movement. Of the internal organs, some exist for the sake of nourishment and others for safety. Of exterior motions, some are conveyed to the interior intelligent places of perception while others, not falling under the power of apprehension, are unperceived, either because the affected bodies are too earth-like or because the movements are too feeble. The painful movements tend to arouse nature, while the pleasurable lull nature into remaining within herself.

iii. Theages
On the Virtues

The principles of all virtue are three: knowledge, power and deliberate choice. Knowledge indeed is that by which we contemplate and form a judgment of things; power is a certain strength of nature from which we derive our subsistence, and which gives stability to our actions; and deliberate choice is, as it were, the hand of the soul by which we are impelled to, and lay hold on, the objects of our choice.

The soul is divided into reasoning power, anger and desire. Reasoning power rules knowledge, anger deals with impulse, and desire bravely rules the soul's affections. When these three parts unite into one action, exhibiting a composite energy, then concord and virtue result in the soul. When sedition divides them, then discord and vice appear.

When the reasoning power prevails over the irrational part of the soul, then endurance and continence are produced; endurance indeed in the retention of pains, but continence in the absence of pleasures. But when the irrational parts of the soul prevail over the reasoning part of the soul, then are produced effeminacy in flying from pain, and incontinence in being vanquished by the pleasures. When however the better part of the soul prevails, the less excellent part is governed; the former leads, and the latter follows, and both consent and agree, and then in the whole soul is generated virtue and all the goods. Again, when the appetitive part of the soul follows the reasoning, then is produced temperance; when this is the case with the irascible, courage appears; and when it takes place in all the parts of the soul, then the result is justice. Justice is that which separates all the vices and all the virtues of the soul from each other. Justice is an established order and organization of the parts of the soul, and the perfect and supreme virtue; in this every good is contained, while the other goods of the soul cannot subsist without it. Hence Justice possesses great influence both among Gods and men. It contains the bond by which the whole and the universe are held together, and also that by which the Gods and men are connected (cf. Plato, *Gorgias* 507e). Among the celestials it is called Themis, and among the terrestrials it is called Dike, while among men it is called the Law. These are but symbols indicative that justice is the supreme virtue. Virtue, therefore, when it consists in contemplating and judging, is called wisdom; when in sustaining dreadful things, is called courage; when in restraining pleasure, it is called temperance; and when in abstaining from injuring our neighbors, justice.

Obedience to virtue according to, and transgression thereof contrary to right reason, tends toward decorousness, and its opposite. Propriety is that which ought to be. This requires neither addition nor detraction, being what it should be. The improper is of two kinds: excess and defect. The excess is over-scrupulousness, and its deficiency, laxity. Virtue however is a habit of propriety. Hence it is both a climax and a medium of which are proper things. They are

media because they fall between excess and deficiency; they are cli-
maxes because they endure neither increase nor decrease, being
just what they ought to be.

iv. Euryphamus
Concerning Human Life

The perfect life of man falls short indeed of the life of God because
it is not self-perfect, but surpasses that of irrational animals, participating as it does of virtue and felicity. For neither is God in want of
external causes—as he is naturally good and happy, and is perfect
from himself—nor is he in want of any irrational animal. For beasts
being destitute of reason, they are also destitute of the sciences pertaining to actions. But the nature of man partly consists of his own
proper deliberate choice, and partly is in want of the assistance
derived from divinity. For that which is capable of being fashioned
by reason, which has an intellectual perception of things beautiful
and base, can from earth erect itself and look to heaven, and with
the eye of intellect can perceive the highest Gods—that which is
capable of all this likewise receives assistance from the Gods.

But in consequence of possessing will, deliberate choice, and a
principle of such a kind as enables it to study virtue, and to be agitated by the storms of vice, to follow, and also to apostatize from the
Gods—it is likewise able to be moved by itself. Hence it may be
praised or blamed, partly by the Gods, and partly by men, according as it applies itself zealously either to virtue or vice.

For the whole reason of the thing is as follows: Divinity introduced man into the world as a most exquisite being, to be honored
reciprocally with himself, and as the eye of the orderly systematiza-
tion of everything. Hence also man gave things names, himself
becoming the character of them. He also invented letters, through
these procuring a treasury of memory. He imitated the established
order of the universe, by laws and judicial proceedings, organizing
the communion of cities. For no human work is more honorable in
the eyes of the world, nor more worthy of notice by the Gods, than
proper constitution of a city governed by good laws, distributed in an
orderly fashion throughout the state. For though by himself no man
amounts to anything, and by himself is not able to lead a life conforming to the common concord, and to the proper organization of
a state; yet he is well adapted to the perfect system of society.

Human life resembles a properly tuned and cared-for lyre. Every lyre requires three things: apparatus, tuning, and musical skill of the player. By apparatus we mean preparation of all the appropriate parts: the strings, the plectrum and other instruments cooperating in the tuning of the instrument. By tuning we mean the adaptation of the sounds to each other. The musical skill is the motion of the player in consideration of the tuning. Human life requires the same three things. Apparatus is the preparation of the physical basis of life, riches, renown, and friends. Tuning is the organizing of these according to virtue and the laws. Musical skill is the mingling of these according to virtue and the laws, virtue sailing with a prosperous wind and no external resistance. For felicity does not consist in being driven from the purpose of voluntary intentions, but in obtaining them; nor in virtue lacking attendants and servers, but in completely possessing its own proper powers which are adapted to actions.

For man is not self-perfect, but imperfect. He may become perfect partly from himself, and partly from some external cause. Likewise, he may be perfect either according to nature or to life. According to nature he is perfect if he becomes a good man, as the virtue of everything is the climax and perfection of the nature of that thing. Thus the virtue of the eyes is the climax and perfection of their nature, and this is also true of the virtue of the ears. Thus too the virtue of man is the climax and perfection of the nature of man. But man is perfect according to life when he becomes happy. For felicity is the perfection and completion of human goods. Hence, again, virtue and prosperity become parts of the life of man.

Virtue, indeed, is a part of him so far as he is soul; but prosperity, so far as he is connected with body; but both parts of him, so far as he is an animal. For it is the province of virtue to use in a becoming manner the goods which are conformable to nature, but of prosperity to impart the use of them. The former, indeed imparts deliberate choice and right reason, but the latter imparts energies and actions. For to wish what is beautiful in conduct, and to endure things of a dreadful nature, is the proper business of virtue. But it is the work of prosperity to render deliberate choice successful, and to cause actions to arrive at the desired end. For a general conquers in conjunction with virtue and good fortune. The pilot sails well in conjunction with art and prosperous winds; the eye sees well in conjunction with acuteness of vision and light. So the life of man reaches its perfection through virtue and prosperity.

v. Crito
On Prudence and Prosperity

God fashioned man in a way such as to declare, not through the want of power or deliberate choice, that man is incapable of impulsion to beauty of conduct. In man was implanted a principle such as to combine the possible with the desirable; so that while man is the cause of power and of the possession of good, God causes reasonable impulse and incitation. So God made man tend to heaven, gave him an intellective power, implanted in him a sight called Intellect, which is capable of beholding God. For without God, it is impossible to discover what is best and most beautiful; and without Intellect we cannot see God, since every mortal nature's establishment implies a progressive loss of [immortal] Intellect. It is not God, however, who effected this, but generation, and that impulse of the soul which lacks deliberate choice.

PART III

PLATO: PHILOSOPHY AS THE REGROWTH OF WINGS

Plato (c.428–348 B.C.E.), the founder of the Academy at Athens, is regarded as the supreme spokesman of the Hellenic philosophical tradition. He exercised great artistry in the presentation of his ideas and became a source of inspiration to many forms of mysticism. In a certain respect Plato can also be viewed as one of the most important Pythagorean thinkers in Greece.

It is usually held that the European philosophical tradition consists of a series of footnotes to Plato; and yet there exist some trustworthy scholars who question the European claim of having exclusive rights to the classical Hellenic inheritance in general and of Plato (be he regarded as "Pythagorean," "Socratic," or even "Neoplatonic") in particular. The ancient Hellenes, this group are wont to argue, have been uncritically identified as "Westerners" by precisely those Western rationalists and humanists who, by reason of their own intellectual poverty, ceaselessly tried to invent—in retrospective—their own glorious past. In this way, it is claimed, they sought to find a kind of "archetypal" support for their rationalistic program of "enlightenment," which was set up in contradistinction to the hated "Oriental darkness" (exemplified especially by the Islamic, and to a lesser extent, traditional Byzantine civilizations). For this sinister purpose the philosophy of Plato was artificially separated not only from its Egyptian and Orphic mythological roots, but from the later Middle Platonic and Neoplatonic traditions of exegesis too. Now, an understanding of Plato depends largely on an interpretation of his thought; but this interpretation need not necessarily be "Western"—even though the "official" view remains that of an amalgam of biases from late Christian (Protestant), Humanist and partly corrupted Classicist sources.

For Plato, philosophy was a practice of and for death; a discipline of immortality aimed at the purification and separation of the soul—which was no longer regarded as the illusory phantom (*eidolon*) of the body, but as the immortal *psuche*—and which was now considered as the very essence of the being. By shifting the emphasis from the mortal body to the immortal soul, Plato initiated a philosophically oriented *paideia*, the final goal of which was a learning to live according to the highest metaphysical truth and virtue, to be attained by imitating God, the cause of all blessedness. Through an association with that which is divine—the good, beautiful and orderly (*kosmios*)—the philosopher attained to divinity and orderliness (*kosmios*). This was a way of life based on philosophy as presented by Pythagoras; but it would be wrong to suppose that Plato was in this way the only and inevitable route for all the earlier Hellenic and Oriental traditions that passed down to late antiquity.

Among the basic premises of Plato's philosophy was the distinction between two orders of reality, Being and Becoming. The real noetic world, the realm of Being (or Being, Life, and Intelligence, according to the later commentators) contained the immaterial, eternal and unchanging Forms (*eide*). The realm of Becoming, by contrast, contained the shifting phenomena of the world, which were but imperfect imitations or copies of the Forms, i.e., the world of Becoming contained all sensible things about which no certain scientific knowledge was possible. The Platonic Forms were noetic paradigms, archetypes, and universals arranged in a hierarchy, crowned by the Form of the Good (or Beauty). They constituted the only true objects of divine knowledge. In the myth of *Phaedrus* they were contemplated by the charioteers of souls before they crashed into the world of Becoming, and were thereafter unable to contemplate the Ideas directly. In principle, the Platonic Forms or Ideas, were "Platonic" and somewhat "new" only in respect of their systematic rational formulation and philosophical expression. In their mythological and theological dresses (intimately related to corresponding hieratic rites), the so-called theory of Ideas and Archetypes can be traced back to the ancient Egyptian and Sumerian cosmogonies. Plato received this doctrine in its semi-Pythagorean form, along with conceptions of the ultimate metaphysical principles (the One, Limit, and Unlimited), Form and Matter—woven together through numerical harmony and the doctrine of the tripartite soul. But one ought to remember that Pythagoras, as a son of Apollo or even Apollo himself incarnated in human form (and thus tantamount to the Egyptian Horus), was "nameless" and his personal identity a mystery. It should also be noted that Plato wanted to be seen as an heir to Parmenides, a priest of Apollo the Healer, although he somewhat transformed or even rationally distorted both the Parmenidian *paradosis* and the primordial vision of the ancient sages.

According to Plato, the visible cosmos is "a shrine brought into being for the everlasting gods" (*ton aidion theon gegonos agalma*), a living and self-moved creature modeled according to the pattern of the Intelligible Living Being (i.e., the realm of Ideas, *kosmos noetos*) that is forever existent. The divine Demiurge models the world of Becoming on the world of Being, described as a complex system of Forms containing within itself all subordinate Forms whose likeness one can trace here below. Plato drew a close correspondence between macrocosm and microcosm, that is, between the structure of the entire noetic, psychic and material cosmos and the structure of the human being. The cosmological and metaphysical circles of Sameness and Difference were thus present both in the World Soul and the human soul. But, due to its broken wings the human soul had to leave the divine procession and descend to the realm of *genesis*. The task of the philosopher was thus to regrow his wings and to pass from the shadows of the sensible world to the divine realm, and to contemplate not the remote images, or shadows, but the Forms, or realities, themselves. This was the spiritual and intellectual way of recollection (*anamnesis*) which constituted the heart of Platonic philosophy.

The ascent, or rather re-ascent, of the soul to its original abode had many stages and demanded both intellectual and erotic training. In this respect, the philosopher was also the ideal lover who was led by examples of beauty in the realm of sense—by symbols and sacred images—to the blissful contemplation of the Form of Beauty itself—a mystical vision of Reality which was incommunicable. Having a daemonic and intermediate nature, Eros was one of the links between the sensible cosmos and the eternal world of the gods. Accordingly, Eros was regarded as a paradigm and pattern for the philosopher, or lover of wisdom, because wisdom was beautiful and beauty was loveable. He was attached to both worlds and could move in both directions: downward and upward. The stages of philosophical ascent led from the love of particular physical beauty to physical beauty in general; thence to beauty of soul separated from the beauty of the body and so on. Finally, the beauty of divine knowledge was reached and the vision of the Form of Beauty itself was granted. In Plato's *Symposium*, the priestess Diotima describes this ascent in terms borrowed from the Eleusinian mysteries, because essentially it is the same ascent, consistent with all religious experience. It is a gradual elevation and illumination comparable to the stages of an initiation where the culminating revelation or the final vision (*epopteia*) transcends discursive thought and reason altogether. No wonder that Plato's *Phaedrus* and *Symposium* provided certain models for the theurgic ascent; and in fact these crucial accounts, masterfully introduced as they are by Plato, themselves imitate the ancient cultic patterns recognizable in Mesopotamian and Egyptian cosmogonical rites. Thus it is that the guide of the soul in philosophy corresponds to the hierophant of the mysteries.

Plato's Dialogues and Letters

Plato stands with Pythagoras, Parmenides, Socrates and Aristotle as one of the most eminent thinkers of the ancient Hellenic tradition. He may be regarded as the father of both Western and Eastern (Byzantine, Islamic) philosophy. Born into a renowned family, he had a wide acquaintance with the scholars and sages of his time. He traveled extensively abroad and—according to numerous testimonies—studied in the Egyptian temples (or so-called Houses of Life), in this respect following the example of such men as Solon, Thales of Miletus, and Pythagoras. At the age of forty Plato founded the Academy in Athens. He himself was a disciple and admirer of Socrates, who became the main character and spokesman of his dialogues. Being both a mathematician in the Pythagorean fashion and a master of dialectics, Plato believed the cosmos to be pervaded by divine goodness and beauty. He developed the theory of Ideas, or Forms, which were regarded as the archetypal principles, divine numbers, and formative forces of the entire reality at all ontological levels. The Form of the Good itself was beyond Being (*epekeina tes ousias*); however, every concrete being depended on, and was turned towards, this supernal Sun, the source of truth and beauty, life and intelligence.

Plato's writings allowed him to lead his students at the Academy to metaphysical insights through dialectical exercises, scientific studies, meditations, rational speculations, and mythical imagination. As a perfect stylist he used both rational discourse and poetical imagery; but he never subordinated meaning to the outer form.

Presented here are but a few excerpts from the well-known dialogues of Plato. They concern Pythagorean cosmology; mythologized accounts of the human soul and its destiny; the main task and nature of philosophy (understood as a love of wisdom and preparation for death); the crucial role of Eros in the ascent to the realm of the eternal Ideas; and the impotence of human language to give adequate expression to profound metaphysical, or theological, truths.

The excerpts from the *Seventh Letter* were rendered by L.A. Post (1925); from *Timaeus* by B. Jowett (1953, 4th ed.); from *Phaedrus* by R. Hackforth (1952); from *Phaedo* by H. Tredennick (1954); from *Theaetetus* by F.M. Cornford (1935); and from *Symposium* by M. Joyce (1935).

i. *Seventh Letter* 342c–344d

... For everything that exists there are three classes of objects through which knowledge about it must come; the knowledge itself is a fourth, and we must put as a fifth entity the actual object of knowledge which is the true reality. We have then, first, a name, second, a description, third, an image, and fourth, a knowledge of the object. Take a particular case if you want to understand the meaning of what I have just said; then apply the theory to every object in the same way. There is something for instance called a circle, the name of which is the very word I just now uttered. In the second place there is a description of it which is composed of nouns and verbal expressions. For example the description of that which is named "round" and "circumference" and "circle" would run as follows: the thing which has everywhere equal distances between its extremities and its center. In the third place there is the class of object which is drawn and erased and turned on the lathe and destroyed—processes which do not affect the real circle to which these other circles are all related, because it is different from them. In the fourth place there are knowledge and understanding and correct opinion concerning them, all of which we must set down as one thing more that is found not in sounds nor in shapes of bodies, but in minds, whereby it evidently differs in its nature from the real circle and from the aforementioned three. Of all these four, understanding approaches nearest in affinity and likeness to the fifth entity, while the others are more remote from it.

The same doctrine holds good in regard to shapes and surfaces, both straight and curved, in regard to the good and the beautiful and the just, in regard to all bodies artificial and natural, in regard to fire and water and the like, and in regard to every animal, and in regard

to every quality of character, and in respect to all states active and passive. For if in the case of any of these a man does not somehow or
other get hold of the first four, he will never gain a complete understanding of the fifth. Furthermore these four [names, descriptions,
bodily forms, concepts] do as much to illustrate the particular quality of any object as they do to illustrate its essential reality because of
the inadequacy of language. Hence no intelligent man will ever be so
bold as to put into language those things which his reason has contemplated, especially not into a form that is unalterable—which must
be the case with what is expressed in written symbols.

Again, however, the meaning of what has just been said must be
explained. Every circle that is drawn or turned on a lathe in actual
operations abounds in the opposite of the fifth entity, for it everywhere touches the straight, while the real circle, I maintain, contains in itself neither much nor little of the opposite character.
Names, I maintain, are in no case stable. Nothing prevents the
things that are now called round from being called straight and the
straight round, and those who have transposed the names and use
them in the opposite way will find them no less stable than they are
now. The same thing for that matter is true of a description, since it
consists of nouns and of verbal expressions, so that in a description
there is nowhere any sure ground that is sure enough. One might,
however, speak forever about the inaccurate character of each of
the four! The important thing is that, as I said a little earlier, there
are two things, the essential reality and the particular quality, and
when the mind is in quest of knowledge not of the particular but of
the essential, each of the four confronts the mind with the
unsought particular, whether in verbal or in bodily form. Each of
the four makes the reality that is expressed in words or illustrated in
objects liable to easy refutation by the evidence of the senses. The
result of this is to make practically every man a prey to complete
perplexity and uncertainty.

Now in cases where as a result of bad training we are not even
accustomed to look for the real essence of anything but are satisfied
to accept what confronts us in the phenomenal presentations, we
are not rendered ridiculous by each other—the examined by the
examiners, who have the ability to handle the four with dexterity
and to subject them to examination. In those cases, however, where
we demand answers and proofs in regard to the fifth entity, anyone
who pleases among those who have skill in confutation gains the vic-

tory and makes most of the audience, who think that the man who was first to speak or write or answer has no acquaintance with the matters of which he attempts to write or speak. Sometimes they are unaware that it is not the mind of the writer or speaker that fails in the test, but rather the character of the four—since that is naturally defective. Consideration of all of the four in turn—moving up and down from one to another—barely begets knowledge of a naturally flawless object in a naturally flawless man. If a man is naturally defective—and this is the natural state of most people's minds with regard to intelligence and to what are called morals—while the objects he inspects are tainted with imperfection, not even Lynceus could make such a one see.

To sum it all up in one word, natural intelligence and a good memory are equally powerless to aid the man who has not an inborn affinity with the subject. Without such endowments there is of course not the slightest possibility. Hence all who have no natural aptitude for and affinity with justice and all the other noble ideals, though in the study of other matters they may be both intelligent and retentive—all those too who have affinity but are stupid and unretentive—such will never any of them attain to an understanding of the most complete truth in regard to moral concepts. The study of virtue and vice must be accompanied by an inquiry into what is false and true of existence in general and must be carried on by constant practice throughout a long period, as I said in the beginning. Hardly after practicing detailed comparisons of names and definitions and visual and other sense perceptions, after scrutinizing them in benevolent disputation by the use of question and answer without jealousy, at last in a flash understanding of each blazes up, and the mind, as it exerts all its powers to the limit of human capacity, is flooded with light.

For this reason no serious man will ever think of writing about serious realities for the general public so as to make them a prey to envy and perplexity. In a word, it is an inevitable conclusion from this that when anyone sees anywhere the written work of anyone, whether that of a lawgiver in his laws or whatever it may be in some other form, the subject treated cannot have been his most serious concern—that is, if he is himself a serious man. His most serious interests have their abode somewhere in the noblest region of the field of his activity. If, however, he really was seriously concerned with these matters and put them in writing, "then surely" not the gods, but mortals "have utterly blasted his wits" (*Iliad*, 7.360).

ii. *Timaeus* 27c–31b

TIMAEUS: All men, Socrates, who have any degree of right feeling, at the beginning of every enterprise, whether small or great, always call upon God. And we, too, who are going to discourse of the nature of the universe, how created or how existing without creation, if we be not altogether out of our wits, must invoke the aid of gods and goddesses and pray that our words may be above all acceptable to them and in consequence to ourselves. Let this, then, be our invocation of the gods, to which I add an exhortation of myself to speak in such manner as will be most intelligible to you, and will most accord with my own intent.

First then, in my judgment, we must make a distinction and ask, What is that which always is and has no becoming, and what is that which is always becoming and never is? That which is apprehended by intelligence and reason is always in the same state, but that which is conceived by opinion with the help of sensation and without reason is always in a process of becoming and perishing and never really is. Now everything that becomes or is created must of necessity be created by some cause, for without a cause nothing can be created. The work of the creator, whenever he looks to the unchangeable and fashions the form and nature of his work after an unchangeable pattern, must necessarily be made fair and perfect, but when he looks to the created only and uses a created pattern, it is not fair or perfect. Was the heaven then or the world, whether called by this or by any other more appropriate name—assuming the name, I am asking a question which has to be asked at the beginning of an inquiry about anything—was the world, I say, always in existence and without beginning, or created, and had it a beginning? Created, I reply, being visible and tangible and having a body, and therefore sensible, and all sensible things are apprehended by opinion and sense, and are in a process of creation and created. Now that which is created must, as we affirm, of necessity be created by a cause. But the father and maker of all this universe is past finding out, and even if we found him, to tell of him to all men would be impossible. This question, however, we must ask about the world. Which of the patterns had the artificer in view when he made it— the pattern of the unchangeable or of that which is created? If the world be indeed fair and the artificer good, it is manifest that he must have looked to that which is eternal, but if what cannot be said without blasphemy is true, then to the created pattern. Everyone will see that he must have looked to the eternal, for the world is the fairest of creations and he is the best of causes. And having been created in this way, the world has been framed in the likeness of that which is apprehended by reason and mind and is unchangeable, and must therefore of necessity, if this is admitted, be a copy of something. Now it is all-important that the beginning of everything should be according to nature. And in speaking of the copy and the original we may assume that words are akin to the matter which they describe; when they relate to the lasting and permanent and intelligible, they ought to be lasting and unalterable, and, as far as their nature allows, irrefutable and invincible—nothing less. But when they express only the copy or likeness and not the eternal things themselves, they need only be likely and analogous to the former words. As being is to becoming, so is truth to belief. If then, Socrates, amidst the many opinions about the gods and the generation of the universe, we are not able to give notions which are altogether and in every respect exact and consistent with one another, do not be surprised. Enough if we adduce probabilities as likely as any others, for we must remember that I who am the speaker and you who are the judges are only mortal men, and we ought to accept the tale which is probable and inquire no further.

SOCRATES: Excellent, Timaeus, and we will do precisely as you bid us. The prelude is charming and is already accepted by us; may we beg of you to proceed to the strain?

TIMAEUS: Let me tell you then why the creator made this world of generation. He was good, and the good can never have any jealousy of anything. And being free from jealousy, he desired that all things should be as like himself as they could be. This is in the truest sense the origin of creation and of the world, as we shall do well in believing on the testimony of wise men. God desired that all things should be good and nothing bad, so far as this was attainable. Wherefore also finding the whole visible sphere not at rest, but moving in an irregular and disorderly fashion, out of disorder he brought order, considering that this was in every way better than the other. Now the deeds of the best could never be or have been other than the fairest, and the creator, reflecting on the things which are by nature visible, found that no unintelligent creature taken as a whole could ever be fairer than the intelligent taken as a whole, and again that intelligence could not be present in anything which was devoid of soul. For which reason, when he was framing the universe, he put intelligence in soul, and soul in body, that he might be the creator of a work which was by nature fairest and best. On this wise, using the language of probability, we may say that the world came into being—a living creature truly endowed with soul and intelligence by the providence of God.

This being supposed, let us proceed to the next stage. In the likeness of what animal did the creator make the world? It would be an unworthy thing to liken it to any nature which exists as a part only, for nothing can be beautiful which is like any imperfect thing. But let us suppose the world to be the very image of that whole of which all other animals, both individually and in their tribes, are portions. For the original of the universe contains in itself all intelligible beings, just as this world comprehends us and all other visible creatures. For the deity, intending to make this world like the fairest and most perfect of intelligible beings, framed one visible animal comprehending within itself all other animals of a kindred nature. Are we right in saying that there is one world, or that they are many and infinite? There must be one only if the created copy is to accord with the original. For that which includes all other intelligible creatures cannot have a second or companion; in that case there would be need of another living being which would include both, and of which they would be parts, and the likeness would be more truly said to resemble not them, but that other which included them. In order then that the world might be solitary, like the perfect animal, the creator made not two worlds or an infinite number of them, but there is and ever will be one only-begotten and created heaven.

37c–44c

TIMAEUS: When the father and creator saw the creature which he had made moving and living, the created image of the eternal gods, he rejoiced, and in his joy determined to make the copy still more like the original, and as this was an eternal living being, he sought to make the universe eternal, so far as might be. Now the nature of the ideal being was everlasting, but to bestow this attribute in its fullness upon a creature was impossible. Wherefore he resolved to have a moving image of eternity, and when he set in order the heaven, he made this image eternal but moving according to number, while eternity itself rests in unity, and this image we call time. For there were no days and nights and months and years before the heaven was created, but when he constructed the heaven he created them also. They are all parts of time, and the past and future are created species of time, which we unconsciously but wrongly transfer to eternal being, for we say that it "was," or "is," or "will be," but the truth is that "is" alone is properly attributed to it, and that "was" and "will be" are only to be spoken of becoming in time, for they are motions; but that which is immovably the same forever cannot become older or younger by time, nor can it be said that it came into being in the past, or has come into being now, or will come into being in the future, nor is it subject at all to any of those states which affect moving and sensible things and of which generation is the cause. These are the forms of time, which imitates eternity and revolves according to a law of number. Moreover, when we say that what has become *is* become and what becomes *is* becoming, and that what will become *is* about to become and that the nonexistent *is* nonexistent—all these are inaccurate modes of expression. But perhaps this whole subject will be more suitably discussed on some other occasion.

Time, then, and the heaven came into being at the same instant in order that, having been created together, if ever there was to be a dissolution of them, they might be dissolved together. It was framed after the pattern of the eternal nature—that it might resemble this as far as was possible, for the pattern exists from eternity, and the created heaven has been and is and will be in all time. Such was the mind and thought of God in the creation of time. The sun and moon and five other stars, which are called the planets, were created by him in order to distinguish and preserve the numbers of time, and when he had made their several bodies, he placed them in the orbits in which the circle of the other was revolving—in seven orbits seven stars. First, there was the moon in the orbit nearest the earth, and the next the sun, in the second orbit above the earth, then came the morning star and the star said to be sacred to Hermes, moving in orbits which have an equal swiftness with the sun, but in an opposite direction, and this is the reason why the sun and Hermes and Lucifer[1] regularly overtake and are overtaken by each other. To enumerate the places which he assigned to the other stars and to give all the reasons why he assigned them, although a secondary matter, would give more trouble than the primary. These things at some future time, when we are at leisure, may have the consideration which they deserve, but not at present.

Now, when each of the stars which were necessary to the creation of time had come to its proper orbit, and they had become living creatures having bodies fastened by vital chains, and learned their appointed task—moving in the motion of the diverse, which is diagonal and passes through and is governed by the motion of the same—they revolved, some in a larger and some in a lesser orbit, those which had the lesser orbit revolving faster, and those which had the larger more slowly. Now by reason of the motion of the same, those which revolved fastest appeared to be overtaken by those which moved slower although they really overtook them, for the motion of the same made them all turn in a spiral, and, because some went one way and some another, that which receded most slowly from the sphere of the same, which was the swiftest, appeared to follow it most nearly. That there might be some visible measure of their relative swiftness and slowness as they proceeded in their eight courses, God lighted a fire, which we now call the sun, in the second from the earth of these orbits, that it might give light to the whole of heaven, and that the animals, as many as nature intended, might participate in number, learning arithmetic from the revolution of the same and the like. Thus, then, and for this reason the night and the day were created, being the period of the one most intelligent revolution. And the month is accomplished when the moon has completed her orbit and overtaken the sun, and the year when the sun has completed his own orbit. Mankind, with hardly an exception, have not remarked the periods of the other stars, and they have no name for them, and do not measure them against one another by the help of number, and hence they can scarcely be said to know that their wanderings, being of vast number and admirable

---

1. Phosphoros, or the Morning Star. This is an example of a regrettable fashion, once current among Western scholars, of rendering Greek names by their Latin equivalents.

for their variety, make up time. And yet there is no difficulty in see-ing that the perfect number of time fulfills the perfect year when all the eight revolutions, having their relative degrees of swiftness, are accomplished together and attain their completion at the same time, measured by the rotation of the same and equally moving. After this manner, and for these reasons, came into being such of the stars as in their heavenly progress received reversals of motion, to the end that the created heaven might be as like as possible to the perfect and intelligible animal, by imitation of its eternal nature.

Thus far and until the birth of time the created universe was made in the likeness of the original, but inasmuch as all animals were not yet comprehended therein, it was still unlike. Therefore, the creator proceeded to fashion it after the nature of the pattern in this remaining point. Now as in the ideal animal the mind per-ceives ideas or species of a certain nature and number, he thought that this created animal ought to have species of a like nature and number. There are four such. One of them is the heavenly race of the gods; another, the race of birds whose way is in the air; the third, the watery species; and the fourth, the pedestrian and land crea-tures. Of the heavenly and divine, he created the greater part out of fire, that they might be the brightest of all things and fairest to behold, and he fashioned them after the likeness of the universe in the figure of a circle, and made them follow the intelligent motion of the supreme, distributing them over the whole circumference of heaven, which was to be a true cosmos or glorious world spangled with them all over. And he gave to each of them two movements—the first, a movement on the same spot after the same manner, whereby they ever continue to think consistently the same thoughts about the same things, in the same respect; the second, a forward movement, in which they are controlled by the revolution of the same and the like—but by the other five motions they were unaf-fected, in order that each of them might attain the highest perfec-tion. And for this reason the fixed stars were created, to be divine and eternal animals, ever abiding and revolving after the same man-ner and on the same spot, and the other stars which reverse their motion and are subject to deviations of this kind were created in the manner already described. The earth, which is our nurse, clinging around the pole which is extended through the universe, he framed to be the guardian and artificer of night and day, first and eldest of gods that are in the interior of heaven. Vain would be the attempt to tell all the figures of them circling as in dance, and their juxtapositions, and the return of them in their revolutions upon themselves, and their approximations, and to say which of these deities in their conjunctions meet, and which of them are in opposition, and in what order they get behind and before one another, and when they are severally eclipsed to our sight and again reappear, sending terrors and intimations of the future to those who cannot calculate their movements—to attempt to tell of all this without a visible representation of the heavenly system would be labor in vain. Enough on this head, and now let what we have said about the nature of the created and visible gods have an end.

To know or tell the origin of the other divinities is beyond us, and we must accept the traditions of the men of old time who affirm themselves to be the offspring of the gods—that is what they say— and they must surely have known their own ancestors. How can we doubt the word of the children of the gods? Although they give no probable or certain proofs, still, as they declare that they are speaking of what took place in their own family, we must conform to custom and believe them. In this manner, then, according to them, the genealogy of these gods is to be received and set forth.

Oceanus and Tethys were the children of Earth and Heaven, and from these sprang Phorcys and Cronus and Rhea, and all that generation, and from Cronus and Rhea sprang Zeus and Hera, and all those who are said to be their brethren, and others who were the children of these.

Now, when all of them, both those who visibly appear in their revolutions as well as those other gods who are, of a more retiring nature, had come into being, the creator of the universe addressed them in these words. Gods, children of gods, who are my works and of whom I am the artificer and father, my creations are indissoluble, if so I will. All that is bound may be undone, but only an evil being would wish to undo that which is harmonious and happy. Wherefore, since ye are but creatures, ye are not altogether immortal and indissoluble, but ye shall certainly not be dissolved, nor be liable to the fate of death, having in my will a greater and mightier bond than those with which ye were bound at the time of your birth. And now listen to my instructions. Three tribes of mortal beings remain to be created— without them the universe will be incomplete, for it will not contain every kind of animal which it ought to contain, if it is to be perfect. On the other hand, if they were created by me and received life at my hands, they would be on an equality with the gods. In order then that they may be mortal, and that this universe may be truly universal, do ye, according to your natures, betake yourselves to the formation of animals, imitating the power which was shown by me in creating you. The part of them worthy of the name immortal, which is called divine and is the guiding principle of those who are willing to follow justice and, you—of that divine part I will myself sow the seed, and having made a beginning, I will band the work over to you. And do ye then interweave the mortal with the immortal and make and beget living creatures, and give them food and make them to grow, and receive them again in death.

Thus he spoke, and once more into the cup in which he had previously mingled the soul of the universe he poured the remains of the elements, and mingled them in much the same manner; they were not, however, pure as before, but diluted to the second and third degree. And having made it he divided the whole mixture into souls equal in number to the stars and assigned each soul to a star, and having there placed them as in a chariot he showed them the nature of the universe and declared to them the laws of destiny, according to which their first birth would be one and the same for all—no one should suffer a disadvantage at his hands. They were to be sown in the instruments of time severally adapted to them, and— to come forth the most religious of animals, and as human nature was of two kinds, the superior race was of such and such a character, and would hereafter be called man. Now, when they should be implanted in bodies by necessity and be always gaining or losing some part of their bodily substance, then, in the first place, it would be necessary that they should all have in them one and the same faculty of sensation, arising out of irresistible impressions; in the second place, they must have love, in which pleasure and pain mingle—also fear and anger, and the feelings which are akin or opposite to them. If they conquered these they would live righteously, and if they were conquered by them, unrighteously. He who lived well during his appointed time was to return and dwell in his native star, and there he would have a blessed and congenial existence. But if he failed in attaining this, at the second birth he would pass into a woman, and if, when in that state of being, he did not desist from evil, he would continually be changed into some brute who resembled him in the evil nature which he had acquired, and would not cease from his toils and transformations until he helped the revolution of the same and the like within him to draw in its train the turbulent mob of later accretions made up of fire and air and water and earth, and by this victory of reason over the irrational returned to the form of his first and better state. Having given all these laws to his creatures, that he might be guiltless of future evil in any of them, the creator sowed some of them in the earth, and some in the moon, and some in the other instruments of time. And when he had sown them he committed to the younger gods the fashioning of their mortal bodies, and desired them to furnish what was still lacking to the human soul, and having made all the suitable additions, to rule over them, and to pilot the mortal animal in the best and wisest manner which they could and avert from him all but self-inflicted evils.

When the creator had made all these ordinances he remained in his own accustomed nature, and his children heard and were obedient to their father's word, and receiving from him the immortal principle of a mortal creature, in imitation of their own creator they borrowed portions of fire and earth and water and air from the world, which were hereafter to be restored—these they took and welded them together, not with the indissoluble chains by which they were themselves bound, but with little pegs too small to be visible, making up out of all the four elements each separate body, and fastening the courses of the immortal soul in a body which was in a state of perpetual influx and efflux. Now these courses, detained as in a vast river, neither overcame nor were overcome, but were hurrying and hurried to and fro, so that the whole animal was moved and progressed, irregularly however and irrationally and anyhow, in all the six directions of motion, wandering backward and forward, and right and left, and up and down, and in all the six directions. For great as was the advancing and retiring flood which provided nourishment, the affections produced by external contact caused still greater tumult—when the body of anyone met and came into collision with some external fire or with the solid earth or the gliding waters, or was caught in the tempest borne on the air—and the motions produced by any of these impulses were carried through the body to the soul. All such motions have consequently received the general name of "sensations," which they still retain. And they did in fact at that time create a very great and mighty movement; uniting with the ever-flowing stream in stirring up and violently shaking the courses of the soul, they completely stopped the revolution of the same by their opposing current and hindered it from predominating and advancing, and they so disturbed the nature of the other or diverse that the three double intervals [that is, between 1, 2, 4, 8] and the three triple intervals [that is, between 1, 3, 9, 27], together with the mean terms and connecting links which are expressed by the ratios of 3:2 and 4:3 and of 9:8—these, although they cannot be wholly undone except by him who united them, were twisted by them in all sorts of ways, and the circles were broken and disordered in every possible manner, so that when they moved they were tumbling to pieces and moved irrationally, at one time in a reverse direction, and then again obliquely, and then upside down, as you might imagine a person who is upside down and has his head leaning upon the ground and his feet up against something in the air, and when he is in such a position, both he and the spectator fancy that the right of either is his left, and the left right. If, when powerfully experiencing these and similar effects, the revolutions of the soul come in contact with some external thing, either of the class of the same or of the other, they speak of the same or of the other in a manner the very opposite of the truth, and they become false and foolish, and there is no course or revolution in them which has a guiding or directing power. And if again any sensations enter in violently from without and drag after them the whole vessel of the soul, then the courses of the soul, though they seem to conquer, are really conquered.

And by reason of all these affections, the soul, when incased in a mortal body, now, as in the beginning, is at first without intelligence, but when the flood of growth and nutriment abates and the courses of the soul, calming down, go their own way and become steadier as time goes on, then the several circles return to their natural form and their revolutions are corrected, and they call the same and the other by their right names and make the possessor of them to become a rational being. And if these combine in him with any true nurture or education, he attains the fullness and health of the perfect man, and escapes the worst disease of all, but if he neglects education he walks lame to the end of his life and returns imperfect and good for nothing to the world below.[2]

iii. *Phaedrus* 244a–253c

SOCRATES: Now you must understand, fair boy, that whereas the preceding discourse was by Phaedrus, son of Pythocles, of Myrrhinus, that which I shall now pronounce is by Stesichorus, son of Euphemus, of Himera. This then is how it must run.

"False is the tale" that when a lover is at hand favor ought rather to be accorded to one who does not love, on the ground that the former is mad, and the latter sound of mind. That would be right if it were an invariable truth that madness is an evil, but in reality, the greatest blessings come by way of madness, indeed of madness that is heaven-sent. It was when they were mad that the prophetess at Delphi and the priestesses at Dodona achieved so much for which both states and individuals in Greece are thankful; when sane they did little or nothing. As for the Sibyl and others who by the power of inspired prophecy have so often foretold the future to so many, and guided them aright, I need not dwell on what is obvious to everyone. Yet it is in place to appeal to the fact that madness was accounted no shame nor disgrace by the men of old who gave things their names; otherwise they would not have connected that greatest of arts, whereby the future is discerned, with this very word "madness," and named it accordingly. No, it was because they held madness to be a valuable gift, when due to divine dispensation, that they named that art as they did, though the men of today, having no sense of values, have put in an extra letter, making it not *manic* but *mantic.* That is borne out by the name they gave to the art of those sane prophets who inquire into the future by means of birds and other signs; the name was *oionoistic* which by its components indicated that the prophet attained understanding and information by

2. For more on Plato's cosmology see Francis MacDonald Cornford, *Plato's Cosmology: The Timaeus of Plato* (Indianapolis and Cambridge, Mass.: Hackett Publishing Company, 1997).

a purely human activity of thought belonging to his own intelligence, though a younger generation has come to call it *oionistic,* lengthening the quantity of the *o* to make it sound impressive. You see then what this ancient evidence attests. Corresponding to the superior perfection and value of the prophecy of inspiration over that of omen reading, both in name and in fact, is the superiority of heaven-sent madness over man-made sanity.

And in the second place, when grievous maladies and afflictions have beset certain families by reason of some ancient sin, madness has appeared among them, and breaking out into prophecy has secured relief by finding the means thereto, namely by recourse to prayer and worship, and in consequence thereof rites and means of purification were established, and the sufferer was brought out of danger, alike for the present and for the future. Thus did madness secure, for him that was maddened aright and possessed, deliverance from his troubles.

There is a third form of possession or madness, of which the Muses are the source. This seizes a tender, virgin soul and stimulates it to rapt passionate expression, especially in lyric poetry, glorifying the countless mighty deeds of ancient times for the instruction of posterity. But if any man come to the gates of poetry without the madness of the Muses, persuaded that skill alone will make him a good poet, then shall he and his works of sanity with him be brought to nought by the poetry of madness, and behold, their place is nowhere to be found.

Such then is the tale, though I have not told it fully, of the achievements wrought by madness that comes from the gods. So let us have no fears simply on that score; let us not be disturbed by an argument that seeks to scare us into preferring the friendship of the sane to that of the passionate. For there is something more that it must prove if it is to carry the day, namely that love is not a thing sent from heaven for the advantage both of lover and beloved. What we have to prove is the opposite, namely that this sort of madness is a gift of the gods, fraught with the highest bliss. And our proof assuredly will prevail with the wise, though not with the learned.

Now our first step toward attaining the truth of the matter is to discern the nature of soul, divine and human, its experiences, and its activities. Here then our proof begins.

All soul is immortal,[3] for that which is ever in motion is immortal. But that which while imparting motion is itself moved by something else can cease to be in motion, and therefore can cease to live; it is only that which moves itself that never intermits its motion, inasmuch as it cannot abandon its own nature; moreover this self-mover is the source and first principle of motion for all other things that are moved. Now a first principle cannot come into being, for while anything that comes to be must come to be from a first principle, the latter itself cannot come to be from anything whatsoever; if it did, it would cease any longer to be a first principle. Furthermore, since it does not come into being, it must be imperishable, for assuredly if a first principle were to be destroyed, nothing could come to be out of it, nor could anything bring the principle itself back into existence, seeing that a first principle is needed for anything to come into being.

The self-mover, then, is the first principle of motion, and it is as impossible that it should be destroyed as that it should come into being were it otherwise; the whole universe, the whole of that which comes to be, would collapse into immobility, and never find another source of motion to bring it back into being.

And now that we have seen that that which is moved by itself is immortal, we shall feel no scruple in affirming that precisely that is the essence and definition of soul, to wit, self-motion. Any body that has an external source of motion is soulless, but a body deriving its motion from a source within itself is animate or *besouled* which implies that the nature of soul is what has been said.

And if this last assertion is correct, namely that "that which moves itself" is precisely identifiable with soul, it must follow that soul is not born and does not die.

---

3. Or "the soul as a whole (*psuche pasa*) is immortal," as suggested by Ulrich von Wilamovitz-Moellendorf. Since the time of Hermeias of Alexandria, the interpreters have disputed over whether the meaning of *psuche pasa* is "all soul" or "every soul." In 246b6, *psuche pasa* appears as a complete being having wings, which stands in contrast to the soul which has lost its wings. The translation of *psuche pasa* as "the soul as a whole," stresses the difference between the complete immortal and incomplete mortal. As Yoav Rinon explains (p. 558): "The immortal has both a body and a soul which exist forever as a complete phenomenon. By contrast, the living being which is an outcome of an arbitrary connection between body and soul, has only a temporal completeness, which merely serves as a means for the new growth of the wings." See Yoav Rinon, "The Rhetoric of Jacques Derrida II: Phaedrus," *The Review of Metaphysics*, vol. XLVI, 3 (1993): 537–558.

As to soul's immortality then we have said enough, but as to its nature there is this that must be said. What manner of thing it is would be a long tale to tell, and most assuredly a god alone could tell it but what it resembles, that a man might tell in briefer compass. Let this therefore be our manner of discourse. Let it be likened to the union of powers in a team of winged steeds and their winged charioteer. Now all the gods' steeds and all their charioteers are good, and of good stock, but with other beings it is not wholly so. With us men, in the first place, it is a pair of steeds that the charioteer controls; moreover one of them is noble and good, and of good stock, while the other has the opposite character, and his stock is opposite. Hence the task of our charioteer is difficult and troublesome.

And now we must essay to tell how it is that living beings are called mortal and immortal. All soul has the care of all that is inanimate, and traverses the whole universe, though in ever-changing forms. Thus when it is perfect and winged it journeys on high and controls the whole world, but one that has shed its wings sinks down until it can fasten on something solid, and settling there it takes to itself an earthly body which seems by reason of the soul's power to move itself. This composite structure of soul and body is called a living being, and is further termed "mortal"; "immortal" is a term applied on no basis of reasoned argument at all, but our fancy pictures the god whom we have never seen, nor fully conceived, as an immortal living being, possessed of a soul and a body united for all time. Howbeit, let these matters, and our account thereof, be as God pleases; what we must understand is the reason why the soul's wings fall from it, and are lost. It is on this wise.

The natural property of a wing is to raise that which is heavy and carry it aloft to the region where the gods dwell, and more than any other bodily part it shares in the divine nature, which is fair, wise, and good, and possessed of all other such excellences. Now by these excellences especially is the soul's plumage nourished and fostered, while by their opposites, even by ugliness and evil, it is wasted and destroyed. And behold, there in the heaven Zeus, mighty leader, drives his winged team. First of the host of gods and daemons he proceeds, ordering all things and caring therefore, and the host follows after him, marshaled in eleven companies. For Hestia abides alone in the gods' dwelling place, but for the rest, all such as are ranked in the number of the twelve as ruler gods lead their several companies, each according to his rank.

Now within the heavens are many spectacles of bliss upon the highways whereon the blessed gods pass to and fro, each doing his own work, and with them are all such as will and can follow them, for jealousy has no place in the choir divine. But at such times as they go to their feasting and banquet, behold they climb the steep ascent even unto the summit of the arch that supports the heavens, and easy is that ascent for the chariots of the gods, for they are well balanced and readily guided. But for the others it is hard, by reason of the heaviness of the steed of wickedness, which pulls down his driver with his weight, except that driver have schooled him well.

And now there awaits the soul the extreme of her toil and struggling. For the souls that are called immortal, so soon as they are at the summit, come forth and stand upon the back of the world, and straightway the revolving heaven carries them round, and they look upon the regions without.

Of that place beyond the heavens none of our earthly poets has yet sung, and none shall sing worthily. But this is the manner of it, for assuredly we must be bold to speak what is true, above all when our discourse is upon truth. It is there that true being dwells, without color or shape, that cannot be touched; reason alone, the soul's pilot, can behold it, and all true knowledge is knowledge thereof. Now even as the mind of a god is nourished by reason and knowledge, so also is it with every soul that has a care to receive her proper food; wherefore when at last she has beheld being she is well content, and contemplating truth she is nourished and prospers, until the heaven's revolution brings her back full circle. And while she is borne round she discerns justice, its very self, and likewise temperance, and knowledge, not the knowledge that is neighbor to becoming and varies with the various objects to which we commonly ascribe being, but the veritable knowledge of being that veritably is. And when she has contemplated likewise and feasted upon all else that has true being, she descends again within the heavens and comes back home. And having so come, her charioteer sets his steeds at their manger, and puts ambrosia before them and draught of nectar to drink withal.

Such is the life of gods. Of the other souls that which best follows a god and becomes most like thereunto raises her charioteer's head into the outer region and is carried round with the gods in the revolution, but being confounded by her steeds she has much ado to discern the things that are; another now rises, and now sinks, and by reason of her unruly steeds sees in part, but in part sees not. As for the rest, though all are eager to reach the heights and seek to follow, they are not able; sucked down as they travel they trample and tread upon one another, this one striving to outstrip that. Thus confusion ensues, and conflict and grievous sweat. Whereupon, with their charioteers powerless, many are lamed, and many have their wings all broken, and for all their toiling they are balked, every one, of the full vision of being, and departing therefrom they feed upon the food of semblance.

Now the reason wherefore the souls are fain and eager to behold the plain of Truth, and discover it, lies herein—to wit, that the pasturage that is proper to their noblest part comes from that meadow, and the plumage by which they are borne aloft is nourished thereby.

Hear now the ordinance of Necessity. Whatsoever soul has followed in the train of a god, and discerned something of truth, shall be kept from sorrow until a new revolution shall begin, and if she can do this always, she shall remain always free from hurt. But when she is not able so to follow, and sees none of it, but meeting with some mischance comes to be burdened with a load of forgetfulness and wrongdoing, and because of that burden sheds her wings and falls to the earth, then thus runs the law. In her first birth she shall not be planted in any brute beast, but the soul that hath seen the most of being shall enter into the human babe that shall grow into a seeker after wisdom or beauty, a follower of the Muses and a lover; the next, having seen less, shall dwell in a king that abides by law, or a warrior and ruler; the third in a statesman, a man of business, or a trader; the fourth in an athlete, or physical trainer, or physician; the fifth shall have the life of a prophet or a Mystery priest; to the sixth that of a poet or other imitative artist shall be fittingly given; the seventh shall live in an artisan or farmer; the eighth in a Sophist or demagogue; the ninth in a tyrant.

Now in all these incarnations he who lives righteously has a better lot for his portion, and he who lives unrighteously a worse. For a soul does not return to the place whence she came for ten thousand years, since in no lesser time can she regain her wings, save only his soul who has sought after wisdom unfeignedly, or has conjoined his passion for a loved one with that seeking. Such a soul, if with three evolutions of a thousand years she has thrice chosen this philosophical life, regains thereby her wings, and speeds away after three thousand years; but the rest, when they have accomplished their first life, are brought to judgment, and after the judgment some are taken to be punished in places of chastisement beneath the earth, while others are borne aloft by Justice to a certain region of the heavens, there to live in such manner as is merited by their past life in the flesh. And after a thousand years these and those alike come to the allotment and choice of their second life, each choosing according to her will; then does the soul of a man enter into the life of a beast, and the beast's soul that was aforetime in a man goes back to a man again. For only the soul that has beheld truth may enter into this our human form—seeing that man must needs understand the language of forms, passing from a plurality of perceptions to a unity gathered together by reasoning—and such understanding is a recollection of those things which our souls beheld aforetime as they journeyed with their god, looking down upon the things which now we suppose to be, and gazing up to that which truly is.

Therefore is it meet and right that the soul of the philosopher alone should recover her wings, for she, so far as may be, is ever near in memory to those things a god's nearness whereunto makes him truly god. Wherefore if a man makes right use of such means of remembrance, and ever approaches to the full vision of the perfect mysteries, he and he alone becomes truly perfect. Standing aside from the busy doings of mankind, and drawing nigh to the divine, he is rebuked by the multitude as being out of his wits, for they know not that he is possessed by a deity.

Mark therefore the sum and substance of all our discourse touching the fourth sort of madness—to wit, that this is the best of all forms of divine possession, both in itself and in its sources, both for him that has it and for him that shares therein—and when he that loves beauty is touched by such madness he is called a lover. Such a one, as soon as he beholds the beauty of this world, is reminded of true beauty, and his wings begin to grow; then is he fain to lift his wings and fly upward; yet he has not the power, but inasmuch as he gazes upward like a bird, and cares nothing for the world beneath, men charge it upon him that he is demented.

Now, as we have said, every human soul has, by reason of her nature, had contemplation of true being; else would she never have entered into this human creature; but to be put in mind thereof by things here is not easy for every soul. Some, when they had the vision, had it but for a moment; some when they had fallen to earth consorted unhappily with such as led them to deeds of unrighteousness, wherefore they forgot the holy objects of their vision. Few indeed are left that can still remember much, but when these discern some likeness of the things yonder, they are amazed, and no longer masters of themselves, and know not what is come upon them by reason of their perception being dim.

Now in the earthly likenesses of justice and temperance and all other prized possessions of the soul there dwells no luster; nay, so dull are the organs wherewith men approach their images that hardly can a few behold that which is imaged, but with beauty it is otherwise. Beauty it was ours to see in all its brightness in those days when, amidst that happy company, we beheld with our eyes that blessed vision, ourselves in the train of Zeus, others following some other god; then were we all initiated into that mystery which is rightly accounted blessed beyond all others; whole and unblemished were we that did celebrate it, untouched by the evils that awaited us in days to come; whole and unblemished likewise, free from all alloy, steadfast and blissful were the spectacles on which we gazed in the moment of final revelation; pure was the light that shone around us, and pure were we, without taint of that prison house which now we are encompassed withal, and call a body, fast bound therein as an oyster in its shell.

There let it rest then, our tribute to a memory that has stirred us to linger awhile on those former joys for which we yearn. Now beauty, as we said, shone bright amidst these visions, and in this world below we apprehend it through the clearest of our senses, clear and resplendent. For sight is the keenest mode of perception vouchsafed us through the body; wisdom, indeed, we cannot see thereby—how passionate had been our desire for her, if she had granted us so clear an image of herself to gaze upon—nor yet any other of those beloved objects, save only beauty; for beauty alone this has been ordained, to be most manifest to sense and most lovely of them all.

Now he whose vision of the mystery is long past, or whose purity has been sullied, cannot pass swiftly hence to see beauty's self yonder, when he beholds that which is called beautiful here; wherefore he looks upon it with no reverence, and surrendering to pleasure he essays to go after the fashion of a four-footed beast, and to beget offspring of the flesh, or consorting with wantonness he has no fear nor shame in running after unnatural pleasure. But when one who is fresh from the mystery, and saw much of the vision, beholds a godlike face or bodily form that truly expresses beauty, first there come upon him a shuddering and a measure of that awe which the vision inspired, and then reverence as at the sight of a god, and but for fear of being deemed a very madman he would offer sacrifice to his beloved, as to a holy image of deity. Next, with the passing of the shudder, a strange sweating and fever seizes him. For by reason of the stream of beauty entering in through his eyes there comes a warmth, whereby his soul's plumage is fostered, and with that warmth the roots of the wings are melted, which for long had been so hardened and closed up that nothing could grow; then as the nourishment is poured in, the stump of the wing swells and hastens to grow from the root over the whole substance of the soul, for aforetime the whole soul was furnished with wings. Meanwhile she throbs with ferment in every part, and even as a teething child feels an aching and pain in its gums when a tooth has just come through, so does the soul of him who is beginning to grow his wings feel a ferment and painful irritation. Wherefore as she gazes upon the boy's beauty, she admits a flood of particles streaming therefrom—that is why we speak of a "flood of passion"—whereby she is warmed and fostered; then has she respite from her anguish, and is filled with joy. But when she has been parted from him and become parched, the openings of those outlets at which the wings are sprouting dry up likewise and are closed, so that the wing's germ is barred off. And behind its bars, together with the flood aforesaid, it throbs like a fevered pulse, and pricks at its proper outlet, and thereat the whole soul round about is stung and goaded into anguish; howbeit she remembers the beauty of her beloved, and rejoices again. So between joy and anguish she is distraught at being in such strange case, perplexed and frenzied; with madness upon her she can neither sleep by night nor keep still by day, but runs hither and thither, yearning for him in whom beauty dwells, if haply she may behold him. At last she does behold him, and lets the flood pour in upon her, releasing the imprisoned waters; then has she refreshment and respite from her stings and sufferings, and at that moment tastes a pleasure that is sweet beyond compare. Nor will she willingly give it up. Above all others does she esteem her beloved in his beauty;

mother, brother, friends, she forgets them all. Nought does she reck of losing worldly possessions through neglect. All the rules of conduct, all the graces of life, of which aforetime she was proud, she now disdains, welcoming a slave's estate and any couch where she may be suffered to lie down close beside her darling, for besides her reverence for the possessor of beauty she has found in him the only physician for her grievous suffering.

Hearken, fair boy to whom I speak. This is the experience that men term love (*eros*) but when you hear what the gods call it, you will probably smile at its strangeness. There are a couple of verses on love quoted by certain Homeric scholars from the unpublished works, the second of which is remarkably bold and a trifle astray in its quantities. They run as follows:

> Eros, cleaver of air, in mortals' speech is he named,
> But, since he must grow wings, Pteros the celestials call him.

You may believe that or not, as you please; at all events the cause and the nature of the lover's experience are in fact what I have said.

Now if he whom Love has caught be among the followers of Zeus, he is able to bear the burden of the winged one with some constancy, but they that attend upon Ares, and did range the heavens in his train, when they are caught by Love and fancy that their beloved is doing them some injury, will shed blood and not scruple to offer both themselves and their loved ones in sacrifice. And so does each lover live, after the manner of the god in whose company he once was, honoring him and copying him so far as may be, so long as he remains uncorrupt and is still living in his first earthly period, and in like manner does he comport himself toward his beloved and all his other associates. And so each selects a fair one for his love after his disposition, and even as if the beloved himself were a god he fashions for himself as it were an image, and adorns it to be the object of his veneration and worship.

Thus the followers of Zeus seek a beloved who is Zeus-like in soul; wherefore they look for one who is by nature disposed to the love of wisdom and the leading of men, and when they have found him and come to love him they do all in their power to foster that disposition. And if they have not aforetime trodden this path, they now set out upon it, learning the way from any source that may offer of finding it for themselves, and as they follow up the trace within themselves of the nature of their own god their task is made easier, inasmuch as they are constrained to fix their gaze upon him, and reaching out after him in memory they are possessed by him, and from him they take their ways and manners of life, in so far as a man can partake of a god. But all this, mark you, they attribute to the beloved, and the draughts which they draw from Zeus they pour out, like bacchants, into the soul of the beloved, thus creating in him the closest possible likeness to the god they worship.

Those who were in the train of Hera look for a royal nature, and when they have found him they do unto him all things in like fashion. And so it is with the followers of Apollo and each other god. Every lover is fain that his beloved should be of a nature like to his own god, and when he has won him, he leads him on to walk in the ways of their god, and after his likeness, patterning himself thereupon and giving counsel and discipline to the boy. There is no jealousy or petty spitefulness in his dealings, but his every act is aimed at bringing the beloved to be every whit like unto himself and unto the god of their worship.

So therefore glorious and blissful is the endeavor of true lovers in that mystery rite, if they accomplish that which they endeavor after the fashion of which I speak, when mutual affection arises through the madness inspired by love.

iv. *Phaedo* 66b–69d

"All these considerations," said Socrates, "must surely prompt serious philosophers to review the position in some such way as this. 'It looks as though this were a bypath leading to the right track. So long as we keep to the body and our soul is contaminated with this imperfection, there is no chance of our ever attaining satisfactorily to our object, which we assert to be truth. In the first place, the body provides us with innumerable distractions in the pursuit of our necessary sustenance, and any diseases which attack us hinder our quest for reality. Besides, the body fills us with loves and desires and fears and all sorts of fancies and a great deal of nonsense, with the result that we literally never get an opportunity to think at all about anything. Wars and revolutions and battles are due simply and solely to the body and its desires. All wars are undertaken for the acquisition of wealth, and the reason why we have to acquire wealth is the body, because we are slaves in its service. That is why, on all these accounts, we have so little time for philosophy. Worst of all, if we do obtain any leisure from the body's claims and turn to some line of inquiry, the body intrudes once more into our investigations, interrupting, disturbing, distracting, and preventing us from getting a glimpse of the truth. We are in fact convinced that if we are ever to have pure knowledge of anything, we must get rid of the body and contemplate things by themselves with the soul by itself. It seems, to judge from the argument, that the wisdom which we desire and upon which we profess to have set our hearts will be attainable only when we are dead, and not in our lifetime. If no pure knowledge is possible in the company of the body, then either it is totally impossible to acquire knowledge, or it is only possible after death, because it is only then that the soul will be separate and independent of the body. It seems that so long as we are alive, we shall continue closest to knowledge if we avoid as much as we can all contact and association with the body, except when they are absolutely necessary, and instead of allowing ourselves to become infected with its nature, purify ourselves from it until God himself gives us deliverance. In this way, by keeping ourselves uncontaminated by the follies of the body, we shall probably reach the company of others like ourselves and gain direct knowledge of all that is pure and uncontaminated— that is, presumably, of truth. For one who is not pure himself to attain to the realm of purity would no doubt be a breach of universal justice.' Something to this effect, Simmias, is what I imagine all real lovers of learning must think themselves and say to one another. Don't you agree with me?"

"Most emphatically, Socrates."

"Very well, then," said Socrates, "if this is true, there is good reason for anyone who reaches the end of this journey which lies before me to hope that there, if anywhere, he will attain the object to which all our efforts have been directed during my past life. So this journey which is now ordained for me carries a happy prospect for any other man also who believes that his mind has been prepared by purification."

"It does indeed," said Simmias.

"And purification, as we saw some time ago in our discussion, consists in separating the soul as much as possible from the body, and accustoming it to withdraw from all contact with the body and concentrate itself by itself, and to have its dwelling, so far as it can, both now and in the future, alone by itself, freed from the shackles of the body. Does not that follow?"

"Yes, it does," said Simmias.

"Is not what we call death a freeing and separation of soul from body?"

"Certainly," he said.

"And the desire to free the soul is found chiefly, or rather only, in the true philosopher. In fact the philosopher's occupation consists precisely in the freeing and separation of soul from body. Isn't that so?"

"Apparently."

"Well then, as I said at the beginning, if a man has trained himself throughout his life to live in a state as close as possible to death, would it not be ridiculous for him to be distressed when death comes to him?"

"It would, of course."

"Then it is a fact, Simmias, that true philosophers make dying their profession, and that to them of all men death is least alarming. Look at it in this way. If they are thoroughly dissatisfied with the body, and long to have their souls independent of it, when this happens would it not be entirely unreasonable to be frightened and distressed? Would they not naturally be glad to set out for the place where there is a prospect of attaining the object of their lifelong desire—which is wisdom—and of escaping from an unwelcome association? Surely there are many who have chosen of their own free will to follow dead lovers and wives and sons to the next world, in the hope of seeing and meeting there the persons whom they loved. If this is so, will a true lover of wisdom who has firmly grasped this same conviction—that he will never attain to wisdom worthy of the name elsewhere than in the next world—will he be grieved at dying? Will he not be glad to make that journey? We must suppose so, my dear boy; that is, if he is a real philosopher; because then he will be of the firm belief that he will never find wisdom in all its purity in any other place. If this is so, would it not be quite unreasonable, as I said just now, for such a man to be afraid of death?"

"It would, indeed."

"So if you see anyone distressed at the prospect of dying," said Socrates, "it will be proof enough that he is a lover not of wisdom but of the body. As a matter of fact, I suppose he is also a lover of wealth and reputation—one or the other, or both."

"Yes, you are quite right."

"Doesn't it follow, Simmias," he went on, "that the virtue which we call courage belongs primarily to the philosophical disposition?"

"Yes, no doubt it does," he said.

"Self-control, too, as it is understood even in the popular sense—not being carried away by the desires, but preserving a decent indifference toward them—is not this appropriate only to those who regard the body with the greatest indifference and spend their lives in philosophy?"

"Certainly," he said.

"If you care to consider courage and self-control as practiced by other people," said Socrates, "you will find them illogical."

"How so, Socrates?"

"You know, don't you, that everyone except the philosopher regards death as a great evil?"

"Yes, indeed."

"Isn't it true that when a brave man faces death he does so through fear of something worse?"

"Yes, it is true."

"So in everyone except the philosopher courage is due to fear and dread, although it is illogical that fear and cowardice should make a man brave."

"Quite so."

"What about temperate people? Is it not, in just the same way, a sort of self-indulgence that makes them self-controlled? We may say that this is impossible, but all the same those who practice this simple form of self-control are in much the same case as that which I have just described. They are afraid of losing other pleasures which they desire, so they refrain from one kind because they cannot resist the other. Although they define self-indulgence as the condition of being ruled by pleasure, it is really because they cannot resist some pleasures that they succeed in resisting others, which amounts to what I said just now—that they control themselves, in a sense, by self-indulgence."

"Yes, that seems to be true."

"I congratulate you on your perception, Simmias. No, I am afraid that, from the moral standpoint, it is not the right method to exchange one degree of pleasure or pain or fear for another, like coins of different values. There is only one currency for which all these tokens of ours should be exchanged, and that is wisdom. In fact, it is wisdom that makes possible courage and self-control and integrity or, in a word, true goodness, and the presence or absence of pleasures and fears and other such feelings makes no difference at all, whereas a system of morality which is based on relative emotional values is a mere illusion, a thoroughly vulgar conception which has nothing sound in it and nothing true. The true moral ideal, whether self-control or integrity or courage, is really a kind of purgation from all these emotions, and wisdom itself is a sort of purification. Perhaps these people who direct the religious initiations are not so far from the mark, and all the time there has been an allegorical meaning beneath their doctrine that he who enters the next world uninitiated and unenlightened shall lie in the mire, but he who arrives there purified and enlightened shall dwell among the gods. You know how the initiation practitioners say, 'Many bear the emblems, but the devotees are few'?[4] Well, in my opinion these devotees are simply those who have lived the philosophical life in the right way—a company which, all through my life, I have done my best in every way to join, leaving nothing undone which I could do to attain this end. Whether I was right in this ambition, and whether we have achieved anything, we shall know for certain, if God wills, when we reach the other world, and that, I imagine, will be fairly soon."

v. *Theaetetus* 155d–155e

SOCRATES: That shows that Theodorus was not wrong in his estimate of your nature. This sense of wonder is the mark of the philosopher. Philosophy indeed has no other origin, and he was a good genealogist who made Iris the daughter of Thaumas.

Do you now begin to see the explanation of all this which follows from the theory we are attributing to Protagoras? Or is it not yet clear?

THEAETETUS: I can't say it is yet.

SOCRATES: Then perhaps you will be grateful if I help you to pen-

4. Or: "Many are the narthex-bearers, but few are *bakchoi*" (*Phaed.* 69c; cf. *Orphicorum fragmenta* 5, 235). See Walter Burkert, *Ancient Mystery Cults* (Cambridge, Mass.: Harvard University Press, 1987), p.34.

etrate to the truth concealed in the thoughts of a man—or I should say, of men—of such distinction.

THEAETETUS: Of course I shall be very grateful.

SOCRATES: Then just take a look round and make sure that none of the uninitiated overhears us. I mean by the uninitiated the people who believe that nothing is real save what they can grasp with their hands and do not admit that actions or processes or anything invisible can count as real.

176a–177a

THEODORUS: If you could convince everyone, Socrates, as you convince me, there would be more peace and fewer evils in the world.

SOCRATES: Evils, Theodorus, can never be done away with, for the good must always have its contrary; nor have they any place in the divine world, but they must needs haunt this region of our mortal nature. That is why we should make all speed to take flight from this world to the other, and that means becoming like the divine so far as we can, and that again is to become righteous with the help of wisdom. But it is no such easy matter to convince men that the reasons for avoiding wickedness and seeking after goodness are not those which the world gives. The right motive is not that one should seem innocent and good—that is no better, to my thinking, than an old wives' tale—but let us state the truth in this way. In the divine there is no shadow of unrighteousness, only the perfection of righteousness, and nothing is more like the divine than any one of us who becomes as righteous as possible. It is here that a man shows his true spirit and power or lack of spirit and nothingness. For to know this is wisdom and excellence of the genuine sort; not to know it is to be manifestly blind and base. All other forms of seeming power and intelligence in the rulers of society are as mean and vulgar as the mechanic's skill in handicraft. If a man's words and deeds are unrighteous and profane, he had best not persuade himself that he is a great man because he sticks at nothing, glorying in his shame as such men do when they fancy what others say of them. They are no fools, no useless burdens to the earth, but men of the right sort to weather the storms of public life.

Let the truth be told. They are what they fancy they are not, all the more for deceiving themselves, for they are ignorant of the very thing it most concerns them to know—the penalty of injustice. This is not, as they imagine, stripes and death, which do not always fall on the wrongdoer, but a penalty that cannot be escaped.

THEODORUS: What penalty is that?

SOCRATES: There are two patterns, my friend, in the unchangeable nature of things, one of divine happiness, the other of godless misery—a truth to which their folly makes them utterly blind, unaware that in doing injustice they are growing less like one of these patterns and more like the other. The penalty they pay is the life they lead, answering to the pattern they resemble. But if we tell them that, unless they rid themselves of their superior cunning, that other region which is free from all evil will not receive them after death, but here on earth they will dwell for all time in some form of life resembling their own and in the society of things as evil as themselves, all this will sound like foolishness to such strong and unscrupulous minds.

vi. *Symposium* 201c–204b

"No, no, dear Agathon. It's the truth you find unanswerable, not Socrates. And now I'm going to leave you in peace, because I want to talk about some lessons I was given, once upon a time, by a Mantinean woman called Diotima—a woman who was deeply versed in this and many other fields of knowledge. It was she who brought about a ten years' postponement of the great plague of Athens on the occasion of a certain sacrifice, and it was she who taught me the philosophy of Love. And now I am going to try to connect her teaching—as well as I can without her help—with the conclusions that Agathon and I have just arrived at. Like him, I shall begin by stating who and what Love is, and go on to describe his functions, and I think the easiest way will be to adopt Diotima's own method of inquiry by question and answer. I'd been telling her pretty much what Agathon has just been telling me—how Love was a great god, and how he was the love of what is beautiful, and she used the same arguments on me that I've just brought to bear on Agathon to prove that, on my own showing, Love was neither beautiful nor good.

"'Whereupon, my dear Diotima,' I asked, 'are you trying to make me believe that Love is bad and ugly?'

"'Heaven forbid,' she said. 'But do you really think that if a thing isn't beautiful it's therefore bound to be ugly?'

"'Why, naturally.'

"'And that what isn't learned must be ignorant? Have you never heard of something which comes between the two?'

"'And what's that?'

"'Don't you know,' she asked, 'that holding an opinion which is in fact correct, without being able to give a reason for it, is neither true knowledge—how can it be knowledge without a reason?—nor ignorance—for how can we call it ignorance when it happens to be true? So may we not say that a correct opinion comes midway between knowledge and ignorance?'

"'Yes,' I admitted, 'that's perfectly true.'

"'Very well, then,' she went on, 'why must you insist that what isn't beautiful is ugly, and that what isn't good is bad? Now, coming back to Love, you've been forced to agree that he is neither good nor beautiful, but that's no reason for thinking that he must be bad and ugly. The fact is that he's between the two.'

"'And yet,' I said, 'it's generally agreed that he's a great god.'

"'It all depends,' she said, 'on what you mean by "generally." Do you mean simply people that don't know anything about it, or do you include the people that do?'

"'I meant everybody.'

"At which she laughed, and said, 'Then can you tell me, my dear Socrates, how people can agree that he's a great god when they deny that he's a god at all?'

"'What people do you mean?' I asked her.

"'You for one, and I for another.'

"'What on earth do you mean by that?'

"'Oh, it's simple enough,' she answered. 'Tell me, wouldn't you say that all the gods were happy and beautiful? Or would you suggest that any of them were neither?'

"'Good heavens, no!' said I.

"'And don't you call people happy when they possess the beautiful and the good?'

"'Why, of course.'

"'And yet you agreed just now that Love lacks, and consequently longs for, those very qualities?'

"'Yes, so I did.'

"'Then, if he has no part in either goodness or beauty, how can he be a god?'

"'I suppose he can't be,' I admitted.

"'And now,' she said, 'haven't I proved that you're one of the people who don't believe in the divinity of Love?'

"'Yes, but what can he be, then?' I asked her. 'A mortal?'

"'Not by any means.'

"'Well, what then?'

"'What I told you before—halfway between mortal and immortal.'

"'And what do you mean by that, Diotima?'

"'A very powerful spirit, Socrates, and spirits, you know, are halfway between god and man.'

"'What powers have they, then?' I asked.

"'They are the envoys and interpreters that ply between heaven and earth, flying upward with our worship and our prayers, and descending with the heavenly answers and commandments, and since they are between the two estates they weld both sides together and merge them into one great whole. They form the medium of the prophetic arts, of the priestly rites of sacrifice, initiation, and incantation, of divination and of sorcery, for the divine will not mingle directly with the human, and it is only through the mediation of the spirit world that man can have any intercourse, whether waking or sleeping, with the gods. And the man who is versed in such matters is said to have spiritual powers, as opposed to the mechanical powers of the man who is expert in the more mundane arts. There are many spirits, and many kinds of spirits, too, and Love is one of them.'

"'Then who were his parents?' I asked.

"'I'll tell you,' she said, 'though it's rather a long story. On the day of Aphrodite's birth the gods were making merry, and among them was Resource, the son of Craft. And when they had supped, Need came begging at the door because there was good cheer inside. Now, it happened that Resource, having drunk deeply of the heavenly nectar—for this was before the days of wine—wandered out into the garden of Zeus and sank into a heavy sleep, and Need, thinking that to get a child by Resource would mitigate her penury, lay down beside him and in time was brought to bed of Love. So Love became the follower and servant of Aphrodite because he was begotten on the same day that she was born, and further, he was born to love the beautiful since Aphrodite is beautiful herself.

"'Then again, as the son of Resource and Need, it has been his fate to be always needy; nor is he delicate and lovely as most of us believe, but harsh and arid, barefoot and homeless, sleeping on the naked earth, in doorways, or in the very streets beneath the stars of heaven, and always partaking of his mother's poverty. But, secondly, he brings his father's resourcefulness to his designs upon the beautiful and the good, for he is gallant, impetuous, and energetic, a mighty hunter, and a master of device and artifice—at once desirous and full of wisdom, a lifelong seeker after truth, an adept in sorcery, enchantment, and seduction.

"'He is neither mortal nor immortal, for in the space of a day he will be now, when all goes well with him, alive and blooming, and now dying, to be born again by virtue of his father's nature, while what he gains will always ebb away as fast. So Love is never altogether in or out of need, and stands, moreover, midway between ignorance and wisdom. You must understand that none of the gods are seekers after truth. They do not long for wisdom, because they are wise—and why should the wise be seeking the wisdom that is already theirs? Nor, for that matter, do the ignorant seek the truth or crave to be made wise. And indeed, what makes their case so hopeless is that, having neither beauty, nor goodness, nor intelligence, they are satisfied with what they are, and do not long for the virtues they have never missed.'

"'Then tell me, Diotima,' I said, 'who are these seekers after truth, if they are neither the wise nor the ignorant?'

"'Why, a schoolboy,' she replied, 'could have told you that, after what I've just been saying. They are those that come between the two, and one of them is Love. For wisdom is concerned with the loveliest of things, and Love is the love of what is lovely. And so it follows that Love is a lover of wisdom, and, being such, he is placed between wisdom and ignorance—for which his parentage also is responsible, in that his father is full of wisdom and resource, while his mother is devoid of either'."

"So much I gathered, gentlemen, at one time and another from Diotima's dissertations upon Love. And then one day she asked me, 'Well, Socrates, and what do you suppose is the cause of all this longing and all this love? Haven't you noticed what an extraordinary effect the breeding instinct has upon both animals and birds, and how obsessed they are with the desire, first to mate, and then to rear their litters and their broods, and how the weakest of them are ready to stand up to the strongest in defense of their young, and even die for them, and how they are content to bear the pinch of hunger and every kind of hardship, so long as they can rear their offspring?

"'With men,' she went on, 'you might put it down to the power of reason, but how can you account for Love's having such remarkable effects upon the brutes? What do you say to that, Socrates?'

"Again I had to confess my ignorance."

"'Well,' she said, 'I don't know how you can hope to master the philosophy of Love, if *that's* too much for you to understand.'

"'But, my dear Diotima,' I protested, 'as I said before, that's just why I'm asking you to teach me—because I realize how ignorant I am. And I'd be more than grateful if you'd enlighten me as to the cause not only of this, but of all the various effects of Love.'

"'Well,' she said, 'it's simple enough, so long as you bear in mind what we agreed was the object of Love. For here, too, the principle holds good that the mortal does all it can to put on immortality. And how can it do that except by breeding, and thus ensuring that there will always be a younger generation to take the place of the old?

"'Now, although we speak of an individual as being the same so long as he continues to exist in the same form, and therefore assume that a man is the same person in his dotage as in his infancy, yet, for all we call him the same, every bit of him is different, and every day he is becoming a new man, while the old man is ceasing to exist, as you can see from his hair, his flesh, his bones, his blood, and all the rest of his body. And not only his body, for the same thing happens to his soul. And neither his manners, nor his disposition, nor his thoughts, nor his desires, nor his pleasures, nor his sufferings, nor his fears are the same throughout his life, for some of them grow, while others disappear.

"'And the application of this principle to human knowledge is even more remarkable, for not only do some of the things we know increase, while some of them are lost, so that even in our knowledge we are not always the same, but the principle applies as well to every single branch of knowledge. When we say we are studying, we really mean that our knowledge is ebbing away. We forget, because our knowledge disappears, and we have to study so as to replace what we are losing, so that the state of our knowledge may seem, at any rate, to be the same as it was before.

"'This is how every mortal creature perpetuates itself. It cannot, like the divine, be still the same throughout eternity; it can only leave behind new life to fill the vacancy that is left in its species by obsolescence. This, my dear Socrates, is how the body and all else that is temporal partakes of the eternal; there is no other way. And so it is no wonder that every creature prizes its own issue, since the whole creation is inspired by this love, this passion for immortality.'

"'Well, Diotima,' I said, when she had done, 'that's a most impressive argument. I wonder if you're right.'

"'Of course I am,' she said with an air of authority that was almost professorial. 'Think of the ambitions of your fellow men, and though at first they may strike you as upsetting my argument, you'll see how right I am if you only bear in mind that men's great incentive is the love of glory, and that their one idea is "To win eternal mention in the deathless roll of fame."

"'For the sake of fame they will dare greater dangers, even, than for their children; they are ready to spend their money like water and to wear their fingers to the bone, and, if it comes to that, to die.

"'Do you think,' she went on, 'that Alcestis would have laid down her life to save Admetus, or that Achilles would have died for the love he bore Patroclus, or that Codrus, the Athenian king, would have sacrificed himself for the seed of his royal consort, if they had not hoped to win "the deathless name for valor," which, in fact, posterity has granted them? No, Socrates, no. Every one of us, no matter what he does, is longing for the endless fame, the incomparable glory that is theirs, and the nobler he is, the greater his ambition, because he is in love with the eternal.

"'Well then,' she went on, 'those whose procreancy is of the body turn to woman as the object of their love, and raise a family, in the blessed hope that by doing so they will keep their memory green, "through time and through eternity." But those whose procreancy is of the spirit rather than of the flesh—and they are not unknown, Socrates—conceive and bear the things of the spirit. And what are they? you ask. Wisdom and all her sister virtues; it is the office of every poet to beget them, and of every artist whom we may call creative.

"'Now, by far the most important kind of wisdom,' she went on, 'is that which governs the ordering of society, and which goes by the names of justice and moderation. And if any man is so closely allied to the divine as to be teeming with these virtues even in his youth, and if, when he comes to manhood, his first ambition is to be begetting, he too, you may be sure, will go about in search of the loveliness—and never of the ugliness—on which he may beget. And hence his procreant nature is attracted by a comely body rather than an ill-favored one, and if, besides, he happens on a soul which is at once beautiful, distinguished, and agreeable, he is charmed to find so welcome an alliance. It will be easy for him to talk of virtue to such a listener, and to discuss what human goodness is and how the virtuous should live—in short, to undertake the other's education.

"'And, as I believe, by constant association with so much beauty, and by thinking of his friend when he is present and when he is away, he will be delivered of the burden he has labored under all these years. And what is more, he and his friend will help each other rear the issue of their friendship—and so the bond between them will be more binding, and their communion even more complete than that which comes of bringing children up because they have created something lovelier and less mortal than human seed.

"'And I ask you, who would not prefer such fatherhood to merely human propagation, if he stopped to think of Homer, and Hesiod, and all the greatest of our poets? Who would not envy them their immortal progeny, their claim upon the admiration of posterity?

"'Or think of Lycurgus,' she went on, 'and what offspring he left behind him in his laws, which proved to be the saviors of Sparta and, perhaps, the whole of Hellas. Or think of the fame of Solon, the father of Athenian law, and think of all the other names that are remembered in Grecian cities and in lands beyond the sea for the noble deeds they did before the eyes of all the world, and for all the diverse virtues that they fathered. And think of all the shrines that have been dedicated to them in memory of their immortal issue, and tell me if you can think of *anyone* whose mortal children have brought him so much fame.

"'Well now, my dear Socrates, I have no doubt that even you might be initiated into these, the more elementary mysteries of Love. But I don't know whether you could apprehend the final revelation, for so far, you know, we are only at the bottom of the true scale of perfection.

"'Never mind,' she went on, 'I will do all I can to help you understand, and you must strain every nerve to follow what I'm saying.

"'Well then,' she began, 'the candidate for this initiation cannot, if his efforts are to be rewarded, begin too early to devote himself to the beauties of the body. First of all, if his preceptor instructs him as he should, he will fall in love with the beauty of one individual body, so that his passion may give life to noble discourse. Next he must consider how nearly related the beauty of any one body is to the beauty of any other, when he will see that if he is to devote himself to loveliness of form it will be absurd to deny that the beauty of each and every body is the same. Having reached this point, he must set himself to be the lover of every lovely body, and bring his passion for the one into due proportion by deeming it of little or of no importance.

"'Next he must grasp that the beauties of the body are as nothing to the beauties of the soul, so that wherever he meets with spiritual loveliness, even in the husk of an unlovely body, he will find it beautiful enough to fall in love with and to cherish—and beautiful enough to quicken in his heart a longing for such discourse as tends toward the building of a noble nature. And from this he will be led to contemplate the beauty of laws and institutions. And when he discovers how nearly every kind of beauty is akin to every other he will conclude that the beauty of the body is not, after all, of so great moment.

"'And next, his attention should be diverted from institutions to the sciences, so that he may know the beauty of every kind of knowledge. And thus, by scanning beauty's wide horizon, he will be saved from a slavish and illiberal devotion to the individual loveliness of a single boy, a single man, or a single institution. And, turning his eyes toward the open sea of beauty, he will find in such contemplation the seed of the most fruitful discourse and the loftiest thought, and reap a golden harvest of philosophy, until, confirmed and strengthened, he will come upon one single form of knowledge, the knowledge of the beauty I am about to speak of.

"'And here,' she said, 'you must follow me as closely as you can. Whoever has been initiated so far in the mysteries of Love and has viewed all these aspects of the beautiful in due succession, is at last drawing near the final revelation. And now, Socrates, there bursts upon him that wondrous vision which is the very soul of the beauty he has toiled so long for. It is an everlasting loveliness which neither comes nor goes, which neither flowers nor fades, for such beauty is the same on every hand, the same then as now, here as there, this way, as that way, the same to every worshiper as it is to every other.

"'Nor will his vision of the beautiful take the form of a face, or of hands, or of anything that is of the flesh. It will be neither words, nor knowledge, nor a something that exists in something else, such as a living creature, or the earth, or the heavens, or anything that is—but subsisting of itself and by itself in an eternal oneness, while every lovely thing partakes of it in such sort that, however much the parts may wax and wane, it will be neither more nor less, but still the same inviolable whole.

"'And so, when his prescribed devotion to boyish beauties has carried our candidate so far that the universal beauty dawns upon his inward sight, he is almost within reach of the final revelation. And this is the way, the only way, he must approach, or be led toward, the sanctuary of Love. Starting from individual beauties, the quest for the universal beauty must find him ever mounting the heavenly ladder, stepping from rung to rung—that is, from one to two, and from two to *every* lovely body, from bodily beauty to the beauty of institutions, from institutions to learning, and from learning in general to the special lore that pertains to nothing but the beautiful itself—until at last he comes to know what beauty is.

"'And if, my dear Socrates,' Diotima went on, 'man's life is ever worth the living, it is when he has attained this vision of the very soul of beauty. And once you have seen it, you will never be seduced again by the charm of gold, of dress, of comely boys, or lads just ripening to manhood; you will care nothing for the beauties that used to take your breath away and kindle such a longing in you, and many others like you, Socrates, to be always at the side of the beloved and feasting your eyes upon him, so that you would be content, if it were possible, to deny yourself the grosser necessities of meat and drink, so long as you were with him.

"'But if it were given to man to gaze on beauty's very self—unsullied, unalloyed, and freed from the mortal taint that haunts the frailer loveliness of flesh and blood—if, I say, it were given to man to see the heavenly beauty face to face, would you call his,' she asked me, 'an unenviable life, whose eyes had been opened to the vision, and who had gazed upon it in true contemplation until it had become his own forever?

"'And remember,' she said, 'that it is only when he discerns beauty itself through what makes it visible that a man will be quickened with the true, and not the seeming, virtue—for it is virtue's self that quickens him, not virtue's semblance. And when he has brought forth and reared this perfect virtue, he shall be called the friend of god, and if ever it is given to man to put on immortality, it shall be given to him.'

"This, Phaedrus—this, gentlemen—was the doctrine of Diotima. I was convinced, and in that conviction I try to bring others to the same creed, and to convince them that, if we are to make this gift our own, Love will help our mortal nature more than all the world. And this is why I say that every man of us should worship the god of Love, and this is why I cultivate and worship all the elements of Love myself, and bid others do the same. And all my life I shall pay the power and the might of Love such homage as I can. So you may call this my eulogy of Love, Phaedrus, if you choose; if not, well, call it what you like."

PART IV

NEOPLATONIC HERMENEUTICS AND THE WAY TO GOD

By "Neoplatonism" is meant that current of late Platonic philosophy proceeding from Plotinus (204–270 C.E.)—the renowned student of the Alexandrian sage Ammonius, who transmitted a complex metaphysical system dependent on the One as ultimate principle. In a sense, Neoplatonism was a prolongation of the Middle Platonic and Neopythagorean traditions (represented, among others, by Moderatus of Gades and Numenius of Apamea), and was based on a creative exegesis of Plato and Aristotle, especially Plato's philosophy as it was propounded outside of the Dialogues in his oral teachings. Just as Sufism can be viewed as an elaborated interpretation of the Quran and *ahadith* (the sayings of the Prophet of Islam), so Neoplatonism can be regarded—ultimately and in principle—as an enlarged interpretation of Plato's *Parmenides* and *Timaeus*. The Neoplatonists thus considered themselves, without contradiction, as Platonists pure and simple; and yet they endeavored to show the presence of the same metaphysical truths not merely in Plato, but in Pythagoras, Parmenides, Empedocles, and Aristotle, as also in Homer, Hesiod, the Orphic poems, the *Chaldean Oracles*, and the entire Mediterranean mythology, which, according to certain of them, contained the elements of a perennial theology that marked the path of salvation for initiates.

The Neoplatonists took little interest in Plato's political theory, choosing rather to focus upon certain selected aspects of his metaphysics. They situated the Platonic doctrine of the noetic Forms (*eide*) and particulars within an elaborate and complex hierarchy in which each level of reality not only reflected and imitated the one above, but remained, simultaneously, as the transcendental principle, that which had proceeded from the principle, and that which had returned back to the principle. That is, remaining (*mone*) in, proceeding (*proodos*) from, and coming back (*epistrophe*) to the archetypal source were all considered as inseparable and atemporal

109

modes of an ontological instant. The very existence and order of each thing depended on unity; and the cause was always more perfect and more simple than its effect. Each level of manifested reality was ontologically good and immanently sacred as an image (*eikon*) of its prior; but being merely an image it had also to be regarded as an inferior shadow. The lower images were darkened by virtue of their distance from the archetypal Sun; they had thus to be finally transcended.

Convinced that all perennial truths were known by Plato, the Neoplatonists tried to extract various metaphysical doctrines from the hints he dropped in obscure passages of his Dialogues, sometimes utilizing certain conceptions drawn from Aristotle, the Stoics, and various of the mystery cults. Their metaphysical approach to reality required that contemplation of the multi-dimensional noetic cosmos—or the realm of Ideas—and mystical union could not be separated. The metaphysical, hermeneutical (or exegetic), and religious (or theurgic) aspects of Neoplatonism were understood to form a complex unity based on dialectical analysis, symbolical interpretation, and elevation (*anagoge*).

It was Plotinus who identified metaphysical realities with states of consciousness; his three Hypostases—the One, Intellect, and Soul—may thus be viewed either cosmologically as metacosmic and macrocosmic realities respectively, or soteriologically, as the microcosmic dimensions of the human being and levels of ascent. The higher divine realities being transcendent, ineffable, and barely expressible, the Neoplatonists used both analogical and apophatic means of approaching the One.

The vast majority of Neoplatonic philosophers were descendants of Syria, Phoenicia, Egypt, and Anatolia—these being the most civilized and wealthiest areas of the Roman Empire. Plotinus was born in Lycopolis (modern Asyut) in Upper Egypt. His famous pupil Porphyry (c.232–c.305 C.E.), who edited his *Enneads*, was a Phoenician from Tyre. He translated his Phoenician name Malchos into Greek Basileus, but later took the name of Porphyry (*Porphyrios*) because of its relationship with kingship and royal symbolism. Iamblichus (c.245–c.325 C.E.) was a Syrian of Arab origin. In his name (*ya-mliku*), the second element has the root meaning "king," *malik.* He traced his ancestry to Sampsigeramos, the founder of the line of priest-kings in Emesa, and Monimos, a god worshiped in Emesa. Hierocles (end of 4th century–first half of 5th century C.E.), a student of Plutarch of Athens (who died around 431 C.E.), and the author of a surviving commentary on the *Golden Verses*, lived in Alexandria, the famous Greco-Egyptian metropolis. Hermeias (5th century C.E.) also resided for a time in Alexandria and was a pupil of Syrianus, a teacher and official successor (*diadochos*) of the Platonic School in Athens, who most likely traced his ancestry to Syria. Proclus (c.412–485 C.E.), another pupil of Syrianus and one of the greatest philosophers among the later Neoplatonists, was a Lycian from Xanthus in Asia Minor, born in Constantinople. Marinus (5th century C.E.), the author of the *Vita Procli* (*Life of Proclus*), was a Samaritan from Neapolis (modern Nablus) in Palestine.

The very name of Damascius (c.462–c.537 C.E.) suggests his likely Syrian roots. He was the last official successor (*diadochos*) of the Platonic School (or Academy) in Athens before it was summarily closed in 529 C.E. (at least as a public institution) by the edict of Justinian, the Byzantine Christian Emperor, who prohibited the teaching of Hellenic philosophy. Thereafter Damascius, along with other devoted Neoplatonists (Simplicius among them) departed for Persia, or rather Mesopotamia, in hope of establishing the Platonic Academy in Ctesiphon, the capital of the Persian Sassanid Empire. Three years later they left the court of Shah Khusro I Anushirwan and perhaps settled in the North Mesopotamian town of Harran, where Damascius set up the Academy and where Simplicius wrote his Aristotelian commentaries. If this hypothesis is correct, the Sabians of Harran, who survived well into Islamic times and influenced the philosophy and science of the Abbasid dynasty, may be regarded (at least partly) as the descendants and heirs of these Neoplatonists and other Pagan intellectual refugees from all over the Empire. In any case, it is well established that the School of Harran played a crucial role in the transmission of Hellenic theology, philosophy, theurgy—as well as certain Hermetic doctrines—to the Arab world.

Plotinus the Egyptian (as Proclus labeled him) thought that the summit of the soul remained at the unfallen level, where it contemplated the divine Intellect eternally, despite all the plays of the lower soul on the stage of the material world. Plotinus and his pupil Porphyry regarded the intellectual virtues as highest; and since the crown of virtue was to lose all human qualities and acquire divine qualities—thus reaching the level of unity, simplicity, and perfection—they treated philosophy as the best means to approach the divine realm. Iamblichus, however, explicitly denied this. For this reason Plotinus was never to become the supreme authority for the later Neoplatonists, who agreed with Iamblichus that it was not usually knowledge that united to the gods (though an innate gnosis was united to its cause from the beginning), but unspeakable theurgy through the assistance of the gods themselves. Since religious activities seemed to be more effective for this purpose, Iamblichus clearly separated rational philosophical exposition from the liturgy and theurgic ascent. As a Pythagorean he allotted mathematics a central role in the highest form of worship and stressed that the theurgic mysteries were solar mysteries—the ascent to the noetic Fire and the supreme Sun. Theurgists, as "the true athletes of Fire," differed from conventional philosophers by their dependence on "the perfect operation of the unspeakable acts correctly performed, acts which are beyond understanding; and on the power of the unutterable symbols which are intelligible only to the gods" (*De myster.* II.XI.96–97).

Iamblichus and his followers revived Pythagorean sacred mathematics, developed the allegorical exegesis of Plato and used the *Chaldean Oracles* in support of their sacramental attitudes.[1] In addition, Iamblichus built up the logical structure of Neoplatonic metaphysics into its final form. He was particularly concerned to classify the Platonic Dialogues and deduce their correct order of reading, such that they properly reflected the process of spiritual ascent. In accord with Iamblichus, Hierocles of Alexandria believed the *Golden Verses* of Pythagoras to contain the general principles of all philosophy; they showed the way for beginners in philosophy and led them

1. This name of the *Chaldean Oracles* was granted to a collection of philosophical oracles, or simply "utterances" (*ta logia*), "handed down by the gods" (*theoparodata*) to a certain Julian the Chaldean and his son, Julian the Theurgist, in the late 2nd century C.E. Chaldean theology largely reflects its Middle Platonic origins, but also had spiritual affinities with Syrian, or Assyrian, and Babylonian wisdom. Chaldean religious practice included a complex ascent ritual involving purifications, invocations, visualizations, sacred objects, theurgic instruments and formulas, prayers, hymns, animations of statues and contemplations.

on to the assimilation to God though the cultivation of truth and virtue.

Proclus, the successor of the Platonic School in Athens, also put theurgy above philosophy; but he viewed each as comprising an integral and complex unity, since philosophy itself was a reversion to the One, though achieving only an incomplete union. Proclus elaborated a vast and elaborate metaphysical structure of reality based on a creative exegesis of the first two hypotheses of Plato's *Parmenides.* He believed that Plato's Dialogues (the written texts) microcosmically reflected the structure of the entire noetic cosmos, and thus tried to reveal the hidden meaning of Plato using such resourceful hermeneutical methods as the theory of metaphysical symbolism, later adapted by Dionysius the Areopagite, his tacit admirer and imitator.

According to Proclus, all Hellenic theology (or metaphysics) was derived from the secret doctrines of Pythagoras and Orpheus. Both he and Hermeias were devoted pupils of the great master Syrianus and were firmly convinced that the highest praise belonged to those who revealed the truth. But the truth itself existed independently of its interpreters: the inspired poets concealed the truth behind a veil (*parapetasma*) of symbols and riddles, but the philosophers put it into a more scientific dress on the level of discursive thought.

For Proclus, the ascent of the soul was a gathering of itself into a unity by dialectical exercises, allegorical interpretations, and contemplations, along with piety, asceticism, and the providential support of the gods. This unity (*henosis*) was the henad of soul. Proclus expounded a participative theory of the Forms in the One (*to hen*) which proceeded from it and were present not only in the Intellect, but in each hypostasis below the One, and within all the irradiations of each hypostasis. Following Iamblichus and Syrianus, he named these unities "henads" and identified them with the traditional Hellenic gods. Thus Proclus believed that "all the gods are henads above being and transcend the multiplicity of beings and are the summits of beings" (*In Parm.* 6.1066 27–28). Since the ineffable One is God, these ineffable henads were regarded as having a supra-ontological quality, or rather, a mysterious and apophatic seal, of being divine, which is necessarily possessed by anything real. They were the supreme instances of theophany, unspeakable symbols (*sunthemata*) which constituted and pervaded all levels of manifestation. The gods could thus be known indirectly by a reading and interpreting of signs, i.e., by a studying of the orders (*taxeis*) of reality in the visible cosmos and within the soul. However, the henad of the soul was not the intellect, but a participated One. This was the reason why it was beyond the scope of intellectual vision and had to be accomplished by theurgy.

Proclus several times quoted Theodorus of Asine with approval when he said that "all things pray except the First" (e.g. *In Tim.* I.213.3). All things in their ultimate essence were immersed in ineffable unity with the First. Thus, Damascius, who glorified the fathomless divine silence and emphasized the absolute transcendence of the First, even began to speak of the divine Nothingness. In the presence of this "silence of silence" (*sige sigon*), the tearing to pieces of Dionysus symbolized the creative irradiation of the divine in the world. But this Dionysian aspect of divine activity was eternally correlated with the harmonizing and integrating activity of Apollo, which led all back to the ineffable simplicity of the Source (*pege*).

1. Porphyry
On the Life of Plotinus

Porphyry, the disciple of Plotinus, presented the *Life of Plotinus* as an introduction to his edition of the *Enneads*. Conforming to the rules of the genre, the *Life* was modeled as an icon of the ideal philosopher and virtuous sage, who was to be admired and imitated by his disciples. However, Porphyry also presented a portrait of Plotinus as he really knew him. The excerpts reproduced here reveal Plotinus' relationship with magic and his god-like status among the other spiritual heroes (both mythical and historically attested) of Greek antiquity.

These selected excerpts were translated by Stephen MacKenna and were first published in 1917.

10. Among those making profession of Philosophy at Rome was one Olympius, an Alexandrian, who had been for a little while a pupil of Ammonius.

This man's jealous envy showed itself in continual insolence, and finally he grew so bitter that he even ventured sorcery, seeking to crush Plotinus by star-spells. But he found his experiments recoiling upon himself, and he confessed to his associates that Plotinus possessed "a mighty soul, so powerful as to be able to hurl every assault back upon those that sought his ruin." Plotinus had felt the operation and declared that at that moment Olympius' "limbs were convulsed and his body shriveling like a money-bag pulled tight." Olympius, perceiving on several attempts that he was endangering himself rather than Plotinus, desisted.

In fact Plotinus possessed by birth something more than is accorded to other men. An Egyptian priest who had arrived in Rome and, through some friend, had been presented to the philosopher, became desirous of displaying his powers to him, and he offered to evoke a visible manifestation of Plotinus' presiding spirit. Plotinus readily consented and the evocation was made in the Temple of Isis, the only place, they say, which the Egyptian could find pure in Rome.

At the summons a Divinity appeared, not a being of the spirit-ranks, and the Egyptian exclaimed: "You are singularly graced; the guiding-spirit within you is not of the lower degree but a God." It was not possible, however, to interrogate or even to contemplate this God any further, for the priest's assistant, who had been holding the birds to prevent them flying away, strangled them, whether through jealousy or in terror. Thus Plotinus had for indwelling spirit a Being of the more divine degree, and he kept his own divine spirit unceasingly intent upon that inner presence. It was this preoccupation that led him to write his treatise upon *Our Tutelary Spirit*, an essay in the explanation of the differences among spirit-guides.

Amelius was scrupulous in observing the day of the New-Moon and other holy-days, and once asked Plotinus to join in some such celebration: Plotinus refused: "It is for those Beings to come to me, not for me to go to them."[2] What was in his mind in so lofty an utterance we could not explain to ourselves and we dared not ask him....

---

2. A hierarchy of souls exists, and Plotinus here asserts that his soul is that of a superior rank, which transcends the level of religious rituals. This means that he has realized his self-identity with the Supreme Principle, which is the source of all the gods and daemons. It is thus for them to come to their own Principle, represented by Plotinus as Perfect Man—to express the matter in Sufi terms. Compare the famous sayings by Abu Yazid al-Bastami (d.874 C.E.), such as *Subhani* ("Glory be to me"), instead of *Subhana' Llah* ("Glory be to God"). According to S.H. Nasr: "Those who have died to their ego have gained thereby the right to assert with such saints as Hallaj and Bastami their 'union' with the Divine and to express through their ecstatic utterances such sayings as 'I am the Truth' or 'Glory be unto me.' In such cases, it was not the individual Sufi but God in them who uttered such ecstatic sayings" ("God," in *Islamic Spirituality: Foundations*, ed. S.H. Nasr [New York: SCM Press, 1985], p.322).

22. But why talk, to use Hesiod's phrase, "About Oak and Rock"?[3] If we are to accept the evidence of the wise—who could be wiser than a God? And here the witness is the same God that said with truth:

> "I have numbered the sands and taken the measure of the sea; I understand the dumb and hear where there has been no speech."[4]

Apollo was consulted by Amelius, who desired to learn where Plotinus' soul had gone. And Apollo, who uttered of Socrates that great praise, "Of all men, Socrates the wisest"—you shall hear what a full and lofty oracle Apollo rendered upon Plotinus.

> I raise an undying song, to the memory of a gentle friend, a hymn of praise woven to the honey-sweet tones of my lyre under the touch of the golden plectrum.
>
> The Muses, too, I call to lift the voice with me in strains of many-toned exultation, in passion ranging over all the modes of song:
>
> even as of old they raised the famous chant to the glory of Aeacides in the immortal ardors of the Homeric line.
>
> Come, then, Sacred Chorus, let us intone with one great sound the utmost of all song, I Phoebus, Bathychaites,[5] singing in the midst.
>
> Celestial! Man at first but now nearing the diviner ranks! the bonds of human necessity are loosed for you and, strong of heart, you beat your eager way from out the roaring tumult of the fleshly life to the shores of that wave-washed coast free from the thronging of the guilty, thence to take the grateful path of the sinless soul:
>
> where glows the splendor of God, where Right is throned in the stainless place, far from the wrong that mocks at law.
>
> Oft-times as you strove to rise above the bitter waves of this blood-drenched life, above the sickening whirl, toiling in the midmost of the rushing flood and the unimaginable turmoil, oft-times, from the Ever-Blessed, there was shown to you the Term still close at hand:
>
> Oft-times, when your mind thrust out awry and was like to be rapt down unsanctioned paths, the Immortals themselves pre-

3. Hesiod, *Theogony* 35.
4. Herodotus, *Histories* I.47.
5. I.e. "of the thick hair."

vented, guiding you on the straight going way to the celestial spheres, pouring down before you a dense shaft of light that your eyes might see from amid the mournful gloom.

Sleep never closed those eyes: high above the heavy murk of the mist you held them; tossed in the welter, you still had a vision; still you saw sights many and fair not granted to all that labor in wisdom's quest.

But now that you have cast the screen aside, quitted the tomb that held your lofty soul, you enter at once the heavenly consort:

where fragrant breezes play, where all is unison and winning tenderness and guileless joy, and the place is lavish of the nectar-streams the unfailing Gods bestow, with the blandishments of the Loves, and delicious airs, and tranquil sky:

where Minos and Rhadamanthus dwell, great brethren of the golden race of mighty Zeus; where dwell the just Aeacus, and Plato, consecrated power, and stately Pythagoras and all else that form the Choir of Immortal Love, that share their parentage with the most blessed spirits, there where the heart is ever lifted in joyous festival.

O Blessed One, you have fought your many fights; now, crowned with unfading life, your days are with the Ever-Holy.

Rejoicing Muses, let us stay our song and the subtle windings of our dance; thus much I could but tell, to my golden lyre, of Plotinus, the hallowed soul.

23. Good and kindly, singularly gentle and engaging: thus the oracle presents him, and so in fact we found him. Sleeplessly alert— Apollo tells—pure of soul, ever striving towards the divine which he loved with all his being, he labored strenuously to free himself and rise above the bitter waves of this blood-drenched life: and this is why to Plotinus—God-like and lifting himself often, by the ways of meditation and by the methods Plato teaches in the Banquet,[6] to the first and all-transcendent God—that God appeared, the God who has neither shape nor form but sits enthroned above the Intellectual-Principle and all the Intellectual-Sphere.

"There was shown to Plotinus the Term ever near": for the Term, the one end, of his life was to become Uniate, to approach to the God over all: and four times, during the period I passed with him, he achieved this Term, by no mere latent fitness but by the ineffable Act.

6. See Diotima's speech in Plato's *Symposium* 210–211.

To this God, I also declare, I Porphyry, that in my sixty-eighth year I too was once admitted and entered into Union.

We are told that often when he was leaving the way, the Gods set him on the true path again, pouring down before him a dense shaft of light; here we are to understand that in his writing he was over-looked and guided by the divine powers.

"In this sleepless vision within and without," the oracle says, "your eyes have beheld sights many and fair not vouchsafed to all that take the philosophic path": contemplation in man may some-times be more than human, but compare it with the True-Knowing of the Gods and, wonderful though it be, it can never plunge into the depths their divine vision fathoms.

Thus far the Oracle recounts what Plotinus accomplished and to what heights he attained while still in the body: emancipated from the body, we are told how he entered the celestial circle where all is friendship, tender delight, happiness, and loving union with God, where Minos and Rhadamanthus and Aeacus, the sons of God, are enthroned as judges of souls—not, however, to hold him to judgment but as welcoming him to their consort to which are bid-den spirits pleasing to the Gods—Plato, Pythagoras, and all the peo-ple of the Choir of Immortal Love, there where the blessed spirits have their birth-home and live in days filled full of "joyous festival" and made happy by the Gods.

2. Plotinus
Enneads

Plotinus is commonly regarded as the founder of Neoplatonism. And yet the term itself was actually invented by 18th century European scholars who sought to distinguish—and sometimes abuse—that form of the late Platonic tradition inaugurated by Plotinus, and developed in slightly dif-ferent ways by Porphyry, Iamblichus, Proclus, and Damascius. But this pur-ported line of demarcation between the so-called Middle Platonists, Neopythagoreans and Neoplatonists is in fact quite arbitrary and unclear. What *is* evident is that it now seems likely that the inner structure of Hermeticism, Neopythagoreanism and Neoplatonism have some hidden Egyptian parallels that can be traced back at least as far as the theological systems of the 18th dynasty (1551–1292 B.C.E.), if not to those that belong to the very age of the Pyramids.

Plotinus, "a man in whom Plato lived again," according to Augustine, saw himself as a faithful interpreter of Plato, though, at the same time, he adapted certain doctrines of Stoic and Peripatetic origin while paying little attention to Plato's mathematical and political interests. Accordingly, he ignored the early Socratic dialogues of Plato and turned to the metaphysical subjects, which included contemplation, dialectical ascent to the noetic cosmos, and mystical union with the ultimate divine principle.

Plotinus was born in Lycopolis (modern Asyut) in Upper Egypt. It is not clear whether he belonged to a Greek or a Hellenized Egyptian family, but in any event his education and culture were thoroughly Hellenic. At the age of twenty-eight Plotinus started to study philosophy in Alexandria. He spent eleven years with a mysterious master called Ammonius, nicknamed (perhaps pejoratively) "Saccas" (a man who carries sacks) by later Christian authors. Ammonius wrote nothing at all and our knowledge about his real teachings is uncertain.

In 243 C.E. Plotinus joined the emperor Gordian's expedition against the Persians in hope of making contact with the sages of Persia and India. After the failure of this campaign in Mesopotamia, Plotinus came to Rome where he founded a school of philosophy, initially providing only oral instruction until the year 253 C.E., when he began to write.

Plotinus shared with Plato the conviction that metaphysical, or divine, realities cannot be properly expressed in human terms. The collection of his treatises, entitled the *Enneads* by his disciple Porphyry—who spent six years (from 263 to 268 C.E.) with the master—is thus characterized by a lack of clear structure and division of argument. In addition, Plotinus was quite free with the rules of Greek grammar.

The works of Plotinus were edited by Porphyry in the first decade of the 4th century, just before the death of the editor himself at around 305 C.E. Another disciple of Plotinus, Eustochius, produced a different edition which is not extent. Porphyry divided the treatises of Plotinus into six groups of nine ("Enneads") in accord with the mystical science of numbers practiced by the Pythagoreans and the ancient Egyptian priests. The systematic ordering of the treatises was intended to reflect the progression, or ascent, from the sensible (mortal) realm up to the intelligible (immortal) cosmos and the One.

The excerpts from the *Enneads* presented here were rendered by Stephen MacKenna and were first published by the Medici Society in 1917–1930. This translation was revised by B.S. Page in 1969. From the point of view of stylistic elegance, MacKenna's translation is better than the Greek of Plotinus' original. The more recent translation of the *Enneads* by H.A. Armstrong for the Loeb Classical Library series (in 7 vols, Harvard and London, 1966–1988) is more accurate, but sometimes lacks the poetical beauty of MacKenna's version.

Enneads **III.4.6**

6. What, then, is the achieved Sage?

One whose Act is determined by the higher phase of the Soul.

It does not suffice to perfect virtue to have only this spirit (equivalent in all men) as co-operator in the life: the acting force in the Sage is the Intellective Principle (the diviner phase of the human Soul) which therefore is itself his presiding spirit or is guided by a presiding spirit of its own, no other than the very Divinity.

But this exalts the Sage above the Intellectual Principle as possessing for presiding spirit the Prior to the Intellectual Principle: how then does it come about that he was not, from the very beginning, all that he now is?

The failure is due to the disturbance caused by birth[7]—though, before all reasoning, there exists the instinctive movement reaching out towards its own.

An instinct which the Sage finally rectifies in every respect?

Not in every respect: the Soul is so constituted that its life-history and its general tendency will answer not merely to its own nature but also to the conditions among which it acts.

The presiding spirit, as we read,[8] conducting a soul to the Underworld ceases to be its guardian—except when the soul resumes (in its later choice) the former state of life.

But, meanwhile, what happens to it?

From the passage (in the *Phaedo*) which tells how it presents the soul to judgment we gather that after the death it resumes the form it had before the birth, but that then, beginning again, it is present to the souls in their punishment in the period before their renewed life—a time not so much of living as of expiation.

But the souls that enter into brute bodies, are they controlled by some thing less than this presiding spirit? No: theirs is still a spirit, but an evil or a foolish one.

And the souls that attain to the highest?

Of these higher souls some live in the world of Sense, some above it: and those in the world of Sense inhabit the sun or anoth-

7. Cf. Plato, *Timaeus* 43a–44b.
8. Cf. Plato, *Phaedo* 107de.

er of the planetary bodies;[9] the others occupy the fixed sphere (above the planetary) holding the place they have merited through having lived here the superior life of reason.

We must understand that, while our souls do contain an Intellectual Cosmos, they also contain a subordination of various forms like that of the Cosmic Soul. The World Soul [10] is distributed so as to produce the fixed sphere and the planetary circuits corresponding to its graded powers: so with our souls; they must have their provinces according to their different powers, parallel to those of the World Soul: each must give out its own special act; released, each will inhabit there a star consonant with the temperament and faculty in act within and constituting the principle of the life; and this star or the next highest power will stand to them as God or more exactly as tutelary spirit.

But here some further precision is needed.

Emancipated souls, for the whole period of their sojourn there above, have transcended the Spirit-nature and the entire fatality of birth and all that belongs to this visible world, for they have taken up with them that Hypostasis of the Soul in which the desire of earthly life is vested. This Hypostasis may be described as the distributable Soul,[11] for it is what enters bodily forms and multiplies itself by this division among them. But its distribution is not (arithmetical, not) a matter of magnitudes; wherever it is present, there is the same thing present entire; its unity can always be reconstructed: when living things—animal or vegetal—(distribute themselves and) produce their constant succession of new forms, they do so in virtue of the self-distribution of this phase of the Soul, for it must be as much distributed among the new forms as the propagating originals are. In some cases it communicates its force by permanent presence—the life principle in plants for instance; in other cases it withdraws after imparting its virtue—for instance where from the putridity of dead animal or vegetable matter a multitudinous birth is produced from one organism.

9. See Plato's *Timaeus* 41d–42d, where the Demiurge allots each of the souls before birth to a Star, or an archetype, to which they may re-ascend through the practice of philosophy. This imagery goes back to the Egyptian *Pyramid Texts*, composed at least two thousand years before Plato.

10. Cf. Plato, *Timaeus* 38c–40b.

11. Cf. Plato, *Timaeus* 35a.

A power corresponding to this in the All must reach down and co-operate in the life of our world—in fact the very same power.

If the Soul returns to this Sphere it finds itself under the same spirit or a new, according to the life it is to live. With this spirit it embarks in the skiff of the universe: the "spindle of Necessity"[12] then takes control and appoints the seat for the voyage, the seat of the lot in life.

The Universal circuit is like a breeze, and the voyager, still or stirring, is carried forward by it. He has a hundred varied experiences, fresh sights, changing circumstances, all sorts of events. The vessel itself furnishes incident, tossing as it drives on. And the voyager also acts of himself in virtue of that individuality which he retains because he is on the vessel in his own person and character. Under identical circumstances individuals answer very differently in their movements and desires and acts: hence it comes about that, be the occurrences and conditions of life similar or dissimilar, the result may differ from man to man, as on the other hand a similar result may be produced by dissimilar conditions: this (force of circumstance) it is that constitutes destiny.

IV.3.11–16

11. I think, therefore, that those ancient sages, who sought to secure the presence of divine beings by the erection of shrines and statues,[13] showed insight into the nature of the All; they perceived that, though this Soul is everywhere tractable, its presence will be secured all the more readily when an appropriate receptacle is elaborated, a place especially capable of receiving some portion or

12. Cf. Plato, *Republic* X.616c. Plotinus here uses the traditional image of life as a voyage. See Jean Pepin, "The Platonic and Christian Ulysses," in *Neoplatonism and Christian Thought*, ed. Dominic J. O'Meara (Norfolk, Virginia: International Society for Neoplatonic Studies, 1982), pp.3–18.

13. A reference by Plotinus to the ancient sacramental rituals, which follow basic cosmogonical patterns. The temples, shrines and statues were regarded as the cultic bodies of the gods, their material receptacles, made according to the rules of the revealed sacred science of divine symbols, forms, proportions, materials, and iconography. The animation of statues refers to the descent of the invisible divine light, archetype, or spirit (tantamount to the intelligible "life") into the sacred vehicle (human body, temple, statue, or landscape). The rites of liturgical "animation" or the consecration of divine images, buildings, and mummies were once the

phase of it, something reproducing it, or representing it and serving like a mirror to catch an image of it.

It belongs to the nature of the All to make its entire content reproduce, most felicitously, the Reason-Principles in which it participates; every particular thing is the image within matter of a Reason-Principle which itself images a pre-material Reason-Principle: thus every particular entity is linked to that Divine Being in whose likeness it is made, the divine principle which the Soul contemplated and contained in the act of each creation. Such mediation and representation there must have been since it was equally impossible for the created to be without share in the Supreme, and for the Supreme to descend into the created.

The sun of that sphere—let us return to it as our example—is an Intellectual-Principle, and immediately upon it follows the Soul depending from it, stationary Soul from stationary Intelligence. But the Soul borders also upon the sun of this sphere, and becomes the medium by which it is linked to the over-world; it plays the part of an interpreter between what emanates from that sphere down to this lower universe, and what rises—as far as, through Soul, anything can—from the lower to the highest.

Nothing, in fact, is far away from anything; things are not remote: there is, no doubt, the aloofness of difference and of mingled natures as against the unmingled; but selfhood has nothing to do with spatial position, and in unity itself there may still be distinction.

These Beings (the heavenly bodies) are divine in virtue of cleaving to the Supreme, because, by the medium of the Soul thought of as descending, they remain linked with the Primal Soul, and through it are veritably what they are called and possess the vision of the Intellectual Principle, the single object of contemplation to that soul in which they have their being.

orthodox daily practice of the Egyptian priests. The theurgic animation of statues in Neoplatonism was based on the teaching of the *Chaldean Oracles* and the hieratic rites of the ancient Egyptians, Phoenicians, Assyrians and Babylonians. According to Iamblichus, the gods illuminate heaven, earth, cities, and even holy statues and can enliven them externally, without descent to them. See John F. Finamore, "Julian and the Descent of Asclepius," *Journal of Neoplatonic Studies*, vol. 7, 2:63–86.

12. The souls of men, seeing their images in the mirror of Dionysus as it were,[14] have entered into that realm in a leap downward from the Supreme: yet even they are not cut off from their origin, from the divine Intellect; it is not that they have come bringing the Intellectual Principle down in their fall; it is that though they have descended even to earth, yet their higher part holds for ever above the heavens.[15]

Their initial descent is deepened since that mid-part of theirs is compelled to labor in care of the care-needing thing into which they have entered. But Zeus, the father, takes pity on their toils[16] and makes the bonds in which they labor soluble by death and gives respite in due time, freeing them from the body, that they too may come to dwell there where the Universal Soul unconcerned with earthly needs, has ever dwelt.

For the container of the total of things must be a self-sufficing entity and remain so: in its periods it is wrought out to purpose under its Reason-Principles which are perdurably valid; by these periods it reverts unfailingly, it the measured stages of defined life-duration, to its established character; it is leading the things of this realm to be of one voice and plan with the Supreme. And thus the cosmic content is carried forward to its purpose, everything in its co-ordinate place, under one only Reason-Principle operating alike in the descent and return of souls and to every purpose of the system.

We may know this also by the concordance of the souls with the ordered scheme of the Cosmos; they are not dependent, but, by their descent, they have put themselves in contact, and they stand henceforth in harmonious association with the cosmic circuit—to the extent that their fortunes, their life experiences, their choosing and refusing, are announced by the patterns of the stars—and out

---

14. A reference to the Orphic myth of Dionysus who was torn to pieces by the Titans. Cf. *Orphicorum fragmenta* 209.

15. A reference by Plotinus to the doctrine that the summit of the soul does not descend into the body, but remains above in the noetic realm. On this subject see Hilary Armstrong, "Aristotle in Plotinus: The Continuity and Discontinuity of Psyche and Nous," in *Aristotle and the Later Tradition*, ed. Henry J. Blumenthal and H. Robinson (Oxford: Clarendon Press, 1991), pp.117–127; and Henry J. Blumenthal, "The Psychology of Plotinus and Later Platonism," in *The Perennial Tradition of Neoplatonism* (Leuven: Leuven University Press, 1997), pp.269–290.

16. An adaptation of Plato's *Symposium* 191b5.

of this concordance rises as it were one musical utterance: the music, the harmony, by which all is described, is the best witness to this truth.

Such a consonance can have been procured in one only way:

The All must, in every detail of act and experience, be an expression of the Supreme, which must dominate alike its periods and its stable ordering and the life-careers varying with the movement of the souls as they are sometimes absorbed in that highest, sometimes in the heavens, sometimes turned to the things and places of our earth. All that is Divine Intellect will rest eternally above, and could never fall from its sphere but, poised entire in its own high place, will communicate to things here through the channel of Soul. Soul in virtue of neighborhood is more closely modeled upon the Idea uttered by the Divine Intellect, and thus is able to produce order in the movement of the lower realm, one phase (the World-Soul) maintaining the unvarying march (of the cosmic circuit), the other (the Soul of the Individual) adapting itself to times and seasons.

The depth of the descent, also, will differ—sometimes lower, sometimes less low—and this even in its entry into any given Kind: all that is fixed is that each several soul descends to a recipient indicated by affinity of condition; it moves towards the thing which it There resembled, and enters, accordingly, into the body of man or animal.

13. The Ineluctable,[17] the Cosmic Law is, thus, rooted in a natural principle under which each several entity is overruled to go, duly and in order, towards that place and Kind to which it characteristically tends, that is towards the age of its primal choice and constitution.

In that archetypal world every form of soul is near to the image (the thing in the world of copy) to which its individual constitution inclines it; there is therefore no need of a sender or leader acting at the right moment to bring it at the right moment whether into body or into a definitely appropriate body: of its own motion it descends at the precisely true time and enters where it must. To every soul its own hour; when that strikes it descends and enters the body suitable to it as at the cry of a herald; thus all is set stirring and advancing as by a magician's power or by some mighty traction; it is much as, in

17. What follows is an interpretation of the myth of Plato's *Republic* X.617b.

any living thing, the Soul itself effects the fulfillment of the natural career, stirring and bringing forth, in due season, every element— beard, horn, and all the successive stages of tendency and of output—or, as it leads a tree through its normal course within set periods.

The souls go forth neither under compulsion nor of freewill; or, at least, freedom, here, is not to be regarded as action upon preference; it is more like such a leap of the nature as moves men to the instinctive desire of sexual union, or, in the case of some, to fine conduct; the motive lies elsewhere than in the reason: like is destined unfailingly to like, and each moves hither or thither at its fixed moment.

Even the Intellectual-Principle, which is before all the Cosmos, has, it also, its destiny, that of abiding intact above, and of giving downwards; what it sends down is the particular whose existence is implied in the law (or decreed system) of the universal, for the universal broods closely over the particular; it is not from without that the law derives the power by which it is executed; on the contrary the law is given in the entities upon whom it falls; these bear it about with them. Let but the moment arrive, and what it decrees will be brought to act by those beings in whom it resides; they fulfill it because they contain it; it prevails because it is within them; it becomes like a heavy burden, and sets up in them a painful longing to enter the realm to which they are bidden from within.

14. Thus it comes about that this Cosmos, lit with many lights, gleaming in its souls, receives still further graces, gifts from here and from there, from the gods of the Supreme, and from those other Intellectual-Principles whose nature it is to ensoul. This is probably the secret of the myth[18] in which, after Prometheus had molded woman, the other gods heaped gifts upon her, Hephaistos "blending the clay with moisture and bestowing the human voice and the form of a goddess"; Aphrodite bringing her gifts, and the Graces theirs, and other gods other gifts, and finally calling her by the name (Pandora) which tells of gift and of all giving—for all have

18. A reference to the myth of Prometheus and Pandora in Hesiod, *Works and Days* 60–89; cf. *Theogony* 521–528. On Plotinus' interpretation of myths see Pierre Hadot, "Ouranos, Kronos and Zeus in Plotinus' Treatise Against the Gnostics," in *Neoplatonism and Early Christian Thought: Essays in Honor of A.H. Armstrong*, ed. H.J. Blumenthal and R.A. Marcus (London: Variorum, 1981), pp.124–127.

added something to this formation brought to being by a Promethean, a fore-thinking power. As for the rejection of Prometheus' gift by after-thought, Epimetheus, what can this signify but that the wiser choice is to remain in the Intellectual realm? Pandora's creator is fettered, to signify that he is in some sense held by his own creation; such a fettering is external and the release by Hercules tells that there is power in Prometheus, so that he need not remain in bonds.

Take the myth as we may, it is certainly such an account of the bestowal of gifts upon the Cosmos as harmonizes with our explanation of the universal system.

15. The souls peering forth from the Intellectual Realm descend first to the heavens and there put on a body;[19] this becomes at once the medium by which as they reach out more and more towards magnitude (physical extension) they proceed to bodies progressively more earthy. Some even plunge from heaven to the very lowest of corporeal forms; others pass, stage by stage, too feeble to lift towards the higher the burden they carry, weighed downwards by their heaviness and forgetfulness.

As for the differences among them, these are due to variation in the bodies entered, or to the accidents of life, or to upbringing, or to inherent peculiarities of temperament, or to all these influences together, or to specific combinations of them.

Then again some have fallen unreservedly into the power of the destiny ruling here: some yielding betimes are betimes too their own: there are those who, while they accept what must be borne, have the strength of self-mastery in all that is left to their own act; they have given themselves to another dispensation: they live by the code of the aggregate of beings, the code which is woven out of the Reason-Principles and all the other causes ruling in the Cosmos, out of soul-movements and out of laws springing in the Supreme; a code, therefore, consonant with those higher existences, founded upon them, linking their sequents back to them, keeping unshak-

---

19. A reference to the vehicle (*ochema*) of the soul. On the astral bodies, or vehicles, of the soul in Neoplatonism, see John F. Finamore, *Iamblichus and the Theory of the Vehicle of the Soul* (California: Scholars Press, 1985); G.R.S. Mead, *The Doctrine of the Subtle Body in Western Tradition* (London: Stuart and Watkins, 1967); and H.J. Blumenthal, "Soul Vehicles in Simplicius," in *Platonism in Late Antiquity*, ed. Stephen Gersh and Charles Kannengiesser (Notre Dame, Indiana: University of Notre Dame Press, 1992), pp.173–188.

ably true all that is capable of holding itself set towards the divine nature, and leading round by all appropriate means whatsoever is less natively apt.

In fine all diversity of condition in the lower spheres is determined by the descendent beings themselves.

16. The punishment justly overtaking the wicked must therefore be ascribed to the cosmic order which leads all in accordance with the right.

But what of chastisements, poverty, illness, falling upon the good outside of all justice? These events, we will be told, are equally interwoven into the world order and fall under prediction, and must consequently have a cause in the general reason: are they therefore to be charged to past misdoing?

No: such misfortunes do not answer to reasons established in the nature of things; they are not laid up in the master-facts of the universe, but were merely accidental sequents: a house falls, and anyone that chances to be underneath is killed, no matter what sort of man he be: two squadrons of cavalry are moving in perfect order—or one if you like—but anything getting in the way is wounded or trampled down. Or we may reason that the undeserved stroke can be no evil to the sufferer in view of the beneficent interweaving of the All; or again, no doubt, that nothing is unjust that finds justification in a past history.

We may not think of some things being fitted into a system with others abandoned to the capricious; if things must happen by cause, by natural sequences, under one Reason-Principle and a single set scheme, we must admit that the minor equally with the major is fitted into that order and pattern.

Wrongdoing from man to man is wrong in the doer and must be imputed, but, as belonging to the established order of the universe, is not a wrong even as regards the innocent sufferer; it is a thing that had to be, and, if the sufferer is good, the issue is to his gain. For we cannot think that this ordered combination proceeds without God and justice; we must take it to be precise in the distribution of due, while, yet, the reasons of things elude us, and to our ignorance the scheme presents matter of censure.

IV.4.43–44

43. And the Proficient (the Sage), how does he stand with regard to magic and philter-spells?

In the Soul he is immune from magic; his reasoning part cannot be touched by it, he cannot be perverted. But there is in him the unreasoning element which comes from the (material) All, and in this he can be affected, or rather this can be affected in him. Philter-love, however, he will not know, for that would require the consent of the higher soul to the trouble stirred in the lower. And, just as the unreasoning element responds to the call of incantation, so the adept himself will dissolve those horrible powers by counter-incantations.[20] Death, disease, any experience within the material sphere, these may result, yes; for anything that has membership in the All may be affected by another member, or by the universe of members; but the essential man is beyond harm.

That the effects of magic should not be instantaneous but developed is only in accord with Nature's way.

Even the Celestials, the Daemons, are not on their unreasoning side immune: there is nothing against ascribing acts of memory and experiences of sense to them, in supposing them to accept the traction of methods laid up in the natural order, and to give hearing to petitioners; this is especially true of those of them that are closest to this sphere, and in the degree of their concern about it.

For everything that looks to another is under spell to that: what we look to, draws us magically. Only the self-intent go free of magic. Hence every action has magic as its source, and the entire life of the practical man is a bewitchment: we move to that only which has wrought a fascination upon us. This is indicated where we read:[21] "for the burgher of great-hearted Erechtheus has a pleasant face (but you should see him naked; then you would be cautious)." For what conceivably turns a man to the external? He is drawn, drawn

---

20. See Porphyry's account on the attack of the magician Olympius (*Vita Plot.* 10). On magic in antiquity see Georg Luck, *Arkana Mundi: Magic and the Occult in the Greek and Roman World* (Baltimore and London: Johns Hopkins University Press, 1992), pp.3–131. See also E.A. Wallis Budge, *Egyptian Magic* (New York: Dover Publications, 1971).

21. *Alcibiades I* 132a5, where Plato is adapting Homer's *Iliad* II.547. Plotinus uses the quotation to refer to the physical world in general.

by the arts not of magicians but of the natural order which administers the deceiving draught and links this to that, not in local contact but in the fellowship of the philter.

44. Contemplation alone stands untouched by magic; no man self-gathered falls to a spell; for he is one, and that unity is all he perceives, so that his reason is not beguiled but holds the due course, fashioning its own career and accomplishing its task.

In the other way of life, it is not the essential man that gives the impulse; it is not the reason; the unreasoning also acts as a principle, and finds its premises in emotion. Caring for children, planning marriage—everything that works as bait, taking value by dint of desire—these all tug obviously: so it is with our action, sometimes stirred, not reasonably, by a certain spirited temperament, sometimes as foolishly by greed; political interests, the siege of office, all betray a forth-summoning lust of power; action for security springs from fear; action for gain, from desire; action undertaken for the sake of sheer necessities—that is, for supplying the insufficiency of nature—indicates, manifestly, the cajoling force of nature to the safeguarding of life.

We may be told that no such magic underlies good action, since, at that, Contemplation itself, certainly a good action, implies a magic attraction.

The answer is that there is no magic when actions recognized as good are performed upon sheer necessity with the recollection that the veritable good is elsewhere; this is simply knowledge of need; it is not a bewitchment binding the life to this sphere or to any thing alien; all is permissible under duress of human nature, and in the spirit of adaptation to the needs of existence in general—or even to the needs of the individual existence, since it certainly seems reasonable to fit oneself into life rather than to withdraw from it.

When, on the contrary, the agent falls in love with what is good in those actions, and, cheated by the mere track and trace of the Authentic Good, makes them his own, then, in his pursuit of a lower good, he is the victim of magic. For all dalliance with what wears the mask of the authentic, all attraction towards that mere semblance, tells of a mind misled by the spell of forces pulling towards unreality.

The sorcery of Nature is at work in this; to pursue the non-good as a good, drawn in unreasoning impulse by its specious appearance: it is to be led unknowing down paths unchosen; and what can we call that but magic?

Alone in immunity from magic is he who, though drawn by the alien parts of his total being, withholds his assent to their standards of worth, recognizing the good only where his authentic self sees and knows it, neither drawn nor pursuing, but tranquilly possessing and so never charmed away.

V.3.17

17. But what can it be which is loftier than that existence—a life compact of wisdom, untouched by struggle and error, or than this Intellect which holds the Universe with all there is of life and intellect?

If we answer "The Making Principle," there comes the question, "making by what virtue"? and unless we can indicate something higher there than in the made, our reasoning has made no advance: we rest where we were.

We must go higher—if it were only for the reason that the self-sufficiency of the intellectual-Principle is that of a totality of which each member is patently indigent, and that each has participated in The One and, as drawing on unity, is itself not unity.

What then is this in which each particular entity participates, the author of being to the universe and to each item of the total?

Since it is the author of all that exists, and since the multiplicity in each thing is converted into a self-sufficing existence by this presence of The One, so that even the particular itself becomes self-sufficing, then clearly this principle, author at once of Being and of self-sufficingness, is not itself a Being but is above Being and above even self-sufficing.

May we stop, content, with that?[22] No: the Soul is yet, and even more, in pain. Is she ripe, perhaps, to bring forth, now that in her pangs she has come so close to what she seeks? No: we must call upon yet another spell if anywhere the assuagement is to be found. Perhaps in what has already been uttered, there lies the charm if only we tell it over often? No: we need a new, further, incantation.

---

22. It seems here that Plotinus describes his own experience. However, he is also dependent on such passages of Plato as *Symposium* 210e and *Epistle* VII. 341cd. The "experience" is thus modeled on *a priori* recognized and accepted patterns.

All our effort may well skim over every truth, and through all the verities in which we have part, and yet the reality escape us when we hope to affirm, to understand: for the understanding, in order to its affirmation, must possess itself of item after item; only so does it traverse all the field: but how can there be any such peregrination of that in which there is no variety?

All the need is met by a contact purely intellective. At the moment of touch there is no power whatever to make any affirmation; there is no leisure; reasoning upon the vision is for afterwards. We may know we have had the vision when the Soul has suddenly taken light. This light[23] is from the Supreme and is the Supreme; we may believe in the Presence when, like that other God on the call of a certain man,[24] He comes bringing light: the light is the proof of the advent. Thus, the Soul unlit remains without that vision; lit, it possesses what it sought. And this is the true end set before the Soul, to take that light, to see the Supreme by the Supreme and not by the light of any other principle—to see the Supreme which is also the means to the vision; for that which illumines the Soul is that which it is to see, just as it is by the sun's own light that we see the sun.

But how is this to be accomplished?

Cut away everything.

VI.9.6–11

6.... Any manifold, anything beneath The Unity, is dependent: combined from various constituents, its essential nature goes in need of unity; but unity cannot need itself; it stands unity accomplished. Again, a manifold depends upon all its factors; and furthermore each of those factors in turn—as necessarily inbound with the rest and not self-standing—sets up a similar need both to its associates and to the total so constituted.

23. On light in the philosophy of Plotinus see Algis Uždavinys, "Divine Light in Plotinus and Al-Suhrawardi," *Sacred Web* 10 (2003):73–89; and Frederic M. Schroeder, "Light and the Active Intellect in Alexander and Plotinus," *Hermes* 112 (1984):239–248.

24. See Hans Lewy, "Chaldean Oracles and Theurgy," in *Mysticism, Magic and Platonism in the Late Roman Empire*, ed. Michel Tardieu (Paris: Études Augustiniennes, 1978); and Algis Uždavinys, "Putting on the Form of the Gods: Sacramental Theurgy in Neoplatonism," *Sacred Web* 5 (2000):107–120.

The sovereignly self-sufficing principle will be Unity-Absolute, for only in this unity is there a nature above all need whether within itself or in regard to the rest of things. Unity seeks nothing towards its being or its well-being or its safehold upon existence; cause to all, how can it acquire its character outside of itself or know any good outside? The good of its being can be no borrowing. This is The Good. Nor has it station; it needs no standing-ground as if inadequate to its own sustaining; what calls for such underpropping is the soulless, some material mass that must be based or fall. This is base to all, cause of universal existence and of ordered station. All that demands place is in need; a First cannot go in need of its sequents: all need is effort towards a first principle; the First, principle to all, must be utterly without need. If the Unity be seeking, it must inevitably be seeking to be something other than itself; it is seeking its own destroyer. Whatever may be said to be in need is needing a good, a preserver; nothing can be a good to The Unity, therefore.

Neither can it have will to anything; it is a Beyond-Good, not even to itself a good but to such beings only as may be of quality to have part with it. Nor has it Intellection; that would comport diversity: nor Movement; it is prior to Movement as to Intellection.

To what could its Intellection be directed? To itself? But that would imply a previous ignorance; it would be dependent upon that Intellection in order to knowledge of itself; but it is the self-sufficing. Yet this absence of self-knowing, of self-intellection, does not comport ignorance; ignorance is of something outside—a knower ignorant of a knowable—but in the Solitary there is neither knowing nor anything unknown. Unity, self-present, it has no need of self-intellection: indeed this "self-presence" were better left out, the more surely to preserve the unity; we must eliminate all knowing and all association, all intellection whether internal or external. It is not to be thought of as having but as being Intellection; Intellection does not itself perform the intellective act but is the cause of the act in something else and cause is not to be identified with caused: most assuredly the cause of all is not a thing within that all.

This Principle is not, therefore, to be identified with the good of which it is the source; it is good in the unique mode of being The Good above all that is good.

7. If the mind reels before something thus alien to all we know, we must take our stand on the things of this realm and strive thence to see. But in the looking beware of throwing outward; this Principle does not lie away somewhere leaving the rest void; to those of power to reach, it is present; to the inapt, absent. In our daily affairs we cannot hold an object in mind if we have given ourselves elsewhere, occupied upon some other matter; that very thing, and nothing else, must be before us to be truly the object of observation. So here also; preoccupied by the impress of something else, we are withheld under that pressure from becoming aware of The Unity; a mind gripped and fastened by some definite thing cannot take the print of the very contrary. As Matter, it is agreed,[25] must be void of quality in order to accept the types of the universe, so and much more must the soul be kept formless if there is to be no infixed impediment to prevent it being brimmed and lit by the Primal Principle.

In sum, we must withdraw from all the extern, pointed wholly inwards; no leaning to the outer; the total of things ignored, first in their relation to us and later in the very idea; the self put out of mind in the contemplation of the Supreme; all the commerce so closely There that, if report were possible, one might become to others reporter of that communion.

Such converse, we may suppose, was that of Minos,[26] thence known as the Familiar of Zeus; and in that memory he established the laws which report it, enlarged to that task by his vision There. Some, on the other hand, there will be to disdain such citizen service,[27] choosing to remain in the higher: these will be those that have seen much.

God—we read[28]—is outside of none, present unperceived to all; we break away from Him, or rather from ourselves; what we turn from we cannot reach; astray ourselves, we cannot go in search of another; a child distraught will not recognize its father; to find ourselves is to know our source.

8. Every soul that knows its history is aware, also, that its movement, unthwarted, is not that of an outgoing line; its natural course

25. Cf. Plato, *Timaeus* 50de.
26. Cf. Homer, *Odyssey* XIX.178–179.
27. Cf. Plato, *Republic* VII.519d.
28. Cf. Plato, *Parmenides* 138e4.

may be likened to that in which a circle turns not upon some external but on its own center, the point to which it owes its rise. The soul's movement will be about its source, to this it will hold, poised intent towards that unity to which all souls should move and the divine souls always move, divine in virtue of that movement; for to be a god is to be integral with the Supreme; what stands away is man still multiple, or beast.

Is then this "center" of our souls the Principle for which we are seeking?

We must look yet further: we must admit a Principle in which all these centers coincide: it will be a center by analogy with the center of the circle we know. The soul is not a circle in the sense of the geometric figure but in that its primal nature (wholeness) is within it and about it, that it owes its origin to what is whole, and that it will be still more entire when severed from body.

In our present state—part of our being weighed down by the body, as one might have the feet under water with all the rest untouched—we bear ourselves aloft by that intact part and, in that, hold through our own center to the center of all the centers, just as the centers of the great circles of a sphere coincide with that of the sphere to which all belong. Thus we are secure.

If these circles were material and not spiritual, the link with the centers would be local; they would lie round it where it lay at some distant point: since the souls are of the Intellectual, and the Supreme still loftier, we understand that contact is otherwise procured, that is by those powers which connect Intellectual agent with Intellectual object; indeed soul is closer to the Supreme than Intellect to its object—such is its similarity, identity, and the sure link of kindred. Material mass cannot blend into other material mass: unbodied beings are not under this bodily limitation; their separation is solely that of otherness, of differentiation; in the absence of otherness, it is similars mutually present.

Thus the Supreme as containing no otherness is ever present with us; we with it when we put otherness away. It is not that the Supreme reaches out to us seeking our communion: we reach towards the Supreme; it is we that become present. We are always before it: but we do not always look: thus a choir, singing set in due order about the conductor, may turn away from that center to which all should attend; let it but face aright and it sings with beauty, present effectively. We are ever before the Supreme—cut off is utter dissolution; we can no longer be—but we do not always attend: when we look, our Term is attained; this is rest;[29] this is the end of singing ill; effectively before Him, we lift a choral song full of God.

9. In this choiring, the soul looks upon the wellspring of Life, wellspring also of Intellect, beginning of Being, fount of Good, root of Soul. It is not that these are poured out from the Supreme, lessening it as if it were a thing of mass. At that the emanants would be perishable; but they are eternal; they spring from an eternal principle, which produces them not by its fragmentation but in virtue of its intact identity: therefore they too hold firm; so long as the sun shines, so long there will be light.

We have not been cut away; we are not separate, what though the body-nature has closed about us to press us to itself; we breathe and hold our ground because the Supreme does not give and pass but gives on for ever, so long as it remains what it is.

Our being is the fuller for our turning Thither; this is our prosperity; to hold aloof is loneliness and lessening. Here is the soul's peace, outside of evil, refuge taken in the place clean of wrong; here it has its Act, its true knowing; here it is immune. Here is living, the true; that of today, all living apart from Him, is but a shadow, a mimicry. Life in the Supreme is the native activity of Intellect; in virtue of that silent converse it brings forth gods, brings forth beauty, brings forth righteousness, brings forth all moral good; for of all these the soul is pregnant when it has been filled with God. This state is its first and its final, because from God it comes, its good lies There, and, once turned to God again, it is what it was. Life here, with the things of earth, is a sinking, a defeat, a failing of the wing.[30]

That our good is There is shown by the very love inborn with the soul; hence the constant linking of the Love-God with the Psyches in story and picture; the soul, other than God but sprung

29. A reference to Plato's *Republic* VII.532e3, where what is being described is the culmination of the dialectical ascent. This ultimate contemplation (*theoria*) of the Supreme Good is the end of dialectic, but it is not something we can produce simply by our own effort, as we practice dialectic: the final vision of the Good, or the Beautiful, is not attained but revealed; it comes upon the soul. According to Plato, the Form of the Good is the Sun of the noetic realm and the source of all perception in that realm. But the Supreme Good itself is unknowable and the soul can only touch it through the ineffable union. See Andrew Louth, *The Origins of the Christian Mystical Tradition: From Plato to Denys* (Oxford: Clarendon Press, 1981).

30. Cf. Plato, *Phaedrus* 246c2 and 248c9.

of Him, must needs love. So long as it is There, it holds the heavenly love; here its love is the baser; There the soul is Aphrodite of the heavens; here, turned harlot, Aphrodite of the public ways: yet the soul is always an Aphrodite. This is the intention of the myth which tells of Aphrodite's birth and Eros born with her.[31]

The soul in its nature loves God and longs to be at one with Him in the noble love of a daughter for a noble father; but coming to human birth and lured by the courtships of this sphere, she takes up with another love, a mortal, leaves her father and falls.

But one day coming to hate her shame, she puts away the evil of earth, once more seeks the father, and finds her peace.[32]

Those to whom all this experience is strange may understand by way of our earthly longings and the joy we have in winning to what we most desire—remembering always that here what we love is perishable, hurtful, that our loving is of mimicries and turns awry because all was a mistake, our good was not here, this was not what we sought; There only is our veritable love and There we may unite with it, not holding it in some fleshly embrace but possessing it in all its verity. Any that have seen know what I have in mind: the soul takes another life as it draws nearer and nearer to God and gains participation in Him; thus restored it feels that the dispenser of true life is There to see, that now we have nothing to look for but, far otherwise, that we must put aside all else and rest in This alone, This become, This alone, all the earthly environment done away, in haste to be free, impatient of any bond holding us to the baser, so that with our being entire we may cling about This, no part in us remaining but through it we have touch with God.

Thus we have all the vision that may be of Him and of ourselves; but it is of a self wrought to splendor, brimmed with the Intellectual light, become that very light, pure, buoyant, unburdened, raised to

31. Plotinus refers to Plato's *Symposium* 80de on the subject of the two Aphrodites, and to *Symposium* 203c on the birth of Eros.

32. The motif of seeking the Father, and the symbolism of a spiritual voyage and Homecoming (i.e., to the realm of the gods, the light of *kosmos noetos*, or the Supreme Principle) is common to various trends of Gnostic, Hermetic and Hellenic spirituality of late antiquity. They can be traced back to the different mythological traditions, including the Persian and Chaldean myths, the Homeric poems (allegorized by the Orphics), and the Egyptian accounts of the winged soul (*ba*) who tries to reach the Fields of Peace and thereby return to the abode of spiritual light (*akh*) of her Father Osiris-Ra.

Godhood or, better, knowing its Godhood, all aflame then—but crushed out once more if it should take up the discarded burden.

10. But how comes the soul not to keep that ground?

Because it has not yet escaped wholly: but there will be the time of vision unbroken, the self hindered no longer by any hindrance of body. Not that those hindrances beset that in us which has veritably seen; it is the other phase of the soul that suffers, and that only when we withdraw from vision and take to knowing by proof, by evidence, by the reasoning processes of the mental habit. Such logic is not to be confounded with that act of ours in the vision; it is not our reason that has seen; it is something greater than reason, reason's Prior, as far above reason as the very object of that thought must be.

In our self-seeing There, the self is seen as belonging to that order, or rather we are merged into that self in us which has the quality of that order. It is a knowing of the self restored to its purity. No doubt we should not speak of seeing; but we cannot help talking in dualities, seen and seer, instead of, boldly, the achievement of unity. In this seeing, we neither hold an object nor trace distinction; there is no two. The man is changed, no longer himself nor self-belonging; he is merged with the Supreme, sunken into it, one with it: center coincides with center, for centers of circles, even here below, are one when they unite, and two when they separate; and it is in this sense that we now (after the vision) speak of the Supreme as separate. This is why the vision baffles telling; we cannot detach the Supreme to state it; if we have seen something thus detached we have failed of the Supreme which is to be known only as one with ourselves.

11. This is the purport of that rule of our Mysteries: "Nothing Divulged to the Uninitiate": the Supreme is not to be made a common story, the holy things may not be uncovered to the stranger, to any that has not himself attained to see. There were not two; beholder was one with beheld; it was not a vision compassed but a unity apprehended. The man formed by this mingling with the Supreme must—if he only remember—carry its image impressed upon him: he is become the Unity, nothing within him or without inducing any diversity; no movement now, no passion, no outlooking desire, once this ascent is achieved; reasoning is in abeyance and all Intellection and even, to dare the word, the very self: caught away, filled with God, he has in perfect stillness attained isolation;

all the being calmed, he turns neither to this side nor to that, not even inwards to himself; utterly resting he has become very rest. He belongs no longer to the order of the beautiful; he has risen beyond beauty; he has overpassed even the choir of the virtues; he is like one who, having penetrated the inner sanctuary, leaves the temple images behind him—though these become once more first objects of regard when he leaves the holies; for There his converse was not with image, not with trace, but with the very Truth in the view of which all the rest is but of secondary concern.

There, indeed, it was scarcely vision, unless of a mode unknown; it was a going forth from the self, a simplifying, a renunciation, a reach towards contact and at the same time a repose, a meditation towards adjustment. This is the only seeing of what lies within the holies: to look otherwise is to fail.

Things here are signs; they show therefore to the wiser teachers how the supreme God is known; the instructed priest reading the sign may enter the holy place and make real the vision of the inaccessible.

Even those that have never found entry must admit the existence of that invisible; they will know their source and Principle since by principle they see principle and are linked with it, by like they have contact with like and so they grasp all of the divine that lies within the scope of mind. Until the seeing comes they are still craving something, that which only the vision can give; this Term, attained only by those that have overpassed all, is the All-Transcending.

It is not in the soul's nature to touch utter nothingness; the lowest descent is into evil and, so far, into non-being: but to utter nothing, never. When the soul begins again to mount, it comes not to something alien but to its very self; thus detached, it is in nothing but itself; self-gathered it is no longer in the order of being; it is in the Supreme.

There is thus a converse in virtue of which the essential man outgrows Being, becomes identical with the Transcendent of Being.[33] The self thus lifted, we are in the likeness of the Supreme: if from that heightened self we pass still higher—image to archetype—we have won the Term of all our journeying. Fallen back

33. Cf. Plato, *Republic* VI.509b9.

again, we waken the virtue within until we know ourselves all order once more; once more we are lightened of the burden and move by virtue towards Intellectual-Principle and through the Wisdom in That to the Supreme.

This is the life of gods and of the godlike and blessed among men, liberation from the alien that besets us here, a life taking no pleasure in the things of earth, the passing of solitary to solitary.

3. Porphyry
Letter to Marcella

Porphyry studied with Plotinus for six years and then, following his master's suggestion, set off for Sicily. After Plotinus' death in 270 C.E., Porphyry returned to Rome and assumed leadership of the Neoplatonic school. At the elderly age of 70, Porphyry married Marcella, a widow of his friend, who had seven children. "I admired you because your disposition was suited to true philosophy," said Porphyry to Marcella, thus explaining the reason of their marriage. Porphyry's *Letter to his Wife Marcella* (*Pros Markellan*) was written as a consolation and ethical instruction, addressed to the soul in its ascent to the realm of the divine principles.

The excerpt from Porphyry's *Letter* here reproduced was translated by Alice Zimmern and first appeared as *Porphyry the Philosopher to his Wife Marcella* (London: George Redway, 1896).

Ad Marcel. 11–31

11. Reason tells us that the divine is present everywhere and in all men, but that only the mind of the wise man is sanctified as its temple, and God is best honored by him who knows Him best. And this must naturally be the wise man alone, who in wisdom must honor the Divine, and in wisdom adorn for it a temple in his thought, honoring it with a living statue, the mind molded in His image.... Now God is not in need of any one, and the wise man is in need of God alone. For no one could become good and noble, unless he knew the goodness and beauty which proceed from the Deity. Nor is any man unhappy, unless he has fitted up his soul as a dwelling place for evil spirits. To the wise man God gives the author-

ity of a god. And a man is purified by the knowledge of God, and issuing from God, he follows after righteousness.

12. Let God be at hand to behold and examine every act and deed and word. And let us consider Him the author of all our good deeds. But of evil we ourselves are the authors, since it is we who made choice of it, but God is without blame. Wherefore we should pray to God for that which is worthy of Him, and we should pray for what we could attain from none other. And we must pray that we may attain after our labors those things that are preceded by toil and virtue; for the prayer of the slothful is but vain speech. Neither ask of God what you will not hold fast when you have attained it, since God's gifts cannot be taken from you, and He will not give what you will not hold fast. What you will not require when you are rid of the body, that despise, but practice yourself in that you will need when you are set free, calling on God to be your helper. You will need none of those things which chance often gives and again takes away. Do not make any request before the fitting season, but only when God makes plain the right desire implanted by nature within you.

13. Hereby can God best be reflected, who cannot be seen by the body, nor yet by an impure soul darkened by vice. For purity is God's beauty, and His light is the life-giving flame of truth. Every vice is deceived by ignorance, and turned astray by wickedness. Wherefore desire and ask of God what is in accordance with His own will and nature, well assured that, inasmuch as a man longs after the body and the things of the body in so far does he fail to know God, and is blind to the sight of God, even though all men should hold him as a god. Now the wise man, if known by only few, or, if you will, unknown to all, yet is known by God, and is reflected by his likeness to Him. Let then your mind follow after God, and let the soul follow the mind, and let the body be subservient to the soul as far as may be, the pure body serving the pure soul. For if it be defiled by the emotions of the soul, the defilement reacts upon the soul itself.

14. In a pure body where soul and mind are loved by God, words should conform with deeds: since it is better for you to cast a stone at random than a word, and to be defeated speaking the truth rather than conquer through deceit; for he who conquers by deceit is worsted in his character. And lies are witnesses unto evil deeds. It is impossible for a man who loves God also to love pleasure and the

141

body, for he who loves these must needs be a lover of riches. And he who loves riches must be unrighteous. And the unrighteous man is impious towards God and his fathers, and transgresses against all men. And though he slay whole hecatombs in sacrifice, and adorn the temples with ten thousand gifts, yet is he impious and godless, and at heart a plunderer of holy places. Wherefore we should shun all addicted to love of the body as godless and impure.

15. Do not associate with any one whose opinions cannot profit you, nor join with him in converse about God. For it is not safe to speak of God with those who are corrupted by false opinion. Yea, and in their presence to speak truth or falsehood about God is fraught with equal danger. It is not fitting for a man who is not purified from unholy deeds to speak of God himself, nor must we suppose that he who speaks of Him with such is not guilty of a crime. We should hear and use speech concerning God as though in His presence. Godlike deeds should precede talk of God, and in the presence of the multitude we should keep silence concerning Him, for the knowledge of God is not suitable to the vain conceit of the soul. Esteem it better to keep silence than to let fall random words about God. You will become worthy of God if you deem it wrong either to speak or do or know aught unworthy of Him. Now a man who was worthy of God would be himself a god.

16. You will best honor God by making your mind like unto Him, and this you can do by virtue alone. For only virtue can draw the soul upward to that which is akin to it. Next to God there is nothing great but virtue, yet God is greater than virtue. Now God strengthens the man who does noble deeds. But an evil spirit is the instigator of evil deeds. The wicked soul flies from God, and would fain that His providence did not exist, and it shrinks from the divine law which punishes all the wicked. But the wise man's soul is like God, and ever beholds Him and dwells with Him. If the ruler takes pleasure in the ruled, then God too cares for the wise man and watches over him. Therefore is the wise man blest, because he is in God's keeping. 'Tis not his speech that is acceptable to God, but his deed; for the wise man honors God even in his silence, while the fool dishonors Him even while praying and offering sacrifice. Thus the wise man only is a priest; he only is beloved by God, and knows how to pray.

17. The man who practices wisdom practices the knowledge of God; and he shows his piety not by continued prayers and sacrifices

but by his actions. No one could become well-pleasing to God by the opinions of men or the vain talk of the Sophists. But he makes himself well-pleasing and consecrated to God by assimilating his own disposition to the blessed and incorruptible nature. And it is he who makes himself impious and displeasing to God, for God does not injure him (since the divine nature can only work good), but he injures himself, chiefly through his wrong opinion concerning God. Not he who disregards the images of the gods is impious, but he who holds the opinions of the multitude concerning God. But do you entertain no thought unworthy of God or of His blessedness and immortality.

18. The chief fruit of piety is to honor God according to the laws of our country, not deeming that God has need of anything, but that He calls us to honor Him by His truly reverend and blessed majesty. We are not harmed by reverencing God's altars, nor benefited by neglecting them. But whoever honors God under the impression that He is in need of him, he unconsciously deems himself greater than God. 'Tis not when they are angry that the gods do us harm, but when they are not understood. Anger is foreign to the gods, for anger is involuntary, and there is nothing involuntary in God. Do not then dishonor the divine nature by false human opinions, since you will not injure the eternally blessed One, whose immortal nature is incapable of injury, but you will blind yourself to the conception of what is great and chiefest.

19. Again you could not suppose my meaning to be this when I exhort you to reverence the gods, since it would be absurd to command this as though the matter admitted a question. And we do not worship Him only by doing or thinking this or that, neither can tears or supplications turn God from His purpose, nor yet is God honored by sacrifices nor glorified by plentiful offerings; but it is the godlike mind that remains stably fixed in its place that is united to God. For like must needs approach like. But the sacrifices of fools are mere food for fire, and the offerings they bring help the robbers of temples to lead their evil life. But, as was said before, let your temple be the mind that is within you. This must you tend and adorn, that it may be a fitting dwelling for God. Yet let not the adornment and the reception of God be but for a day, to be followed by mockery and folly and the return of the evil spirit.

20. If, then, you ever bear in mind that wheresoever your soul walks and inspires your body with activity, God is present and over-

looks all your counsels and actions, then will you feel reverence before the unbegotten presence of the spectator, and you will have God to dwell with you. And even though your mouth discourse the sound of some other thing, let your thought and mind be turned towards God. Thus shall even your speech be inspired, shining through the light of God's truth and flowing the more easily; for the knowledge of God makes discourse short.

21. But wheresoever forgetfulness of God shall enter in, there must the evil spirit dwell. For the soul is a dwelling-place, as you have learned, either of gods or of evil spirits. If the gods are present, it will do what is good both in word and in deed; but if it has welcomed in the evil guest, it does all things in wickedness. Whensoever, then, you behold a man doing or rejoicing in that which is evil, know that he has denied God in his heart and is the dwelling-place of an evil spirit. They who believe that God exists and governs all things have this reward of their knowledge and firm faith: they have learnt that God has forethought for all things, and that there exist angels, divine and good spirits, who behold all that is done, and from whose notice we cannot escape. Being persuaded that this is so, they are careful not to fall in their life, keeping before their eyes the constant presence of the gods whence they cannot escape. And they have attained to a wise mode of life, and know the gods and are known by them.

22. On the other hand, they who believe that the gods do not exist and that the universe is not governed by God's providence, have this punishment: they neither believe themselves, nor yet do they put faith in others who assert that the gods exist, but think that the universe is directed by a whirling motion void of reason. Thus they have cast themselves into unspeakable peril, trusting to an unreasoning and uncertain impulse in the events of life; and they do all that is unlawful in the endeavor to remove the belief in God. Assuredly such men are forsaken by the gods for their ignorance and unbelief. Yet they cannot flee and escape the notice of the gods or of justice their attendant, but having chosen an evil and erring life, though they know not the gods, yet are they known by them and by justice that dwells with the gods.

23. Even if they think they honor the gods, and are persuaded that they exist, yet neglect virtue and wisdom, they really have denied the divinities and dishonor them. Mere unreasoning faith without right living does not attain to God. Nor is it an act of piety

to honor God without having first ascertained in what manner He delights to be honored. If, then, He is gratified and won over by libations and sacrifices, it would not be just that while all men make the same requests they should obtain different answers to their prayers. But if there is nothing that God desires less than this, while he delights only in the purifications of the mind, which every man can attain of his own free choice, what injustice could there be? But if the divine nature delights in both kinds of service, it should receive honor by sacred rites according to each man's power, and by the thoughts of his mind even beyond that power. It is not wrong to pray to God, since ingratitude is a grievous wrong.

24. No god is in fault for a man's wickedness, but the man who has chosen it for himself. The prayer which is accompanied by base actions is impure, and therefore not acceptable to God; but that which is accompanied by noble actions is pure, and at the same time acceptable.

There are four first principles that must be upheld concerning God—faith, truth, love, hope. We must have faith that our only salvation is in turning to God. And having faith, we must strive with all our might to know the truth about God. And when we know this, we must love Him we do know. And when we love Him we must nourish our souls on good hopes for our life, for it is by their good hopes good men are superior to bad ones. Let then these four principles be firmly held.

25. Next let these three laws be distinguished. First, the law of God; second, the law of human nature; third, that which is laid down for nations and states. The law of nature fixes the limits of bodily needs, and shows what is necessary to these, and condemns all striving after which is needless and superfluous. Now that which is established and laid down for states regulates by fixed agreements the common relations of men, by their mutual observance of the covenants laid down. But the divine law is implanted by the mind, for their welfare, in the thoughts of reasoning souls, and it is found truthfully inscribed therein. The law of humanity is transgressed by him who through vain opinions know it not, owing to his excessive love for the pleasures of the body. But the conventional law is subject to expediency, and is differently laid down at different times according to the arbitrary will of the prevailing government. It punishes him who transgresses it, but it cannot reach a man's secret thoughts and intentions.

26. The divine law is unknown to the soul that folly and intemperance have rendered impure, but it shines forth in self-control and wisdom. It is impossible to transgress this, for there is nothing in man that can transcend it. Nor can it be despised, for it cannot shine forth in a man who will despise it. Nor is it moved by chances of fortune, because it is in truth superior to chance and stronger than any form of violence. Mind alone knows it, and diligently pursues the search thereafter, and finds it imprinted in itself, and supplies from it food to the soul as to its own body. We must regard the rational soul as the body of the mind, which the mind nourishes by bringing into recognition, through the light that is in it, the thoughts within, which mind imprinted and engraved in the soul in accordance with the truth of the divine law. Thus mind is become teacher and savior, nurse, guardian and leader, speaking the truth in silence, unfolding and giving forth the divine law; and looking on the impressions thereof in itself it beholds them implanted in the soul from all eternity.

27. You must therefore first understand the law of nature, and then proceed to the divine law, by which also the natural law has been prescribed. And if you make these your starting-point you shall never fear the written law. For written laws are made for the benefit of good men, not that they may do no wrong, but that they may not suffer it. Natural wealth is limited, and it is easy to attain. But the wealth desired of vain opinions has no limits, and is hard to attain. The true philosopher therefore, following nature and not vain opinions, is self-sufficing in all things; for in the light of the requirements of nature every possession is some wealth, but in the light of unlimited desires even the greatest wealth is but poverty. Truly it is no uncommon thing to find a man who is rich if tried by the standard of vain opinions. No fool is satisfied with what he possesses; he rather mourns for what he has not. Just as men in a fever are always thirsty through the grievous nature of their malady, and desire things quite opposed to one another, so men whose souls are ill-regulated are ever in want of all things, and experience ever-varying desires through their greed.

28. Wherefore the gods, too, have commanded us to purify ourselves by abstaining from food and from love, bringing those who follow after piety within the law of that nature which they themselves have formed, since everything which transgresses this law is loathsome and deadly. The multitude, however, fearing simplicity in

their mode of life, because of this fear, turn to the pursuits that can best procure riches. And many have attained wealth, and yet not found release from their troubles, but have exchanged them for greater ones. Wherefore philosophers say that nothing is so necessary as to know thoroughly what is unnecessary, and moreover that to be self-sufficing is the greatest of all wealth, and that it is honorable not to ask anything of any man. Wherefore, too, they exhort us to strive, not to acquire some necessary thing, but rather to remain of good cheer if we have not acquired it.

29. Neither let us accuse our flesh as the cause of great evils, nor attribute our troubles to outward things. Rather let us seek the cause of these things in our souls, and casting away every vain striving and hope for fleeting joys, let us become completely masters of ourselves. For a man is unhappy either through fear or through unlimited and empty desire. Yet if he bridle these, he can attain to a happy mind. But in as far as you are in want, it is through forgetfulness of your nature that you feel the want. For hereby you cause to yourself vague fears and desires. And it were better for you to be content and lie on a bed of rushes than to be troubled though you have a golden couch and a luxurious table acquired by labor and sorrow. Whilst the pile of wealth is growing bigger, life is growing wretched.

30. Do not think it unnatural that when the flesh cries out for anything, the soul should cry out too. The cry of the flesh is, "Let me not hunger, or thirst, or shiver," and 'tis hard for the soul to restrain these desires. 'Tis hard, too, for it by help of its own natural self-sufficing to disregard day by day the exhortations of nature, and to teach it to esteem the concerns of life as of little account. And when we enjoy good fortune, to learn to bear ill fortune, and when we are unfortunate not to hold of great account the possessions of those who enjoy good fortune. And to receive with a calm mind the good gifts of fortune, and to stand firm against her seeming ills. Yea, all that the many hold good is but a fleeting thing.

31. But wisdom and knowledge have no part in chance. It is not painful to lack the gifts of chance, but rather to endure the unprofitable trouble of vain ambition. For every disturbance and unprofitable desire is removed by the love of true philosophy. Vain is the word of that philosopher who can ease no mortal trouble. As there is no profit in the physician's art unless it cure the diseases of the body, so there is none in philosophy, unless it expel the troubles of

the soul. These and other like commands are laid on us by the law of our nature.

4. Iamblichus
Exhortation to Philosophy

The philosophy of Iamblichus was an elaboration of the Platonism developed by Plotinus, and a prolongation of the Neopythagorean tradition represented by eminent figures such as Moderatus of Gades, Nicomachus of Gerasa and Numenius of Apamea. Being also an admirer of the divinely inspired Chaldean wisdom, Iamblichus is of basic importance for an understanding of the development of the later Neoplatonic scholasticism.

The *Exhortation to Philosophy*, or *Protreptic to Philosophy* (*Protreptikos epi philosophian*), constitutes the second book of Iamblichus' Pythagorean encyclopedia (*On Pythagoreanism*). In this book Iamblichus describes the nature of the true philosophical life. Philosophy was regarded by him as a path, and to philosophize in the Pythagorean manner meant to reach "firm and unchanging truths strengthened by scientific demonstration through sciences (*mathematon*) and contemplation."

Iamblichus' *Exhortation to Philosophy* was addressed particularly to beginners on the path. The selected excerpts reproduced here have been rendered by Thomas Moore Johnson and were published in 1907 and 1920.

Protrept. 9–10; 12–14; 16–17

9.... Pythagoras, being asked for what purpose or end Deity and nature created us, answered, "that we might contemplate the celestial sphere." And he said that he himself was a contemplator of nature, and in order to exercise this function came into physical life. And also Anaxagoras, being asked why anyone was born and desired to live, answered, "that he might contemplate the heavenly sphere and what it contains, the stars, moon, and sun, because all other things were nothing." So of everything the end or purpose is always better: for on account of the end all things that come into existence are generated, and that for the sake of which anything comes into existence is better and the best of all, and this is the end according to nature, and this end is that which, in the productive order fulfilling itself continuously, is the last to be perfected.

First, therefore, the things which pertain to the human body fulfill or attain the end, then those which pertain to the soul, and thus continuously the end or purpose of that which is better comes later than generation. Hence the soul is later in its entrance into the generated sphere than the body, and of psychical powers wisdom is perfected last. For we may see that this comes last to men in the order of nature, wherefore old age seeks this alone of the goods. Wisdom, therefore, according to nature, is to us an end, and the ultimate end or object for the sake of which we came into this world, i.e. that we may know. Therefore if we were generated, it is plain the purpose and object of our generation was that we may gain insight and learn something. Rightly for this reason did Pythagoras affirm that for the sake of knowing and contemplating was every man made by God. Whether the world or some other nature is to be contemplated may be considered later. This will suffice as a preliminary statement.

If Wisdom is the end according to nature, Wisdom will be the best of all things. Wherefore we should give attention to all other things on account of the goods which are in Wisdom, and of these goods we should bestow care on the corporeal for the sake of the psychical, but cultivate and practice virtue on account of Wisdom in which it resides, for this is the highest. But if one argues that from every science something else is produced, and that it is useful, he is totally ignorant of the primary difference between good and necessary things, and this difference is truly great. For those things which are loved on account of something else, things without which it is impossible to live, must be said to be necessary and concausal things. But the things that are loved *per se*, even though nothing else results from them, are properly called good. For one thing is not to be loved on account of another, and that on account of still another, for this process would continue *ad infinitum*. But it is necessary to stop somewhere. And it is utterly ridiculous, therefore, to require of every thing a utility besides the thing itself, and to ask of what benefit it is to us, and for what it is useful.

Truly may we say, if any one should as it were transport us in thought to the Islands of the Blessed—for there nothing "useful" is wanted, and nothing of all other things would be of any benefit, but alone would remain a life of thought and contemplation, that which we even now call a free life—in such a case who of us would not be justly ashamed if he were unable through his own fault to accept an offer of dwelling in the Islands of the Blessed? Wherefore the benefit of science to men must not be ignored: nor is it by any means a small good which arises from it. For just as we receive the rewards of justice in Hades, as the wise poets say, so do the gifts of Wisdom remain to us in the Islands of the Blessed. And so it is of no importance if Wisdom appears to be of no practical use to anyone. But we affirm that it is not useful but good; and that it should be chosen and sought, not on account of anything else, but *per se* or for its own sake alone. For just as we attend the Olympian festival for the mere pleasure of the spectacle alone, even though we gain nothing from it—for the spectacle is better than much wealth—and as we view the Dionysian performances, not that we may receive anything from the actors—truly we pay largely for the privilege of attending, and we spend much money in seeing many other shows, [which are not of a useful character]—so the contemplation of the universe must be preferred to all things which seem to be useful. Indeed it is not becoming that men should imitate weak women and slaves in contending and running with much ardor and trouble in order to see shows, and yet be unwilling to contemplate the nature and truth of beings without a utilitarian reward. Thus, proceeding from the purpose [design] of nature we have exhorted to the study and acquisition of Wisdom, as to a certain good which is valuable *per se* or for its own sake, even though nothing "useful" to human life should come from it.

10. But indeed that theoretic Wisdom or insight supplies to human life the greatest utilities, one may easily see from the arts. For just as learned physicians and gymnasts must be skilled in a knowledge of nature, so also good law-givers must have a knowledge of nature, and a much greater knowledge than the others. For the first are only artificers of corporeal virtue [strength], but the others are busied with the virtues of the soul, and the felicity and infelicity of the State—much more therefore do they need Philosophy. For even as in other mechanical arts the best instruments are drawn from nature as, for instance, in carpentry the plummet, rule, and compass, the exemplars for which are found in water, light, and the splendors of rays by which we test those things which to the senses appear sufficiently straight and smooth, so likewise it is necessary that the politician should have certain standards drawn from nature and truth, in accordance with which he judges what is just, what is beautiful, and what is useful. For just as in nature the exemplars surpass all the instruments, so here that law is the best which approxi-

mates nearest to the natural or eternal law. This it is not possible for one to enact unless he philosophizes and knows the truth. And of other arts, they know that the instruments and most accurate reasonings are not assumed primarily from themselves but from things secondary, tertiary, and most remote, and the productive principles are drawn from experience.

To the philosopher alone is there a correct representation of those things which are of and from themselves accurate exemplars, immutable Ideas, for he is a spectator of things themselves but not of imitations of these. Just as neither will he be a good carpenter who does not use the rule and other instruments of this kind, but builds with reference to other houses as a rule or model, similarly, if one [without reference to immutable exemplars] establishes laws for states, or does things with reference to other actions, or imitates the human forms of states either of the Lacedaemonians or Cretans or others, he will be neither a good legislator nor an upright man. For it cannot happen that an imitation of that which is not good is good, nor that an imitation of that which is not divine and permanent may be immortal and permanent; but of all artificers and legislators the laws of the philosopher alone are permanent and the actions right and beautiful. For he alone who looks to nature and the divine truly lives, just as a good ruler drawing from immortal and stable sources the principles of living advances and lives according to them himself. This science therefore is both theoretic and productive, as we do all things according to it. For just as sight is neither productive nor causative of anything, since its sole function is to judge and make manifest everything visible, and to afford us the power and opportunity to act, so that by its aid the greatest deeds may be done by us— for deprived of sight we are practically helpless—so also it is plain that though true science is theoretic, we may by means of it do thousands of things, and through it may apprehend some things and avoid others; and briefly, may acquire all good through it....

12. But if our conclusion is to be deduced not only from parts but from a consideration of universal felicity, we distinctly affirm that, in the same manner as Philosophy is related to felicity, so is our moral perfection, having no connection with that which is vile. For all things, partly on account of Felicity and partly on account of Philosophy, are desired and sought by means of which we become happy. We therefore define Felicity to be either intellectual insight or some type of wisdom, or Virtue, or the greatest intellectual pleas-

ure, or all of these. If therefore it is intellectual insight, it is evident that to philosophers alone will come a felicitous life; if it is psychical virtue, or intellectual pleasure, these also the philosophers either alone or above all others will experience. For Virtue is the most valuable and excellent of our possessions, and Wisdom is the most delightful of all things, comparing things with each other. Similarly, if one should say that all these constitute Felicity he would define Wisdom or Insight: wherefore all should philosophize to the extent of their capacity. For Philosophy indeed is the science of living perfectly, and is above all things, to speak briefly, the cause to souls of this perfect life. Yet on this earth, because our race is in an unnatural abode, it is difficult for us to learn and investigate, and scarcely one is able on account of mental sluggishness, [caused by our descent hither,] and the unnatural life, to acquire a perception of this fact. But if saved, we return again to the place whence we came, it is evident that we will learn easily and pleasantly. For now, abandoning the pursuit of things which are truly good, we are devoting all our time to things which are termed "necessary" or "practical," and this is especially the case with all those who seem to the multitude to be most happy. But if we pursue the heavenly way and live in our kindred star, then we will philosophize, living truly, busied with the most profound and marvelous speculations, beholding the beauty in the soul immutably related to Truth, viewing the rule of the Gods with joy, gaining perpetual delight and additional insight from contemplating, and experiencing pure pleasure absolutely unmingled with any pain or sorrow. Pursuing this way, therefore, we will find that Philosophy leads us to total felicity; and hence, since Philosophy is in its nature most excellent, it is fully worthy of our most ardent study.

13. But if it is necessary to use an exhortation to the study of Philosophy drawn from philosophic conceptions, we will thus begin. It seems that those who practice Philosophy rightly are not understood by others to do nothing else than to study how "to die" and "to be dead."[34] And this very rationally. For the multitude do not know in what way and why true philosophers study how "to die," and are worthy of "death," and what kind of a "death" they deserve. And death indeed is nothing else than the release and separation of

---

34. Cf. Plato, *Phaedo* 64a–65d.

the soul from the body, and this is "to die": so that death is merely the existence of the body apart from the soul, and the existence of the soul *per se* or apart from the body. This therefore being so, it is not reasonable that the philosopher should eagerly pursue pleasures so-called—such as, for instance, the pleasures of eating and drinking, or sexual delights. Nor will he consider as of any worth the other services and cares of the body, such as the possession of costly clothing and sandals and other adornments of the body—these he will not deem of any importance but will despise them, and will use them only so far as it is absolutely necessary.

In brief, it seems that the study and business of this man is not concerned with the body, but, so far as he can, he departs from it, and applies himself absolutely to the culture of his soul. And in things of this kind it is plain that the philosopher, acting differently from other men, especially aims and studies to release his soul from an association with the body: and by reason of this fact the multitude thinks that to him who derives no pleasure from corporeal things, and who enjoys none of them, life is not worth living, but that he verges most closely on the state of death who cares nothing for the pleasures which come through and by means of the body. Moreover, in acquiring Wisdom the body is an impediment, if one should take it with him as a companion in the search. But to illustrate this point: neither the sense of sight nor of hearing brings any truth to men. For the poets constantly sing to us that "we nothing accurate hear or see." And if even these senses of the body are neither accurate nor certain, much less are the others: for all the others are inferior to these.

Wherefore, if the soul does not apprehend the truth when it attempts to investigate something in connection with the body— since it is evident that it is then deceived and misled by the body— it is doubtless in the process of thinking, if at all, that any real truth becomes manifest to her. But she thinks and reasons the best, most deeply and perfectly, when none of the senses annoys by its intrusion, neither hearing, nor sight, nor pain, nor any pleasure—and reaches after true being when she is as much as possible alone *per se*, bidding farewell to the body, and as far as possible, becoming free from communication and contact with it. Here, then, the soul of the philosopher most despises the body, and flies from it, and seeks to become and live alone *per se*. But this will be specially evident from the contemplation of Ideas. For absolute Justice, Beauty, and Good, and all other things on which we impress the character of essence or reality—no one ever saw any of these with his eyes nor perceived them by any other senses which act through the body; but whoever has most thoroughly and accurately prepared himself to apprehend intellectually the essence of each object of his investigation, he it is that will approximate the nearest to the knowledge of it. Wherefore he will do this most purely who strives to reach each thing as much as possible by discursive reason alone, and neither takes the sight as an accessory in the processes of the discursive power, nor drags after him any other sense to act in connection with his reasoning power; but using his discursive reason *per se*, in its absolute purity, he will strive to investigate and apprehend everything which is true being, subsisting pure and *per se*, liberated as far as possible from eyes and ears and, speaking summarily, from the whole body, because it only disturbs the soul and does not permit her by its presence to acquire truth and Wisdom. For this man, if any, will attain to true being.

From all the premises, therefore, it necessarily follows that such an inference will be drawn by genuine philosophers, that they will speak to each other thus: It seems that it is only a certain narrow way which will lead us to the end of our journey in this investigation, because so long as we have the body as an associate with reason in our search and our soul is mixed up with such an evil,[35] we shall never fully attain the object of our desires, and this object we affirm to be Truth. For innumerable are the impediments which the body throws in our way, on account of the necessity of providing for its support. Moreover, should any maladies befall it they too impede the ardent pursuit of real being—and it fills us with desires and passions and terrors and vain imaginations of all kinds and a host of frivolities, so that as it is truly said, we can never truly and in reality acquire wisdom or insight through the body. For in fact to wars, seditions, and contentions nothing else than the body and its passions incite us. For all wars arise through the passion for acquiring

---

35. The Neoplatonists regarded the world as a theophany, a manifestation of the divine principles; but in the process of philosophical education, and for mostly didactic purposes, they sometimes equated the mortal lower world of becoming (*genesis*) with an evil that must finally be abandoned and rejected in favor of the immortal intelligible realm of the divine principles.

wealth, and we are compelled to get it on account of the body, because we are enslaved to its service; so that, on account of this, we have no leisure for the study and practice of Philosophy.

But the last and worst of all is, that if any leisure from the exactions of the body should come to us, and we apply our mind to the speculation of any intellectual object, in the very midst of our researches again, at every moment, it interrupts us, creating tumult and disturbance, and confuses us so that we are unable, by reason of its presence, to perceive the truth: but in fact it has been demonstrated that, if we are ever to know anything purely and clearly, we must be liberated from the body, and contemplate with the soul alone the realities of things, i.e. the Ideas. And then, as it appears, we shall have what we desire and profess a love for, namely Wisdom or insight, after "death," as our argument makes clear, but not so long as we "live."

For if it is impossible to attain to pure knowledge while we are associated and connected with the body, one of two things must follow: either we can nowhere at all acquire it, or only after death, for then, but not before, will the soul be by herself, separated from the body. And during our lifetime we shall, I think, make the nearest approach to knowledge, if we abstain as far as possible from intercourse and communication with the body, except so far as is absolutely necessary, and preserve ourselves from infection by its nature, keeping ourselves pure from its pollutions until God himself has liberated us from the corporeal bonds. And thus being pure, and released from the folly of the body, it is right to believe that we shall dwell with others who are similarly pure and genuine: for it is not lawful that the impure should ever associate with the pure. But purification, indeed, as has been said above, consists in the most complete separation of the soul from the body, and the habituation of her to collect and concentrate herself by herself from all parts of the physical frame, and to dwell as far as possible both in the time now present and in the future alone by herself, released from the body as from a prison, working out her deliverance as it were from the shackles of the body. But this is called "death," namely a release and separation of the soul from the body. But chiefly, and indeed only those who philosophize rightly, as we have said, always work in the most strenuous degree to release the soul; and the aim and study of philosophers is neither more nor less than this, the release and separation of the soul from the body.

Wherefore Philosophy, since it brings to us the greatest good, namely a liberation from the chains in which the soul is bound from the date of its birth into time must be sought with the most intense avidity and study. But what is called Fortitude chiefly belongs to those who are disposed to the study of Philosophy; and likewise Temperance, which even the many call by its right name, and which consists in not being agitated by the passions but in moderating them with contempt and composure, belongs only to those who specially despise the body and live in the practice of Philosophy. For if the Fortitude and Temperance of others are examined they will appear to be absurdities. For it is well known that all others deem "death" to be the greatest of evils. It is therefore from fear of greater evils that the brave among the many support death, when they do support it: therefore all except the philosophers are courageous through and by fearing and fear, though it is strange that one should be courageous through fear and timidity. But what about the moderate among them? Are not these affected in the same manner, being temperate through a kind of intemperance? And yet, though we should be disposed to say that it is impossible, still their case in respect of this foolish kind of temperance does come to bear a close resemblance to this: for from mere fear of being deprived of one kind of pleasure and from desire of another, they abstain from some while they are dominated by others; and though they call a subjection to pleasures intemperance, yet at the same time they succeed in mastering some pleasures just because they are mastered by others; and this is analogous to what was said just now, that in a way they are made temperate through intemperance. This, therefore, is not the right road to virtue, namely to change pleasures for pleasures, pains for pains, fear for fear, and the greater too for the less, like so many pieces of money; but Wisdom alone is the coin for which we must exchange all these things, and all that is bought and sold for this and with this—that and that alone is in reality, whether it be fortitude or temperance or justice; and in a word that true virtue only exists when accompanied by wisdom, whether pleasures and fears and all the rest of such things be thrown in or withdrawn: whereas, separated from wisdom and exchanged one for the other, such virtue as this is a mere shadowy sketch and really servile, with no soundness or genuineness about it. But real Virtue is a complete purification from all such things; and Temperance, Justice, Fortitude, and Wisdom itself form the prelude as it were to this purification from pollution.

And indeed those famous men who established the Mysteries for us seem to have been no mean thinkers, but in fact to have obscurely hinted long ago that whoever descends into Hades uninitiated and unpurified shall grovel in the mire; but he who has been purified and initiated shall on his arrival there dwell with the Gods. For there are, say those who write about the Mysteries, many that bear the thyrsus [wand] but few that are bacchanals [true initiates].

> The thyrsus-bearers numerous are seen,
> But few the Bacchuses have always been.[36]

These few are in my opinion no other than the genuine philosophers. If therefore Philosophy alone by reason of its nature causes perfect virtue and purification of the soul, that alone is worthy to be desired and sought. But to the company of the Gods none may go who has not sought wisdom and departed in perfect purity; none but the lover of learning. And this is the reason why true philosophers abstain from the indulgence of all corporeal desires or passions, and persevere in this abstinence, not surrendering themselves to them, and not at all because they fear ruin and poverty, like the vulgar and the lovers of money: nor, again, because they fear disgrace and contempt, like the lovers of power and of honor, do they abstain from these desires. Wherefore those who have any concern for their soul, and do not live subserving their bodies, bid adieu to all such characters as we have mentioned, and walk not in the same path, being assured that these know not where they are going: but they themselves, persuaded that they ought not to act contrary to Philosophy and to its liberating and purifying operations, give themselves up to its direction, and follow whithersoever it leads.

For the lovers of learning know that Philosophy receiving into its care their soul which is a close prisoner in the body and glued to it and forced to contemplate real things through the body, or as it were through the bars of her dungeon, instead of alone, and wallowing in every kind of ignorance, and clearly perceiving that the dire nature of the dungeon arises through the soul's eager desire or appetition to make as much as possible the captive himself an

36. Cf. Plato, *Phaedo* 69cd.

accomplice in his own incarceration—the lovers of learning therefore know that Philosophy receiving their soul into its care in this condition gently endeavors to exhort her and to set her free, by showing her that all observation by the eyes is fallacious and illusive, and that this is likewise the case with perception, the ears and the other senses; and by persuading her to withdraw from them, except just so far as she must use them, and by exhorting her to collect and concentrate herself into herself, and to put no faith in anything but herself, that is, in that portion of real existence in and by itself which she can apprehend in and by herself, but whatsoever she contemplates by different organs varying with varying conditions—she holds none of that to be true, for all such things belong to the realm of sense and of the visible, whereas what she sees herself belongs to the intelligible and invisible.

Thinking, then, that she ought not to oppose herself to this process of liberation, the soul of the true philosopher therefore holds herself aloof from pleasures and passions and fears as far as possible, reflecting that, whenever anyone is violently moved by pleasure or fear or pain or desire, the evil that he contracts from them is not of that slight magnitude that one might think—an attack of sickness, for instance, or some loss incurred by the indulgence of his passions—but he suffers that which is the greatest and extremest of all evils, though he never takes it into account, namely that the soul of every man in the act of feeling some vehement pleasure or pain is at the same time forced into the belief that everything which most excites this feeling is the most vivid and true, though it is not so. And these are, most of all, the visible things.

Wherefore in this "feeling" the soul is most completely manacled by the body, because every pleasure and pain with a nail as it were fastens and rivets the soul to the body, causes her to become corporeal, and to believe that whatever the body asserts is true. For from her conformity of opinions and identity of pleasures with those of the body, she is forced to become like it in her habits and nurture, and of such a character that she can never arrive in Hades pure, but must always depart polluted by the body, so that she speedily falls again into another body, and grows again as if she had been sown there, and hence is deprived of all communion with that which is pure, simple and divine.

On account of these things [i.e., the considerations drawn from the nature and destinies of the soul] therefore the true lovers of wisdom are temperate and firm, and not for the reasons which the multitude assigns: but the soul of the philosopher reasons thus, and does not think that Philosophy ought to liberate her from the body, but that while Philosophy is freeing her she may give herself up to pleasures and pains so as to be again entangled in bonds, condemning herself to endless labor, handling, so to speak, her web in the very opposite way from the example of Penelope; on the contrary, calming the passions to rest, following her reason and in it ever abiding, contemplating that which is true, divine, and beyond the sphere of opinion, and being nourished by it, she deems that she must thus pass her life as long as it lasts, and that after "death" she will go to that which is akin and congenial to herself, and so be delivered from all human evils.

From this course of reasoning it is evident that Philosophy brings to us a release from human or corporeal chains and a deliverance from the incidents of temporal birth [generation], and leads to that which truly is, and to a knowledge of Truth itself and the purification of souls. But if in this above all things there is true felicity, we must cultivate Philosophy most zealously, if we wish to be truly happy. Moreover, it is right to reflect that, since the soul is immortal, it requires our anxious care, not merely for this interval of time which we call "life," but always; and most serious will be the danger if we neglect the soul. For if death were a total annihilation, great would be the gain to the wicked, since they would be liberated by death at once from the body and from their depravity, together with the soul; but now, since the soul proves to be immortal, there is for her no escape from evils, nor salvation, other than by becoming as good and wise as possible.

For the soul descends to Hades with nothing whatever but her education and culture, which as it is said is [according to its kind] either of the greatest aid or of the greatest disadvantage to the soul, at the very outset of her journey thither. For the better soul dwells with the Gods, traverses the heavenly sphere, and receives a better allotment; but he who has been guilty of unjust acts and is full of depravity and impiety, going into the subterranean dungeons receives fitting penalties.

For the sake of these things, therefore, we ought to use our utmost efforts to gain virtue and wisdom in this life. For the contest is noble and the hope great, and on account of these one should believe confidently in the worth of his own soul if through life he has ignored corporeal and mundane pleasures as alien, and considered any participation of them as pernicious to himself, but has given himself to those pleasures which are inherent in learning—and, ornamenting his soul not with anything alien to its essence but with its own connate ornaments, namely wisdom, justice, fortitude, liberty, and truth, he is ready to take the journey into Hades when the appointed time arrives.

These things being so, we should not make the accumulation of riches our highest aim, nor glory and honor, but the acquisition of Wisdom and truth and the way by which the soul may reach the most excellent condition. Things of the greatest worth should not be held in less esteem than those of a trifling character. Neither, therefore, must attention be given to the body, nor to the getting of money, nor to anything else, prior to the care of the soul, which it should be our chief business to bring to the best possible condition. For Virtue does not arise from riches, but from Virtue come riches and all other goods, private and public, to men. This one thing, therefore, must be deemed absolutely true, namely that to a good man neither in life nor after death will any evil come, nor are his affairs neglected by the Gods; so that to him will be given all the goods which contribute to felicity, and he who closely follows the path leading to Virtue will live most happily. Let therefore an exhortation to the study of Philosophy, drawn from the preceding, be of this kind.

14. Next we must draw an exhortation from the life of philosophers of the first rank, the Coryphaeans,[37] according to the teachings of Pythagoras. For these philosophers have never from their childhood known the way to the forum, or where a law court is, or council chamber, or any other political meeting-place; laws and decrees, whether spoken or written, they neither hear nor see. The ambitious striving of political clubs for offices, public meetings, and banquets and revelings with minstrelsy—all these are practices which do not occur to them even in dreams. What has been well or badly transacted in the city, or what infamy may attach to anyone from his ancestors, either by his father's or mother's side, of this he is as ignorant as he is of the number of drops of water in the ocean. And he is even ignorant that he is ignorant of all these particulars,

37. Cf. Plato, *Theaetetus* 173c–177b.

for he does not keep himself aloof from them for the sake of reputation; but in reality it is only his body which dwells and is conversant in the city, while his discursive reason (*dianoia*), deeming all these things trifling and of no value, despises them and soars all abroad, "measuring," as Pindar says, "the regions below the earth and those upon it, star-gazing into heaven's height," and thoroughly investigating all the nature of the beings which each whole contains, but not descending to anything which is near.

It is said, for example, that Thales astronomizing and looking intently upward fell into a well, and a bright and lively Thracian girl taunted him about the accident, saying that in his eagerness to know what was in heaven he could not see what was around him and under his feet. Now the same taunt is good for all students of Philosophy. They are indeed entirely ignorant what their nearest neighbor is about, and almost whether or not he is a human being; but what man is, and what it becomes him, as distinguished from every other creature, to do or suffer, into all this they make diligent inquiry.

Therefore when a philosopher of this kind chances to hold a public or private conversation with anyone, when he is compelled to enter a law-court, or some such place, and engage in a discussion concerning the things before his eyes and under his feet, he is a fruitful subject for merriment, not only to Thracian girls but to the whole company, tumbling into pitfalls and getting into all sorts of embarrassments because of his ignorance, and behaving so awkwardly that people look upon him as a kind of booby. If he is shamefully treated, he does not retaliate, as he has no private grudge, and he is regarded as ridiculously inspired because he knows no evil of anyone and is without any appetite for gossip. When others are praised and eulogized, he is only unfeignedly amused, and is for this also counted as a manifest simpleton. When he hears a tyrant or king praised, it is in his estimation much as if some herdsman, or swineherd, shepherd, or cow-herd, were praised for his large stock of serviceable beasts; with this difference, however, that he thinks of a herd of cattle as less treacherous and ungovernable than the animals tended and milked by a tyrant.

And as for the ruler, he must become even more rude and uncultured than a herdsman, for he is always hard at work and girt in by his stone walls as by the sides of a mountain cavern. When this philosopher hears that some one owns a thousand acres or more, this marvelous possession is for him an unconsidered trifle, since he has been wont to view the whole earth. They who sing of pedigree, how that some are noble because they count seven rich ancestors, are to him of dull and narrow sight, being unable in their ignorance to fix their eyes upon the whole of time or to reflect that everyone has had myriads of forefathers and ancestors, amongst whom are numbered rich and poor, kings and slaves, both barbarians and Greeks. When they boast that in their genealogical tree the five and twentieth ancestor was Hercules the son of Amphitryon, they forget in their petty arithmetic that Amphitryon's five and twentieth ancestor was nobody in particular, and that he in turn had a fiftieth; and the philosopher smiles at their meager reckonings, and fatuous absorption in their own vain and foolish selves.

In all this, however, he is ridiculed by the multitude, in part because he has a proud bearing, as they think, in part because he is ignorant of what is at his feet, and in matters of detail is always at fault.

But when the philosopher leads anyone to take a higher view, and bids him mount out of questions of private injury into the consideration of justice and injustice, as each is in itself and as they differ from each other and from all other things, or when they turn from the question whether the rich king is happy to inquire into kingship and human happiness generally, of what nature they are and what kind of man ought to be happy and escape misery—when such questions as these are to the fore, and that narrow-minded legal personage must give a reason and answer, then he presents a counterpart of the philosopher. For, suspended aloft at such an unusual height and looking into mid-air, he becomes dizzy and dismayed, his want of wit and incoherent babble making him a laughing-stock, not to Thracian girls or any uneducated person, for they do not see the absurdity, but to all whose training has not been that of slaves. Such is the condition and character of each: one is that of the man really, bred in freedom and leisure, who should be given the name philosopher, who surely is not to blame if he is foolish and at a loss when it falls to him to perform some such servile duty as to pack a trunk, or flavor a sauce, or make a fawning speech; the other is the man who can do all these services thoroughly and with dispatch, but who does not know how to don his cloak gracefully, or, by acquiring harmony of language to sing well the true life of the Gods and blessed men.

I think, therefore, if all men were convinced of these things, there would be more peace and less evil in the world. But, indeed, evil cannot be altogether destroyed, for there must always be something opposite to good: it cannot, however, find a place in the home of the Gods, but of necessity flourishes in the mortal nature and this terrestrial region. Wherefore we must endeavor to fly from this world to the other with the utmost haste. Moreover, one should know that flight means becoming like to God as much as possible; and the way to be like God is to become just and holy and wise. But it is difficult to persuade the many that these are the true reasons for shunning evil and seeking Virtue, and not, as they think, in order to have the appearance of goodness. But the notions of the many on this subject are as absurd as an old woman's fable. The real truth may thus be stated: God can never be unjust, but is wholly just, and nothing can be more like Him than the perfectly just man.

By this means we distinguish genuine worth from worthlessness and puerility; for to know the nature of God is wisdom and true virtue, and not to know it is sheer ignorance and vice. All other wisdom [so called] or ability, whether in politics or in the arts, is vulgar and ignoble. It is far better not to allow for a moment that the men who are unjust, profane, or unrighteous in word or deed are men of powerful minds because they are rogues. Such men glory in their name, and imagine that they are spoken of not as good-for-nothing encumbrances but as exemplary citizens. They must be told that their worthlessness is in proportion to their false opinion of their value. They are ignorant of what they most of all should know, that the consequence of injustice is not merely lashes and death, which the wrong-doer sometimes escapes, but a punishment which is inevitable. For in the nature of things there are two types, namely one divine and blessed, the other ungodlike and repulsive; those who live unjustly do not see in the extremity of their folly and blindness that they are becoming like the earthly type and unlike the divine, and their reward is that their life is in harmony with the corresponding type or exemplar.

If we say to them that unless they abandon their unscrupulous ways they, when they die, will not be admitted into the place that is pure of evil, and in this world will be given over to things which are in conformity with their unworthy behavior, they in their abounding cunning and craft will look on us as giving the counsel of fools.

However, one noteworthy thing befalls them. If they are willing to discuss in private their objections to Philosophy, and wait manfully and unflinchingly to see the matter out, then, strange to say, they lose their satisfaction in themselves, their brilliant rhetoric fades, and they become as little children. But if these things are true, and the life of those who devote themselves to the acquisition and practice of Philosophy is more divine and felicitous than any other mode of living, we should do nothing else than to grasp nobly and ardently the principles of Philosophy....

16. Hence, if these things be true, we cannot avoid believing that the real nature of education[38] is not such as some assert, who pretend to infuse into the mind a knowledge of which it was destitute, just as sight might be instilled into blinded eyes, whereas our present reasoning shows us that there is a power inherent in the soul of each person which is the instrument by which each of us is able to learn; and that just as we might suppose it to be impossible to turn the eye round from darkness to light without turning the whole body, so must this faculty or instrument be wheeled round in company with the entire soul away from the world of death and generation, until it is enabled to endure the contemplation of the real world and the brightest part of it, which we call the good. Hence this process of revolution or converting must give rise to an art teaching in what way the change will most easily and most effectually be brought about. Its object will not be to implant in a person the power of seeing, but, on the contrary, it assumes that he possesses it, though he is turned in a wrong direction and does not look toward the right quarter; and its aim is to remedy this defect.

Therefore, though the other so-called virtues of the soul seem to resemble those of the body—inasmuch as they really do not pre-exist in the soul, but are formed in it in the course of time by habit and exercise—the virtue of wisdom does most certainly appertain to a more divine substance, which never loses its actuality, but by change of position becomes useful and serviceable, or else remains useless and injurious. For you must have noticed how keen-sighted are the puny souls of those who have the reputation of being clever but vicious, and how sharply they see through the things to which they are directed, thus proving that their powers of vision are by no

38. Cf. Plato, *Republic* 518b–519b.

means feeble, though they have been compelled to become the servants of wickedness, so that the more sharply they see, the more numerous are the evils which they work. But, if from earliest childhood these characters had been shorn and stripped of those leaden, earth-born weights, which grow and cling to the pleasures of eating, and gluttonous enjoyments of a similar nature, and which keep the eye of the soul turned upon the things below—if they had been released from these snares, and turned around to look at objects that are true, then these very same souls of these very same men would have had as keen an eye for such pursuits as they actually have for those in which they are now engaged. Now, therefore, since we are "born" here, it is evident from the same reasoning what nature the function of Philosophy has and how precious it is. For to cleanse the soul of every taint of generation, and to purify that actuality of it to which the power of reason belongs, is the chief function of Philosophy. This therefore is the best mode of living, namely to live and die practicing justice and the other virtues: and this mode we must follow, if we wish to become truly happy.

17. But if our hearers should be advised from ancient discourses and sacred myths, both of the Pythagoreans and others, from these we will proceed to draw an exhortation. Rightly are those called happy who need nothing, and the life of those who have innumerable desires is dangerous and full of trouble.[39] I should not wonder, indeed, if Euripides is right when he says,

> Who knoweth if to live is to be dead,
> And to be dead is to live?[40]

And one might wonder if we are all really dead, and the body is our tomb, and that part of the soul in which the desires reside is of a nature liable to be over-persuaded and to be swayed continually to and fro. And so some smart Sicilian or Italian turned this into a fable, and, playing with the word, from its susceptibility to all impressions and capacity for holding belief, named it a jar, and the foolish he called uninitiated: in these uninitiated, that part of the soul where the desires are, the licentious and non-retentive portion of it, he compared to a jar full of holes, because there was no possi-

39. Cf. Plato, *Gorgias* 493.
40. *Polyidus*, fr.7.

bility of filling or satisfying it. Wherefore, this thinker shows, contrary to the opinion of the multitude, that of all those in Hades, which signifies the invisible region, the uninitiated are the most miserable, and are forced to carry water into their leaky jar in a sieve perforated just like the other. And by the sieve he represents the soul: and the soul of the foolish he likened to a sieve, because it is full of holes, as incapable of holding anything by reason of its incredulity and forgetfulness, i.e., its inaptitude for receiving and retaining knowledge. This may indeed seem somewhat whimsical; still it shows clearly what I want to prove, namely that one should choose, in preference to a life of insatiable self-indulgence, one that is orderly and regular and ever content and satisfied with what it has.

5. Iamblichus
On the Mysteries of the Egyptians

The actual title of Iamblichus' *De mysteriis* in the manuscripts is *The Reply of the Master Abammon to the Letter of Porphyry to Anebo and the Solution to the Problems raised therein*. The title *On the Mysteries of the Egyptians, Chaldeans, and Assyrians* was the contribution of Marsilio Ficino. In this work, Iamblichus, wearing the mask of an Egyptian priest called Abammon, defends the practice of theurgy (*theourgia*) and answers Porphyry's doubts regarding the efficacy of hieratic art. Iamblichus' philosophical justification of theurgy (which he regarded as essentially Egyptian and Chaldean in origin) was of importance for the later sacramental theology of the Greek Christian Fathers.

The excerpts presented here were translated by Thomas Taylor and published in 1821 under the title *On the Mysteries of the Egyptians, Chaldeans, and Assyrians*.

De myster. VII

I. The doubts also that follow in the next place require for their solution the assistance of the same divinely-wise Muse. But I am desirous, previous to this, to unfold to you the peculiarity of the theology of the Egyptians. For they, imitating the nature of the universe, and the fabricative energy of the Gods, exhibit certain images through symbols of mystic, occult, and invisible intellections; just as nature, after a certain manner, expresses invisible reasons [or productive powers] through visible forms. But the fabricative energy of the Gods delineates the truth of forms, through visible images. Hence the Egyptians, perceiving that all superior natures rejoice in the similitude to them of inferior beings, and thus wishing to fill the latter with good, through the greatest possible imitation of the former, very properly exhibit a mode of theologizing adapted to the mystic doctrine concealed in the symbols.

II. Hear, therefore, the intellectual interpretation of symbols, according to the conceptions of the Egyptians; at the same time removing from your imagination and your ears the image of things symbolical, but elevating yourself to intellectual truth. By *"mire,"* therefore, understand every thing corporeal-formed and material or that which is nutritive and prolific; or such as the material species of nature is, which is borne along in conjunction with the unstable flux of matter; or a thing of such a kind as that which the river of generation receives, and which subsides together with it; or the primordial cause of the elements, and of all the powers distributed about the elements, and which must be antecedently conceived to exist analogous to a foundation. Being, therefore, a thing of this kind, the God who is the cause of generation, of all nature, and of all the powers in the elements, as transcending these, and as being immaterial, incorporeal, and supernatural, unbegotten and impartible, wholly derived from himself, and concealed in himself,—this God precedes all things, and comprehends all things in himself. And because, indeed, he comprehends all things, and imparts himself to all mundane natures, he is from these unfolded into light. Because, however, he transcends all things, and is by himself expanded above them, on this account he presents himself to the view as separate, exempt, elevated, and expanded by himself above the powers and elements in the world. The following symbol, likewise, testifies the truth of this. For by the God *"sitting above the lotus,"* a transcendency and strength which by no means come into contact with the mire, are obscurely signified, and also indicate his intellectual and empyrean empire. For every thing belonging to the lotus is seen to be circular, viz. both the form of the leaves and the fruit; and circulation is alone allied to the motion of intellect, which energizes with invariable sameness, in one order, and according to one reason. But the God is established by himself, and above a dominion and energy of this kind, venerable and holy, superexpanded, and abiding in himself, which his being seated is intended to signify. When the God, also, is represented as *"sailing in a ship,"* it exhibits to us the power which governs the world. As, therefore, the pilot being separate from the ship presides over the rudder of it, thus the sun having a separate subsistence, governs the helm of the whole world. And as the pilot directs all things from the stern, giving from himself a small principle of motion to the vessel; thus, also, by a much greater priority, the God indivisibly imparts supernally from the first principles of nature, the primordial causes of motions. These particulars, therefore, and still more than these, are indicated by the God sailing in a ship.

III. Since, however, every part of the heavens, every sign of the zodiac, all the motion of the heavens, every period of time according to which the world is moved, and all things contained in the wholes of the universe, receive the powers which descend from the sun, some of which are complicated with these wholes, but others transcend a commixture with them, the symbolical mode of signification represents these also, indicating *"that the sun is diversified according to the signs of the zodiac, and that every hour he changes his form."* At the same time, also, it indicates his immutable, stable, never failing, and at once collected communication of good to the whole world. But since the recipients of the impartible gift of the God are variously affected towards it, and receive multiform powers from the sun, according to their peculiar motions, hence the symbolical doctrine evinces through the multitude of the gifts, that the God is one, and exhibits his one power through multiform powers. Hence, likewise, it says that he is one and the same, but that the vicissitudes of his form, and his configurations, must be admitted to exist in the recipients. On this account it asserts "that he is changed every hour, according to the signs of the zodiac," in consequence of these being variously changed about the God, according to the many modes by which they receive him. The Egyptians use prayers to the sun, conformable to these assertions, not only in visions which are seen by the bodily eyes, but also in their more common supplications, all which have such a meaning as this, and are offered to the God conformably to a symbolic and mystic doctrine of this kind. Hence it would not be reasonable in any one to undertake a defense of them.

IV. But the inquiries which follow in the next place, require a more abundant doctrine, in order to their elucidation. At the same time, however, it is necessary to discuss the truth concerning them with brevity. For you inquire *"what efficacy there is in names that are not significant."* They are not, however, as you think, without signification; but let them be indeed unknown to us (though some of them are known to us, the explications of which we receive from the Gods), yet to the Gods all of them are significant, though not according to an effable mode; nor in such a way as that which is significant and indicative with men through imaginations; but either intellectually, conformably to the divine intellect which is in us; or ineffably, and in a way more excellent and simple, and conformably to the intellect which is united to the Gods. It is requisite, therefore, to take away all conceptions derived by an abstraction from sensibles, and all logical evolutions from divine names; and likewise the connascent physical similitudes of language to things which exist in nature. But the intellectual and divine symbolical character of divine similitude must be admitted to have a subsistence in names. And, moreover, though it should be unknown to us, yet this very circumstance is that which is most venerable in it, for it is too excellent to be divided into knowledge. But in those names which we can scientifically analyze, we possess a knowledge of the whole divine essence, power, and order, comprehended in the name. And farther still, we preserve in the soul collectively the mystic and arcane image of the Gods, and through this we elevate the soul to the Gods, and when elevated conjoin it as much as possible with them. But you ask, *"Why, of significant names, we prefer such as are Barbaric to our own?"* Of this, also, there is a mystic reason. For because the Gods have shown that the whole dialect of sacred nations, such as those of the Egyptians and Assyrians, is adapted to sacred concerns; on this account we ought to think it necessary that our conference with the Gods should be in a language allied to them. Because, likewise, such a mode of speech is the first and most ancient. And especially because those who first learned the names of the Gods, having mingled them with their own proper tongue, delivered them to us, that we might always preserve immoveable the sacred law of tradition, in a language peculiar and adapted to them. For if any other thing pertains to the Gods, it is evident that the eternal and immutable must be allied to them.

V. You object, however, *"that he who hears words looks to their signification, so that it is sufficient the conception remains the same, whatever the words may be that are used."* But the thing is not such as you suspect it to be. For if names subsisted through compact it would be of no consequence whether some were used instead of others. But if they are suspended from the nature of things, those names which are more adapted to it will also be more dear to the Gods. From this, therefore, it is evident that the language of sacred nations is very reasonably preferred to that of other men. To which may be added, that names do not entirely preserve the same meaning when translated into another language; but there are certain idioms in each nation which cannot be signified by language to another nation. And, in the next place, though it should be possible to translate them, yet they no longer preserve the same power when translated. Barbarous names, likewise, have much emphasis, great conciseness, and participate of less ambiguity, variety, and multitude. Hence, on all these accounts, they are adapted to more excellent natures. Take away, therefore, entirely those suspicions of yours which fall off from the truth, viz. *"if he who is invoked is either an Egyptian or uses the Egyptian language."* But rather think that as the Egyptians were the first of men who were allotted the participation of the Gods, the Gods when invoked rejoice in the Egyptian rites. Again, however, if all these were the fraudulent devices of enchanters, how is it possible that things which are in the most eminent degree united to the Gods, which also conjoin us with them, and have powers all but equal to those of superior beings, should be phantastic devices, though without them no sacred operation can be effected? But neither *"do these veils [by which arcana are concealed] originate from our passions, which rumor ascribes to a divine nature."* For beginning, not from our passions, but, on the contrary, from things allied to the Gods, we make use of words adapted to them. *"Nor do we frame conceptions of a divine nature, contrary to its real mode of subsistence."* But conformably to the nature which it possesses, and to the truth concerning it, which those obtained who first established the laws of sacred religion, we persevere in our conceptions of divinity. *For if any thing else in religious legal institutions is adapted to the Gods, this must certainly be immutability. And it is necessary that ancient prayers, like sacred asylums, should be preserved invariably the same, neither taking any thing from them, nor adding any thing to them which is elsewhere derived.* For this is nearly the cause at present that both names and prayers have lost their efficacy, because they are continually changed through the innovation and illegality of the Greeks. For the Greeks are naturally studious of novelty, and are carried about every where by their volatility; neither possessing any stability themselves, nor preserving what they have received from others; but rapidly relinquishing this, they transform every thing through an unstable desire of discovering something new. But the Barbarians are stable in their manners, and firmly continue to employ the same words. Hence they are dear to the Gods, and proffer words which are grateful to them; but which it is not lawful for any man by any means to change. And thus much we have said in answer to you concerning names, which though they are inexplicable, and are called Barbaric, yet are adapted to sacred concerns.

VIII

I. Leaving, therefore, these particulars, you wish in the next place that I would unfold to you *"What the Egyptians conceive the first cause to be; whether intellect, or above intellect; whether alone, or subsisting with some other or others; whether incorporeal, or corporeal; and whether it is the same with the Demiurgus, or is prior to the Demiurgus? Likewise, whether all things are from one principle, or from many principles; whether they have a knowledge of matter, or of primary corporeal qualities; and whether they admit matter to be unbegotten, or to be generated?"* I, therefore, will in the first place relate to you the cause why in the books of the ancient writers of sacred concerns many and various opinions concerning these things are circulated, and also why among those that are still living, and are renowned for their wisdom, the opinion on this subject is not simple and one. I say then, that as there are many essences, and these differing from each other, the all-various multitude of the principles of these, and which have different orders, were delivered by different ancient priests. As Seleucus[41] narrates, therefore, Hermes described the principles that rank as wholes in two myriads[42] of books; or, as we are informed by Manetho,[43] he perfectly unfolded these principles in three myriads six thousand five hundred and twenty five volumes. But different

41. Seleucus the Theologian, perhaps a contemporary of Manetho, is mentioned by Porphyry in the *De Abstinentia* II.55.1–2.

42. The "innumerable writings" of Hermes refer to the Thoth literature used by the Egyptian priests. Their number is 20,000 according to Seleucus and 36,525 according to Manetho. See G. Fowden, *The Egyptian Hermes: A Historical Approach to the Late Pagan Mind* (Princeton: Princeton University Press, 1993), p.136.10.

43. Manetho (Manethon, Manethoth) was a chief priest of the Ra temple at Heliopolis and a practical authority in the cult of Sarapis. Manetho's writings on

ancient writers differently explained the partial principles of essences. It is necessary, however, by investigation to discover the truth about all these principles, and concisely to unfold it to you as much as possible. And, in the first place, hear concerning that which is the first subject of your inquiry.

II. Prior to truly existing beings and total principles [or principles that rank as wholes], there is one God, prior to [that deity who is generally believed to be] the first God and king, immoveable, and abiding in the solitude of his own unity. For neither is the intelligible connected with him, nor any thing else; but he is established as the paradigm of the God who is the father of himself, is self begotten, is father alone, and is truly good. For he is something even greater and prior to this, is the fountain of all things, and the root of the first intelligible forms. But from this one deity, the God who is sufficient to himself, unfolds himself into light. For this divinity, also, is the principle and God of Gods, a monad from *The One,* prior to essence, and the principle of essence. For from him entity and essence are derived; and hence, also, he is denominated the principle of intelligibles. These, therefore, are the most ancient principles of all things, which Hermes arranges prior to the ethereal, empyrean, and celestial Gods. He likewise delivered to us the history of the empyrean Gods in one hundred books; of the ethereal in an equal number; and of the celestial in a thousand books.

III. According to another order, however, he arranges the God *Emeph*[44] prior to, and as the leader of, the celestial Gods. And he says that this God is an intellect, itself intellectually perceiving itself, and converting intellections to itself. But prior to this, he arranges the impartible one, which he says is the first paradigm, and which he denominates *Eikton.* In this, also, is contained that which is first intel-

---

Egyptian subjects in Greek (extant only in quotations) include the *History of Egypt, Against Herodotus, Sacred Book, Book of Sothis, On Antiquity and Religion,* and others. His activities were connected with the reigns of Ptolemy I Soter (323–283 B.C.E.) and Ptolemy II Philadelphos (285–246 B.C.E.).

44. Iamblichus' begins his account of Egyptian theology by establishing the supreme triad: the One; the Monad that proceeds from the One; and Essence, or the First Intelligible, deriving from the Monad. The indivisible One, who was worshiped only in silence, was called *Eikton.* After him came *Kheph* (MSS: *Emeph*), and the demiurgic *Nous,* master of truth and wisdom. Since Thomas Taylor anachronistically changed some of the names of the Greek gods into their Latin equivalents, we have restored the Greek originals used by Iamblichus, e.g. "Hephaestus" instead of Taylor's "Vulcan."

lective, and the first intelligible, and which is to be worshiped through silence alone. Besides these, also, other leaders preside over the fabrication of visible natures. For the demiurgic intellect, who is the curator of truth and wisdom, descending into generation, and leading the power of occult reasons into light, is called in the Egyptian tongue Amon; but in consequence of perfecting all things with veracity and artificially, he is called Ptah. The Greeks, however, assume Ptah for Hephaestus, solely directing their attention to the artificial peculiarity of the God. So far, also, as he is effective of good he is called Osiris; and he has other appellations through other powers and energies. With the Egyptians, therefore, there is another domination of the whole elements in generation, and of the powers contained in them; four of these powers being male and four female, which they attribute to the sun. And there is, likewise, another government of the whole of nature about generation, which they assign to the moon. But dividing the heavens into two, or four, or twelve, or six-and-thirty parts, or the doubles of these, they give to the parts a greater or less number of rulers. And over all these they place one ruler, who transcends all the rest. Thus, therefore, the doctrine of the Egyptians concerning principles, proceeding from on high as far as to the last of things, begins from one principle, and descends to a multitude which is governed by this one; and every where an indefinite nature is under the dominion of a certain definite measure, and of the supreme unical cause of all things. But God produced matter by dividing materiality from essentiality; and this being vital, the Demiurgus receiving, fabricated from it the simple and impassive spheres. But he distributed in an orderly manner the last of it into generable and corruptible bodies.

IV. These things, therefore, having been accurately discussed, the solution of the doubts which you have met with in certain books will be manifest. *For the books which are circulated under the name of Hermes contain Hermaic opinions, though they frequently employ the language of the philosophers: for they were translated from the Egyptian tongue by men who were not unskilled in philosophy.*[45] But Chaeremon,[46] and any others who have at all discussed the first causes of mundane

45. See Erik Iversen, *Egyptian and Hermetic Doctrine* (Copenhagen: Museum Tusculanum Press, 1984).

46. In the ancient sources, Chaeremon was called *philosophos* and *hierogrammateus* ("sacred scribe"). *Hierogrammateis* belonged to the class of the ancient Egyptian

natures, have unfolded the last rulers of these. And such as have written concerning the planets, the zodiac, the decans, horoscopes, and what are called powerful and leading planets, these have unfolded the partible distributions of the rulers. The particulars, also, contained in the Calendars comprehend a certain very small part of the Hermaic arrangements. And the causes of such things as pertain to the phases or occulations of the stars, or to the increments and decrements of the moon, are assigned by the Egyptians the last of all. The Egyptians, likewise, do not say that all things are physical. For they separate the life of the soul and the intellectual life from nature, not only in the universe, but also in us. And admitting intellect and reason to subsist by themselves, they say that generated essences were thus fabricated. They likewise arrange the Demiurgus as the primary father of things in generation; and they acknowledge the existence of a vital power, prior to the heavens, and subsisting in the heavens. They also establish a pure intellect above the world, and one impartible intellect in the whole world, and another which is distributed into all the spheres. And these things they do not survey by mere reason alone, but through the sacerdotal theurgy, they announce that they are able to ascend to more elevated and universal essences, and to those that are established above Fate, viz. to God and the Demiurgus; neither employing matter, nor assuming any other thing besides, except the observation of a suitable time.

V. This deific and anagogic path Hermes, indeed, narrated, but Bitys,[47] the prophet of King Ammon, explained it, having found it in the adyta of Sais in Egypt, written in hieroglyphics; and the same

priests whose many functions included the finding of sacred animals, the testing of candidates for priesthood, the interpretation of dreams and omens, and the cultivation of the ancient science of magic. According to Porphyry, Origen "also made use of the books of Chaeremon the Stoic and of Cornutus; from these he learned the allegorical method of interpreting the mysteries of the Greeks, and he applied it to the Jewish scriptures" (*Contra Christianos* fr.39). The Byzantine author Tzetzes says: "For since the most ancient of the sacred scribes wanted to conceal the theory about the nature of the gods, they handed these things down to their own children by way of such allegorical symbols and characters as the sacred scribe Chaeremon says" (*Exegesis in Iliadem* I.97).

47. According to Iamblichus, the prophet Bitys translated to King Ammon the teachings of Hermes (Thoth), inscribed in hieroglyphic characters in a sanctuary at Sais. One class of Egyptian priests, hmw-ntr ("servants of god") were termed *prophetai* by Greek authors, though they were not prophets or officials of oracles, as

prophet also delivered the name of God, which pervades through the whole world.

But there are, likewise, many other co-arrangements of the same things; so that you do not appear to me to act rightly in referring all things with the Egyptians to physical causes. For there are, according to them, many principles and many essences; and also supermundane powers, which they worship through sacerdotal sanctimony. To me, therefore, these things appear to afford common auxiliaries to the solution of all the remaining inquiries. But since it is necessary not to leave any one of them uninvestigated, we shall add them to these problems, and examine them on all sides, in order that we may see where there is any thing futile in your opinions.

VI. You say, therefore, *"that according to many of the Egyptians, that which is in our power depends on the motion of the stars."* What the truth, however, is respecting this, it is necessary to unfold to you from the Hermaic conceptions. For man, as these writings say, has two souls. And one, indeed, is derived from the first intelligible, and participates of the power of the Demiurgus; but the other is imparted from the circulation of the celestial bodies, to which the soul that sees God returns. These things, therefore, thus subsisting, the soul that descends to us from the worlds follows the periods of the worlds; but that which is intelligibly present from the intelligible, transcends the genesiurgic motion, and through this a liberation from fate, and the ascent to the intelligible Gods, are effected. Such theurgy, likewise, as leads to an unbegotten nature is perfected conformably to a life of this kind.

VII. Hence that of which you are dubious is not true, *"that all things are bound with the indissoluble bonds of Necessity,"* which we call Fate. For the soul has a proper principle of circumduction to the intelligible, and of a separation from generated natures; and also of a contact with real being, and that which is divine. *"Nor must we ascribe fate to the Gods, whom we worship in temples and statues, as the dissolvers of fate."* For the Gods, indeed, dissolve fate; but the last

the Greek term suggests. Bitys was regarded as a theurgical authority as is attested by the alchemist Zosimus of Panopolis, who speaks of "the tablet that Bitys (MSS: Bitos) wrote, and Plato the thrice-great (*trismegas*) and Hermes the infinitely great" (On apparatus and furnaces, fr.gr.230–235). King Ammon was the ninth pharaoh in the XXVI dynasty of the Saitan pharaohs.

natures which proceed from them, and are complicated with the generation of the world and with body, give completion to fate. Hence we very properly worship the Gods with all possible sanctity, and the observance of all religious rites, in order that they may liberate us from the evils impending from fate, as they alone rule over necessity through intellectual persuasion. But neither are all things comprehended in the nature of fate, but there is another principle of the soul, which is superior to all nature and generation, and through which we are capable of being united to the Gods, of transcending the mundane order, and of participating in eternal life, and the energy of the supercelestial Gods. Through this principle, therefore, we are able to liberate ourselves from fate. For when the more excellent parts of us energize, and the soul is elevated to natures better than itself, then it is entirely separated from things which detain it in generation, departs from subordinate natures, exchanges the present for another life, and gives itself to another order of things, entirely abandoning the former order with which it was connected.

VIII. What then, is it not possible for a man to liberate himself [from fate] through the Gods that revolve in the heavens, and to consider the same as the leaders of fate, and yet as those that bind our lives with indissoluble bonds? Perhaps nothing prevents this from being the case. For if the Gods comprehend in themselves many essences and powers, there are also in them other immense differences and contrarieties. Moreover, this also may be said, that in each of the Gods, though such as are visible, there are certain intelligible principles through which a liberation to souls from mundane generation is effected. But if some one leaves only two genera of Gods, viz. the mundane and supermundane, the liberation to souls will be effected through the supermundane Gods. These things, therefore, are more accurately discussed in our treatise *Concerning the Gods*, in which it is shown who are the anagogic Gods, and according to what kind of powers they are so; how they liberate from fate, and through what sacred regressions; and what the order is of mundane nature, and how the most perfect intellectual energy rules over this. So that what you add from Homer, "that the Gods are flexible," it is not holy to assert. For the works of the sacred ceremonies of religion have long since been defined by pure and intellectual laws. Subordinate natures, also, are liberated through a greater order and power; and when we abandon inferior natures, we are transferred into a more excellent allotment. This, however, is not effected contrary to any original sacred law, so as to cause the Gods to be changed, through a sacred operation being afterwards performed; but from the first divinity sent souls hither, in order that they might again return to him. Neither, therefore, is any mutation produced through a re-ascent of this kind, nor do the descents and ascents of souls oppose each other. For as generation and this universe are suspended from an intellectual essence; thus, also, in the orderly distribution of souls, the liberation from generation accords with the care employed by them about generation.

6. Hierocles
Commentary on the Golden Verses

Little is known of the life of Hierocles: he and Syrianus were disciples of Plutarch of Athens and adapted the Iamblichean philosophy developed— or simply transmitted—by Aidesius, Priscus and Plutarch of Athens (who is not to be confused with Plutarch of Chaeroneia, a Middle Platonist). Hierocles taught Platonic philosophy in Alexandria, and like Syrianus (who later became a master of Proclus), he argued for a harmony between Plato, Orpheus, Homer and the *Chaldean Oracles*. Following Iamblichus, he interpreted true philosophy as a revelation and a soteriological mission undertaken by superior souls; he also regarded Platonism as a branch of Pythagoreanism, which embraced the basic truths of all philosophy. He claimed that the *Golden Verses* of Pythagoras contained the general principles of philosophy and could thus serve as a starting-point for beginners, providing an elementary initiation into Pythagorean philosophy aimed towards assimilation to God. The *Golden Verses* were thus viewed as an "educational introduction" (*paideutike stoicheiosis*) left by the spiritual master (Pythagoras), who had already ascended on the divine way. The best recent study on Hierocles is in French: Ilsetraut Hadot, *Le probleme du neoplatonisme Alexandrin: Hierocles et Simplicius* (Paris: Études Augustiniennes, 1978).

The excerpts from Hierocles' *Commentary* here reproduced were translated by N. Rowe from the French version of André Dacier, published in 1907.

In Aureum Pythagoreorum carmen commentarius. Introduction

Philosophy is the purification and perfection of human nature: its purification, because it delivers it from the temerity and folly that proceed from matter and because it disengages its affections from the mortal body; and its perfection, because it makes it recover its original felicity by restoring it to the likeness of God.

Now virtue and truth alone can operate these two things: virtue, by driving away the excess of the passions, and truth, by dispelling the darkness of error and by returning the divine form to such as are disposed to receive it.

For this science, therefore, which ought to render us pure and perfect, it is good to have short and certain rules as so many aphorisms of the art, that by their means we may arrive methodically and in due order at happiness, which is our only end.

Amongst all the rules that contain a summary of Philosophy, the Verses of Pythagoras, called the *Golden Verses,* justly hold the first rank, for they contain the general precepts of all Philosophy regarding the *active* as well as the *contemplative* life. By their means everyone may acquire truth and virtue, render himself pure, and happily attain to the Divine Resemblance. As is said in the *Timaeus* of Plato (whom we ought to regard as a very exact master of the doctrine of Pythagoras), after having regained his health and recovered his integrity and his perfection, he may see himself again in his primitive state of innocence and of light.

Pythagoras begins by the precepts of *active* virtue. Before all things, we ought to dissipate and drive away the folly and the laziness that are in us and then apply ourselves to the knowledge of divine things. As an eye that is diseased and not yet healed cannot behold a dazzling and resplendent light, in like manner a soul that is still destitute of virtue cannot fix its view on the beauty and the splendor of truth. Nor is it lawful for impurity to touch the things that are pure.

Practical Philosophy is the mother of virtue, and contemplative virtue is the mother of truth, as we are taught by these very Verses of Pythagoras, where Practical Philosophy is called *Human Virtue* and where the Contemplative is celebrated under the name of *Divine Virtue.* After having finished the precepts of civil virtue by these words: *Practice thoroughly all these things; meditate on them well; thou oughtest to love them with all thy heart*, he continues, *it is they that will put thee in the way of Divine Virtue.*

We must, therefore, first be men and afterwards become God. The Civil Virtues make the man and the sciences lead to Divine Virtue which makes the God. Now according to the rules of the Order, little things must precede the greater if we would make any progress, and this is the reason why in these Verses of Pythagoras the precepts of virtue are the first to teach us that the practice of virtues, which is so necessary in this life, is the way whereby we ought to advance and rise even to the Divine Image. And the order and design proposed in these Verses is to give to those that read them the true character of Philosophy before they are initiated in the other sciences.

They are called *Golden Verses* to signify to us that they are the most excellent and most divine of any of this kind. In like manner we call the *Golden Age* the age that produced the greatest men, and describe the difference of the manners of the several ages by the analogical qualities of metals. Gold being the purest of all metals and free from all the dross found in the other metals that are inferior to it—as silver, iron and brass—is therefore the most excellent, being the only metal that never breeds any rust, whereas the others grow rusty in proportion to the quantity of dross they have mixed in them. Rust, therefore, being the figure and emblem of vice, it was but reasonable that the age in which sanctity and purity reigned and which was exempt from all corruption of manners should be called the *Age of Gold.* Thus these Verses, being every way sovereignly good, have justly deserved the appellation of *Verses Golden and Divine.* We find not in them, as in all other poems, one good verse and another that is not so, but they are all perfectly good, they all equally represent purity of manners, lead to the likeness with God, and discover the most perfect aim of the Pythagorean Philosophy, as will evidently appear by the explanation we are going to give of each Verse in particular....

The excerpt from the commentary on verse 1

In the first place revere the Immortal Gods, as they are established and ordained by the Law.

Since the piety that relates to the Divine Cause is the chief and the guide of all the virtues, the precept concerning that piety is with good reason placed at the head of all the laws prescribed by these Verses. We ought to honor the Gods of this Universe according to the Order in which they are established, and which the Eternal Law that produced them distributed them with their Essences, placing some of them in the first sphere of Heaven, others in the second, others in the third and so on, till all the celestial globes were filled up. To acknowledge and honor them according to the order and station in which they were placed by their Creator and Father is to obey the Divine Law and to render them truly all honor due to them. Nor ought we to extol their dignity above measure any more than to entertain diminishing thoughts about them, but we should take them for what they are, give them the rank they have received, and refer all the honor we render them to God alone who created them and who may properly be called the God of Gods, the most high and most good God. The only way we have to discover and comprehend the majesty of this excellent Being who created the world is to be fully convinced that He is the Cause of the Gods and the Creator of the Rational and Immutable Substances. These are the Substances, these the Gods we here call *Immortal Gods*. They have always the same opinion and the same thoughts of God who created them because they are always intent upon this Supreme God and united with Him. They have received from Him immutably and indivisibly the being and the well-being too, inasmuch as they are the unchangeable and incorruptible Images of the Cause that created them. For it is worthy of God to have produced such Images of Himself as were not capable of change nor of corrupting themselves by their inclinations to ill as are the souls of men, who are the last of all Intelligent Substances, whilst those that are called *Immortal Gods* are the first.

And it is to distinguish them from the souls of men that we here call them *Immortal Gods*, because they never die and never forget, one single moment, either their own Essence or the goodness of the Father who created them. Consider the passions and alterations to which the soul of man is subject: sometimes it remembers its God and the dignity in which it was created, and sometimes it entirely forgets both the one and the other. For this reason the souls of men may justly be called *Mortal Gods*, as dying sometimes to the Divine

Life by their going astray from God and sometimes recovering it again by their return to Him, living thus in this last sense a life divine and in the other dying as much as it is possible for an immortal Essence to participate in death—not by ceasing to be, but by being deprived of well-being. For the death of a Reasonable Essence is ignorance and impiety, which drag after them disorders and revolt of the passions, and the ignorance of good necessarily plunges us into the slavery of ill—a slavery whence it is impossible to be redeemed except by returning to knowledge and to God, which is done by recollection and the faculty of reminiscence.

Now between these *Immortal* and *Mortal Gods*, as I have called them, it is necessary that there should be an Essence superior to man and inferior to God, to be, as it were, a medium and a link to chain the two extremes to one another, to the end that the whole Intelligent Essence might be bound and united together.

This middle Essence, *the Angels*, is never altogether ignorant of God, yet has not always an equally immutable and permanent knowledge of Him, but sometimes a greater, sometimes a less. By this state of knowledge which never absolutely ceases, it is superior to the nature of man, and by this state of knowledge which is not always the same but lessens or increases, it is inferior to the nature of God. It has not raised itself up above the condition of man by its proficiency and improvement in knowledge, and it is not become inferior to the *Gods*. Nor has it been placed in this middle rank by reason of the diminution of the same knowledge, but it is by its nature a mean, a middle Being. For God who created all things established these three Beings, first, second and third, different from one another by their nature; nor can they ever displace themselves nor confound themselves one with another either by vice or by virtue. But being eternal by their nature, they differ according to the rank that has been given them. They were placed in this order because of the causes that produced them. It is Order that contains the three degrees of perfect wisdom, the first, the second and the third. Wisdom is wisdom only because it produces its works in order and perfection, inasmuch as wisdom, order and perfection are always found together and never separate from one another. In like manner, in this Universe the Beings produced by the first thought of God ought to be the first in the world, those that are produced by the second, the second or middle, and those that resemble the end of the thoughts, the last of all rational Beings. This whole reasonable Order with an incorruptible body is the entire and perfect image of God who created it. The Beings that hold the first rank in this world are the pure image of what is most excellent in God; those that hold the middle rank are the middle image of what is middling in God; and those that hold the third, the last rank among the rational Beings, are the last image of what is last in the Divinity. The first of these Orders is here called the *Immortal Gods*, the second *Heroes who are full of goodness and light*, and the third *Terrestrial Daemons*, as we shall see hereafter.

Let us now return to what we were saying. What is the Law? What is the Order that is conformable to it? And lastly, what is the honor rendered in regard to this Order and to this Law? The Law is the Intelligence that has created all things; it is the Divine Intelligence by which all has been produced from all eternity and which likewise preserves it eternally.

The Order conformable to this Law is the rank which God, the Father and Creator of all things, gave the *Immortal Gods* when He created them, and that appoints some of them to be first and others second. For though they are the first in all this Intelligent Order and have received whatever is most excellent, they are different, nevertheless, amongst themselves—some are more, some less, divine than the others. A mark of their superiority or inferiority with regard to the others is the rank and order of the Celestial Spheres, which were distributed amongst them according to their Essence, power and virtue, inasmuch as the Law relates only to their Essence and the Order is only the rank that was given to them suitable to their dignity. For neither were they created fortuitously nor separated and placed by chance, but they were created and placed with order, as different parts and different members of one single *Whole*, which is Heaven.

The excerpt from the commentary on verses 27, 28, and 29

... Repentance is the beginning of Philosophy, the avoiding of all foolish words and actions, and the first step of a life that will no more be subject to repentance. He who prudently deliberates before he acts never falls into involuntary and unforeseen troubles and misfortunes nor ever commits unwittingly any actions whose consequences he can foresee. But he prepares himself to accept whatever can happen contrary to his expectation.

Therefore, neither the hope of what we call goods makes him renounce his real good, nor does the fear of evils incline him to commit real ills. But having his mind continually bent on the rules that God has prescribed, he squares his whole life according to them.

That thou may'st know most assuredly that it is the part of a miserable person indeed to speak and to act without Reason, behold Medea deploring her miseries in our theaters. The fury of a senseless amour spurred her on to betray her parents and to run away with a foreigner. At length, finding herself condemned and forsaken by him, she thought her misfortunes insupportable, and in thought breaks out into imprecation, "Let Heaven's dire thunder on my head be hurled!" after which she falls to committing the most heinous of crimes.

In the first place it is unreasonable and foolish for her to pray that what is done might be undone; and then, like a senseless distracted person indeed, she thinks to heal her ills by other ills, hoping to efface the beginning of her miseries by a yet more miserable end. For she madly endeavors, by the murder of her children, to atone for her marriage, to which she had consented rashly and without reflection.

If you have a mind to see how Homer's Agamemnon behaves, you will find that prince, when he is punished for not having bridled his rage, crying out with tears in his eyes, "I'm lost! undone! and all my strength forsakes me!" And in the ill state of his affairs he quenches with a flood of tears that fire of his eyes which rage had kindled in his prosperity.

This is the life of every foolish and inconsiderate man. He is driven and tossed to and fro by contrary passions, unendurable in prosperity, dejected in adversity, imperious and haughty when he hopes, cowardly and crouching when he fears. Not having the constancy that prudent deliberation inspires, he veers about with every blast of Fortune.

Let us then take sound Reason for our guide in all our actions, imitating Socrates, who says: "You know that I have now accustomed myself not to obey any of mine except that Reason which after due examination appears to be most just and upright." By this expression "any of mine," he means all his senses. And indeed, all the things that are given us to be subservient to Reason—as anger, love, sense, and even the body itself, which is to serve as an instrument to all these faculties—are *ours*, but not its, and we ought to obey none of them except, as Socrates says, sound Reason alone—that is to say, the Rational part of our nature. It is that alone that can see and know what ought to be done and said.

Now to obey sound Reason and to obey God are the same thing, since our Intelligent part is enlightened by the irradiation that is natural and proper to it and wills nothing but what the Law of God requires. A soul well disposed according to God is always of the same mind with God, and whatever it does, it keeps the divinity and splendid brightness that surround it always in sight; whereas the soul disposed in a contrary manner, intent on what is out of God and full of darkness, is carried here and there and wanders without keeping any certain road, being destitute of understanding and fallen from God.

The excerpt from the commentary on verses 67, 68, and 69

… Now by mystical operation I mean the purgative faculty of the luminous body, to the end that of all Philosophy the theory may precede as the Mind, and the practical follow as the Act or Faculty. Now the practical is of two sorts, political or civil and mystical. The first purges us of folly by the means of virtue, and the second cuts off all earthly thoughts by means of the sacred ceremonies.

The public laws are a good pattern of civil Philosophy and the sacrifices offered by cities of the mystical. Now the sublimest pitch of all Philosophy is the contemplative mind; the political mind holds the middle place; and in the last is the mystical. The first, in regard to the two others, holds the place of the eye; and the two last, in regard to the first, hold the place of the hand and of the foot. But they are all three so well linked together that either of the three is imperfect and almost useless without the cooperation of the other two. Therefore we ought always to join together the knowledge that has found out the truth, the faculty that produces virtue, and that which brings forth purity, to the end that the civil actions may be rendered conformable to the mind that presides, and that the holy actions may be answerable to the one and to the other.

Thus you see the end of the Pythagorean Philosophy is that we may become all over wings to soar aloft to the Divine Good, to the end that at the hour of death, leaving upon earth this mortal body and divesting us of its corruptible nature, we may be ready for the celestial voyage, like champions in the sacred combats of Philosophy. For then we shall return to our ancient country and be deified as far as it is possible for men to become *Gods*. And this we are promised in the two following Verses.

The commentary on verses 70 and 71

> And when, after having divested thyself of thy mortal body, thou arrivest in the most pure Ether, thou shalt be a God, immortal, incorruptible, and death shall have no more dominion over thee.

Behold the most glorious end of all our labors! Behold, as Plato says, the glorious combat and the great hope that is proposed to us! Behold the most perfect fruit of Philosophy! This is the greatest work, the most excellent achievement of the Art of Love, that mysterious Art which raises all souls to Divine Goods and establishes them therein and delivers them from afflictions here below, as from the obscure dungeon of mortal life. It exalts to the Celestial Splendors and places in the Islands of the Blest all who have walked in the ways which the foregoing rules have taught them. For them and them alone is reserved the inestimable reward of deification, it not being permitted for any to be adopted into the rank of the *Gods*, but for him alone who has acquired for his soul virtue and truth, and for his spiritual chariot, purity.

Such a man, having thereby become sound and whole, is restored to his primordial state after he has recovered himself by his union with sound Reason, after he has discovered the All-Divine Ornament of this Universe and thus found out the Author and Creator of all things, as much as it is possible for us to find Him. Having arrived after purification to that sublime degree of bliss which the Beings whose nature is incapable of descending into generation always enjoy, he unites himself by his knowledge to this *Whole*, and raises himself up even to God Himself.

But since he has a body that was created with him, he stands in need of a place wherein he may be seated, as it were, in the rank of the stars. And the most suitable place for a body of such a nature is immediately beneath the moon, as being above all terrestrial and corruptible bodies, and beneath all the Celestial. And this place the

Pythagoreans call the *pure Ether—Ether* because it is immaterial and eternal, and *pure* because it is exempt from earthly passions.

What shall he be, then, who is arrived there? He shall be what these Verses promise him, an *Immortal God*. He shall be rendered like the *Immortal Gods* of whom we have spoken in the beginning of this treatise, an *Immortal God*, I say, but not by nature. For how can it be that he who since a certain time only has made any progress in virtue, and whose deification has had a beginning, should become equal to the *Gods* who have been *Gods* from all eternity? This is impossible. Therefore, to make this exception and to mark this difference, the Poet, after he had said *Thou shalt be a God*, adds, *immortal, incorruptible, and death shall have no more dominion over thee*, thereby intimating that it is a deification which proceeds only from our being divested of what is mortal and is not a privilege annexed to our nature and to our Essence, but to which we arrive little by little and by degrees. So this class of Beings makes a third sort of *Gods* who are immortal when they are ascended into Heaven but mortal when they descend upon Earth, and in this way always inferior to the *Heroes who are full of goodness and light*. These last remember God always, but the third sometimes forget Him. For it is not possible that the third kind, though rendered perfect, should ever be superior to the second or equal to the first. But continuing always as the third, they become like the first though they are subordinate to the second, for the resemblance to the *Celestial Gods* is more perfect and more natural in the Beings of the second rank, that is to say, in the *Heroes*.

Thus there is but one and the same perfection common to all Intelligent Beings, which is their resemblance to God who created them. But see what makes the difference: this perfection is always, and always the same, in the Celestial; always too, but not always the same, in the Ethereal (*Heroes*) who are fixed and permanent in their state and condition; and neither always, nor always the same, in the Ethereal (souls of men) who are subject to descend and to come and inhabit the earth.

If any man should assert that the first and most perfect likeness of God is *the copy and the original of the two others*, or that the second is of the third, his assertion would be very just. Our aim is not only to resemble God, but to resemble Him by approaching the nearest we can to this all-perfect Original, or to arrive at the second resemblance. But if, not being able to attain to this most perfect resemblance, we acquire that of which we are capable, we have, as well as the most perfect Beings, all that our nature requires. And we enjoy the perfect fruits of virtue even in this, that we know the measure and extent of our Essence and that we are not dissatisfied with it.

For the perfection of virtue is to keep ourselves within the limits of the Creation, by which all things are distinguished according to their kind, and to submit ourselves to the Laws of Providence that have distributed to each individual the good that is proper for it in regard to its faculties and its virtues.

This is the commentary we have thought fit to make on these *Golden Verses* and that may be called a summary, neither too prolix nor too succinct, of the doctrine of Pythagoras. It was not fitting either that our explanation should imitate the brevity of the text, for then we should have left many things obscure and should not have been able to discover and show the reasons and the beauties of all the precepts, or that it should contain all his Philosophy, for that would have been too large and too tedious a work for a commentary. But we thought it proper to proportion this work, as much as we could, to the sense of these Verses, reciting no more of the general precepts of Pythagoras than what was consonant and might serve to the explanation of these *Golden Verses*, which are properly only a most perfect representation of his Philosophy, an abridgement of his principal tenets and elements of perfection, which they who have walked in the ways of God and whose virtues have raised up to Heaven have left to instruct their descendants. These elements may justly be called the greatest and most excellent mark of the nobility of man, and are not the private opinion of any particular person but the doctrine of the whole sacred body of the Pythagoreans and, as it were, the common voice of all their assemblies. For this reason there was a law which enjoined each of them, every morning when he rose, and every night at his going to bed, to have these Verses read to him as the Oracles of the Pythagorean doctrine, to the end that by continual meditation on these precepts their spirit and energy might shine forth in his life. And this is what we likewise ought to do, that we may make trial, and find what great advantages we should in time gain by so doing.

7. Hermeias
Commentary on Plato's Phaedrus

Hermeias was a Neoplatonist who taught philosophy in Alexandria. Along with Proclus, he was a disciple of Syrianus in Athens. Hermeias' *Commentary on the Phaedrus*, consists of notes based on Syrianus' lectures on Plato's *Phaedrus*. Some additional material is taken from Iamblichus' *Commentary on the Phaedrus*. In the commentary of Hermeias the Platonic theology of the *Phaedrus* is explained and supported by references to Pythagoras, Orpheus, Homer and the *Chaldean Oracles*. Hermeias emphasized the revelatory nature of philosophy and accepted the Platonic assertion that both philosophy and poetry are forms of divinely inspired madness.

The excerpt reproduced here from Hermeias' *Commentary* was translated by Thomas Taylor and included as an additional note in his translation of the *Theology of Plato* by Proclus; it was published in 1816 under the title *The Six Books of Proclus, the Successor: On the Theology of Plato*. As Taylor explains: "The following account of enthusiasm, and of the different kinds of mania mentioned by Plato in the *Phaedrus* (265b), from the Scholia of Hermeias on that dialogue, is extracted from the additional notes to my translation of Proclus on the *Timaeus*."

Since Plato here delivers four kinds of mania, by which I mean enthusiasm, and possession or inspiration from the Gods, viz. the musical, the telestic, the prophetic, and the amatory, previous to the discussion of each, we must first speak about enthusiasm, and show to what part of the soul the enthusiastic energy pertains; whether each part of it possesses this energy; if all enthusiasm is from the Gods; and in what part of the soul it is ingenerated; or whether it subsists in something else more excellent than soul. Where, then, does that which is properly and primarily called enthusiasm subsist, and what is it? Of the rational soul there are two parts, one of which is *dianoia*, but the other *opinion*. Again, however, of *dianoia*, one part is said to be the lowest, and is properly *dianoia*, but another part of it is the highest, which is said to be the intellect of it, according to which the soul especially becomes intellectual, and which some call intellect in capacity. There is also another thing above this, which is the summit of the whole soul, and most allied to *The One*, which likewise wishes well to all things, and always gives itself up to the Gods, and is readily disposed to do whatever they please. This, too, is said to be *the one* of the soul, bears the image of the superessential one, and unites the whole soul. But that these things necessarily thus subsist, we may learn as follows: The rational soul derives its existence from all the causes prior to itself, i.e. from intellect and the Gods. But it subsists also from itself: for it perfects itself. So far, therefore, as it subsists from the Gods, it possesses *the one*, which unites all its powers, and all the multitude of itself, and conjoins them to *The One Itself*, and is the first recipient of the goods imparted by the Gods. It likewise makes all the essence of the soul to be boniform (i.e., a "good-like form"), according to which it is connected with the Gods, and united to them. But so far as it subsists from intellect it possesses an intellectual nature, according to which it apprehends forms, by simple projections, or intuitions, and not discursively; and is conjoined to the intellect which is above itself. And so far as it constitutes itself, it possesses the dianoetic power, according to which it generates sciences and certain theorems, energizes discursively, and collects conclusions from propositions. For that it constitutes or gives subsistence to itself, is evident from its imparting perfection to itself; since that which leads itself to perfection, and imparts to itself well-being, will much more impart to itself existence. For well-being is a greater thing than being. If, therefore, the soul imparts that which is greater to itself, it will much more impart that which is less. Hence that which is primarily, properly, and truly enthusiasm from the Gods, is effected according to this one of the soul, which is above *dianoia*, and above the intellect of the soul; which one is at another time in a relaxed and dormant state. This one, likewise, becoming illuminated [by the Gods], all the life of the soul is illuminated, and also intellect, *dianoia*, and the irrational part, and the resemblance of enthusiasm is transmitted as far as to the body itself.

Other enthusiasms, therefore, are produced about other parts of the soul, certain daemons exciting them, or the Gods also, though not without the intervention of daemons. For *dianoia* is said to energize enthusiastically, when it discovers sciences and theorems in a very short space of time, and in a greater degree than other men. Opinion, likewise, and the fantasy, are said thus to energize when they discover arts, and accomplish admirable works, such, for instance, as Pheidias effected in the formation of statues, and another in another art, as also Homer says (*Odyssey* XI.612) of him who made the belt of Heracles, "that he neither did nor would artificially produce such another." Anger, likewise, is said to energize enthusiastically, when in battle it energizes supernaturally. "Like Ares, when brandishing his spear, he raged" (*Iliad* XV.605).

But if some one, yielding to desire, should eat of that which reason forbids, and through this should unexpectedly become well, you may say that desire also, in this instance, energized enthusiastically, though obscurely; so that enthusiasm is likewise produced about the other parts of the soul. Enthusiasm, however, properly so called, is when this one of the soul, which is above intellect, is excited to the Gods, and is from thence inspired. But at different times it is possessed about the aptitudes of itself, by different Gods; and is more or less possessed when intellect or *dianoia* is that which is moved. As, therefore, when we inquire what philosophy is, we do not always accurately define it, but frequently, from an improper use of the word, call mathematics or physics philosophy and science; we do the like also with respect to enthusiasm. For though it should be the fantasy which is excited, we are accustomed to call the excitation enthusiasm. Moreover, those who ascribe enthusiasm to the temperatures of bodies, or the excellent temperament of the air, or the ascendancy of exhalations, or the aptitudes of times and places, or the agency of the bodies that revolve in the heavens, speak rather of the cooperating and material causes of the thing than of the causes of it properly so called. You have, therefore, for the producing cause of enthusiasm, the Gods; for the material cause, the enthusiastically energizing soul itself, or the external symbols; for the formal cause, the inspiration of the Gods about *the one* of the soul; and for the final cause, good.

If, however, the Gods always wish the soul what is good, why does not the soul always energize enthusiastically? May we not say, that the Gods indeed always wish the soul what is good, but they are also willing that the order of the universe should prevail, and that the soul, through many causes, is not always adapted to enthusiasm, on which account it does not always enthusiastically energize? But some say that the telestic art extends as far as to the sublunary region. If, therefore, they mean that no one of the superlunary and celestial natures energizes in the sublunary region, they evidently assert what is absurd. But if they mean that the Telestae, or mystic operators, are not able to energize above the lunar sphere, we say, that if all the allotments of souls are sublunary, their assertion will be true; but if there are also allotments of souls above the moon, as there are (for some are the attendants of the sun, others of the moon, and others of Saturn, since the Demiurgus disseminated some of them into the earth, others into the moon, and others elsewhere), this being the case, it will be possible for the soul to energize above the moon. For what the whole order of things imparts to the soul for a very extended period of time, this the soul is also able to impart to itself for a short space of time, when assisted by the Gods through the telestic art. For the soul can never energize above its own allotment, but can energize to the extent of it. Thus, for instance, if the allotment of the soul was as far as to philosophy, the soul would be able, though it should not choose a philosophic but some other life, to energize in that life somewhat philosophically. There are also said to be certain supermundane souls. And thus we have shown how the soul energizes enthusiastically.

But how are statues said to have an enthusiastic energy? May we not say, that a statue being inanimate, does not itself energize about divinity, but the telestic art, purifying the matter of which the statue consists, and placing round it certain characters and symbols, in the first place renders it, through these means, animated, and causes it to receive a certain life from the world; and, in the next place, after this, it prepares the statue to be illuminated by a divine nature, through which it always delivers oracles, as long as it is properly adapted. For the statue, when it has been rendered perfect by the telestic art, remains afterwards [endued with a prophetic power] till it becomes entirely unadapted to divine illumination; but he who receives the inspiring influence of the Gods receives it only at certain times, and not always. But the cause of this is, that the soul, when filled with deity, energizes about it. Hence, in consequence of energizing above its own power, it becomes weary. For it would be a God, and similar to the souls of the stars, if it did not become weary. But the statue, conformably to its participations, remains illuminated. Hence the inaptitude of it entirely proceeds into privation, unless it is again, *de novo*, perfected and animated by the mystic operator. We have sufficiently shown, therefore, that enthusiasm, properly so called, is effected about *the one* of the soul, and that it is an illumination of divinity.

In the next place, let us discuss the order and the use of the four manias, and show why the philosopher makes mention of these alone. Is it because there are no other than these, or because these were sufficient for his purpose? That there are, therefore, many other divine inspirations and manias Plato himself indicates as he proceeds, and prior to this, he makes mention of the inspiration from the Nymphs. But there are also inspirations from Pan, from the mother of the Gods, and from the Corybantes, which are elsewhere mentioned by Plato. Here, however, he alone delivers these four manias; in the first place, because these alone are sufficient to the soul, in the attainment of its proper apocatastasis, as we shall afterwards show; and in the next place, because he delivers the proximate steps of ascent to the soul. For the gifts of the Gods to all beings are many and incomprehensible. But now he delivers to us the energies of the Gods which are extended to souls. He delivers, however, these four manias, not as if one of them was not sufficient, and especially the amatory, to lead back the soul to its pristine felicity; but at present the series and regular gradation of them, and the orderly perfection of the soul, are unfolded. As, therefore, it is possible for the tyrannic life, when suddenly changed, to become aristocratic, through employing strenuous promptitude and a divine allotment, but the gradual ascent is from a tyrannic to a democratic, and from this to an oligarchic life, afterwards to a timocratic, and at last to an aristocratic life, but the descent and lapse are vice versa; thus also here, the soul being about to ascend, and be restored to its former felicity, is in the first place possessed with the musical mania, afterwards with the telestic, then with the prophetic, and, in the last place, with the amatory mania. These inspirations, however, conspire with, and are in want of, each other; so abundant is their communion. For the telestic requires the prophetic mania; since the latter interprets many things pertaining to the former. And again, the prophetic requires the telestic mania. For the telestic mania perfects and establishes oracular predictions. Farther still, the prophetic uses the poetic and musical mania. For prophets, as I may say, always speak in verse. And again, the musical uses the prophetic mania spontaneously, as Plato says. But what occasion is there to speak about the amatory and musical manias? For nearly the same persons exercise both these, as, for instance, Sappho, Anacreon, and the like, in consequence of these not being able to subsist without each other. But it is very evident that the amatory mania contributes to all these, since it is subservient to enthusiasm of every kind: for no enthusiasm can be effected without amatory inspiration. And you may see how Orpheus appears to have applied himself to all these, as being in want of, and adhering to, each other. For we learn that he was most telestic, and most prophetic, and was excited by Apollo; and besides this, that he was most poetic, on which account he is said to have been the son of Calliope. He was likewise most amatory, as he himself acknowledges to Musaeus, extending to him divine goods, and rendering him perfect. Hence he appears to have been possessed with all the manias, and this by a necessary consequence. For there is an abundant union, conspiration, and alliance with each other, of the Gods who preside over these manias, viz. of the Muses, Bacchus, Apollo, and Love.

It remains, therefore, that we should unfold the nature of each of the manias, previously observing that those which are internal, and originate from the soul itself, and give perfection to it, are of one kind; but the external energies of them, and which preserve the outward man, and our nature, are of another. The four external, however, are analogous to the four internal manias. Let us consider, therefore, in the first place, the internal, and which alone originate from the soul itself, and let us see what they effect in the soul. In order, likewise, that this may become manifest, and also their arrangement, let us survey from on high, the descent, as Plato says, and defluxion of the wings of the soul. From the beginning, therefore, and at first, the soul was united to the Gods, and its unity to their one. But afterwards the soul departing from this divine union descended into intellect, and no longer possessed real beings unitedly, and in one, but apprehended and surveyed them by simple projections, and, as it were, contacts of its intellect. In the next place, departing from intellect, and descending into reasoning and *dianoia*, it no longer apprehended real beings by simple intuitions, but syllogistically and transitively, proceeding from one thing to another, from propositions to conclusions. Afterwards, abandoning true reasoning, and the dissolving peculiarity, it descended into generation, and became filled with much irrationality and perturbation. It is necessary, therefore, that it should recur to its proper principles and again return to the place from whence it came. To this ascent and apocatastasis, however, these four manias contribute. And the musical mania, indeed, leads to symphony and harmony, the agitated and disturbed nature of the parts of the soul, which were hurried away to indefiniteness and inaptitude, and were filled with abundant tumult. But the telestic mania causes the soul to be perfect and entire, and prepares it to energize intellectually. For the musical mania alone harmonizes and represses the parts of the soul; but the telestic causes the whole of it to energize, and prepares it to become entire, so that the intellectual part of it may energize. For the soul, by descending into the realms of generation, resembles a thing broken and relaxed. And the circle of *the same*, or the intellectual part of it, is fettered; but the circle of *the different*, or the doxastic part, sustains many fractures and turnings. Hence, the soul energizes partially, and not according to the whole of itself. The Dionysiacal inspiration, therefore, after the parts of the soul are coharmonized, renders it perfect, and causes it to energize according to the whole of itself, and to live intellectually. But the Apolloniacal mania converts and coexcites all the multiplied powers, and the whole of the soul, to *the one* of it. Hence Apollo is denominated as elevating the soul from multitude to *the one*. And the remaining mania, the amatory, receiving the soul united, conjoins this one of the soul to the Gods, and to intelligible beauty. As the givers, therefore, of these manias are transcendently united, and are in each other, the gifts also on this account participate of, and communicate with, each other, and the recipient, which is the soul, possesses an adaptation to all the gifts. This, therefore, is the order, and these are the energies and powers within the soul itself, of these four manias.

But let us also consider their external energies on man, and what they outwardly effect about us. The musical mania, therefore, causes us to speak in verse, and to act and be moved rhythmically, and to sing in meter, the splendid deeds of divine men, and their virtues and pursuits; and, through these, to discipline our life, in the same manner as the inward manias coharmonize our soul. But the telestic mania, expelling everything foreign, contaminating, and noxious, preserves our life perfect and innoxious, and banishing an insane and diabolical fantasy, causes us to be sane, entire, and perfect, just as the internal telestic mania makes the soul to be perfect and entire. Again, the prophetic mania contracts into one the extension and infinity of time, and sees, as in one present now, all things, the past, the future, and the existing time. Hence it predicts what will be, which it sees as present to itself. It causes us, therefore, to pass through life in an irreprehensible manner; just as the internal prophetic mania contracts and elevates all the multiplied and many powers and lives of the soul to *the one*, in order that it may in a greater degree be preserved and connected. But the amatory mania converts young persons to us, and causes them to become our friends, being instructive of youth, and leading them from sensible beauty to our psychical beauty, and from this sending them to intelligible beauty; in the same manner as the internal amatory mania conjoins *the one* of the soul to the Gods.

All the above mentioned manias, therefore, are superior to the prudent and temperate energies of the soul. Nevertheless, there is a mania which is coordinate with temperance, and which we say has in a certain respect a prerogative above it. For certain inspirations are produced, according to the middle and also according to the doxastic reasons of the soul, conformably to which artists effect certain things, and discover theorems beyond expectation, as Asclepius, for instance, in medicine, and Heracles in the practic life.

8. Marinus
Proclus or About Happiness

Marinus of Samaria was a pupil and immediate successor of Proclus at the Neoplatonic School in Athens. He was born in Neapolis (Schechem, modern Nablus), a major Hellenized city in Samaria. His master Proclus died in 485 C.E. and Marinus was by then quite old himself. He maintained mathematical and scientific interests at the School and less than a year after the master's death wrote his biography, *Proclus or About Happiness*. The work is an idealized account of the exemplary Neoplatonic sage who possessed all manner of virtue as is possible for a human being and was consequently the happiest of all men. The biography follows a stylistic plan based on the Neoplatonic theory of *eudaimonia*, or "true happiness."

The excerpts reproduced here from the *Vita Procli* were taken from the translation of L.J. Rosan, which was published in his monograph *The Philosophy of Proclus: The Final Phase of Ancient Thought* (New York: Cosmos, 1949).

Vita Procli 10–12; 18–19; 22; 28

10. But after having studied under these Alexandrian teachers[48] and profited from whatever knowledge they had, Proclus one day felt that they no longer were interpreting the text that they were

---

48. In Alexandria Proclus attended the classes of Leonas the Sophist from Isauria, and the grammarian Orion who was of the Egyptian priestly caste. He also learned Aristotelian philosophy under Olympiodorus and mathematics under Heron.

explaining in a spirit worthy of the philosopher (Aristotle), and he began to look down upon these teachers. Remembering then the divine vision which he had in Byzantium and its command, he traveled to Athens, accompanied by the best wishes of all the oracles, the gods who watch over philosophy and the good daemons. The gods led him onward to the guardian of philosophy (Athena) so that the Platonic tradition might be preserved untarnished and pure. This was definitely proved by what happened to him when he first arrived, which was like a sign from the gods that clearly informed him beforehand of the bequest of his father (Apollo) and of the future choice from above regarding the (Platonic) Succession. For when Proclus arrived at the Piraeus, and those in the city were notified of this, Nicolaus (who later became famous as a sophist but who at that time was still studying in Athens) went down to the harbor, received Proclus as a friend, entertained him as a fellow-citizen (since Nicolaus also came from Lycia), and took him to the city. Along the road, Proclus felt tired from walking; and near the Socrateion, although he had not yet known or heard that the place was sacred to Socrates, he asked Nicolaus to remain there with him for a little while to rest, and requested some water if there was any at that place, since he suddenly had become very thirsty. Nicolaus gladly went and brought water, not from anywhere else, but from that sacred place itself, the spring at the monument of Socrates which was close-by; and while Proclus was drinking, Nicolaus recognized this symbolic act and told him that he was actually sitting in the Socrateion and that it was its water which he was drinking for the first time in Athens, whereupon Proclus rose and made obeisance to the monument.

Then they continued to the city, but as they were arriving upon the heights to enter, they met the gate-keeper who was just about ready to place his keys in the locks, so that he said to Proclus, to quote his exact words: "Really, if you had not come, I would have closed them!" What symbolic saying could have been plainer than this, which does not require a Polles, or a Melampus or any other seer to understand its meaning?[49]

---

49. Marinus suggests here that if Proclus had not come, the Platonic tradition would have ended. With Proclus, however, it flourished again and reached its highest metaphysical peaks.

11. Proclus looked down upon even the Athenian rhetoricians, although they solicited him as much as if he had come for this purpose; but the first philosopher he met was Syrianus, son of Philoxenus; also present at the meeting was Lachares, who was absorbed in philosophical learning, a fellow-student of this philosopher, and as much admired for his sophistry as Homer was for his poetry. Now it was about the time of sunset, and the three were conversing together, when, just as the sun was going down, the moon was seen for the first time since the conjunction (of the sun with the moon). Syrianus and Lachares wished to send the youth away, since he was a stranger, so that they could pay homage to the goddess by themselves; but Proclus himself, as he walked away, noticed from the same house the appearance of the moon; and in full sight of both of them, he took off his shoes and worshiped the goddess. Lachares was struck by the independence of the youth and repeated to the philosopher Syrianus that divine statement of Plato's about remarkable characters: "This person will either be a great blessing or just the opposite." In short, these were the various signs from the gods that the philosopher Proclus received when he first arrived at Athens.

12. Syrianus took him to the great Plutarch, son of Nestorius. When the latter saw that the youth was not yet twenty years old and nevertheless had chosen and desired the philosophic life, he was overjoyed and gladly taught him philosophy, although he was otherwise prevented from teaching due to his advanced age....

18. But we shall let this discussion of friendship be a fitting conclusion to our report of Proclus' social virtues, although we have not really done justice to the subject. We now come to his purifying virtues which are quite different from social virtues. For the purpose of these is to purify the soul and to enable it to provide as freely as possible for all human affairs, so that it may become similar to God, which is its goal and highest good, although not every virtue separates the soul from lower things in the same manner, but some more and some less. Even the social virtues are to a certain extent purifying, since on a lower level they make those who possess them better and finer by keeping desires and emotions in general within a fixed limit and by removing all passions and false opinions. But the purifying virtues are superior to these and entirely separate and free the soul from the truly leaden weight of the world of change and hasten its unhindered flight from this world.

The philosopher Proclus practiced these purifying virtues throughout his philosophical career, explaining in his classes just what they were and how they could be obtained, and living his life by them. He always did that which was conducive to separating the soul, and whether in the night-time or day-time, he would pray against evil demons (*apotrope*), bathe himself and use other methods of purification, both Orphic, and Chaldean, such as immersing himself in the sea resolutely every month, or even twice or three times a month. And he did all this not only in the prime of his life, but even in his later years he religiously performed these customary actions.

19. So that he would not be disturbed by them, he indulged in the necessary pleasures of food and drink only to avoid illness; for he partook sparingly of these. He especially refused to eat anything that had life, although whenever there was an occasion which imperatively demanded it, he would taste a little meat for the sake of the rite. Every month he purified himself by the rites of the Great Mother (Cybele), who was honored by the Romans and previously by the Phrygians; and he observed the Egyptian holy days more than the Egyptians themselves. He fasted especially on certain days because of the appearance (of the moon), on the last day of the month (before the new-moon) he fasted without even eating the night before, and he celebrated the day of the new-moon itself splendidly and solemnly. In general, he observed the important holidays of all peoples and of every nation in the way proper to each; and he did not make them an excuse, as others do, for idleness or feasting, but celebrated them entirely by sleepless (prayer) meetings, singing hymns and things like these. This is proved by the contents of his own *Hymns*, which include praises not only of the Greek gods, but also of the god Marnas of Gaza, Asclepius Leontuchus of Ascalon, Thyandrites who is also honored greatly by the Arabs, Isis who is still honored at Philae, and many other non-Greek gods. For, as this most pious man always used to say, it befits the philosopher not to observe the rites of any one city or of only a few nations, but to be the minister of the whole world in common (*koine hierophantes tou holou kosmou*). In this pure and holy manner, therefore, Proclus constantly practiced continence....

22. Advancing serenely and calmly through these purifying virtues as if they were degrees of mystic initiation, he arrived at the higher virtues above them by means of his excellent nature and intelligent training. For after being purified and rising above the

world of change, he looked down on "the many who carry the narthex" and became one of the true bacchants.[50] But by his own eyes he saw those truly blessed visions of Reality, no longer obtaining this knowledge by reasoning or demonstration, but as if by vision and by simple and immediate perceptions of the intuitive faculty (*haplais epibolais tes noeras energeias*), viewing the ideal forms in the Divine Mind. By this means he reached that virtue, which could no longer be called prudence in the human sense (*phronesis*) but rather true wisdom (*sophia*) or even some more reverent name.

While he was absorbed with this, Proclus learned with ease all of Greek and non-Greek theology and also that truth which had been hidden in the form of myths; he explained all these in a very enthusiastic manner to all who wished and were able to understand, and brought them into harmony. He went through all the writings of previous authors and whatever he found that was fruitful he would select and combine, but whatever he discovered was trivial he would discard as disgraceful, and whatever seemed to contradict good doctrine he would refute with arguments and proofs. In his lectures he was able to discuss each doctrine sensibly and he mentioned all of them in his writings. He had an unbounded love of work; sometimes he would teach five or more classes a day, write on the average about seven hundred lines of prose, visit with other philosophers and then in the evening give lectures that were not based on any text; in addition to all this he would sleeplessly worship the gods every night, and bow in prayer to the sun when it arose, at midday and when it set....

28. As I said before, as a result of this work he obtained the higher and more perfect theurgical virtues and no longer remained on the level of the merely intellectual virtues. Therefore he did not live according to just one of the two divine characteristics, but both: by means of his mind alone he aspired towards what was higher, and by means of a not merely social but rather providential attention (*pronoia*) he cared for those things which were lower. He went to Chaldaic gatherings and (prayer) meetings, employed silent tops for strophalomancy,[51] and in general practices various things of this

---

50. Cf. Plato's *Phaedo* 69cd.

51. From *strophalos*, "top," and *mantike*, "divination." A top was rotated and events predicted according to its motion. According to Stephen Gersh, the Byzantine

kind. He learned their significance and use from Asclepigeneia, the daughter of Plutarch; for she alone had preserved from (her grandfather) Nestorius, and through the intermediary of her father, the knowledge of the (religious) Orgies and the whole theurgic science. But the philosopher Proclus proceeded step by step; first he was cleansed by the Chaldean purification; then he held converse, as he himself mentions in one of his works, with the luminous apparitions of Hecate which he conjured up himself; then he caused rain-falls by correctly moving the wryneck bird-wheel;[52] by this means he saved Athens from a severe drought. He proposed means to prevent earthquakes; he tested the divinatory powers of the tripod; and even wrote verses about his own destiny. For at the age of forty he seemed to have said the following verses in a dream:

> Here a divine super-heavenly brilliance has glistened,
> Issuing forth from a fervid and fiery fountain!

At the beginning of his forty-second year, he seemed to have cried aloud the following verses:

> My soul has arrived, and breathes forth the force of fire;
> Extending my mind, it rises in flame to the heavens;
> The circles of stars resonates with immortality.

writer Michael Psellus "discusses the function of a magical instrument known as Hecate's top (*Hekatikos strophalos*) which he describes as a golden disc with a sapphire set in the center and engraved with symbols to be rotated by the magician with a leather thong while making his invocations. As the disc turns he emits 'meaningless or animal cries,' coupled with laughter and whipping of the air." Psellus' account refers specifically to the ritual of the so-called "Chaldeans." See S. Gersh, *From Iamblichus to Eriugena: An Investigation of the Prehistory and Evolution of the Pseudo-Dionysian Tradition* (Leiden: E.J.Brill, 1978), p.293.

52. The wryneck or *iunx* had a special cry and was attached to a turning wheel to predict events from its voice. According to Ruth Majercik, the name *iunx* originally designated a certain bird (the wryneck), which was bound to a wheel by a magician and spun around as a means of attracting an unfaithful lover. Sometimes the wheel itself was called an *iunx*. Under the influence of Plato's spiritualization of Eros, the word *iunx* came to mean the binding force between man and the gods. The *Chaldean Oracles* describe *iunges* as "couriers" between the Father and matter (fr.78). *Iunges* are identified with the thoughts, or Ideas, of the Father (fr.77). See Ruth Majercik, *The Chaldean Oracles* (Leiden: E.J.Brill, 1989), p.9.

In addition, he was convinced that he belonged to the Hermaic tradition; and he believed, according to a dream he once had, that he possessed the soul of the Pythagorean philosopher Nicomachus.

9. Proclus
Commentary on Plato's Alcibiades I

Proclus was the most important philosopher in Late Hellenic Neoplatonism. The intellectual legacy of "the great Proclus" (*ho megas Proklos*) dominated all subsequent Hellenic thought in Late Antiquity. Directly, or indirectly, his metaphysical system was transmitted (sometimes under the mask of Dionysius the Areopagite and Aristotle) to the Byzantine, Western European and Islamic civilizations.

Proclus was born in Byzantium (Constantinople), but his parents were Lycians from Xanthus. At first Proclus studied under the Egyptian grammarian Orion, the sophist Leonas, Olympiodorus the Peripatetic, and Heron in Alexandria; but, according to Marinus, the goddess Athena turned him toward philosophy. He departed for the Neoplatonic School at Athens to study under Plutarch of Athens and Syrianus. After the death of Syrianus, Proclus assumed the leadership of the School.

Many of Proclus' important works have survived but are little known to contemporary readers. He was the first thinker to place Neoplatonic philosophy in a strictly systematic form. Following Iamblichus and Syrianus, he was concerned to harmonize Platonism with the *Chaldean Oracles* and the teachings of Orpheus—these being regarded as sources of divine revelation. Proclus maintained that his elaborated metaphysics was the true, though hidden, meaning of Plato's philosophy, which he regarded as a prolongation and scientific development of the Homeric, Pythagorean and Orphic secret doctrines. He viewed the philosophy of Aristotle as belonging to the Lesser Mysteries, which were to be accomplished before approaching the Greater Mysteries of Plato. According to A.C. Lloyd:

> Proclus moved in important political circles, but like other leading Platonists he was a champion of pagan worship against imperial policy and found himself more than once in trouble. There is no doubt of his personal faith in religious practices. A vegetarian diet, prayers to the sun, the rites of a Chaldean initiate, even the observance of Egyptian holy days were scrupulously practiced. He is said

to have got his practical knowledge of theurgy from a daughter of Plutarch, and according to his own claim he could conjure up luminous phantoms of Hecate.[53]

The Neoplatonic tradition was based on both an oral transmission and written commentaries on selected dialogues of the "divine" Plato. Since the time of Iamblichus, the fixed order of reading the dialogues of Plato under the tutelage of a master was established—the sequence of study reflecting the various stages of spiritual ascent (*anagoge*). The prescribed order ran as follows: *Alcibiades I, Gorgias, Phaedo, Cratylus, Theaetetus, Sophist, Politicus, Phaedrus, Symposium, Philebus, Timaeus,* and *Parmenides. Alcibiades I* was placed first for it was regarded as providing the initial ethical basis for later self-knowledge.

The excerpts of Proclus' *Commentary on Alcibiades I,* as reproduced here, were translated by William O'Neil, *Proclus: Alcibiades I: A Translation and Commentary* (The Hague: Martinus Nijhoff, 1965).

In Alcib. 4–11

Hence we should reckon this to be the most valid starting-point both for all philosophy and for the system of Plato, namely, as we said, the clear and unadulterated knowledge of ourselves determined in scientific terms and "securely established by causal reasoning."[54] From what other source indeed, should one begin one's own purification and perfection than from where the god at Delphi exhorted us? For as the public notice warned those entering the precincts of the Eleusinian mysteries not to pass within the inner shrine if they were profane and uninitiated, so also the inscription "Know Thyself" on the front of the Delphi sanctuary indicated the manner, I presume, of ascent to the divine and the most effective path towards purification, practically stating clearly to those able to understand, that he who has attained the knowledge of himself, by beginning at the beginning, can be united with the god who is the revealer of the whole truth and guide of the purgative life; but he who does not know who he is, being uninitiated and profane[55] is unfit to partake of the providence of Apollo.

53. A.C. Lloyd, "The Later Neoplatonists," in *Cambridge History of Later Greek and Early Medieval Philosophy,* ed. A.H. Armstrong (Cambridge, UK.: Cambridge University Press, 1970), p.305.

54. Cf. Plato, *Meno* 98a3.

55. Cf. Plato, *Phaedo* 69c.

Let this then be the start of philosophy, and of the teaching of
Plato viz. the knowledge of ourselves. For I think it befits the familiar friend[56] of Apollo to begin the perfection of the imperfect from
the same starting-point as the god himself bids. Since Socrates also,
who asserts that he is the "fellow-slave of the swans"[57] and has no
less than they received the gift of prophecy from the god, is said to
have begun his impulse towards philosophy by coming upon the
Pythian inscription and considering it to be the bidding, as it were,
of Apollo himself. We also then, obedient to god, must start from
there; and we must enquire in which dialogue especially Plato has
this aim in mind, viz. the consideration of our being, in order that
therefrom we may make our very first start upon the works of Plato.
Now could we name any other prior to the *Alcibiades* and the conversation of Socrates related therein? Where else shall we say that
the nature of our being is similarly demonstrated; or enquiry made
into man and his nature; or the meaning of the Delphic inscription
thoroughly investigated? Or how, before this, could we examine
anything else, either of the things that are or come to be when we
have heard Socrates himself say: "It seems ridiculous to me to consider the properties of other beings, when I do not know myself?"[58]
Nothing is nearer to us than our selves; if then we do not perceive
what is nearest, what means is there of ascertaining the more
remote, and what is naturally perceived through our agency? But if
you reflect that not only does this subject receive considerable elucidation in this dialogue but also that this is the first conversation
that Socrates initiates with *Alcibiades* and that it is he himself who
says that the beginnings of perfection depend on the consideration
of ourselves, you will no longer doubt that all who are anxious for
perfection must begin from here. Each one of us and of mankind
in general is more or less clearly subject to the very same misfortunes as the son of Kleinias. Held bound by the forgetfulness incident to generation and sidetracked by the disorder of the irrational
forms of life, we do not know ourselves, and we think we know many
things of which we are unaware, by reason of the innate notions
present in us according to our being;[59] we stand in need of the same

56. I.e. Plato; cf. Diogenes Laertius, *Lives of the Eminent Philosophers* III.45.
57. Cf. Plato, *Phaedo* 85b.
58. Cf. Plato, *Phaedrus* 229e.
59. Cf. Proclus, *The Elements of Theology*, propositions 194–5.

assistance, in order both to keep ourselves from excessive conceit and to light upon the care appropriate to us.

Well, it has already been observed that the knowledge of ourselves must precede all other enquiries and practically the whole of philosophical study. But perhaps someone might reproach us for so casual an assertion that this is the object of the *Alcibiades*, since accounts by many other famous commentators have described its purpose, some one way, some another. Nevertheless I would be ashamed of myself, if, while discerning that the supreme subject in the dialogue, which requires greater scientific knowledge and embraces all the problems, is the disclosure of the nature of our being, and that this extends through all the main sections of the work, I were to make the secondary, less important and more particular aspects objects of the aforesaid composition. For neither is it appropriate to refer the purpose of the dialogue to Alcibiades alone, as some have supposed (since scientific consideration views what is general and extends to all similar states); nor to put forward the tools of philosophical discussion as aims of the conversation, e.g. exhortation, elicitation or refutation, but to observe to what end these tend; nor, standing aside from the considerations in hand, to transfer the enquiry to other forms of being, divine or spirit-like, in no way appropriate to us (for the object must be proper to the first beginnings of philosophical consideration, since Socrates says that this is the first time he has approached the youth); nor to devise some altogether different and adventitious purpose for the dialogue, casting aside that to which Socrates himself bears witness. If the knowledge of ourselves must precede all other considerations, how could there be any other end of this first conversation more to the point than the knowledge of ourselves?

Exhortations therefore and dissuasions, refutation, elicitation, praise and blame, fulfill the function of indispensable means; for without these it is not possible to know oneself: exhortation is needed towards what is really good, and dissuasion from what is really evil: elicitation for the advancement of unperverted notions, and refutation for purification from twofold ignorance:[60] praise to make those undergoing perfection feel at home, and blame to benefit

60. Cf. *Prolegomena to Platonic Philosophy*, p.211, 3–5 Hermann: "Simple ignorance is when one is unaware of the essence and knows that one is unaware: twofold ignorance is when one is both unaware of the essence and does not recognize this unawareness."

them and cure their bad habits. As, therefore, in the mystic rites[61] there are preliminary cleansings, sprinklings with lustral water and purifications which are practiced for secret rites and communion with the divine, so also the work of philosophical perfection seems to me to purge and prepare those on the path towards it for their self-knowledge, and the intuitive consideration of our being. Hence this and no other is the object of the dialogue; but of the matters demonstrated therein, some precede, and others are consequent upon this purpose, as conclusions implicit in this end. The removal of twofold ignorance and the exhortation and suchlike come first, and then follows the demonstration of virtue and happiness and the condemnation of the many crafts as not knowing either themselves or what belongs to them or absolutely anything at all, and such material of this nature as is offered in additional evidence at the end of the dialogue. But the chief purpose and principal object of the whole conversation is the consideration of our being.

Even if one should say that the purpose of the dialogue is the care of ourselves and the knowledge thereof, although his assertion is correct, let him note that it is appropriate that this should accrue to us as an end and as the benefit that results from what is demonstrated, but the object of enquiry and the purpose of the syllogisms is a problem,[62] viz. the knowledge of ourselves. For it is one thing to know the aim of the dialogue, and another the good that derives from such a purpose. Admittedly, as we have said elsewhere about the dialogues, each one must possess what the whole cosmos possesses;[63] and an analogous part must be assigned therein to the good, part to the intellect, part to the soul, part to the form and

---

61. A reference to contemporary theurgy. See A. Sheppard, "Proclus' Attitude to Theurgy," *Classical Quarterly* 32, 1 (1982):212–224; and G. Shaw, "The Geometry of Grace: A Pythagorean Approach to Theurgy," in *The Divine Iamblichus: Philosopher and Man of Gods*, ed. H.J. Blumenthal and E.G. Clark (Bristol, 1993), pp.116–137.

62. The sense of the word "problem" here seems to be "a subject for intellectual enquiry." Cf. *Proleg. Phil. Plat.* p.212, 33–8 Hermann: "It is natural for the problem to be compared to the Intellect; for just as the Intellect is undivided, and is apprehended like a center-spot, while around the Intellect are the processes of discursive reasoning like a circumference unfolding around its center, so it is with the problem, and around it the demonstrations are unfolded like a circumference, desiring to seek out the answer that is emitted by it."

63. Cf. *Proleg. Phil. Plat.* p.210, 21–6 Hermann: "Now since we have learned that the dialogue is a cosmos and the cosmos a dialogue, we shall find as many constituents

part to the underlying nature itself. Let it then be stated that in this work proportionate to the good is conformity to the divine[64] through the care of ourselves, to the intellect the knowledge of ourselves, to the soul the wealth of demonstrations leading us to this conclusion, and practically the whole syllogistic part of the dialogue; for the form there remains the style of the diction and the interweaving of the figures of speech, and of the literary forms, and what else belongs to stylistic ability; and for the matter the persons and the time and what is called by some the plot. Now these exist in every dialogue, but as regards the question under discussion, the object of this work is the knowledge of our being, and we are lovers of this knowledge in order that we may attain our own perfection. As among the causative principles themselves the intellect depends on the good, so likewise in this matter, the object of enquiry in the dialogue is closely united with the purpose of the conversation; and the purpose is just such as we have said.

Let so much be placed on record by us in regard to the purpose, since we have already shown that the beginning of our perfection must be the pure knowledge of ourselves. This dialogue is the beginning of philosophy, as indeed is the knowledge of ourselves; and for this reason scattered throughout it is the exposition of many considerations of logic, the elucidation of many points of ethics and such matters as contribute to our general investigation concerning happiness, and the outline of many doctrines leading us to the study of natural phenomena or even to the truth concerning divine matters themselves, in order that as it were in outline in this dialogue the one, common and complete plan of all philosophy may be comprised, being revealed through our actual first turning towards ourselves. It seems to me that this is why the divine Iamblichus[65]

---

of the dialogues as the cosmos. Now in the universal cosmos there are matter, form, nature that implants form in matter, soul, intellect and divinity; and in the dialogue analogous to matter are the characters, the time and the place ... to form the style ... to soul the demonstrations ... and to intellect the subject of enquiry. There is another way also of showing how the constituents of the dialogue are analogous to those in the cosmos. There are six causes in the case of each thing that comes into being, the material, formal, efficient, final, exemplary and instrumental. Analogous to the material are the characters, the time and the place, to the formal the style, to the efficient the soul, to the instrumental the demonstrations, to the exemplary the subjects of enquiry, to the final the good."

64. Cf. Plato, *Theaetetus* 176b.

gives it the first position among the ten dialogues in which he considers the whole of Plato's philosophy is embraced, their whole subsequent development having been, as it were, anticipated in this seed. But which are the ten and how they should be arranged and how they are summarized in the two subsequent to them, we have elaborated principally in other writings.

256–258

One should not be surprised if, while stating that what is in accordance with nature is more extensive than what is contrary to it, and that the latter is constrained within a small compass, we assert that the majority of men lack knowledge and are evil, and that the knowledgeable are very few. For life in conjunction with the body is not natural to souls, nor the life that produces generation, but on the contrary the life which is separate, immaterial and incorporeal is more appropriate to them. When they are in the world of process, they resemble those who spend their time in a plague-ridden spot, but when they are outside the world of process, just as Plato himself says, they resemble those who dwell in "a meadow."[66] Just as therefore there is nothing surprising in the fact that in places of pestilence more people suffer from disease than are in a natural state of health, so also it is no cause for surprise that in the world of process there are more souls that are depraved and in the grip of the emotions than otherwise. Indeed the contrary would be surprising—if any souls clothed in such bodies, encompassed in such bonds, and enmeshed in so much change, abstain and remain both pure and free from emotion. Looking at such souls and at one who lived a life that was immaterial among things implicated in matter, and unde-

65. Cf. *Proleg. Phil. Plat.* p.219, 24–9 Hermann: "We relate what divine Iamblichus did. Now he divided all the dialogues into twelve, some of which he termed physical, and others theological; again he reduced the twelve to two, the *Timaeus* and the *Parmenides*, the *Timaeus* as head of the physical and the *Parmenides* as head of the theological dialogues." Ten dialogues are then given in the following order: first the *Alcibiades* (because therein we learn the knowledge of ourselves) and last the *Philebus* (because its subject is the Good); in between come the *Gorgias, Phaedo, Cratylus, Theaetetus, Phaedrus, Symposium, Timaeus,* and *Parmenides.* The probable inclusion of the *Sophist* and the *Statesman* brings the number up to twelve.

66. The "meadow" is the meeting place of souls coming up from earth and down from heaven. Cf. Plato, *Republic* X.614e–616b.

filed among things mortal, a judge would, I think, say: "Wonder possesses me how you have drunk this potion and no whit been charmed."[67] For truly oblivion, error and ignorance are like some use of drugs that drags souls down to the abode of dissimilarity.[68] Why then be surprised if in their way of life there are many who are wolves, many who are swine and many who have put on the likeness of some other kind of irrational animal,[69] since the earthy regions are the residence of Circe[70] and many souls are ensnared by her draught on account of their immoderate desire? Wonder rather at this—if any here are free from the influence of potion and charm and in their natures are followers of Hermes,[71] passing over to reason and knowledge. Just as we should not be surprised if we should see souls being punished in Tartarus (since that place was designed for them), so also if in the world of process the majority are subject

67. Cf. Homer, *Odyssey* X.326.

68. Cf. Plato, *Statesman* 273d.

69. The question of whether men's souls literally entered beasts, or whether this was meant metaphorically is controversial. Porphyry and Iamblichus made a firm distinction between the rational and irrational soul and refused to allow transmigration from one kind to the other. Proclus quotes contemporary opposing views *In Tim.* p.294, 22ff: "It is customary to enquire what is meant by the descent of souls into irrational animals: some consider that the so-called bestial lives are mere assimilations of men to beasts (for it is not possible that a rational substance should become the soul of a beast), others even concede that this substance enters into irrational beings (for, they assert, all souls are the same in kind, so that these become wolves and leopards and jelly-fish)." Proclus then gives his own opinion, which is a compromise between the opposing views: "But the true account says that although the human soul enters into beasts, yet they retain their own appropriate life which the entered soul as it were transcends, while at the same time bound by affinity to it." Proclus admits that man's soul can enter beasts, but that it remains rational and transcendent, and the beasts retain their own life: man's soul does not actually inform the body of a beast. See *In Remp.* II. p.309–28ff: "Let us state, then, that at any rate according to the opinion of Plato the soul transfers into irrational animals on account of similarity in way of life, a position which we too affirm, but not that the soul inhabits their bodies (for the differentiations in natural structure militate against such reduced status) but solely by condition of life is tied to their soul which has animated its own body and has no additional need of the human soul."

70. Cf. Proclus, *In Crat.* p.22, 8–10: "Circe, who contrives the whole of life in the region of the four elements, and at the same time makes the place beneath the moon harmonious with her spells." Compare the position of Hecate as mistress of the evil demons, who inhabit the sublunary zone. These demons are likened to beasts of the earth who lure the soul to an "animal" life.

71. I.e., persons of reason guided by the divine Intellect. See Proclus, *In Tim.* I.p.148, 5;

to the emotions and devoid of understanding and knowledge, since the world of process requires such souls. As therefore in heaven they have all the form of the good, as in Tartarus they are all depraved, so in the world of process the majority are depraved, and the minority are good, since the world of process is near the worse end of the two extremes, not the better and more divine.

10. Proclus
Theology of Plato

The *Theology of Plato* (*Eis ten Platonos theologian*) is the most important work by Proclus in that it presents his entire metaphysical system as based on the Neoplatonic exegesis of Plato. Herein he explained the main principles of his metaphysical hermeneutics and his fundamental claim that the philosophy of Plato had an essential and esoteric dimension which was expounded in the past by Plotinus the Egyptian and his later successors—each of whom belonged to the Golden Chain of transmission.

According to Proclus, to be real was to be one, i.e., to possess an appropriate divine henad, which, however, was ineffable; but the first principles—or the gods—could be studied indirectly by observing the hierarchy of orders that constituted the series, or chains (*seirai*), of manifestation understood as theophany. Most of the *Theology of Plato* was devoted to the various triads of the intelligible world (i.e., noetic, noetic-noeric, and noeric), which Proclus explained by a metaphysical and cosmological interpretation of the first and second hypotheses of Plato's *Parmenides*.

The excerpts of the *Theology of Plato* as reproduced here were translated by Thomas Taylor and first published in 1816.

Plat. Theol. I.1

O Pericles, to me the dearest of friends, I am of opinion that the whole philosophy of Plato was at first unfolded into light through the beneficent will of superior natures, exhibiting the intellect concealed in them, and the truth subsisting together with beings, to souls conversant with generation (so far as it is lawful for them to participate of such supernatural and mighty good); and again, that

and Galen, *Protrep.* p.23 where Hermes is contrasted with the Goddess of Chance.

afterwards having received its perfection, returning as it were into itself, and becoming unapparent to many[72] who professed to philosophize, and who earnestly desired to engage in the investigation of true being, it again advanced into light. But I particularly think that the mystic doctrine respecting divine concerns, which is purely established on a sacred foundation, and which perpetually subsists with the gods themselves, became thence apparent to such as are capable of enjoying it for a time, through one man, whom I should not err in calling the primary leader and hierophant of those true mysteries, into which souls separated from terrestrial places are initiated, and of those entire and stable visions, which those participate who genuinely embrace a happy and blessed life. But this philosophy shone forth at first from him so venerably and arcanely, as if established in sacred temples, and within their adyta, and being unknown to many who have entered into these holy places, in certain orderly periods of time, proceeded as much as was possible for it into light, through certain true priests, and who embraced a life corresponding to the tradition of such mystic concerns. It appears likewise to me, that the whole place became splendid, and that illuminations of divine spectacles every where presented themselves to the view.

These interpreters of the *epopteia* (or mystic speculations) of Plato, who have unfolded to us all-sacred narrations of divine concerns, and who were allotted a nature similar to their leader, I should determine to be the Egyptian Plotinus, and those who received the theory from him; I mean Amelius and Porphyry, together with those in the third place who were produced like virile statues from these, viz.: Iamblichus and Theodorus,[73] and any others, who after these, following this divine choir, have energized about the doctrines of Plato with a divinely-inspired mind. From these, he (Syrianus) who, after the gods, has been our leader to everything beautiful and good, receiving in an undefiled manner the most genuine and pure light

72. On the esoteric history of Platonism, as understood by the Neoplatonists, see John Glucker, *Antiochus and the Late Academy* (Vandenhoeck and Ruprecht in Gottingen, 1978), pp.296–329.

73. Theodorus of Asine, Iamblichus' pupil and rival. Theodorus was influenced by both Numenius and Porphyry. Among the later Neoplatonists, only Theodorus accepted Plotinus' doctrine of an unfallen part of the soul.

of truth in the bosom of his soul, made us a partaker of all the rest of Plato's philosophy, communicated to us that arcane information which he had received from those more ancient than himself, and caused us, in conjunction with him, to be divinely agitated about the mystic truth of divine concerns.

To this man, therefore, should we undertake to return thanks adequate to the benefits which we have received from him, the whole of time would not be sufficient. But if it is necessary, not only that we should have received from others the transcendent good of the Platonic philosophy, but that we should leave to posterity monuments of those blessed spectacles of which we have been spectators, and emulators to the utmost of our ability, under a leader the most perfect of the present time, and who arrived at the summit of philosophy; perhaps we shall act properly in invoking the gods, that they will enkindle the light of truth in our soul, and in supplicating the attendants and ministers of better natures to direct our intellect and lead it to the all-perfect, divine, and elevated end of the Platonic theory. For I think that every where he who participates in the least degree of intelligence, will begin his undertakings from the Gods, and especially in explications respecting the Gods: for we can no otherwise be able to understand a divine nature than by being perfected through the light of the Gods; nor divulge it to others unless governed by them, and exempt from multiform opinions, and the variety which subsists in words, preserving at the same time the interpretation of divine names. Knowing therefore this, and complying with the exhortation of the Platonic *Timaeus*, we in the first place establish the Gods as leaders of the doctrine respecting themselves. But may they in consequence of hearing our prayers be propitious to us, and benignantly approaching, guide the intellect of our soul, and lead it about the Hestia[74] of Plato, and to the arduous sublimities of this speculation; where, when arrived, we shall receive all the truth concerning them, and shall obtain the best end of our parturient conceptions of divine concerns, desiring to know something respecting them, inquiring about them of others, and, at the same time, as far as we are able, exploring them ourselves.

---

74. We have restored the original Hestia instead of Taylor's "Vesta."

I.2

And thus much by way of preface. But it is necessary that I should unfold the mode of the proposed doctrine, what it is requisite to expect it will be, and define the preparatives which a hearer of it ought to possess; that being properly adapted, he may approach, not to our discourses, but to the intellectually elevated and deific philosophy of Plato. For it is proper that convenient aptitudes of auditors should be proposed according to the forms of discourses, just as, in the mysteries, those who are skillful in concerns of this kind, previously prepare receptacles for the Gods, and neither always use the same inanimate particulars, nor other animals, nor men, in order to procure the presence of the divinities; but that alone out of each of these which is naturally capable of participating in divine illumination is by them introduced to the proposed mystic rites.

The present discourse, therefore, will first of all be divided by me into three parts. In the beginning, considering all those common conceptions concerning the Gods, which Plato summarily delivers, together with the power and dignity every where of theological axioms; but in the middle of this work, speculating on the total orders of the Gods, enumerating their peculiarities, defining their progressions after the manner of Plato, and referring every thing to the hypotheses of theologists; and, in the end, speaking concerning the Gods which are in different places celebrated in the Platonic writings, whether they are supermundane or mundane, and referring the theory respecting them to the total genera of the divine orders.

In every part of this work, likewise, we shall prefer the clear, distinct, and simple, to the contraries of these. And such things as are delivered through symbols, we shall transfer to a clear doctrine concerning them; but such as are delivered through images we shall transmit to their exemplars. Such things too as are written in a more affirmative way, we shall examine by causal reasonings; but such as are composed through demonstrations, we shall investigate; and besides this, explain the mode of truth which they contain, and render it known to the hearers. And of things enigmatically proposed, we shall elsewhere discover perspicuity, not from foreign hypotheses, but from the most genuine writings of Plato. But with respect to the things which immediately occur to the hearers, of these we shall contemplate the consent with things themselves. And from all these particulars, one perfect form of the Platonic theology will present itself to our view, together with its truth which pervades through the whole of divine intellections, and the one intellect which generated all the beauty of this theology, and the mystic evolution of this theory. Such, therefore, as I have said, will be my present treatise.

But the auditor of the proposed dogmas is supposed to be adorned with the moral virtues, and to be one who has bound by the reason of virtue all the illiberal and inharmonious motions of the soul, and harmonized them to the one form of intellectual prudence: for, as Socrates says, it is not lawful for the pure to be touched by the impure. But every vicious man is perfectly impure; and the contrary character is pure. He must likewise have been exercised in all the logical methods, and have contemplated many irreprehensible conceptions about analyses, and many about divisions, the contraries to these, agreeably, as it appears to me, to the exhortation of Parmenides to Socrates. For prior to such a contest in arguments, the knowledge of the divine genera, and of the truth established in them, is difficult and impervious. But in the third place, he must not be unskilled in physics. For he who has been conversant with the multiform opinions of physiologists, and has after a manner explored in images the causes of beings, will more easily advance to the nature of separate and primary essences. An auditor therefore of the present work, as I have said, must not be ignorant of the truth contained in the phenomena, nor unacquainted with the paths of erudition, and the disciplines which they contain; for through these we obtain a more immaterial knowledge of a divine essence. But all these must be bound together in the leader intellect. Being likewise a partaker of the dialectic of Plato, meditating on those immaterial energies which are separate from corporeal powers, and desiring to contemplate by intelligence in conjunction with reason [true] beings, our auditor must genuinely apply himself to the interpretation of divine and blessed dogmas, and fill his soul, according to the Oracle, with profound love; since, as Plato somewhere observes, for the apprehension of this theory, a better assistant than love cannot be obtained.

He must likewise be exercised in the truth which pervades through all things, and must excite his intelligible eye to real and perfect truth. He must establish himself in a firm, immovable, and safe kind of divine knowledge, and must be persuaded not to admire any thing else, nor even to direct his attention to other things, but must hasten to divine light with an intrepid reasoning energy, and with the power of an unwearied life; and in short, must propose to himself such a kind of energy and rest as it becomes him to possess who intends to be such a coryphaeus as Socrates describes in the *Theaetetus*. Such then is the magnitude of our hypothesis, and such the mode of the discourses about it. Before, however, I enter on the narration of the things proposed, I wish to speak about theology itself, its different modes, and what theological forms Plato approves, and what he rejects; that these being previously known, we may more easily learn in what follows, the auxiliaries of the demonstrations themselves.

I.3

All, therefore, that have ever touched upon theology, have called things first, according to nature, Gods; and have said that the theological science is conversant about these. And some, indeed, have considered a corporeal essence as that alone which has any existence, and have placed in a secondary rank with respect to essence, all the genera of incorporeal natures, considering the principles of things as having a corporeal form, and evincing that the habit in us by which we know these, is corporeal. But others, suspending indeed all bodies from incorporeal natures, and defining the first *huparxis*[75] to be in soul, and the powers of soul, call (as it appears to me) the best of souls, Gods; and denominate the science which proceeds as far as to these, and which knows these, theology. But such as produce the multitude of souls from another more ancient principle, and establish intellect as the leader of wholes, these assert that

---

75. According to L. Siorvanes, *ousia* means the reality of a thing, its substance, while *huparxis* is pure existence. The term *huparxis* is broad enough to cover the level of pure unity as the hidden foundation of all manifested realities and the level of the divine reality, uncontaminated by any qualifications, even that of substantive being. See Lucas Siorvanes, *Proclus: The Neo-Platonic Philosophy and Science* (Edinburgh: Edinburgh University Press, 1996), p.110. For Thomas Taylor, it is "the summit of any nature, or blossom, as it were, of its essence."

the best end is a union of the soul with intellect, and consider the intellectual form of life as the most honorable of all things. They doubtless too consider theology, and the discussion of intellectual essence, as one and the same. All these, therefore, as I have said, call the first and most self-sufficient principles of things, Gods, and the science respecting these, theology.

The divine narration however, of Plato alone, despises all corporeal natures with reference to principles. Because, indeed, every thing divisible and endued with interval, is naturally unable either to produce or preserve itself, but possesses its being, energy and passivity through soul, and the motions which soul contains. But Plato demonstrates that the psychical essence [i.e. the essence pertaining to soul] is more ancient than bodies, but is suspended from an intellectual hypostasis. For every thing which is moved according to time, though it may be self-moved, is indeed of a more ruling nature than things moved by others, but is posterior to an eternal motion. He shows, therefore, as we have said, that intellect is the father and cause of bodies and souls, and that all things both subsist and energize about it, which are allotted a life conversant with transitions and evolutions.

Plato, however, proceeds to another principle entirely exempt from intellect, more incorporeal and ineffable, and from which all things, even though you should speak of such as are last, have necessarily a subsistence. For all things are not naturally disposed to participate of soul, but such things only as are allotted in themselves a more clear or obscure life. Nor are all things able to enjoy intellect and being, but such only as subsist according to form. But it is necessary that the principle of all things should be participated in by all things, if it does not desert any thing, since it is the cause of all things which in any respect are said to have a subsistence. Plato having divinely discovered this first principle of wholes, which is more excellent than intellect, and is concealed in inaccessible recesses; and having exhibited these three causes and monads, and evinced them to be above bodies, I mean soul, the first intellect, and a union above intellect, produces from these as monads, their proper numbers; one multitude indeed being uniform, but the second intellectual, and the third psychical. For every monad is the leader of a multitude co-ordinate to itself. But as Plato connects bodies with souls, so likewise he connects souls with intellectual forms, and these again with the unities of beings. But he converts all things to one imparticipable unity. And having run back as far as to this unity, he considers himself as having obtained the highest end of the theory of wholes; and that this is the truth respecting the Gods, which is conversant with the unities of beings, and which delivers their progressions and peculiarities, the contact of beings with them, and the orders of forms which are suspended from these unical hypostases.

But he teaches us that the theory respecting intellect, and the forms and the genera revolving about intellect, is posterior to the science which is conversant with the Gods themselves. Likewise that the intellectual theory apprehends intelligibles, and the forms which are capable of being known by the soul through the projecting energy of intellect; but that the theological science transcending this, is conversant with arcane and ineffable *huparxeis*, and pursues their separation from each other, and their unfolding into light from one cause of all: whence, I am of opinion, that the intellectual peculiarity of the soul is capable of apprehending intellectual forms, and the difference which subsists in them, but that the summit, and, as they say, flower of intellect and *huparxis*, is conjoined with the unities of beings, and through these, with the occult union of all the divine unities. For as we contain many gnostic powers, through this alone we are naturally capable of being conjoined with and participating in this occult union. For the genus of the Gods cannot be apprehended by sense, because it is exempt from all bodies; nor by opinion and *dianoia*, for these are divisible and come into contact with multiform concerns; nor by intelligence in conjunction with reason, for knowledge of this kind belongs to true beings; but the *huparxis* of the Gods rides on beings, and is defined according to the union itself of wholes. It remains, therefore, if it be admitted that a divine nature can be in any respect known, that it must be apprehended by the *huparxis* of the soul, and through this, as far as it is possible, be known. For we say that every where things similar can known by their similar; viz. the sensible by sense, the doxastics by opinion, the dianoetic by *dianoia*, and the intelligible by intellect. So that the most unical nature must be known by *The One*, and the ineffable by that which is ineffable.

Indeed, Socrates in the [*First*] *Alcibiades* rightly observes that the soul entering into herself will behold all other things, and deity itself. For verging to her own union, and to the center of all life, laying aside multitude, and the variety of the all-manifold powers which she contains, she ascends to the highest watchtower of beings. And as in the most holy of the mysteries, they say that the mystics at first meet with the multiform and many-shaped genera, which are hurled forth before the Gods, but on entering the interior parts of the temple, unmoved, and guarded by the mystic rites, they genuinely receive in their bosom divine illumination, and divested of their garments, as they would say, participate of a divine nature; the same mode, as it appears to me, takes place in the speculation of wholes. For the soul when looking at things posterior to herself, beholds the shadows and images of beings, but when she converts herself to herself she evolves her own essence, and the reasons which she contains. And at first indeed, she only as it were beholds herself; but, when she penetrates more profoundly into the knowledge of herself, she finds in herself both intellect, and the orders of beings. When however, she proceeds into her interior recesses, and into the adytum as it were of the soul, she perceives with her eye closed, the genus of the Gods, and the unities of beings. For all things are in us psychically, and through this we are naturally capable of knowing all things, by exciting the powers and the images of wholes which we contain.

And this is the best employment of our energy, to be extended to a divine nature itself, having our powers at rest, to revolve harmoniously round it, to excite all the multitude of the soul to this union, and laying aside all such things as are posterior to *The One*, to become seated and conjoined with that which is ineffable, and beyond all things. For it is lawful for the soul to ascend, till she terminates her flight in the principle of things; but arriving thither, beholding the place which is there, descending thence, and directing her course through beings; likewise, evolving the multitude of forms, exploring their monads and their numbers, and apprehending intellectually how each is suspended from its proper unity, then we may consider her as possessing the most perfect science of divine natures, perceiving in a uniform manner the progressions of the Gods into beings, and the distinctions of beings about the Gods. Such then according to Plato's decision is our theologist; and theology is a habit of this kind, which unfolds the *huparxis* itself of the Gods, separates and speculates their unknown and unical light from the peculiarity of their participants, and, announces it to such as are worthy of this energy, which is both blessed and comprehends all things at once.

I.4

After this all-perfect comprehension of the first theory, we must deliver the modes according to which Plato teaches us mystic conceptions of divine natures. For he appears not to have pursued every where the same mode of doctrine about these; but sometimes according to a deific energy, and at other times dialectically, he evolves the truth concerning them. And sometimes he symbolically announces their ineffable peculiarities, but at other times he recurs to them from images, and discovers in them the primary causes of wholes. For in the *Phaedrus* being inspired by the Nymphs, and having exchanged human intelligence for a better possession, fury, he unfolds with a divine mouth many arcane dogmas concerning the intellectual Gods, and many concerning the liberated rulers of the universe, who lead upwards the multitude of mundane Gods to the monads which are intelligible and separate from [mundane] wholes. But relating still more about those Gods who are allotted the world, he celebrates their intellections, and mundane fabrications, their unpolluted providence and government of souls, and whatever else Socrates delivers entheastically [or according to a divinely-inspired energy] in that dialogue, as he clearly asserts, ascribing at the same time this fury to the deities of the place.

But in the *Sophist*, dialectically contending about being, and the separate hypostasis of *The One* from beings, and doubting against those more ancient than himself, he shows how all beings are suspended from their cause, and the first being, but that being itself participates of the unity which is exempt from the whole of things, that it is a passive one, but not *The One* itself, being subject to and united to *The One*, but not being that which is primarily one. In a similar manner too, in the *Parmenides*, he unfolds dialectically the progressions of being from *The One*, and the transcendency of *The One*, through the first hypotheses, and this as he asserts in that dialogue, according to the most perfect division of this method. And again, in the *Gorgias*, he relates the fable concerning the three demiurgi [or fabricators] and their demiurgic allotment, which indeed is not only a fable, but a true narration. But in the *Banquet*, he speaks concerning the union of Love. And in the *Protagoras*, about the distribution of mortal animals from the Gods, in a symbolical manner concealing the truth respecting divine natures, and as far as to mere indication unfolding his mind to the most genuine of his hearers.

If likewise, you are willing that I should mention the doctrine delivered through the mathematical disciplines, and the discussion of divine concerns from ethical or physical discourses, of which many may be contemplated in the *Timaeus*, many in the dialogue called the *Politicus*, and many may be seen scattered in other dialogues; here likewise to you who are desirous of knowing divine concerns through images, the method will be apparent. For all these shadow forth the powers of things divine. The *Politicus*, for instance, the fabrication in the heavens. But the figures of the five elements delivered in geometrical proportions in the *Timaeus*, represent in images the peculiarities of the Gods who ride on the parts of the universe. And the divisions of the psychical essence in that dialogue shadow forth the total orders of the Gods.

I omit to mention that Plato composes polities, assimilating them to divine natures, and to the whole world, and adorns them from the powers which it contains. All these therefore, through the similitude of mortal to divine concerns, exhibit to us in images, the progressions, orders, and fabrications of divine natures. And such are the modes of theologic doctrine employed by Plato,

It is evident however, from what has been already said, that they are necessarily so many in number. For those who treat of divine concerns in an indicative manner, either speak symbolically and fabulously, or through images. But of those who openly announce their conceptions, some frame their discourses according to science, but others according to inspiration from the Gods. And he who desires to signify divine concerns through symbols is Orphic, and in short, accords with those who write fables concerning the Gods.[76] But he who does this through images is Pythagoric. For the mathematical disciplines were invented by the Pythagoreans, in order to a reminiscence of divine concerns, at which, through these as images they endeavor to arrive. For they refer both numbers and figures to the

76. Thomas Taylor anachronistically renders *muthoi* ("myths") as "fables." On the different modes of Neoplatonic theology and exegesis, see John Dillon, "Image, Symbol and Analogy: Three Basic Concepts of Neoplatonic Allegorical Exegesis," in *The Significance of Neoplatonism*, ed. R. Baine Harris (Old Dominion University, 1976), pp.247–262.

Gods, according to the testimony of their historians. But the entheastic character, or he who is under the influence of divine inspiration, unfolding the truth itself by itself concerning the Gods, most perspicuously ranks among the highest initiators. For these do not think proper to unfold the divine orders, or their peculiarities to their familiars, through certain veils, but announce their powers and their numbers, in consequence of being moved by the Gods themselves. But the tradition of divine concerns according to science, is the illustrious prerogative of the philosophy of Plato. For Plato alone, as it appears to me, of all those who are known to us, has attempted methodically to divide and reduce into order, the regular progression of the divine genera, their mutual difference, the common peculiarities of the total orders, and the distributed peculiarities in each. But the truth of this will be evident when we frame preliminary demonstrations about the *Parmenides*, and all the divisions which it contains.

At present we shall observe that Plato does not admit all the fabulous figments of dramatic composition, but those only which have reference to the beautiful and the good, and which are not discordant with a divine essence. For that mythological mode which indicates divine concerns through conjecture is ancient, concealing truth under a multitude of veils, and proceeding in a manner similar to nature, which extends sensible figments of intelligibles, material, of immaterial, partible, of impartible natures and images, and things which have a false being, of things perfectly true. But Plato rejects the more tragical mode of mythologizing of the ancient poets, who thought proper to establish an arcane theology respecting the Gods, and on this account devised wanderings, sections, battles, lacerations, rapes and adulteries of the Gods,[77] and many other such symbols of the truth about divine natures, which this theology conceals; this mode he rejects, and asserts that it is in every respect most foreign from erudition. But he considers those mythological discourses about the Gods, as more persuasive, and more adapted to truth and the philosophic habit, which assert that a divine nature is the cause of all good, but of no evil, and that it is void of all mutation, ever preserving its own order immutable, and comprehending

---

77. On Proclus' theory of Homeric and Platonic myths see Robert Lamberton, *Homer the Theologian: Neoplatonist Allegorical Reading and the Growth of the Epic Tradition* (California: University of California Press, 1986).

in itself the fountain of truth, but never becoming the cause of any deception to others. For such types of theology, Socrates delivers in the *Republic*.

All the fables therefore of Plato, guarding the truth in concealment, have not even their externally apparent apparatus discordant with our undisciplined and unperverted anticipation respecting the Gods. But they bring with them an image of the mundane composition, in which both—the apparent beauty is worthy of divinity, and a beauty more divine than this, is established in the unapparent lives and powers of the Gods. This, therefore, is one of the mythological modes respecting divine concerns, which from the apparently unlawful, irrational, and, inordinate, passes into order and bound, and regards as its scope the composition of the beautiful and good.

But there is another mode which he delivers in the *Phaedrus*. And this consists in every where preserving theological fables, unmixed with physical narrations, and being careful in no respect to confound or exchange theology, and the physical theory with each other. For, as a divine essence is separate from the whole of nature, in like manner, it is perfectly proper that discourses respecting the Gods should be pure from physical disquisitions. For a mixture of this kind is, says he, laborious: and to make physical passions the end of mythological conjecture, is the employment of no very good man; such for instance, as considering through his [pretended] wisdom, Chimaera, Gorgon, and things of a similar kind, as the same with physical figments. Socrates, in the *Phaedrus*, reprobating this mode of mythologizing, represents its patrons as saying under the figure of a fable, that Orithya sporting with the wind Boreas and being thrown down the rocks, means nothing more than that Orithya, who was a mortal, was ravished by Boreas through love. For it appears to me that fabulous narrations about the gods should always have their concealed meaning more venerable than the apparent. So that if certain persons introduce to us physical hypotheses of Platonic fables, and such as are conversant with sublunary affairs, we must say that they entirely wander from the intention of the philosopher, and that those hypotheses alone, are interpreters of the truth contained in these fables, which have for their scope a divine, immaterial, and separate hypostasis, and which looking to this, make the compositions and analyses of the fables, adapted to our inherent anticipations of divine concerns.

I.5

As we have therefore enumerated all these modes of the Platonic theology, and have shown what compositions and analyses of fable are adapted to the truth respecting the Gods, let us consider, in the next place, whence, and from what dialogues principally, we think the dogmas of Plato concerning the Gods may be collected, and by a speculation of what types or forms we may be able to distinguish his genuine writings, from those spurious compositions which are ascribed to him.

The truth then concerning the Gods pervades, as I may say, through all the Platonic dialogues, and in all of them conceptions of the first philosophy, venerable, clear, and supernatural, are disseminated, in some indeed, more obscurely, but in others more conspicuously; conceptions which excite those that are in any respect able to participate of them, to the immaterial and separate essence of the Gods. And, as in each part of the universe, and in nature herself, the demiurgus of all that the world contains, established resemblances of the unknown *huparxis* of the Gods, that all things might be converted to a divine nature, through their alliance with it, in like manner I am of opinion, that the divine intellect of Plato weaves conceptions about the Gods in all his writings, and leaves nothing deprived of the mention of divinity, that from the whole of them, a reminiscence of wholes may be obtained, and imparted to the genuine lovers of divine concerns.

If however, it be requisite to lay before the reader those dialogues out of many, which principally unfold to us the mystic discipline about the gods, I should not err in ranking among this number, the *Phaedo* and the *Phaedrus*, the *Banquet*, and the *Philebus*, and together with these, the *Sophist* and *Politicus*, the *Cratylus* and the *Timaeus*. For all these are full through the whole of themselves, as I may say, of the divine science of Plato. But I should place in the second rank after these, the fable in the *Gorgias*, and that in the *Protagoras*; likewise the assertions about the providence of the Gods in the *Laws* and, such things as are delivered about the Fates, or the mother of the Fates, or the circulations of the universe in the tenth book of the *Republic*. Again, you may, if you please, place in the third rank those Epistles, through which we may be able to arrive at the science about divine natures. For in these, mention is made of the three kings; and very many other divine dogmas worthy of the

Platonic theory are delivered. It is necessary therefore, looking to these, to explore in these each order of the Gods.

Thus from the *Philebus*, we may receive the science respecting the one good, and the two first principles of things, together with the triad which is unfolded into light from these. For you will find all these distinctly delivered to us by Plato in that dialogue. But from the *Timaeus*, you may obtain the theory about intelligibles, a divine narration about the demiurgic monad: and the most full truth about the mundane Gods. But from the *Phaedrus*, [you may acquire a scientific knowledge of] all the intelligible and intellectual genera, and of the liberated orders of Gods, which are proximately established above the celestial circulations. From the *Politicus*, you may obtain the theory of the fabrication in the heavens, of the uneven periods of the universe, and the intellectual causes of those periods. But from the *Sophist*, the whole sublunary generation, and the peculiarity of the Gods who are allotted the sublunary region, and preside over its generations and corruptions. But with respect to each of the Gods, we may obtain many conceptions adapted to sacred concerns from the *Banquet*, many from the *Cratylus*, and many from the *Phaedo*. For in each of these dialogues, more or less mention is made of divine names, from which it is easy for those who are exercised in divine concerns to discover by a reasoning process the peculiarities of each.

It is necessary however, to evince that each of the dogmas accords with Platonic principles, and the mystic traditions of theologists. For all the Grecian theology is the progeny of the mystic tradition of Orpheus; Pythagoras first of all learning from Aglaophemus the orgies of the Gods, but Plato in the second place receiving an all-perfect science of the divinities from the Pythagoric and Orphic writings. For in the *Philebus* referring the theory about the two species of principles [bound and infinity] to the Pythagoreans, he calls them men dwelling with the Gods, and truly blessed. Philolaus therefore, the Pythagorean, has left us in writing many admirable conceptions about these principles, celebrating their common progression into beings, and their separate fabrication of things. But in the *Timaeus*, Plato endeavoring to teach us about the sublunary Gods, and their order, flies to theologists, calls them the sons of the Gods, and makes them the fathers of the truth about those divinities. And lastly, he delivers the orders of the sublunary Gods proceeding from wholes, according to the progression delivered by them of the intellectual kings. Again, in the *Cratylus* he follows the traditions of theologists, respecting the order of the divine processions. But in the *Gorgias,* he adopts the Homeric dogma, respecting the triadic hypostasis of the demiurgi. And in short, he every where discourses concerning the Gods agreeably to the principles of theologists; rejecting indeed, the tragical part of mythological fiction, but establishing first hypotheses in common with the authors of fables.

11. Proclus
Commentary on the Timaeus of Plato

Proclus' *Commentary on the Timaeus of Plato* (*Eis ton Platonos Timaion*) is a profound and extensive interpretation of Platonic, or rather, Pythagorean cosmogony and cosmology, including views on the World Soul and heavenly bodies. According to Marinus, this commentary was produced by Proclus in a very short length of time, when (at the age of 28) he still studied with his master Syrianus.

In the Neoplatonic curriculum, physics was first taught at the Aristotelian level and later at the more advanced level of Plato's *Timaeus.* Two dialogues, the *Timaeus* and the *Parmenides,* were regarded as being at the summit of all Neoplatonic studies, and as the source of their entire theology, metaphysics, and cosmology. The whole of philosophy, according to Proclus, was divided into theory about the intelligible and sensible realities: the one was grasped by intellect (*noetos*), the other by the senses (*aisthetos*). The *Parmenides* summarized inquiry into intelligibles; and the *Timaeus* inquiry into the sensible cosmos. Proclus agreed with the "divine" Iamblichus that the whole of Plato's theory (and consequently, the whole of Neoplatonic theory) could be deduced from the *Timaeus* and the *Parmenides.*

The *Commentary on the Timaeus of Plato in Five Books* was translated by Thomas Taylor and first published in 1820.

In Tim. I.1.1–1.8

That the design of the Platonic *Timaeus* embraces the whole of physiology, and that it pertains to the theory of the universe, discussing this from the beginning to the end, appears to me to be clearly evident to those who are not entirely illiterate. For this very treatise of the Pythagoric *Timaeus Concerning Nature,* is written after the

Pythagoric manner; and Plato being thence impelled, applied himself to write the *Timaeus*, according to Sillographus.[78] On this account we have prefixed the treatise of *Timaeus* to these Commentaries, in order that we may know what the *Timaeus* of Plato says that is the same with what is asserted in the treatise of *Timaeus* [the Locrian],[79] what it adds, and in what it dissents. And that we may investigate not in a careless manner the cause of this disagreement. All this dialogue, likewise, through the whole of itself, has physiology for its scope, surveying the same things in images and in paradigms, in wholes and in parts. For it is filled with all the most beautiful boundaries of physiology, assuming things simple for the sake of such as are composite, parts for the sake of wholes, and images for the sake of paradigms, leaving none of the principal causes of nature uninvestigated.

But that the dialogue deservedly embraces a design of this kind, and that Plato alone preserving the Pythagoric mode in the theory concerning nature, has prosecuted with great subtlety the proposed doctrine, ought to be considered by those who are more sagacious and acute. For since, in short, physiology receives a threefold division, and one part of it is conversant with matter and material causes, but another part also adds the investigation of form, and evinces that this is the more principal cause; and again, since a third part demonstrates that these have not the relation of causes, but of con-causes, and admits that there are other causes, which are properly so called, of things generated by nature, viz. the effective, paradigmatic and final cause; this being the case, among the multitude of physiologists prior to Plato, that directed their attention to matter, there was a diversity of opinion respecting the subject of things. For Anaxagoras, who appears to have seen, while the rest were asleep, that intellect is the first cause of generated natures,[80] made no use of intellect in his explanation of things, but rather employed certain airs and ethers as the causes of things that are generated, as Socrates says in the *Phaedo*[81] But of those posterior to Plato, who were the patrons of a sect, not all, but such of them as were more accurate than the rest,[82] thought fit to survey physical form in conjunction

---

78. Timon, who was called Sillographus from writing scurrilous comic poems.

79. This treatise, attributed to Timaeus of Locri (see *On the World and the Soul* in the present anthology) has been transmitted to us through Proclus.

with matter, referring the principles of bodies to matter and form. For if they any where mention the producing cause, as when they say that nature is a principle of motion,[83] they rather take away its efficacious and properly effective power [than allow the existence of it] by not granting that it contains the reasons [or productive principles] of the things effected by it, but admitting that many things are generated causally. To which we may add, that they do not acknowledge that there is a pre-existing producing cause of, in short, all physical things, but of those only that are borne along in generation. For of eternal natures they[84] clearly say that there is no effective cause; in asserting which they are ignorant that they must either give subsistence to the whole of heaven from chance, or evince that what is causal is itself productive of itself.

Plato however alone, following the Pythagoreans, delivers indeed, as the concauses of natural things, a universal recipient, and material form,[85] which are subservient to causes properly so called in the generation of things.[86] But prior to these, he investigates principal causes, viz. the producing cause, the paradigm, and the final cause. Hence also, he places a demiurgic intellect over the universe, and an intelligible cause in which the universe primarily subsists, and *The Good*, which is established prior to the producing cause, in the order of the desirable. For since that which is moved by another thing, is suspended from the power of that which moves, as it is evidently not adapted either to produce, or perfect, or save itself, in all these it is in want of a producing cause, and is conducted by it. It is fit, therefore, that the concauses of natural things should be suspended from true causes, from which they are produced, with a view to which they are fabricated by the father of all things, and for the sake of which they were generated; justly, therefore, are all these delivered, and investigated with accuracy by Plato; and the remaining two, form and the subject-matter, suspended

80. Cf. Plato, *Republic* III.390b12.
81. Cf. Plato, *Phaedo* 98c.
82. Aristotle and his followers.
83. Cf. Aristotle, *Physics* II.192b13.
84. The Epicureans.
85. Cf. Plato, *Timaeus* 51a.
86. Cf. Plato, *Philebus* 27a.

from these. For this world is not the same with the intelligible or intellectual worlds, which, according to some, subsist in pure forms; but one thing in it has the relation of reason and form, and another, of a subject. But that Plato very properly delivers all these causes of the fabrication of the world, viz. *The Good*, the intelligible paradigm, the maker, form, and the subject nature, is evident from the following considerations. For if he had spoken concerning the intelligible Gods, he would have evinced that *The Good* alone is the causes of these; for the intelligible number is from this cause. But if concerning the intellectual Gods, he would have shown that *The Good* and the intelligible are the causes of these. For the intellectual multitude proceeds from the intelligible unities, and the one fountain of beings. And if he had spoken concerning the supermundane Gods, he would have produced them from the intellectual and total fabrication, from the intelligible Gods, and from the cause of all things. For this cause gives subsistence to all things of which secondary natures are generative, but in a primary, ineffable, and inconceivable manner. But since he discusses mundane affairs and the whole world, he gives to it matter and form, descending into it from the supermundane Gods, suspends it from the total fabrication, assimilates it to intelligible animals, and demonstrates it to be a God by the participation of *The Good*; and thus he renders the whole world an intellectual, animated God.[87] This, therefore, and such as this, is, as we have said, the scope of the *Timaeus*.

This however being the case, the order of the universe is appropriately indicated in the beginning of the dialogue, through images; but in the middle of it, the whole fabrication of the world is delivered; and in the end, partial natures, and the extremities of fabrication, are woven together with wholes. For the resumption of the discourse about a polity, and the narration respecting the Atlantic island, unfold through images the theory of the world. For if we direct our attention to the union and multitude of mundane natures, we must say that the polity which Socrates summarily discusses, is an image of their union, establishing as its end the communion which pervades through all things; but that the war of the Atlantics with the Athenians, which Critias narrates, is an image of

87. Cf. Plato, *Timaeus* 30b and 34b.

the division of mundane natures, and especially of the opposition according to the two co-ordinations of things.[88] But if we divide the universe into the celestial and sublunary regions, we must say that the [Socratic] polity is assimilated to the celestial order; for Socrates says that the paradigm of it is established in the heavens;[89] but the war of the Atlantics, to generation, which subsists through contrariety and mutation. These things therefore, for the reasons we have mentioned, precede the whole of physiology.

But after this, the demiurgic, paradigmatic and final causes of the universe are unfolded in consequence of the pre-existence of which, the universe is fabricated both according to the whole and the parts of it. For the corporeal nature of it is fashioned with forms, and divided by divine numbers; soul also is produced from the Demiurgus, and is filled with harmonic reasons, and divine and demiurgic symbols;[90] and the whole animal is woven together conformably to the united comprehension of it in the intelligible world. The parts likewise of it, are arranged in a becoming manner in the whole, both such as are corporeal and such as are vital. For partial souls being introduced into the world, are arranged about their leading Gods, and through their vehicles become mundane,[91] imitating their presiding deities. Mortal animals likewise, are fabricated and vivified by the celestial Gods; where also man is surveyed, and the mode of his subsistence, and through what causes he was constituted. Man indeed is considered prior to other things, either because the theory respecting him pertains to us who make him the subject of discussion, and are ourselves men; or because man is a microcosm,[92] and all such things subsist in him partially, as the world contains divinely and totally. For there is an intellect in us which is in energy, and a rational soul proceeding from the same father, and the same vivific Goddess, as the soul of the universe;[93]

---

88. The Limit (*peras*) and the Unlimited (*apeiron*) are the two most basic and universal principles of Pythagorean cosmology. The cosmos is compounded of elements, summarized in the Table of Opposites, preserved by Aristotle in his *Metaphysics*: Limit–Unlimited; Odd–Even; One–Plurality; Right–Left; Male–Female; Rest–Moving; Straight–Crooked; Light–Darkness; Good–Bad; Square–Oblong.

89. Cf. Plato, *Republic* IX.592b.

90. *Chaldean Oracles* fr.108.

91. *Chaldean Oracles* fr.40.

92. Cf. Plato, *Philebus* 29a.

93. *Chaldean Oracles* fr.36.

also an etherial vehicle analogous to the heavens, and a terrestrial body derived from the four elements,[94] and with which likewise it is co-ordinate. If therefore, it is necessary that the universe should be surveyed multifariously, in the intelligible, and in the sensible world, paradigmatically, iconically, totally and partially, it will be well, if the nature of man is perfectly discussed in the theory of the universe.

You may also say that conformably to the Pythagoric custom, it is necessary to connect the discussion of that which surveys with that which is surveyed. For since we are informed what the world is, it is requisite I think to add also, what that is which considers these things, and makes them the subject of rational animadversion. But that Plato directs his attention likewise to this, is evident from what he says near the end of the dialogue,[95] that it is necessary that the intellect of him who intends to obtain a happy life, should be assimilated to the object of his intellection. For the universe is always happy; and our soul will likewise be happy, when it is assimilated to the universe; for thus it will be led back to its cause. For as the sensible man is to the universe, so is the intelligible man to animal itself. But there secondary natures always adhere to such as are first, and parts subsist in unproceeding union with their wholes, and are established in them. Hence, when the sensible man is assimilated to the universe, he also imitates his paradigm after an appropriate manner, becoming a world through similitude to the world, and happy through resemblance to that blessed god [the universe.] The ends also of fabrication are subtly elaborated by Plato, according to genus and species, and also what pertains to meteors, together with productions in the earth, and in animals, such things as are preternatural, and such as are according to nature; in which part of the *Timaeus*, likewise, the principles of medicine are unfolded. For the physiologist ends at these; since he is a surveyor of nature. For a subsistence according to nature, exists together with nature; but the preternatural is a departure from nature. It is the business, therefore, of the physiologist to understand in how many modes this aberration subsists, and how it becomes terminated in moderation and a natural condition. But it is the province of the medical art to

94. Cf. Plato, *Timaeus* 73e.
95. Cf. Plato, *Timaeus* 90d.

unfold such particulars as are consequent to these. And in these things especially, Plato has something in common with other physiologists. For they were conversant with the most material, and the ultimate works of nature, neglecting the whole heaven, and the orders of the mundane Gods, in consequence of directing their attention to matter; but they bade farewell to forms and primary causes.

It also appears to me that the daemoniacal Aristotle, emulating as much as possible the doctrine of Plato, thus arranges the whole of his discussion concerning nature, perceiving that the things which are common to every thing that has a natural subsistence are, form and a subject, that from whence the principle of motion is derived, motion, time, and place; all which are delivered by Plato in this dialogue, viz. interval, and time which is the image of eternity, and is consubsistent with the universe; the various species of motion; and the concauses of things which have a natural subsistence. But with respect to the things peculiar to substances according to an essential division, of these Aristotle discusses in the first place such as pertain to the heavens, in a way conformably to Plato;[96] so far as he calls the heaven unbegotten, and a fifth essence. For what difference is there between calling it a fifth element, or a fifth world, and a fifth figure, as Plato denominates it?[97] But in the second place, he discusses such things as are common to every thing that has a generated subsistence. And with respect to things of this kind, Plato deserves to be admired, for having surveyed with much accuracy the essence and powers of them, and for having rightly preserved their harmony and contrarieties. And of these, such indeed as pertain to meteors, Plato has delivered the principles, but Aristotle has extended the doctrine respecting them beyond what is fit. But such as pertain to the theory of animals, are distinguished by Plato according to all final causes and concauses, but by Aristotle are scarcely, and but in few instances, surveyed according to form. For his discussion for the most part stops at matter; and making his exposition of things that have a natural subsistence from this, he shows to us that he deserts the doctrine of his preceptor. And thus much concerning these particulars.

In the next place it is requisite to speak of the form and character of the dialogue, and to show what they are. It is universally

96. Aristotle, *De Caelo* I.3.270b22.
97. Cf. Plato, *Timaeus* 55c.

acknowledged, then, that Plato receiving the treatise of the Pythagoric Timaeus, which was composed by him after the Pythagoric manner, began to write his *Timaeus*. Again, it is also acknowledged by those who are in the smallest degree conversant with the writings of Plato, that his manner is Socratic, philanthropic, and demonstrative. If, therefore, he has any where mingled the Pythagoric and Socratic peculiarity, he appears to have done this in the present dialogue. For there are in it from the Pythagoric custom, elevation of conception, the intellectual, the divinely inspired, the suspending every thing from intelligibles, the bounding wholes in numbers, the indicating things mystically and symbolically, the anagogic, the transcending partial conceptions, and the enunciative or unfolding into light. But from the Socratic philanthropy, the sociable, the mild, the demonstrative, the contemplating beings through images, the ethical, and every thing of this kind. Hence it is a venerable dialogue; forms its conceptions supernally from the first principles; and mingles the demonstrative with the enunciative. It also prepares us to understand physics, not only physically, but likewise theologically. For Nature herself who is the leader of the universe, being suspended from, and inspired by the Gods, governs the corporeal-formed essence. And she neither ranks as a Goddess, nor is without a divine peculiarity, but is illuminated by the truly-existing Gods.

If, likewise, it be requisite that discourses should be assimilated to the things of which they are the interpreters, as Timaeus himself says,[98] it will be fit that this dialogue also should have the physical, and should also have the theological; imitating nature, which is the object of its contemplation. Farther still, according to the Pythagoric doctrine, things receive a threefold division into intelligibles, things physical, and such as are the media between these, and which are usually called mathematical. But all things may be appropriately surveyed in all. For such things as are media, and such as are last, pre-subsist in intelligibles after a primordial manner, and both these subsist in the mathematical genera; first natures indeed iconically, but such as rank as the third, paradigmatically. In physical entities, also, there are images of the essences prior to

---

98. Cf. Plato, *Timaeus* 29b.

them. This, therefore, being the case, Timaeus, when he constitutes the soul, very properly indicates its powers, its productive principles, and its elements through mathematical names. But Plato defines its peculiarities by geometrical figures, and leaves the causes of all these primordially pre-existing in the intelligible and demiurgic intellect.

I.1.11–1.14

Nature, therefore, is the last of the causes which fabricate this corporeal-formed and sensible essence. She is also the boundary of the extent of incorporeal essences, and is full of reasons and powers through which she directs and governs mundane beings. And she is a Goddess indeed, in consequence of being deified, but she has not immediately the subsistence of a deity. For we call divine bodies Gods, as being statues of Gods. But she governs the whole world by her powers, containing the heavens indeed in the summit of herself, but ruling over generation through the heavens; and every where weaving together partial natures with wholes. Being however such, she proceeds from the vivific Goddess [Rhea.] [For according to the Chaldean oracle] "Immense Nature is suspended from the back of the Goddess";[99] from whom all life is derived, both that which is intellectual, and that which is inseparable from the subjects of its government. Hence, being suspended from thence, she pervades without impediment through, and inspires all things; so that through her, the most inanimate beings participate of a certain soul, and such things as are corruptible, remain perpetually in the world, being held together by the causes of forms which she contains. For again the Oracle says, "Unwearied Nature rules over the worlds and works, and draws downward, that Heaven may run an eternal course," &c.[100] So that if some one of those who assert that there are three demiurgi, is willing to refer them to these principles, viz. to the demiurgic intellect, to soul, and to total nature [or to nature considered as a whole] he will speak rightly, through the causes which have been already enumerated.[101] But he will speak erroneously, if he supposes that there are three other demiurgi of

99. *Chaldean Oracles* fr.54.
100. *Chaldean Oracles* fr.70.
101. Proclus, *Theology of Plato* V.14.

the universe, beyond soul. For the Demiurgus of wholes is one, but more partial powers distribute his whole fabrication into parts. We must not therefore admit such an assertion, whether it be Amelius or Theodorus [Asineus][102] who wishes to make this arrangement; but we must be careful to remain in Platonic and Orphic hypotheses.

Moreover, those who call nature demiurgic art, if indeed they mean the nature which abides in the Demiurgus, they do not speak rightly; but their assertion is right, if they mean the nature which proceeds from him. *For we must conceive that art is triple, one kind subsisting in the artist, in unproceeding union; another, proceeding indeed, but being converted to him; and a third being that which has now proceeded from the artist, and subsists in another thing.* The art therefore, which is in the Demiurgus, abides in him, and is himself, according to which the sensible world is denominated the work of the artificer, and the work of the artificer of the fiery world.[103] But the intellectual soul is art indeed, yet art which at the same time both abides and proceeds. And nature is art which proceeds alone; on which account also it is said to be the organ of the Gods, not destitute of life, nor alone alter-motive, but having in a certain respect the self-motive, through the ability of energizing from itself. For the organs of the Gods are essentialized in efficacious reasons, are vital, and concur with the energies of the Gods.

As we have therefore shown what nature is according to Plato, that it is an incorporeal essence, inseparable from bodies, containing the reasons or productive principles of them, and incapable of perceiving itself, and as it is evident from these things that the dialogue is physical, which teaches us concerning the whole mundane fabrication,—it remains that we should connect what is consequent with what has been said. For since the whole of philosophy is divided into the theory concerning intelligible[104] and mundane natures, and this very properly, because there is also a twofold world, the intelligible and the sensible, as Plato himself says in the course of the dialogue,[105]—this being the case, the *Parmenides* comprehends the discussion of intelligibles, but the *Timaeus* that of mundane

102. Cf. Plato, *Timaeus* 42d.
103. *Chaldean Oracles* fr.32.
104. Cf. Proclus, *In Parm.* 641.16ff.
105. Plato, *Parmenides* 30c.

natures. For the former delivers to us all the divine orders, but the latter all the progressions of mundane essences. But neither does the former entirely omit the theory of the natures contained in the universe, nor the latter the theory of intelligibles; because sensibles are in intelligibles paradigmatically, and intelligibles in sensibles iconically. But the one is exuberant about that which is physical, and the other about that which is theological, in a manner appropriate to the men from whom the dialogues are denominated: to Timaeus, for he wrote a treatise of this kind about the universe; and to Parmenides, for he wrote about truly-existing beings. The divine Iamblichus, therefore, says rightly that the whole theory of Plato is comprehended in these two dialogues, the *Timaeus* and *Parmenides*. For every thing pertaining to mundane and supermundane natures, obtains its most excellent end in these, and no order of beings is left uninvestigated. To those also who do not carelessly inspect these dialogues, the similitude of discussion in the *Timaeus* to that in the *Parmenides*, will be apparent. For as Timaeus refers the cause of every thing in the world to the first Demiurgus, so Parmenides suspends the progression of all beings from *The One*. And this is effected by the former, so far as all things participate of the demiurgic providence; but by the latter, so far as beings participate of a uniform *huparxis*, [or of an *huparxis* which has the form of *The One*.] Farther still, as Timaeus, prior to physiology, extends through images the theory of mundane natures, so Parmenides excites the investigation of immaterial forms, prior to theology. For it is requisite after having been exercised in discussions about the best polity, to be led to the knowledge of the universe; and after having contended with strenuous doubts about forms, to be sent to the mystic theory of the unities [of beings].

I.1.30

[*Tim.* 17bc] SOCRATES: Let it be so. And to begin: the sum of what was said by me yesterday is this: what kind of polity appeared to me to be the best, and of what sort of men such a polity ought to consist.

Some, considering the resumption of a polity from a more ethical point of view, say that it indicates to us that those who apply themselves to the theory of wholes, ought to be adorned in their manners. But others think that it is placed before us as an image of the orderly distribution of the universe. And others, as an indication of the whole of theology. *For it was usual with the Pythagoreans, prior to scientific doctrine, to render manifest the proposed objects of enquiry, through similitudes and images; and after this, to introduce through symbols the arcane indication respecting them.*[106] For thus, after the excitation of the intellection of the soul, and the purification of its eye, it is requisite to introduce the whole science of the things which are the subjects of discussion. Here, therefore, the concise narration of a polity, prior to physiology, iconically places us in the fabrication of the universe; but the history of the Atlantics accomplishes this symbolically. For it is usual with fables to indicate many things through symbols. So that the physiologic character pervades through the whole of the dialogue; but differently in different places, according to the different modes of the doctrine which is delivered. And thus much concerning the scope of the proposed words.

That in the present discussion, however, the summary repetition of a polity very properly takes place, may be multifariously inferred. For the political science subsists primarily in the Demiurgus of the universe, as we may learn in the *Protagoras*.[107] And true virtue shines forth in this sensible world. Hence also Timaeus says that the world is known and is friendly to itself through virtue.[108]

I.1.33–1.34

The discourse about a polity, and the conglomerated and concise repetition, in a summary way, of the genera contained in it, contributes to the whole narration of the mundane fabrication. For it is possible from these as images to recur to wholes. This very thing also was in a remarkable degree adopted by the Pythagoreans, who investigated the similitudes of beings from analogies, and betook themselves from images to paradigms; which likewise is now in a prefatory manner effected by Plato, who points out to us, and gives us to survey in human lives those things which take place in the universe. For the polities of worthy men are assimilated to the celestial

106. Cf. Iamblichus, *On the Pythagorean Life* 66.
107. Plato, *Protagoras* 31d.
108. Plato, *Timaeus* 34b.

order. It is necessary, therefore, that we also should refer the images which are now mentioned [to their paradigms], and in the first place, what is said about the division of the genera. For this section of genera imitates the demiurgic division in the world, according to which incorporeal natures are not able to pass into the nature of bodies, nor mortal bodies to leave their own essence, and migrate into an incorporeal hypostasis. According to which, also, mortal natures remain mortal; immortal natures eternally continue to be never-failing; and the different orders of them have paradigmatic causes pre-subsisting in wholes. For if you are willing to arrange the whole city analogous to the whole world; since it must not be said that man is a microcosm, and a city not; and to divide it into two parts, the upper city and the lower, and to assimilate the former to the heavens, and the latter to generation, you will find that the analogy is perfectly appropriate. Likewise, according to a division of it into three parts, you may assume in the city, the mercenary, the military, and the guardian: but in the soul, the epithymetic (bestial) part, which procures the necessities of the body; the irascible part, whose office is to expel whatever is injurious to the animal, and is also ministrant to our ruling power; and the rational part, which is essentially philosophic and has a regal authority over the whole of our life.

II.1.210–1.214

All things therefore, both abide in, and convert themselves to the Gods, receiving this power from the divinities, together with twofold impressions according to essence; the one, that they may abide there, but the other that, having proceeded, they may convert themselves [to their causes]. And these things we may survey not only in souls, but also in inanimate natures. For what else ingenerates in these a sympathy with other powers, but the symbols which they are allotted by nature, some of which are allied to *this*, but others to *that* series of Gods? For nature being supernally suspended from the Gods, and distributed from their orders, inserts also in bodies impressions of their alliance to the divinities. In some indeed, inserting solar, but in others lunar impressions, and in others again, the symbol of some other God. And these indeed, convert themselves to the Gods; some, as to the Gods simply, but others as to particular Gods; nature thus perfecting her progeny according to different peculiarities of the divinities. The Demiurgus of the universe therefore, by a much greater priority, impressed these symbols in souls, by which they might be able to abide in themselves, and again convert themselves to the sources of their being. And through the symbol of unity indeed he conferred on them stability; but through intellect, he imparted to them the power of conversion.

But to this conversion prayer is of the greatest utility. For it attracts to itself the beneficence of the Gods, through those ineffable symbols which the father of souls has disseminated in them.[109] It likewise unites those who pray with those to whom prayer is addressed; conjoins the intellect of the Gods with the words of those who pray; excites the will of those who perfectly comprehend good to the abundant communication of it; is the fabricator of divine persuasion; and establishes in the Gods all that we possess.

To a perfect and true prayer however, there is required in the first place, a knowledge of all the divine orders to which he who prays approaches. For no one will accede to the Gods in a proper manner, unless he has a knowledge of their peculiarities. Hence also the oracle admonishes, *that a fire-heated conception has the first order in sacred worship.*[110] But in the second place, there is required a conformation of our life with that which is divine; and this accompanied with all purity, chastity, discipline, and order, through which our concerns being introduced to the Gods, we shall attract their beneficence, and our souls will become subject to them. In the third place, contact is necessary, according to which we touch the divine essence with the summit of our soul, and verge to a union with it. But there is yet farther required, an approximating adhesion: for thus the oracle calls it, when he says, *the mortal approximating to fire will possess a light from the Gods.*[111] For this imparts to us a greater communion with, and a more manifest participation of the light of the Gods. In the last place, union succeeds establishing *the one* of the soul in *The One* of the Gods, and causing our energy to become one with divine energy; according to which we are no longer ourselves, but are absorbed as it were in the Gods, abiding in divine light, and circularly comprehended by it. And this is the best end of true prayer, in order that the conversion of the soul may be conjoined

109. *Chaldean Oracles* fr.95.
110. *Chaldean Oracles* fr.139.
111. *Chaldean Oracles* fr.121; 126.

with its permanency, and that every thing which proceeds from *The One* of the Gods may again be established in *The One*, and the light which is in us may be comprehended in the light of the Gods.

Prayer therefore, is no small part of the whole ascent of souls. Nor is he who possesses virtue superior to the want of the good which proceeds from prayer; but on the contrary the ascent of the soul is effected through it, and together with this, piety to the Gods, which is the summit of virtue. *Nor in short, ought any other to pray than he who is transcendently good, as the Athenian guest [in Plato] says. For to such a one, converse with the Gods becomes most efficacious to the attainment of a happy life.* But the contrary is naturally adapted to befall the vicious.[112] For it is not lawful for the pure to be touched by the impure.[113] Hence, it is necessary that he who generously enters on the exercise of prayer, should render the Gods propitious to him, and should excite in himself conceptions full of intellectual light. For the favor and benignity of more exalted beings is the most effectual incentive to their communication with our natures. And it is requisite to continue without intermission in the worship of divinity. For [according to the oracle] the rapid[114] Gods perfect the mortal constantly employed in prayer. It is also necessary to observe a stable order in the performance of divine works; to exert those virtues which purify and elevate the soul from generation, together with faith, truth, and love;[115] to preserve this triad and hope of good, this immutable reception of divine light, and segregation from every other pursuit, that thus becoming *alone*, we may associate with solitary *deity*,[116] and not endeavor to conjoin ourselves with multitude to *The One*. For he who attempts this, effects the very contrary, and separates himself from the Gods. For as it is not lawful in conjunction with non-entity to associate with being; so neither is it possible with multitude to be conjoined with *The One*. Such therefore are the particulars which ought first to be known concerning prayer; viz. that the essence of it congregates and binds souls to the Gods, or rather, that it unites all secondary to primary natures. For as the great Theodorus says, all things pray except the first.

112. Cf. Plato, *Laws* IV.716d.
113. Cf. Plato, *Phaedo* 67b.
114. The noetic, or intelligible, gods.
115. *Chaldean Oracles* fr.140.
116. *Chaldean Oracles* fr.46.

The perfection however of prayer, beginning from more common goods, ends in divine union, and gradually accustoms the soul to divine light. But its efficacious energy both replenishes us with good, and causes our concerns to be common with those of the Gods. With respect to the causes of prayer too, we may infer, that so far as they are *effective*, they are the efficacious powers of the Gods, converting and calling upwards the soul to the Gods themselves. But that so far as they are final or *perfective*, they are the immaculate goods of the soul, which they derive as the fruits of being established in the Gods. That so far also as they are *paradigmatical*, they are the primordial causes of beings, which proceed from *The Good*, and are united to it, according to one ineffable union. But that so far as they are *formal*, they assimilate souls to the Gods, and give perfection to the whole of their life. And that so far as they are material, they are the impressions or symbols inserted by the Demiurgus in the essences of souls, in order that they may be excited to a reminiscence of the Gods who produced them, and whatever else exists.

Moreover, we may likewise define the modes of prayer which are various, according to the genera and species of the Gods. For prayer is either demiurgic, or cathartic, or vivific. And the *demiurgic* is such as that which is offered for the sake of showers and winds. For the demiurgi are the causes of the generation of these. And the prayers of the Athenians for winds procuring serenity of weather are addressed to these Gods. But the *cathartic* prayer is that which is offered for the purpose of averting diseases originating from pestilence, and other contagious distempers, such as we have written in our temples. And the *vivific* prayer is that with which we worship the Gods, who are the causes of vivification, on account of the origin and maturity of fruits. Hence prayers are of a perfective nature, because they elevate us to these orders of the Gods. And he who considers such prayers in a different manner, fails in properly apprehending the nature and efficacy of prayer. But again, with reference to the things for which we pray: those prayers, which regard the salvation of the soul, obtain the first place; those which pertain to the good temperament of the body, the second; and those rank in the third place, which are offered for the sake of external concerns. And lastly, with respect to the division of the times in which we offer up prayers, it is either according to the seasons of the year, or the centers of the solar revolution; or we establish multiform prayers according to other such-like conceptions.

III.2.24–2.28

Let us, therefore, if you think fit, discuss the theory of the proposed words physically. The first analogy then, according to which nature inserts harmony in her works, and according to which the Demiurgus adorns and arranges the universe, is one certain life, and one reason, proceeding through all things; which first, indeed, connects itself, but afterwards the natures in which it exists; and according to which sympathy is ingenerated in all mundane essences, as existing in one animal, and governed by one nature. This life, therefore, which is the bond of wholes, total nature [or nature which ranks as a whole] and the one soul of the world constitute. The one intellect likewise generates it; and always more excellent beings insert in mundane natures a greater and more perfect union. Let it be said, therefore, that the habit which predominates in material subjects, that material form, and the powers of the middle elements, are bonds. All these however, have the relation of *things without which* the primary bond is not participated, and are analogous to the middle in mathematical entities, through which habitude subsists in the extremes. But the life of which we are speaking, which collects and unites all things, and is suspended indeed from its proper causes, but binds the things in which it is inherent, is truly analogy, and preserves both its own union and the union of its participants. Again, therefore, a bond is threefold. For the common powers of the elements are one bond; the one cause of bodies is another; and a third is that which is the middle of both the others, which proceeds indeed from the cause of bodies, but employs the powers that are divided about body. And this is the strong bond, as the theologist says, which is extended through all things, and is connected by the golden chain. For Zeus after this, constitutes the golden chain,[117] according to the admonitions of Night.

> But when your pow'r around the whole has spread
> A strong coercive bond, a golden chain
> Suspend from ether (Orph. fr. 121; *Chald. Oracl.* fr. 203).

Physical analogy then being a thing of this kind, let us survey in what things, and through what, it is naturally adapted to be established. As Plato therefore says, it subsists in numbers, masses, and

117. As Thomas Taylor explains, this golden chain may be said to be the series of unities proceeding from the One and extending as far as matter itself; and the light

powers. Physical *numbers*, however, are material forms divided about the subject [i.e., about body]. But *masses* are the extensions of these forms, and the separations or intervals of them about matter. And *powers* are the things which connect, and give form [or specific distinction] to bodies. For form is one thing, and the power proceeding from it is another. For form indeed is impartible and essential, but becoming extended, and dilated into bulk it emits, as if it were a blast from itself, material powers, which are certain qualities. Thus, for instance, in fire, the form and essence of it is impartible, and is truly the image of the cause of fire. For in partible natures there is that which is impartible. But from the form in fire which is impartible, a separation and extension of it take place about matter, from which the powers of fire are exerted, such as heat, or refrigeration, or moisture, or something else of the like kind. And these qualities are indeed essential, but are by no means the essence of fire. For essences are not from qualities, nor are essence and power the same; but every where the essential precedes power; and from that being one, a multitude of powers proceeds, and that which is divided, from that which is indivisible; just as from one power many energies proceed. For by how much more each thing proceeds, by so much more is it multiplied and divided, conformably to [the characteristic of] its principle and cause, which is impartible and indivisible. As in every body, therefore, there is this triad, I mean number, bulk, and power; analogy and the physical bond, occupy from on high the numbers, masses, and powers of bodies, and likewise congregate their partible essences, and unite them for the purpose of producing the one completion of the world. They also insert communion in forms, symmetry in masses, and harmony in powers. And thus all things are rendered effable and consentaneous to each other.[110] But this analogy proceeds from the middle to the first, and from the third to the middle; from the first also to the middle, and from this to the last; and again, from the last to the middle, and from this to the first. Because, likewise, a bond of this kind

proceeding from the Sun is an image of this chain. According to E.R. Dodds: "Both *seira* (a term derived ultimately, via Orphism, from Homer) and *taxis* here refer to transverse series or strata of reality; for the vertical series, consisting of a single principle repeated at different levels of reality, develops not from a monad but from a henad." See Proclus, *The Elements of Theology*, trans. E.R. Dodds (Oxford: Clarendon Press, 1992), pp.208–209.

imparts progression and conversion to bodies, it begins indeed from the middle, in consequence of being connective, and the cause of union, and is defined according to this peculiarity. But it proceeds from the first through the middle, to the last, as extending and unfolding itself, as far as to the last of things. And it recurs from the last to the first, as converting all things through harmony to the intelligible cause, from which the division of nature, and the separation and interval of bodies were produced. For by converting them to this cause, according to one circle, one order, and one series, secondary being suspended from primary natures, it causes the world to be one,[119] and most similar to the intelligible [paradigm]. For as there all things are truly united to each other, so here all things are adapted to each other. And as intelligibles proceeding from *The Good* are again converted to it, through the goodness which is in them, and through the intelligible monads; thus also sensibles proceeding from the Demiurgus, are again converted to him, through this bond, which is distributed and pervades through all of them, and binds all things together. For in this respect it imitates the intelligible. But it subsists intellectually in intellect, totally in wholes, and partially in partial natures.

After the same manner, therefore, as the intelligible, the sensible world has all things, according to all its parts. For fire, so far as it is tangible, participates of earth, and earth, so far as it is visible, participates of fire, and each participates of moisture. For earth indeed is conglutinated and connected through moisture, and its dissipated nature is united through it; but fire is nourished and increased by it. So that the extremes are the middle, in order that what is said may become physically manifest in things that are known by us. The extremes, therefore, are in a certain respect the middle, as preserving through it their proper idea, and remaining such as they are. And moisture itself, so far as it is colored, participates of fire, and so far as it is reinvigorated through heat. But again, so far as it is tangible, it participates of earth. So that each of the extremes gives perfection to moisture. These things, however, will shortly after become more known to us.

118. Cf. Plato, *Republic* VIII.546bc.
119. Cf. Plato, *Timaeus* 30d.

But through this harmony and analogy, in the first place, sameness presents itself to the view, and in the next place union. For bodies themselves according to their own nature are partible, and are subdued by difference and strife. These, however, at the same time through harmony, are leagued in friendship with sameness, and through sameness with union. For through analogy the universe is completely rendered one, this having the power of making things that are divided to be one, of congregating things that are multiplied, and connecting things that are dissipated. Hence, theologists surveying the causes of these things in the Gods, enclose Aphrodite with Ares, and surround them with Hephaestian bonds; the difference which is in the world being connected through harmony and friendship. All this complication and connection likewise has Hephaestus for its cause, who through demiurgic bonds connects sameness with difference, harmony with discord, and communion with contrariety. And this being effected, Apollo, Hermes, and each of the Gods laugh. But their laughter gives subsistence to mundane natures, and inserts efficacious power in the bonds. Let these things, however, as it is said, be preserved in sacred silence. But now, from what has been discussed, let thus much be manifest to us, that the physical bond being Hephaestian and demiurgic, (for the one and all-perfect Demiurgus comprehends also the production which is through necessity, as being Hephaestian and Dionysiacal, and causing each of the parts of the universe to be a whole,) is collective of contraries, and connective of material things; uniting their essences, measuring their masses, and harmonizing their powers. It likewise makes all things to be in all, and exhibits the same things in each other, according to all possible modes, empyreally, aerially, aquatically, and terrestrially.

12. Proclus
Commentary on the Chaldean Oracles

On the Chaldean Philosophy (*Ek tes Chaldaikes Philosophias*) is a commentary of Proclus' on the *Chaldean Oracles*, which describes the theurgic ascent of the soul and its apotheosis through mystical union with the gods and the One itself. The *Chaldean Oracles* (*ta logia*) were a collection of philosophical oracles or metaphysical assertions, produced in the 2nd century C.E., probably in Syria. They purported to transmit revelations of the gods regarding various cosmological and theurgic doctrines. The utterances were collected into a single book and put into verse by the "Chaldeans"— Julian the Chaldean or his son Julian the Theurgist, the author of the rather mysterious treatises *Theourgica* and *Telestica*. The *Chaldean Oracles* provided a metaphysical teaching, clothed in Middle Platonic dress, which asserted that every creature possessed an ontological symbol (*sumbolon* or *sunthema*) that came directly from the gods, and which led every being back to its divine origin through the theurgic ascent. The establishment of the *Chaldean Oracles* as theological authority or "holy scripture," gave the Neoplatonists (especially Iamblichus, Syrianus, and Proclus) a new way of reading and explaining the texts of Plato.

The only extant excerpt of Proclus' *On the Chaldean Philosophy* was translated by Thomas M. Johnson and published in 1907 and 1920. The fragments of the *Chaldean Oracles* were first translated by Thomas Taylor as "Collection of the Chaldean Oracles," *Classical Journal* XVI–XVII (1817–1818). For an excellent recent translation and commentary on the oracles, see Ruth Majercik, *The Chaldean Oracles* (Leiden: E.J. Brill, 1989).

1. The eternal orders are the temples and habitations of the Gods, and the paternal order is the all-receptive temple of the Father which receives and unites ascending souls. The angelic order in a characteristic way leads souls upward to the celestial region, "appearing about the soul," according to the Oracle, i.e., illuminating it thoroughly, and causing it to be full of undefiled fire, which imparts to it an immutable and tranquil order and power, through or by which it is not rushed into material disorder, but is united with the light of divine things: this, further, retains it in its native place, and causes it to be unmixed with matter, elevating the spirit by heat and raising it on high by means of the anagogic life. For the heating of the spirit is the imparting of life. But it is wholly elevated by hastening into the celestial region, just as by gravitating downward

it is carried into matter or the region of generation. But the end of ascents is the participation in divine fruits and the filling the soul with divine fire, which is the contemplation of God, the soul being placed in the presence of the Father.

The soul celebrating divine things is perfected, according to the Oracle, placing before and carrying to the Father the ineffable symbols of the Father, which the Father placed in the soul in the first progression of essence. For such are the intellectual and invisible hymns of the ascending soul, awakening the memory of harmonic reasons, which bear the inexpressible images in it of the divine powers.

2. [The immortal depth of the soul should be the leader, but vehemently extend all your eyes upwards.—*Chaldean Oracles*]

The Oracle says that the depth of the soul is its triadic gnostic powers, namely intelligible, discursive, and doxastic or opinionative, but that all the eyes are its triadic gnostic activities. For the eye is the symbol of knowledge, but life of desire: and each of these is a triad. But the earth, from which it is necessary that the heart be raised, signifies all material and mutable things in generation, i.e., the terrestrial life and every corporeal form. To which follows, the Oracle adds, the contemplation of the paternal monad, the pure joy in reference to this contemplation, and a steady tranquility from this intelligible survey.

From these it is evident that the good of this contemplation is mixed from the apprehension and the joy which naturally accompanies it. For every life having an energy which is by its nature easily and quickly liberated is allotted a connate or coordinate pleasure. The hymn of the Father does not consist of compound discourses or the preparation of sacred rites. For being alone incorruptible he does not receive a corruptible hymn. Let us not therefore imagine that we may persuade the Master of true discourses by a strange hurricane of words, nor by show or parade adorned with artificial rites: for God loves the simple, unadorned beauty of form. Let us therefore consecrate this hymn to God as an assimilation to or becoming like him: let us leave this earthly sphere, which is of a transient nature: let us come to the true end: let us know the Master: let us love the Father: let us obey the one calling: let us run to the hot, flying from the cold. Let us become fire: let us travel through fire. We have a quick and easy way to the ascent to the Father. The Father will guide, pointing out the ways of fire: let us not flow with the humble stream of Lethe, the river of oblivion.

3. The body is the root of evil, just as the Intellect is the root of Virtue. For Virtue blossoms for souls in the celestial region, but evil comes to souls from the worse, in the region of matter. The casting into the material region the evil which is eliminated from our nature will enable the soul to go wherever it may aspire. It is now temporarily allotted to the whole of generation or the material nature, since evils are here and of necessity revolve in and around this place. And our body is a part of generation or the sphere of time and sense, but another part, namely the soul, is able to act unsubdued by the power of generation, but cannot conquer the whole of generation, unless we destroy the being or essence of it.

Into the material sphere, therefore, we must cast jealousy and envy, whence the soul drew them. For material things have matter as a nurse. And "the not extinguishing" or restraining the tendency of the mind to the worse does not refer to a mere temporary disappearance of it, just as all the affections which are restrained in a certain being are contained in it and fill it with their own heat. But instead of restraining, cast it out, not keeping within you that which is only dammed up. On account of which the Oracle adds: "Do not defile the spirit through that which is within and hidden." But envy is material: for it dwells with the privation of goods. And privation coexists with unproductive matter. But the theurgic race is beneficent, and devoted to a zealous imitation of the goodness of God, but it is not drawn down to the contentiousness and enmity of men. But these affections are enclosed in souls, imparting to the spirit a certain material character, and filling it with material privation and lifelessness.

4. The soul consisting according to its discursive reason knows or cognizes true or divine beings. But establishing itself in the intellectual life of its peculiar essence, it knows all things by simple and impartible intuitions. Ascending to the One, and folding up and laying aside all multitude which is in itself, it actualizes itself enthusiastically and is united to the super-intellectual summit. For everywhere the similar is naturally united to the similar, and every cognition through similitude binds to that which is known the knower: to the sensible or object of sense-perception the perceptive cognition; to cognizable objects discursive reason; to intelligible objects intelligible cognition; and therefore also to that which is prior to intellect the flower of the intellect is correspondent. For as in other things not intellect, but the cause superior to intellect is highest, so in souls the first form of energy is not intellectual but

that which is more divine than the intellect. And every soul and every intellect have twofold activities, the unical activities which are better than intellection, and the intelligible activities. It is necessary therefore to apprehend this intelligible, which exists per se, and the summit of existence, our eyes being closed to all other lives and powers. For as we apprehend intellect by becoming intellectual form, so becoming uniform we ascend to union, standing on the characteristic summit of intellect—since even the eye does not otherwise see the sun than by becoming solar-formed, but not by the light from fire.

Moreover, it is plain that this intelligible cannot be apprehended by a reasoning process. But, as the Oracle says, if you apply your intellect, you will come by intellectual intuitions into contact with this intelligible, and thus you will apprehend it as understanding some particular things, i.e., you cannot grasp this intelligible by laying hold of it according to a certain measure of form and knowledge. For however simple such intellections may be, they are deprived of the unific simplicity of the intelligible, and are carried into secondary conditions of the intellect, proceeding into a multitude of intelligible things. For no object of knowledge is known through or by an inferior knowledge: neither therefore is that which is above intellect known through intellect. For all at once the intellect hurls or projects itself to a certain thing, and pronounces that this or that is apprehended, which dictum is the second from the intelligible. But if by the flower of our intellect we apprehend this intelligible, established on the summit of the first intelligible triad, are we united by a certain relation to the One which is uncoordinated with all things, and imparticipable? For if the first Father is said by the Oracle to hastily withdraw himself from Intellect and Power, what is that which lacks nothing that it should thus be withdrawn, but is withdrawn or isolated from all things simply, and is celebrated as the God of all? Is this not also said by the Oracle in another place about the Primary Father? And as for the first power of the sacred reason: what is that which is above this, and does not participate in this, and is said by the Oracle to be sacred? And if the reason shining forth is named by the Oracle as a more ineffable reason, it is necessary that prior to reason Silence should subsist as a reason or productive principle, and prior to every sacred reason the deifying cause.

As therefore beyond the intelligibles are the reasons or productive principles of intelligibles, things being united, so the productive principle in them subsists from another more ineffable unity, though there is a reason of the Silence prior to intelligibles, but a Silence of silent intelligibles. Perhaps, therefore, this flower of the intellect is not the flower of our whole soul. But this, i.e., the flower of the intellect, is the most unific of our intellectual life, and the flower of the soul is the one of all the psychical powers, they being multiform. For we are not intellect alone, but discursive reason and opinion and attention and will, and prior to these powers we are one essence and many, partible and impartible. And the one shining forth is twofold: one or the flower of the soul being the first of our powers, the other being the whole essence of the center and of all the all-various powers about it; but this, i.e., the flower of the soul, alone unites us to the Father of the intelligibles. For the one is intellectual, but this is apprehended by the Paternal Intellect according to the unity (*henad*) which is in it. But the unity (*henad*) to which all the psychical powers verge and in which they unite and center alone naturally leads us to the Principle which is beyond all beings, and is the unifying power of all that is in us. So that we are rooted or planted essentially in this Principle, and by being rooted, even though we may descend from the intelligible region, we will not be estranged from our cause.

5. Philosophy says that a forgetfulness of eternal reasons is the cause of the departure of the soul from the Gods, and that a reminiscence of the knowledge of the eternal reasons or Ideas is the cause of the return to them, but the Oracles assert that the forgetfulness and reminiscence of the paternal symbols are respectively the causes of the departure and return. Both statements are in harmony. For the soul is constituted from intellectual reasons and divine symbols, of which the former proceed from the intellectual species, but the latter from the divine unities: and we are images of the intellectual essences, but statues of the unknown symbols. And just as every soul is a fullness (*pleroma*) of forms, but subsists wholly or simply according to one cause, thus also it indeed participates in all symbols, through which it is united to divine things, but the summit of the soul in the one is separated or divided, so that every multitude in the soul is led into one summit. For it is necessary to know that every soul differs from every other soul according to form or specifically, and that there are as many souls as there are species of

souls. For there is first indeed according to one form a hypostasis of many individual, unific forms about matter and the composites of beings, there being one subject nature participating variously in the same form: then the essence of the soul is reason and simple form, and to this extent one soul will differ in no respect from another essentially, but will differ according to form, for by character alone will it differ. But it is form alone. Whence it is evident that every soul, even though it is replete to the same degree with the same reasons, yet is allotted a form distinct from others, just as the solar form characterizes the solar soul, and another form another soul.

13. Proclus
Commentary on Plato's Parmenides

The first Platonist who unequivocally adopted the metaphysical interpretation of Plato's *Parmenides* (following in certain respects the Neopythagorean and Middle Platonic traditions) was Plotinus. For the later Neoplatonists (beginning especially with Iamblichus) the true spiritual life consisted in reading, meditating and commenting on the *Parmenides*, which was viewed as the theological dialogue par excellence. Syrianus and Proclus further elaborated the metaphysical interpretation of the *Parmenides* and claimed that the entire structure of reality could be deduced from the first and the second hypotheses of the *Parmenides*, which respectively negate and affirm attributes of the One (cf. the *via negativa* and *via affirmativa* of later Christian mystical theology, eg. Dionysios the Areopagite). They regarded each characteristic of the One, denied or asserted, as representing a distinct class of the gods. Proclus developed a coherent and systematic scientific theology based on the theological (and allegorical) exegesis of Plato's *Parmenides*. He connected the dialectical procedures of Plato's *Parmenides* to the mystical ascent of the soul to the One. Finally, however, even the dialectical method itself had to be left aside at the threshold of the One. Mystical union was approached through that "silence" which transcends all discursive reasoning and rational thought.

The *Commentary on Plato's Parmenides* (*Eis ton Platonos Parmeniden*) by Proclus was divided into two major parts: the first was devoted to the Platonic Forms, or Ideas; and the second, to the One. The extant commentary, however, extends only to the end of the first hypothesis of *Parmenides* (142b).

Proclus' *Commentary on Plato's Parmenides*, has been translated by Glenn R. Morrow and John M. Dillon (Princeton: Princeton University

Press, 1987). The excerpts presented below were translated by J. Dillon from *In Parm.* VII—extant only in the medieval Latin translation of Moerbeke. See *Procli Commentarium in Parmenidem, pars ultima adhuc inedita, interprete Guillelmo de Moerbeke*, ed. R. Klibansky, L. Labowsky (London, 1953). See also Carlos Steel, Friedrich Rumbach, and Gregory MacIsaac, "The Final Section of Proclus' Commentary on the 'Parmenides': A Greek Retroversion of the Latin Translation," *Documenti e studi sulla tradizione filosofica Medievale* VIII (1997):211–268.

In Parm. VII.35–36

"*It cannot then be even to the extent of being one, for then it would be a thing that is and participates in being; but it seems that the One neither is one nor exists at all if one is to believe such an argument as this.*" "*There seems to be no way out of it.*" (Plato, *Parmenides* 141e)

It has been said that the One does not participate in being in the way that "many" and "whole" and "part" and "shape" and so forth, do; then, that it does not exist even in that way that the first Being does. But the One that is lower than the One itself is said to participate in being inasmuch as it is bound up with it. And so he adds these words, "the One is not even one." For he knows that *one* has two meanings—in one sense it transcends, in the other it is coordinate with, *is*. In the latter sense, it is in a way comparable with existence as participating and being participated in by it. But in the former, it is incomparable and is imparticipable by everything.

So he shows that the first One is not like the One that coexists with Being. For if it can truthfully be said of it that it "is one," this "being one" involves "being"; of the transcendent One he says that it is not even possible to say that it is one. For the One of which we say "is one" is really the One that goes with Being. So we must not say that it is the One, for the "being one" that belongs to the one that goes with "being" and has a part in existence and has not remained "one" but has turned into "One Being."

VII.39–76

For if the first One participated in Being in some way, although it is higher than Being and produces it, it would be a one which took over the mode of reality which belongs to Being. But it is not a one, and is the cause not just of Being but of everything, though of Being before the rest. And if everything must participate in its cause, there must be a "one," other than the simply One, in which Being participates; and this "one" is the principle of beings. This is also how Speusippus understands the situation (presenting his views as the doctrines of the ancients). What does he say?

> For they held that the One is higher than being and is the source of being; and they delivered it even from the status of a principle. For they held that, given the One, in itself, conceived as separated and alone without the other things, with no additional element, nothing else would come into existence. And so they introduced the Indefinite Dyad as the principle of beings. (fr. 48 Taran)

So he too, testifies that this was the opinion of the ancients about the One; it is snatched up[120] beyond existence, and next after it comes the Indefinite Dyad. Here too, then, Plato proves this One to be beyond the existent and beyond the unity that is in the existent and beyond the whole One Being.

In the Second Hypothesis he is going to say that the One Being, too, is a principle. It is constituted by distinct predicates, "one" and "being," and beyond it, he says, is the One Itself. For the unity that has existence through the unity of the One Being is not the One, but a particular one; yet in no case is the particular identical with the undifferentiated character ... or Being.[121] But this too presents difficulty, because the "one" and the "being" must clearly be two, and so they cannot be purely one. For two are not one. So here we have something that is both one and not one; but this is not purely one, as what is both equal and not equal is not simply equal. So it is right to preserve the simplicity of the purely One, placing it beyond the "one" which is in "being" and beyond that "one" which is constituted by "one" and "being."

Having got so far, he rightly observes that, since the One is such, as we have described, it is unknown to all particular kinds of knowledge and is inexpressible and unutterable. For what is first nameable and knowable is the one that is one by existing, and, in general,

120. *Sursum raptum est*, probably translates *apo herpasthe*. This is Chaldean terminology; cf. *Chaldean Oracles* fr.3.
121. Cf. *In Parm.* 1096.21ff. There is a lacuna in the Latin MSS here.

any character unifying, though not participated by, its series. To give an analogy: sense-perception helps us to reach some knowledge of the cosmic gods, for it sees their visible dwelling places and thereby reminds us of their characters; but it does not in the least help us to know the gods that are beyond the heavens. In the same way, intellect and knowledge of being help us to attain to the One Being; but our powers of knowing kinds of being do not in the least help us towards union with the One itself, except in so far as they are a kind of predisposition to the upward movement towards it. For it is not participated in any way or by any kind of being.

"If," Plato says, "one is to believe an argument like this." Proceeding by means of negations, we have declared the One to be exalted above everything; above intelligible and intellectual objects, above the hyper-cosmic and cosmic gods, above the nature that is made divine.

"If," then, "one can believe an argument like this," the One is imparticipable. Obviously the reasoning is human and therefore particular. But neither does divine reason say anything but that the One is imparticipable. For as we have said before, everything strives to imitate the One by way of its own highest element. For souls, what is imparticipable is the first Soul: this is the universal which unites souls into a kind. Again, for intellectual substance the imparticipable is the divine Intellect, which is the universal uniting intellects into a kind. And in the same way, for all the divine henads the imparticipable is the One itself.

Whence, indeed, do the second in rank derive their imparticipability except from the One? For transcendence belongs to what comes first more than to what follows. So the One transcends the kinds of existence more than the universal Intellect transcends souls, or the universal Soul, bodies. So if the first, divine Intellect is imparticipable, it is obvious that the One itself is not on a level with any being.

But what is belief? It looks as if Plato were opposing the argument because, as he himself says, belief founded on persuasion is weaker than knowledge got by learning. But perhaps "belief" here is not the same as the belief we have spoken of elsewhere in connection with sense-perception, but is what the theologians[122] mean

---

122. The Chaldeans; cf. frs.46–48. The Chaldean triad of virtues is mentioned *In Parm.* 927.26 ff. *Pistis* may be translated both as "belief" and as "faith."

when they speak of the preservation of love, truth, and firm and immutable faith in the first principles, and say that faith binds and unites us to the One. These words, then, are to be believed, and to be relied on steadfastly and constantly, not assented to doubtfully and as a matter of opinion.

But suppose he did speak doubtfully when he said, "If one is to believe such reasoning"; this would not be strange, when he is trying by means of negations to hint at the supreme reality of the One. For one cannot allow that reason may entirely grasp it. Even the purest forms of knowledge are unable to comprehend it. The nearer they get to it and the more they attain to what is connatural to them, the more they find that it remains beyond the scope of their own operations, though they achieve participation in whatever can be comprehended.

But whatever they apprehended, they desire something greater than that because of the travail inborn in them, the yearning for the supereminence of the One; and that is why there exists in us so great a devotion to it. But this yearning is always repulsed as falling short of its object, for knowledge is struggling to gainsay the peculiar inapproachability of the One.

"And if a thing does not exist, can this non-existent have anything that either belongs to it or is of it?" "How could it?" (Parm. 142k)

It is obvious that everything which stands in a relation to something must first itself be something and must exist on its own account (cf. *Soph.* 247a ff.), for how could the non-existent endow anything else with existence? This is the nature of real relations. So if it has been shown that the One is beyond existence, nothing at all, such as a name or description, belongs to it, nor will there be a single thing, such as knowledge or sensation, that is of it. For if so, it would be knowable and sensible and nameable and expressible and would stand in relation to something else. But what stands in a relation has some kind of existence. For even the intelligible stands in a certain relation to the intellect, and the knowable to knowledge, inasmuch as they are mutually coordinate. But that which transcends all cannot, as has been shown, be susceptible of even a hint of relationship to anything else.

But what is meant by the careful addition of "this non-existent"? What is the meaning of "not being"? It has various meanings. For what does not exist in any way at all, and what has come to be, and "rest" and "movement" (this follows from the properties of "other"—and the One itself: all of these "are not" (cf. *Soph.* 255a ff.), but not everything that "is not" is unknown and inexpressible. "Rest" and "movement" are known, and so in general are all the things that "are not" which belong to the sphere of the intelligible. For just that is meant by calling them intelligible. Neither is "what has come to be" unapprehended, for, as the *Timaeus* says (27d ff.), that is the object of sense and opinion. The things that "are not" which are unknown are (a) the One itself and (b) what does not exist in any way at all; the former as superior to all knowledge of kinds of existence, the latter as falling short of any possibility whatever of being apprehended. Thus in the *Republic* (V, 477a ff.), Socrates called non-existent what does not exist in any way at all, and said that it was unknown. [He distinguished it from the "not being" of what has come to be], which is the object of opinion and comes after perfect being which is the object of real knowledge. And on the other hand, he called the Good non-existent because it is above being. He says that it is superior to being and existence and better than intelligible objects, and that it is the light of truth which brings the intelligible before the intellect (509b).

So "non-existent" and "beyond belief" can be taken in two ways. And this is correct. For the soul is tormented by the unlimitedness and indefiniteness of the totally non-existent; it experiences difficulty in grasping it and is happy to be ignorant of it, fearing to step out into the limitless and measureless. But it mounts towards the incomprehensible super-eminence of the One itself, borne in its direction by a longing for its nature, revolving round it, wanting to embrace it, seeking with supreme passion to be present to it, unifying itself as far as possible and purging all its own multiplicity so that somehow it may become perfectly one. Impotent to comprehend its incomprehensibility or to know the unknown, yet according to the manner of its own procession, it loves its inexpressible apprehension of participation in the One. For in order to receive something, the soul must first coexist with that thing; but what would it mean to touch the intangible?

Thus the One transcends all analyzable knowledge and intellection and all contact. And only unification brings us near the One, since just because it is higher than any existence, it is unknown. And this is why in the *Letters* (*Ep.* VII, 341c) Plato speaks of "a learning different from all other kinds of learning." Such is the One. But the totally non-existent is unknown as falling away from all things in its indefiniteness and as incapable of having real subsistence.

So it is ridiculous to say that because it is not an object of knowledge or opinion, the One is the same as the totally non-existent. For the totally non-existent is nothing, since one cannot apply the expression "something" to it, the opposite of which is "nothing" (cf. *Soph.* 237c). But it is impossible to say that this is the One, for "nothing"—i.e., "not a thing" is the negation of "one" as well as of everything else. Indeed Plato did not deny "one" absolutely of the One, but the "one" of "being one," as well as "being."

> "*Therefore no name or description or knowledge or sensation or opinion applies to it.*" "*Apparently not.*" (*Parm.* 142a)

You could distinguish these negations into two kinds, and say that the One is declared to be (a) inexpressible, and (b) unknowable. Make a further division of the expressible and the knowable, and you will say that it is inexpressible in two ways, unknowable in three.

For the expressible is expressible either by a description or by a name; but the name is prior, and the description is by nature posterior to the name. For the name imitates the simplicity and unity of objects, but the description their complexity and variety of aspects. So the name is related to the single thing as signifying the whole subject at once; but the description circles round the essence of the thing and unfolds its complexity. The thing is the starting-point for both name and description, but the secret essences of intelligible objects, which are united with One, are preserved "in god-nourished silence":[123] they imitate the inexpressibleness and unutterableness of the One. But the One has its place above the silence and the intellect and the knowledge of the intellect, which form a triad.

Again what can be known is the object either of [sense-perception or of] opinion or of scientific knowledge. For all cognition is either without concepts or with concepts; and, if the latter, it either

---

123. Chaldean terminology; cf. *Chaldean Oracles* fr.16. A reference to the "paternal silence," *In Parm.* 1171.6.

brings in causes or makes no mention of causes. So we have three kinds of cognition: sense perception, opinion, and scientific knowledge. And so what is completely unapprehended by us is neither scientifically knowable nor judgeable nor perceptible.

Now, starting from the kinds of cognition in ourselves, we must also take their totalities and realize that all being known is denied of the One. For how could what is beyond all that exists be sensibly perceived? And how could it be the object of opinion, when it is not such as in one way to be, and in another way not? And how can what has no cause be an object of science?

So it is rightly said in the *Letters* (VII, 341c), as we have said, that it is to be learned in a different way; that when we have given much care and attention to it, a divine light is kindled in us through which there comes about—in such a way as is possible to us—a glimpse of it, which makes us participate in it in respect of that part of ourselves that is most divine. But the most divine thing in us is the One in us, which Socrates called the illumination of the soul, just as he called the truth itself light. This illumination is our individual light, and so, if it is not impious to say this, here also like is apprehensible by like: as the sensible is by sensation, the opiniable by opinion, the knowable by science, so by the One in ourselves do we apprehend the One, which by the brightness of its light is the cause of all beings, by which all participate in the One.

Take, then, all sense-perception, not merely ours but that of the demons, and that of the cosmic gods, and that of the sun itself, and that of the "absolute" gods, and that of the assimilative gods,[124] and the very fount of sense-perception that is its demiurgic cause.[125] "For with the intellect he lays hold of the intelligible, but sensation he applies to the worlds" (*Chald. Or.* fr. 8). If you consider step by step this whole series which springs from the fount of sensation, you will find not one member of it to have knowledge of the One. Just as, in Homer, Zeus is said to be invisible even to the perception of the Sun, "which has the most penetrating light." (*Iliad* 14.343–344). And Plato says that the One is known by no sensation, for, he says, no being senses it evidently not even the divine sensation, nor the primary cause of sensation; nor, in general, is there any mode of

---

124. The *apolutoi* and the *aphomoiotikoi*.

125. On the demiurgic, as opposed to the paternal cause, see Proclus, *The Elements of Theology*, prop. 157.

cognition in the divine Intellect that is coordinate with the One. Neither, therefore, does the demiurgic sense-perception perceive the One, for even that is a perception of things existent.

Secondly, consider opinion; first, ours, then that of the demons, then that of the angels, then that of the cosmic gods, then that of the absolute gods (for these, inasmuch as even they have something to do with the world, contain the rational principles of sensible objects), then that of the assimilative gods (for in these are the causes of the cosmic gods); and, finally, the demiurgic opinion, Opinion itself, for this is the fount of all opinion and is the primary cause of the things that exist in the world, and from it the circle of difference has its origin. Consider this whole series and say: the One is unknowable to all forms of opinion.

There remains knowledge. Do not regard only what we have; for it is particular and there is nothing venerable about it—it does not know the One—but regard also the knowledge of demons, which sees the kinds of existence; and the angelic knowledge, which sees what is prior to these; and that of the cosmic gods (by which they follow their "absolute" leaders); and that of the absolute gods themselves, which operates transcendently in the sphere of the intelligible; and, higher still, that of the assimilative gods, through which they are the first to assimilate themselves to the intellectual gods; and in addition to these, consider the original knowledge which is united to the intelligible themselves, which in the *Phaedrus* (247d) is also called "knowledge itself"; and, above all these, consider the intelligible union which lies hidden and unutterable in the interior recess of Being itself. Consider all these kinds of knowledge and understanding of existence, and you will see that they all fall short of the One. For they are all knowledge of Being and not of the One. But the argument has shown that the One is above Being. Therefore all cognition, whether it is knowledge, or opinion, or sense-perception, is of something secondary and not of the One.

But we have said that the [One is also inexpressible] ... so much the more [do we say] that it is unknowable to any reason-principle that comprehends a multiplicity (?)....[126]

Names may be human or demonic or angelic or divine—for there are divine names, as the *Cratylus* says (400d), which the gods

---

126. A lacuna exists here of some considerable extent.

use in addressing each other, and in the *Phaedrus* (255c) Socrates, himself divinely inspired, says, "whom Zeus named *Himeros* when he was in love with Ganymede." And the *Timaeus* (36c) says, referring to the Demiurge, "He named the circles of identity and difference."[127] For I believe that these passages agree with the theologians inasmuch as they signify by the words quoted that there is also an order of divine names.

All these things belong to what comes after the One, and not to the One itself. No attribute of other things is applicable to the One. For they are all inferior and fall short of its transcendent super-eminence. What could be made commensurable with it, since it is not among the kinds of existence but is beyond them all alike? For if a thing is commensurable with anything else, this means that there are some things that agree with it more and some less; but the One transcends all things equally. So none of the things that come after it is commensurable with it, or corresponds to its nature, or can be compared with it.

Further, every name which can be properly said to be such by nature corresponds to what is named and is the logical image of the object. So there is no name of the One but—as somebody has said[128]—it is even beyond breath. But the first of the things that emanate from it is represented by the rough breathing with which we utter "*hen.*" Itself, it is unnamable, just as the breathing by itself is silent. The second is represented by the utterable vowel which now becomes utterable with the breathing, and it itself becomes both utterable and unutterable, unspeakable and speakable; for the procession of the second order of existence has to be mediated. Third comes *hen* which contains the unsoundable breathing and the soundable force of *e* and the letter that goes with this, the consonant *n*, which represents in a converse way the same thing as the breathing.[129] And the whole is a triad formed in this way: from this one derives a dyad, but behind the dyad there is a monad. But the

---

127. Cf. Proclus, *In Crat.* 19.24 ff.

128. A reference to Theodorus of Asine. Cf. Proclus, *In Tim.* II.274.10 ff, where the doctrine on the letters of the One is attributed to Theodorus.

129. Presumably in the sense that consonants are non-sonant, even as the rough breathing is, but conversely.

first principle is beyond everything and not merely beyond this triad which is the first thing that comes after it.

This, then, is the context of his argument which deduces the trinity by way of the names from the first principle. While he is theologizing in this way, he is thinking only of the very first development of names, declaring that "one" is the very first of names, which is subordinate to the simplicity of the One. He is working purely with an understanding of what is designated and he discovers these two assuming to themselves utterable sounds, and prior to these, and given these, he discovers thirdly that prior breathing which is the silent symbol of Being (*huparxis*).

Clearly we must first enquire how it is that no name of the One is really spoken. We shall learn that if names are natural, the first principle has no name, not even the name "one," understanding that everything that is by nature a name of something has meaning as being congruous to its object, either by analysis into simple names or by reduction to its letters. If this is so, then "one" has to be reduced to its letters, since it cannot be analyzed into any simpler name. So the letters of which it is composed will have to represent something of its nature. But each of them will represent something different, and so the first principle will not be one. So if it had a name, the One would not be one. This is proved from the rules about names which are plainly stated in the *Cratylus* (390d).

The question arises, however, how it is that we call it "one" when the thing itself is altogether unnameable? We should rather say that it is not the One that we call "one" when we use this name, but the understanding of unity which is in ourselves. For everything that exists—beings with intellect, with soul, with life, and inanimate objects and the very matter that goes with these—all long for the first cause and have a natural striving towards it. And this fact shows us that the predilection for the One does not come from knowledge, since if it did, what has no share in knowledge could not seek it; but everything has a natural striving after the One, as also has the soul.

What else is the One in ourselves except the operation and energy of this striving? It is therefore this interior understanding of unity, which is a projection and as it were an expression of the One in ourselves, that we call "the One." So the One itself is not nameable, but the One in ourselves. By means of this, as what is most appropriate to it, we first speak of it and make it known to our own peers.

Since there are two activities in us, the one appetitive and the other reflective (the former existing also in those beings that are inferior to ourselves, but the latter only in those that are conscious of their appetites), that abiding activity that is common to all may not be absent from our own souls, but these must be responsive to the energies that concern the first principle, and so the love of the One must be inextinguishable. This is indeed why this love is real, even though the One is incomprehensible and unknowable. But consciousness labors and falls short when it encounters the unknown. So silent understanding is before that which is put into language, and desire is before any understanding, before that which is inexpressible as well as before that which is analyzable.

Why, then, do we call the understanding of unity within ourselves "one" and not something else? Because, I should say, unity is the most venerable of all the things we know. For everything is preserved and perfected by being unified,[130] but perishes and becomes less perfect when it lacks the virtue of cleaving together and when it gets further away from being one. So disintegrated bodies perish, and souls which multiply their powers die their own death. But they revive when they recollect themselves and flee back to unity from the division and dispersal of their powers.

Unity, then, is the most venerable thing, which perfects and preserves everything, and that is why we give this name to the concept that we have of the first principle. Besides, we noticed that not everything participates in other predicates, not even in existence, for there are things which in themselves are not existents and do not have being. And much less does everything participate in life or intellect or rest or movement. But in unity, everything.

Even if you mention "many," this cannot exist without having a share in some sort of unity. For no multitude can be infinite, so if a multitude occurs, it will be finite. But a finite multitude is a number, and a number is some one thing. For "three" or "four" (and so for any of the numbers) is a sort of unity. It is indeed not a monad, but at any rate it is a unity, for it is a kind, and a kind always participates in unity, for it unites its members. Or how could we say that "three" is one number and "four" another, if they were not distinguished from one another as distinct unities? So everything participates in some unity, and that is why "one" seems to be the most important of predicates.

130. Cf. Plotinus, *Enneads* VI.9.1.

It was therefore correct to give the name "one" to the conception which we have of the first principle. And as we know that unity is common to everything and preserves everything, this will guide us in naming that which is the cause and the desire of all things. For it had to be named either after all things or after those that come next after it; so it can be named "one" after all things.[131]

Why do we not say that the other names also are names of the concepts that we have, and not of the things themselves—e.g., "intellect," "the intelligible," and so on? I would say because the concepts of other things give knowledge of the things of which they are concepts, and they arise in us cognitively; and for this reason they are sometimes (though not always) projected into language. But our concept and apprehension of the One, i.e., our travail, is in our nature per se, and not in the manner of a perception[132] or cognition. The other concepts, being cognitions, coexist with their objects and are capable of naming them, for their objects can somehow be grasped by them. This concept, however, is not cognitive and does not grasp the One, but is essentially an operation of nature and a natural desire of unity. This is proved by the fact that the desire of everything is desire of the One, but if our concept were of something known, then its object would only be the object of desire to the cognitive powers and not to things without knowledge.

From this it is clear that the One and the Good are the same.[133] For each is the object of desire to all things, just as nothingness and evil are what all things shun. And if the One and the Good are different, then either there are two principles or, if the One is before the Good, how can the desire of the One but be higher than the desire of the Good? But how can it be better, if it is not good? Or if the Good is before the One, since it will not be one it will be both good and not good. If, then, the One is the same as the Good, then it is right that it should be an object of desire before any cognition and that the apprehension of it should not be of the same kind as of knowable things. This is why our concepts of these really name

131. Cf. Proclus, *Platonic Theology* III.21, p.74.5–11 Saffrey-Westerink.

132. *Kat' epibolen* (*secundum adiectionem*). An Epicurean term, *epibole*, was taken up by later Platonists, beginning with Iamblichus, which has the general meaning of an act of "attention" or "apprehension."

133. Cf. Proclus, *In Parm.* VI.1097.10ff.

their objects, for they know them; but this other apprehension desires something unknown and, impotent to comprehend it, it applies the name "one," not to the unknown—for how could it?—but to itself, as somehow divining the reality of what transcends itself and everything else. But it is unable to reflect on the One itself, for, as we have said, the desire of the One, the incessant movement of striving, is in all things by nature and not by representation. Even the divine Intellect, as I have said before, does not know the One by direct vision[134] (i.e. intuitively) or intellectually, but is united with it, "drunk with its nectar" (*Symp.* 203b), for its nature, and what is in it, is better than all knowledge ...[135] Thus the One is the desire of all, and all are preserved by it and are what they are through it, and in comparison with it, as with the Good, nothing else has value for anything.

So Socrates says at the beginning that it is knowable, but immediately adds a qualification, saying how it is knowable, namely, "to him who inclines his own light towards it" (*Rep.* VII, 540a). What does he mean by "light," except the One that is in the soul?[136] For he said that the Good can be compared with the sun, and that this light is like a seed from the Good planted in souls. Besides, before speaking of the light, he too made it quite clear that the way to it is by negations: "As if in battle one has to rob it of everything and separate it from everything" (*Rep.* VII, 534b).

So it is right that it should not be possible to apply a name to it, as if one could be made to fit what is beyond all things. But to it "one" only can be applied if one desires to express what not only Plato but the gods, too, have called inexpressible. For they themselves have given oracles to this effect.[137] "For all things, as they come from one and revert to one, are divided, intellectually, into many bodies." They counsel us to get rid of multiplicity of soul, to conduct our mind upwards and bring it to unity, saying, "Do not retain in your intellect anything which is multiple," but "direct the thought of the soul towards the One." The gods, knowing what concerns them, tend upwards towards the One by means of the One in

---

134. *Epibletikos*, transliterated by Moerbeke. This word means "intuitively" and was first used in this sense by Iamblichus, *Protrept.* 18.2.

135. A lacuna in the manuscript.

136. On the One of the soul, see Proclus, *In Parm.* 1071.25–33.

137. The following quotations from the *Chaldean Oracles* do not survive in Greek.

themselves. And this precisely is their theological teaching; through the voice of the true theologians they have handed down to us this hint regarding the first principle. They call it in their own language, *Ad*, which is their word for "one"; so it is translated by people who know their language.[138] And they duplicate it in order to name the demiurgic intellect of the world, which they call *Adad*, "worthy of all praise." They do not say that it comes immediately next to the One, but only that it is comparable to the One by way of proportion; for as the former is to the intelligible, so the latter is to the whole visible[139] world, and for that reason the former is called simply *Ad*, but the other which duplicates it is called *Adad*. Orpheus has also pronounced which god was first named, saying: "The gods called phanes by name first on great Olympus" (fr. 85 Kern). He himself speaks of things that existed before phanes and symbolically applies names taken from the lowest levels of reality: "Time" and "Ether" and "Chaos" (fr. 60 Kern), and, if you will, "the Egg," but he never says that the gods used these names. For these were not their names but he transferred to them names that belong to other things.

If, then, one must give a name to the first principle, "one" and "good" seem to belong to it; for these characters can be seen to pervade the whole of existence. Yet it is beyond every name. This feature of the One is reproduced, but in a different way, by the last of all things, which also cannot be represented by a name of its own; how could it, since it has no determinate nature? But it is named *dexamene*, i.e., "receptacle," and *titheene*, i.e., "nurse," and "matter" and "the underlying," after the things that come before it, just as the first is named after the things that come after it.

"Therefore it is not named or spoken or judged or known, and nothing perceives it." "Apparently not." (Parm. 142a)

It is stated clearly in the *Letters* (VII, 342a–344a) that no name can with certainty comprehend an intelligible object, nor can a visible

---

138. A piece of true Chaldean lore, though not attested in the surviving fragments of the *Chaldean Oracles*. The terms *hapax epekeina* and *dis epekeina*, for the supreme God and Demiurge respectively, may allude to Ad and Adad. On Adad see, Macrobius, *Sat.* I.23.17, where he gives *unus unus* as a translation of Adad.

139. Reading *visibilia* for MS *invisibilia*.

picture, nor a definition, nor any rational knowledge of it. The intellect alone is capable of grasping an intelligible essence certainly and perfectly. Plato works out the argument for one example, the circle.

For when does this mere name "circle" grasp the whole essence of the intelligible circle? When we hear the name, what do we know but the name?

Nor does an impression drawn in the dust by a geometrician comprehend it. For this is merely one of the copies multiplying it, not first known by reasoning but by sense and imagination.

Nor yet the definition, which does indeed circle round its essential nature; but it is complex and composite and so cannot seize upon the simplicity of that essence.

Nor does the theory of it grasp it, even if it meditates a thousand times things that themselves belong accidentally to the circle, and one might as well call it knowledge of these other things.

All these are about it but are not itself. But the intellect and intellectual knowledge knows the essence itself and comprehends the Form itself even by simple intuition. So it alone is capable of knowing the circle. And similarly for "the equal" and "the unequal" and the other characters severally.

If, then, we have shown that names and definitions and rational knowledge are worthless for grasping intelligible objects, what should we say about them with regard to the One? Surely that all names and all discourse and all rational knowledge fall short of it? So the One is not nameable or expressible or knowable or perceptible by anything that exists. This is why it is beyond the grasp of all sensation, all judgment, all science, all reasoning, all names.

But, you will say, what is the difference between this and what he has already said? For he said before that there is no apprehension of the One. But there he said that the One [is not knowable] by others[140]... He is showing by this very insistence that it is not unknowable because of the weakness of other things, but by its own nature. By what he said before, he indicated the inferiority of other things in relation to the One, but here its super-excellence with regard to itself.

---

140. According to John Dillon, Klibansky's supplement here seems unjustified; but there is some corruption or lacuna in the manuscript.

But we must attend to the fact that when he says that the One is not known, by "knowledge" he means "rational knowledge." Before, he mentioned three things—rational knowledge, opinion, and sensation—and as in this sentence he takes up two that are the same as in the previous one, namely sensation and opinion, it is obvious that by the third, "knowledge," he means only rational knowledge, so that if there is a divinely inspired knowledge that is better than rational knowledge and which leads the One in ourselves towards that One, obviously the argument did not eliminate this, and learning it is the "final discipline," as Socrates rightly says (*Rep.* VI, 505a), because it is discipline in the final knowledge. But this final knowledge is not science, but is higher than science.

> *"Is it possible that all this holds true of the One?"*
> *"I should say not."* (*Parm.*142a)

To all his negative propositions he now appends this very unexpected conclusion, which raises a grave doubt. In what sense is it impossible that these things should hold true of the One? Are not all the foregoing arguments dismissed by this single remark?

Some people[141] have therefore been persuaded by this passage to say that the First Hypothesis reaches impossible conclusions, and so that the One is not a real subject. For they associate all the negations into one hypothetical syllogism: "If the One exists, it is not a whole, it has not a beginning, middle, or end, it has no shape," and so on, and after all the rest, "It has no existence, is not existence, is not expressible, is not nameable, is not knowable." Since these are impossibilities, they concluded that Plato himself is saying that the One is an impossibility. But this was really because they themselves held that there is no One that is imparticipable by existence and, therefore, that the One is not different from Being nor from the One-Being, and that "one" has as many modes as being, and that the One that is beyond Being is a mere name.

In reply to this interpretation, it must be stated that impossibility must lie either in the premise or in the reasoning. But the deduction was a necessary one, as every consequent statement was always proved by what went before, and the premise was true. For there

---

141. Origen the Platonist. Cf. Proclus, *In Parm.* 1065.1ff.

must be a One that is simply one, as we have shown both from what is said in the *Sophist* and also from objective necessity.

So the hypothesis does not lead to a conclusion that is impossible or that conflicts with Platonic doctrine. What more need we say to these people, who are already refuted by what is said about dialectic in the *Republic* (VII, 534b ff), namely, that it treats of the cause of all the intelligibles, which approach differs in no way from the negative method?

If this view is true, where does Plato discuss the One negatively? Not in the Second Hypothesis, where he discusses "all" affirmatively, nor in the third, where he discusses "all" negatively. The alternative remains, that the discussion of the One is either in this hypothesis, or nowhere. But the latter is unlikely, as Socrates said in that passage that it was the main subject of dialectic.

But others admit[142] the validity of the hypothesis, because the *Republic* also says about the first principle that it is what is beyond intellect, and the intelligible and beyond existence (VI, 509b), and these are what Plato here denies of the One, while in the Second Hypothesis he begins by affirming existence. So if the first does not deal with the One that is beyond Being, what other hypothesis is there besides it that does so? And so their reply to this doubt is that Parmenides believes all the foregoing conclusions to be true, but that this statement is not the close of the discussion of the First Hypothesis, but is put down as the starting-point of the Second; in order to show the way to the Second Hypothesis, he says that someone may find these conclusions impossible as concerning the One. He had to bring in what was needed to pass over to the Second Hypothesis so that we should not find anything superfluous. For these things only seem impossible because of the inexpressibleness of the One, since it is obvious to any one that, as far as truth goes, they are not impossible. For possible premises do not lead to impossible conclusions, but the premise is possible, unless the really-One is incapable of being real. The Stranger in the *Sophist* reminds us of this (245a-b) where he refutes those who say that the first is the whole, by showing that the really-One is not a whole. If the premise is granted that there is the absolutely-One, then everything follows necessarily from this by necessary hypothetical syllogisms. So this statement, "These things are impossible," is made as a constructive

---

142. The sequence of three authorities culminates in Syrianus; one may thus conjecture that this refers to Porphyry.

introduction, in order to show the way to the Second Hypothesis, because they are impossible on account of the super-excellence of the One. For what is to follow is more commensurate with our understanding and easier to communicate to us than what has gone before, as it has more affinity with our minds. Plato himself in the *Letters* (II, 312e) replies to someone who asks what the first principle is, that such a question is unsuitable. For nothing that has any affinity with us should be attributed to the first principle, and one should absolutely not ask "what is it like?" That is dealt with in the Second Hypothesis, which asks what the One Being is like and shows that it is a whole, that it is a finite and infinite manifold, that it is in motion and at rest, and that it is everything, in due order, that agrees with these characters. But the First Hypothesis which takes the absolutely-One for its subject does not tell us what it is like, but removes everything from it and assigns nothing to it because nothing that has any affinity with us ought to be said of it. From this it is obvious that what has been said will seem impossible (though, as has been shown, it is all possible), because it is so far from our own nature and so totally foreign to Plato's own rule for speaking about the first principle.

This, then, is the argument of these people. But others,[143] later than these, think that this conclusion is a generalization which contains all the previous negations. For just as there are conclusions rounding off every theorem, so this conclusion is appended to the rest, "that all these things are impossible of the One," namely, "many," "whole," "shape," "being in itself or another," the various genera of Being, "like" and "unlike," "equal" and "unequal," the property of being older than, younger than, and the same age as itself, the three- and nine-foldness of the parts of time, and after all these, also participation in substance, being existence itself, being participable by existence, expressibleness, knowableness. All of these, as has been shown, are impossible of the One. This is why he asks if it is possible to say these things which he has asked about of the One, and Aristotle denies it. For whatever you add to "one," any kind of existent whatever, is something other than one. If "one" has something else added to it besides what it itself is, it becomes "something that is one" instead of being simply "one," just as, if "animal" has something else added to it besides what it itself is, it becomes "a

143. Perhaps Iamblichus.

particular animal." And so with everything considered in itself: "good," or "equal" or "like," or "whole," if they have anything else added to them they are no longer just those characters themselves but have become "something good," "something equal," "something that is like"—in general one should say the same about all these characters considered in themselves as about "one." This is, then, a single negation summing up all the rest and added to them. The One, not being one among all things, is the cause of all.[144] So the general negation represents at the same time the whole progression of all from the One and the manifestation of individual beings taken together and separately in the order that appears fitting. And this interpretation, too, is correct.

Of these solutions, the former aims at literary consistency, while the latter does not depart from the consideration of reality. However, following our Master, we must also say that negative propositions in the sphere of the existent have different meanings according to their subject matter. Sometimes they have only a privative, sometimes also specific[145] significance. For example, we say "is not" in speaking of rest because it is not movement or identity or difference, and similarly we say "is not" in speaking of movement because it is not any of the other things; and in general each thing is in a single way, inasmuch as it is itself, but in many ways it is not, inasmuch as it is distinguished from other things. But though we deny other things of it, these negative propositions are in a particular way tied up with positive propositions. For it does also participate in each of the other things, yet it keeps its own integrity and is what it is. In this case, then, the negative propositions are specific, for not being that, it will be the other; now this is intellectual form. For it has been shown that it is the character of difference as distributed[146] in this sphere that makes "not being" true in it; this is what constitutes negation here.

On the other hand, in speaking of sensible objects we say that Socrates is not a horse and not a lion, and is not any of the other things, for he lacks all the other characters. For, being one particular thing, he is not an infinite number of others, and in him there

---

144. Cf. Proclus, *In Parm.* 1075.17–34; 1076.30–32. See also Plotinus, *Enneads* VI.9.6: "That which is cause of all is none of those things [of which it is cause]."

145. *Specionaliter*, presumably translating *eidetikos*.

146. Cf. Plato, *Sophist* 255e.

are lacks, which are nothing but lacks, of all of those characters. For he does not in a particular way participate in the other things, as we said was true of intelligibles. And this non-participation is not due to the purity of the idea "Socrates," but to the weakness of a material and corporeal subject, which is incapable of a simultaneous participation in everything. For this reason negative propositions in the intelligible sphere really express something about the predicates. The same holds true also of negative propositions about objects of sense; but in the former case they are specific, while in the latter they are merely privative.

But negative propositions about the One do not really express anything about the One. For nothing at all applies to it, either specifically or privatively, but, as we have said, the name "one" names our conception of it, not the One itself, and so we say that the negation also is about our conception, and none of the negative conclusions that have been stated is about the One, but because of its simplicity, it is exalted above all contrast and all negation. So he rightly added at the end that these negative propositions do not express anything about the One.

It is not the same thing to refer to the One and to express something about the One. The argument does not express anything about the One, for it is indefinable. So the negative propositions that have been stated do not express anything about the One, but do refer to the One. This is why they resemble neither those which occur in the intelligible sphere nor those which are about the objects of sense. For the former are about the same things of which the negations also are predicated, while the latter do not in any way express anything about the One.

This, then, is the solution of our first doubt. But from another point of view one must say that he first denies everything of the One, thinking that negations are more suited to it than assertions, and keeping the hypothesis which says "is" of the One. But since, as he advances, he has taken away from it not only everything else but also participation in substance and Being, which itself is of high value, and has shown that it is neither expressible nor knowable, now at the end he rightly removes from it even the negations themselves. For if the One is not expressible and if it has no definition, then how will the negations be true for it? For every proposition says that "this" belongs to "that." [But as nothing can belong to the

269

One], it is totally unnameable. But there has to be some name as the subject of a negative proposition, and so even the negations are not true of the One, but negations are truer than assertions; yet even they fall short of the simplicity of the One. Indeed all truth is in it, but it is itself better than all truth. So how would it be possible to say anything true about it?

He is therefore right in ending with the removal even of the negatives, saying that it is impossible that they should express anything about the One, which is inexpressible and unknowable. And one should not wonder that Plato, who always respects the principles of contradiction, says here that both the assertions and the denials are false of the One at the same time. For with regard to what can be said, assertion and denial make the distinction between true and false: but where no proposition is possible, what kind of assertion would be possible? It is clear to me that he too, who after Plato refused to admit a One above Intelligence for the reason that he was convinced of the validity of the principle of contradiction, and saw that the One was inexpressible and unspeakable, stopped short at the intellectual cause and the Intellect, [making that] the cause superior to all things;[147]... however, by asserting that the Intellect is the cause, he eliminates providence; for it is providence that is characteristic of the One that is beyond Intellect, not mere thought such as is proper to Intellect. And by abolishing providence he does away with creation, for what can provide for nothing is sterile. And by rejecting creation he is rejecting the hypothesis of the Ideas according to which the Demiurge fashions his work, and consequently—not to enumerate everything—he does away with the whole of dialectics ...[148] introducing new doctrines into his inherited philosophy. In order to escape this, we say that, for the inexpressible, contradictory propositions are both false, that they make the distinction between true and false only in the sphere of the expressible, and that in no sphere are they ever both true.

To give, as they say, the third cup to Zeus the Preserver,[149] we take the negative propositions about the One as generating positive

147. A gap of eight letters. It is to Aristotle that reference is being made.

148. Once again, a gap of eight letters.

149. A proverbial expression, used by Plato at *Philebus* 66d, *Republic* IX.583b, and *Ep*. VII.340a.

propositions, as has often been said; but do not think that the One has the power of generating all things, both productivity and existence having been removed from it. For power is a middle term between these ... the last negation referring to the One removes also such negations from it.[150] And "these things are not possible of the One" means that even the power of generating all things, which we said was a characteristic of negation, does not belong to the One, and therefore, even if it is said to generate and to produce, these expressions are transferred to it from the sphere of the existent, since they are the most distinguished names of powers. But it is better than all these names, just as it is better than the things that are named by us. Indeed, if I am to state my opinion, positive propositions apply rather to the monads of kinds of being, for the power of generating things is in these. The first principle is before every power and before assertions.

Next, then, let us take up the fourth way of solving the problem. The soul ascending to the level of Intellect ...[151] ascends with her multitude of faculties, but sheds everything that dissipates her activities. Now going further and having arrived there she comes to rest in the One Being, and she approaches the One itself and becomes single, not becoming inquisitive or asking what it is not and what it is, but everywhere closing her eyes, and contracting all her activity and being content with unity alone. Parmenides, then, is imitating this and ends by doing away both with the negations and with the whole argument, because he wants to conclude the discourse about the One with the inexpressible. For the term of the progress towards it has to be a halt; of the upward movement, rest; of the arguments that it is inexpressible and of all knowledge, a unification. For all these reasons it seems to me that he ends by removing the negations also from the One. For this whole dialectical method, which works by negations, conducts us to what lies before the threshold of the One, removing all inferior things and by this removal dissolving the impediments to the contemplation of the One, if it is possible to speak of such a thing. But after going

150. There is some corruption in the text here.

151. A gap of eight letters, but no apparent break in sense. Perhaps simply an epithet of Intellect.

through all the negations, one ought to set aside this dialectical method also, as being troublesome and introducing the notion of the things denied with which the One can have no neighborhood. For the intellect cannot have a pure vision when it is obstructed intelligizing the things that come after it, nor the soul distracted by deliberation, of the things that are lower than the soul, nor in general is it possible to have perfect vision with deliberation. Deliberation is the mark of thought's encounter with difficulties: this is why Nature produces and knowledge says what it says without deliberation. It deliberates only when it is doubtful and falls short of being knowledge.

Just as there deliberation ought to be eliminated from our activity, although it is brought to perfection by deliberation, so here all dialectical activity ought to be eliminated. These dialectical operations are the preparation for the strain towards the One, but are not themselves the strain. Or rather, not only must it be eliminated, but the strain as well. Finally, when it has completed its course, the soul may rightly abide with the One. Having become single and alone in itself, it will choose only the simply One.

This seems to be the point of the last question that Parmenides asks when he concludes this long development of the argument about the One. And so it is right that Aristotle also, following him, [passes from] the nature of Being to the inexpressible itself; for by means of a negation he too removes all the negations. It is with silence, then, that he brings to completion the study of the One.

14. Damascius
Commentary on Plato's Phaedo

Damascius belonged to a small, closed Neoplatonic community by birth and upbringing. As a young student in Alexandria, he moved among the circles of the most eminent Hellenic philosophers and theurgists of his time. He studied rhetoric under Theo at Alexandria, and mathematics under Marinus at Athens. He also studied philosophy with Zenodotus and Ammonius, the son of Hermeias. Damascius knew Aedesia, Hermeias' widow; the Egyptian philosopher-theurgist Asclepiodotus, and his family; Severinus, a distinguished citizen of Damascus with whom he read

Isocrates and the poets; and the great master Isidorus, who was Damascius' predecessor on the Athenian chair.

Damascius was the last official head (*diadochos*) of the Neoplatonic School at Athens. After its restoration by Plutarch of Athens, the wealthy School had stood as a firm bastion of Hellenic philosophy, religion, and culture. Under the leadership of Damascius, the School prospered until the edict of the Emperor Justinian, who set himself the task of extirpating "paganism," and who by a decree issued in 529 C.E. prohibited philosophical teaching. It seems that the School was then closed, although Olympiodorus mentions that at around 560 C.E. the Academy was still in possession of part of its endowment. At any rate, Damascius—who had already endured several waves of persecution—departed for Ctesiphon on the banks of the Tigris, the capital of the Persian Empire. According to a recent hypothesis, he set up the Academy in the North Mesopotamian city of Harran, *hellenon polis*, which had a Greco-Aramaic ethnic history. Harran remained for a long time as a potent symbol of "paganism," where Hermes-Thoth and Plato were duly venerated and the Babylonian moon god Sin worshiped.

Damascius composed several important philosophical works, among them the magnificent (but now neglected and little known) *On the First Principles* (*Damaskiou diadochou aporiai kai luseis peri ton proton archon* or *De principiis*), as well as a commentary on Plato's *Parmenides*. He placed an ineffable Principle above the One and emphasized its inaccessibility not only to conceptual thought, but even to divine intellection. He did not hesitate to criticize Proclus in favor of Iamblichus. His *Commentary on Plato's Phaedo* (wrongly attributed in times past to Olympiodorus) was a course of lectures in which various doctrines of Plato (including the famous definition of philosophy as a preparation for death) were explained, with occasional reference to the Orphic myths. Using Proclus as a starting-point for the discussion, he developed his own ideas—critical or supplementary—assuming that the reader had Proclus' basic work and his own side by side.

The excerpts here reproduced from Damascius' *Commentary on Plato's Phaedo*, were translated by L.G. Westerink and published as *The Greek Commentaries on Plato's Phaedo, vol. II, Damascius* (Amsterdam, Oxford, and New York: North-Holland Publishing Company, 1977).

In Phaed. 3–19. Dionysus and the Titans (Phaed. 61c2–62c4)

3. Creation being twofold, either indivisible or divided, the latter, according to the commentator, is ruled by Dionysus,[152] and therefore divided, the former by Zeus; each of the two has his own multitude of subordinates, Zeus of Olympian Gods, Dionysus of Titans; and in both cases we have a monad as well as a triad of Creators.[153]

4. What he says about a monad and a triad is true, but we must maintain that the Titans who plot against Dionysus belong to another divine character, because no manifold opposes or destroys its own monad, otherwise it would destroy itself also. Besides, it is not to the Titans, but to the other Gods that Zeus says [Orph. fr. 208]:

Hearken, ye Gods, this is the King I give you.

So long, indeed, as Dionysus sits on the throne of Zeus, he is undivided[154] ... to the Titans that he is divided and undergoes a metamorphosis in the way of ... but in the Titanic way. In fact, even ... when he is divided, he is still made whole ... is more according to his nature. Let us say, therefore ... the forms or of the whole, though only ... his own as Titanic ... because they are dispersed or intermediate and constitute the universe, but not the whole, as belonging to the sphere of Dionysus. Hence he can be said to be at the same

---

152. Dionysus, son of Zeus and Persephone, was enthroned by Zeus as king of the Gods. Hera plotted against him with the Titans. Neglecting Apollo's warnings he rose from his Father's throne to join the Titans, who had disguised themselves as Bacchants, carrying the thyrsus. They handed him a thyrsus instead of his royal scepter, and some toys, among which was a mirror. While he was contemplating his face in the mirror, they attacked him, tore him to pieces and devoured his flesh. His heart was saved by Athena, and Apollo gathered what was left of the limbs. The Titans were burnt by the lightning-bolts of Zeus; out of their ashes man was created. Dionysus was reborn from Semele.

153. The demiurgic triad in relation to Zeus is the triad of the three sons of Kronos: Zeus-Poseidon-Pluto; subordinate to the one transcendent Zeus, the Creator of the *Timaeus*, is the intramundane Zeusian triad of the celestial, the marine and the chtonic Zeus. The triad Helios-Apollo-Dionysus, which might also be considered, is not identified with Dionysus as a whole.

154. The manuscript is damaged at this point and following (as indicated by the ellipsis points). It seems that the symbols of the prison (the body or the material world), the Titans (guilt and disintegration of the individual soul), and also that of

time indivisible and divisible, for such is the nature of the universe, which has rather the character of an aggregate and is held together by a totality whose parts are distinct.

5. Why are the Titans said to plot against Dionysus?—Because they initiate a mode of creation that does not remain within the bounds of the multiform continuity of Dionysus.

6. Their punishment consists in the checking of their dividing activities. Such is all chastisement: it aims at restraining and reducing erroneous dispositions and activities.

7. Tradition knows three kinds of punishments inflicted on the Titans: lightning-bolts, shackles, descents into various lower regions. This last kind is in the nature of a retribution, as it aggravates their leaning towards division and uses their shattered remains for the constitution of individuals, human and otherwise; the second is coercive, checking their powers of division; the first is purificatory and makes them whole, though only by participation. All three should be regarded as imposed upon each, though the myth distributes them, for each possesses higher, intermediate and lower powers.

8. In what sense are men created from the fragments of the Titans?—From the fragments, because their life is reduced to the utmost limit of differentiation; of the Titans, because they are the lowest of Creators and in immediate contact with their creation. For Zeus is the "Father of men and Gods," the Titans of men only, not of Gods, and they cannot even be called fathers, but have become men themselves, and not simply themselves, but their dead bodies, and even of these only the fragments, the fragmentary condition of our existence being thus transferred to those who are its causes.

9. The Titanic mode of life is the irrational mode, by which rational life is torn asunder.

It is better to acknowledge its existence everywhere, since in any case at its source there are Gods, the Titans; then also on the plane of rational life, this apparent self-determination, which seems to aim at belonging to itself alone and neither to the superior nor to

Dionysus (the world Mind, or rather, divine Intellect, divided in creation) were already used by Xenocrates. For Porphyry, Dionysus symbolizes the world Mind, and the Titans its vestiges in the material world. For Damascius, the Dionysiac and the Titanic orders are fundamentally different, the Dionysiac form being characterized by unity, the Titanic form by dispersal.

the inferior, is wrought in us by the Titans; through it we tear asunder the Dionysus in ourselves, breaking up the natural continuity of our being and our partnership, so to speak, with the superior and the inferior. While in this condition, we are Titans; but when we recover that lost unity, we become Dionysus and we attain what can be truly called completeness.

10. What is the "kind of custody" [*Phaed.* 62b3–4]?—Viewed as the guarding power, it is Dionysus himself, who loosens the shackle for whom he will, since he is also the cause of individual life. Viewed as the object of the custody, on the other hand, it is the experience itself of being bound in the body, which has befallen us of necessity as an act of justice; for by actualizing her own separate existence the soul has been locked up in a body which, though her own, has also many wants, to make her feel her dependence on the common form and teach her what it is to be an individual.

11. Dionysus is the cause of deliverance only; therefore this God is also named Lyseus, and Orpheus says [fr. 232]:

> And men shall bring to thee rich hecatombs,
> yearly, in season, and celebrate thy rites,
> seeking deliverance from their forebears' sins;
> and thou, their Lord, shalt free whomever thou wilt
> from weary toil and agony unrelieved.

The guarding power, however, in the most comprehensive sense, is Zeus, or, more immediately, the Young Gods, or, most directly, the generative Gods, who have also the power to destroy.

It should be observed that Dionysus, too, is a God in charge of creation, because of his connection with rebirth.

12. [62b4–5] It is the Gods who appoint the term of the imprisonment, as long as it is better for embodied souls to be under restraint, in view of the final goal, which is deliverance by Dionysus. This measure and this appointed term we can never know; therefore, if we free ourselves, such a way of gaining our freedom is not release, but flight, because we still need to be kept in custody.

13. [62b4] Socrates qualifies suicide now as "unlawful" [61c10], then as "impious" [62a6], then again as "undue" [62b4]. The first term measures it by the standard imposed by the Gods, the second by the standard of what we owe to the Gods, while the notion of what is "due" seems to include both.

14. In the mystic account the ruling principle is the monad of the Young God; in the philosophical demonstration, inasmuch as this latter develops the esoteric reason, it is the multitude of the Gods to whom Plato [*Tim.* 42d6] gives the corresponding name of the "Young Gods"; their king he makes the Sun [*Rep.* VI 509d2–3], who, according to Orpheus [fr. 172, 212] is closely connected with Dionysus through the intermediary of Apollo.

Rather, we should make the Sun king of the Gods in so far as he is identical with Zeus, while in his quality of Dionysus he is divided over the world, and as Apollo he holds an intermediate position, gathering the dividedness of Dionysus and standing by the side of Zeus.

15. If the exoteric account is a development of the esoteric reason, just as the manifold is of its own monad, how can the occult reason still be so? A monad heading an exoteric manifold cannot be occult itself, because multitude and monad belong to the same kind. Therefore the truth seems to be rather that in each of the two cases the monad as well as the manifold are both exoteric and occult; but in the one case Plato discusses in philosophical terms the unlawfulness of suicide and the reason for which it is forbidden, in the other he informs us of the symbol by which the commandment was expressed, without explaining its nature (since he was not allowed to do so), only stating that it was given in a mystic form. One who considers this contrary to reason does not know the nature of symbolical utterance; therefore it is described as "deep" and "not easy to grasp": "not easy to grasp" for the profane and among the profane, "deep," because it is not a cause, but the source of all causality.

16. The Young Gods imprison souls in bodies, when they have modeled living organisms fit to receive a soul, "borrowing parts" from the elements [*Tim.* 42e6—43a6]; when, on the other hand, returning what they have borrowed, they decompose the organisms, at that moment they free the souls from their shackles.

17. [62b7] "Care" is the direct providence that bestows on each, according to circumstances and set limits, what is best for him.

18. [62b7–8] Socrates combines the two notions, that "the Gods take care of us" and that "we are their possessions," not only in imitation of the processes of emanation and reversion, but also to establish the major of his hypothetical syllogism all the more secure-

ly. For if we were their possessions and they did not take care of us, or conversely, escape would not be punishable; it follows that, both being true, we are liable to punishment.

19. [62cl–4] How can Socrates draw inferences with regard to the Gods on the analogy of the human situation, though they are obviously not subject to our emotions?—The inference is based on rational behavior in the fields of social life and household administration, since it is evident that all regulating care has its prototype in the Gods. Anger and punishment, however, should be given a different meaning, when applied to them, anger being a withholding of their own light, punishment a secondary, coercive form of providence towards the erring soul.

In Phaed. 119–124. *Purification the Way to God (Phaed. 67a6–b2)*

119. The final goal for the philosopher committed to social life is contact with the God who extends his providence to all things; for the one on the way to purification contact with the God who transcends all things and is with himself alone; for the contemplative philosopher contact with the God who is united with the principles superior to himself and wishes to be theirs rather than his own; therefore Plato says: "to touch the Pure without being pure" [b2].

120. One who is purifying himself and endeavoring to assimilate himself to the Pure must in the first place discard pleasure and pain as far as possible; secondly, the food of which he partakes should be simple, avoiding all luxury, and it should also be in accordance with the laws of justice and temperance (that is to say, free from the taint of bloodshed) and with divine command and ancestral custom (for a diet that, in defiance of religious law, offends against animal life and coarsens the vital spirit, will make the body unruly towards the soul and unfit to enter into contact with God); thirdly, he must suppress the aimless motion of irrational appetite (what indeed could arouse desire or anger in one who has disengaged himself from all external things?), but if anything of the kind should ever stir in waking or sleeping, it must be quelled speedily by reason; fourthly, he must detach himself from sense-perception and imagination, except in so far as it is necessary to make use of them; in the fifth place, the man who wants to be set free from the plurality of genesis must dissociate himself from the multifarious variety of opinion; the sixth and last precept is to escape from the complexity of discursive reason and seek the simpler forms of demonstration and division as a preparation for the undivided activity of the intellect.

121. The same relation that exists between education and life in society (the function of education being to quiet down the wild turmoil of birth and to make the soul fit to attain complete harmony), exists also between the life of purification and the life of contemplation: purification checks the downward trend to prepare us for the effort of ascension, and this is also the aim of the purifying ceremonies that precede sacred rites. If one is to be united with the higher powers, it is necessary to detach oneself from lower influences first.

122. Any disposition on our part inevitably assimilates us to one particular category of beings in the universe. If we are pure, we join the pure, if impure, the impure, i.e., matter-bound demons in the latter case, the Gods in the former, or, if our condition is intermediate, the intermediate kinds. In each case similarity is the binding force that unites things of one kind to form a continuous whole, as water does with water and air with air. Therefore, when approaching God, we should strengthen our likeness to him, as far as it lies in our power, through purity; for, as Plato says, "it is unlawful to touch the Pure without being pure." It is called "unlawful," because God must not be soiled by an impure contact; at the same time it is impossible, since darkness can never approach light.

123. Purity is threefold: of the soul, of the body, of external things. We must strive for all of these, so that everything, not only ourselves, but our tools also, may be flooded by divine illumination, that no demoniac darkness may settle on our soiled tools, turning away our sight from the Gods, and that our soul may travel lighter on her way to the divine and, so far from being burdened by those tools, may derive strength from them for the upward journey, since she is still tied to them as far as natural life is concerned. If, on the other hand, we come to God with an impure mind, though pure externally, we lose our pains; for then the soul by her way of life remains chained to the evil genii she resembles.

124. [67b1] Are pure and true identical, as Plato says?—"Pure" means that a thing is separate from everything else, and "true" that it is exactly what it is, and this is apparently the reason why it is necessary to become pure first, before we can attain truth. Therefore, since we are not yet pure, because we have not yet died, it is said that "we shall know the truth when he have arrived yonder" [69d5–6].

In Phaed. 165–172. Philosophy is Initiation (Phaed. 69c3–d2)

165. Dialectical thought should either start from the divine riddles, developing the mysterious truth in them, or come to rest in them and derive its final confirmation from their symbolical indications, or it should combine the two, as Socrates does here. The whole discussion consisting of two problems, the ban on suicide, and, in spite of this, the necessity of detaching oneself from the body, he makes the divine mysteries the starting-point for the first [62b2–6] and the final point of the second.

166. In this, he imitates the mystic and cosmic cycle of souls. Having fled the undivided Dionysian life and fixed their actual existence on the level of the Titanic and confined way of life, they are in shackles and in "custody" [62b4]; but when they submit to their punishment and take care of themselves, then, cleansed from the taints of Titanic existence and gathered together, they become Bacchus, that is to say, they become whole again, as the Dionysus who remains above is whole.

167. In the mysteries the first stage used to be general purifying ceremonies, followed by more secret ones, after which conjunction took place, then initiation, and finally vision. Analogous to these stages are the several degrees of virtues, the ethical and social virtues correspondingly to the public purifying rites, the purificatory virtues, in which all the extraneous is discarded, to the more secret purifications, speculative activity on the reflective level to conjunction, integration of its results to form an indivisible whole to initiation, simple intuition of simple forms to vision.

168. The object of the initiatory rites is to take souls back to a final destination, which was also the starting-point from which they first set out on their downward journey, and where Dionysus gave them being, seated on his father's throne, that is to say, firmly established in the integral Zeusian life. It follows necessarily that the initiate will "live with the Gods," in accordance with the design of the initiating Gods. Initiatory rites are twofold: those here below, which are a kind of preparation, and those in the hereafter, of which there are, in my opinion, again two kinds, those that purify the pneumatic body (as rites here below do the "shell-like" body) and those that purify the astral body. In other words, the way upward through initiation has three degrees, as also has the way through philosophy: the philosophers' way to perfection takes three thousand years, as it is said in the *Phaedrus* [249a3–5], the number thousand representing a full life and a complete period. Therefore the "uninitiated,"

because farthest remote from his destination, "lies in slime," both here and even more, hereafter, where his place is in the "dregs of creation," Tartarus itself. Of course the text mentions only the extremes, but there is also a wide range of intermediate states. The ways by which philosophy leads us upwards can be thought of in analogous terms, though the communion achieved through them is not perfect or equal to the mystic union. If it is true that a man who pursues philosophy without eagerness will not have the benefit of its results, it is no less true that neither will a man who follows the way of initiation without total commitment reap its fruits.

169. [69c6] The word "to lie" describes the helplessness that makes the soul dependent on external impulses, because it has become like a body, while "living with the Gods" means belonging to their community and sharing in their government. But if so, what is the sense of the Oracle [fr. 130.2], "They rest in God, breathing the midday rays"? Here the condition is a higher one, surpassing all power of self-movement, as it were a supernatural form of being moved from without.

170. [69c8–d1] The fennel-stalk symbolizes matter-bound and divided creation, because it is a spurious form, being "a tree, yet not a tree."

A better reason is its utterly broken continuity, which has made the plant an attribute of the Titans: they offer it to Dionysus instead of his paternal scepter, and thus they entice him into divided existence; further, the Titans are represented as bearing the fennel-stalk and Prometheus steals the fire in one, which means either that he forces down the celestial light into the world of process, or that he leads forth the soul to incarnation, or that he calls forth into the generated world the whole of divine illumination, which is itself ungenerated. This is, in fact, why Socrates too calls the masses "bearers of the fennel-stalk" with the Orphic term, because they lead the Titanic life.

171. The first Bacchus is Dionysus, whose ecstasy manifests itself in dancing [*basis*] and shouting [*iache*], that is, in every form of movement, of which he is the cause according to the *Laws* [II.679a5–d4]; but one who has dedicated himself to Dionysus, having become of his lineage, shares his name also. And when a man leads a Dionysian life, his troubles are already elided and he is free from his bonds and released from custody, or rather from the confined form of life; such a man is the philosopher in the stage of purification.

172. To some philosophy is primary, as to Porphyry and Plotinus and a great many other philosophers; to others hieratic practice, as to Iamblichus, Syrianus, Proclus, and the hieratic school generally. Plato, however, recognizing that strong arguments can be advanced from both sides, has united the two into one single truth by calling the philosopher a "Bacchus"; for by using the notion of a man who has detached himself from genesis as an intermediate term, we can identify the one with the other. Still, it remains evident that he intends to honor the philosopher by the title of Bacchus, as we honor the Intelligence by calling it God, or profane light by giving it the same name as to mystic light.

15. Damascius
On the First Principles

Damascius, though a thoroughly Hellenic philosopher by education and culture, was closely connected with his Near Eastern background. He collected and systematized popular tales and paradoxical accounts of miracles, treating such stories as the vehicles of spiritual truths and the symbolic veils of divine mysteries. He and his master Isidore were even known to have made an eight month pilgrimage from Alexandria to Athens—through Arabia, Palestine, Syria, and Asia Minor—visiting sacred temple sites along the way.

Damascius attempted to establish a kind of perennial philosophy (albeit dressed in late Neoplatonic garb), from which, however, his aggressive enemies and Christians persecutors—whom he regarded as servants of the Typhonian darkness—were excluded. Certain references from his treatise *On the First Principles* show that Damascius had at least some indirect knowledge of ancient Babylonian cosmogony, as it was contained in the cuneiform tablets called the *Enuma elish*.

The excerpt here reproduced from Damascius' *On the First Principles* was translated by Thomas Taylor and first published in 1816, as an additional note to his translation of the *Theology of Plato*, by Proclus.

De principiis I.316.20–I.324.15

The theology contained in the Orphic rhapsodies concerning the intelligible Gods is as follows: *Time* is symbolically placed for the one principle of the universe; but *ether* and *chaos*, for the two posterior to this one; and *being*, simply considered, is represented under the symbol of an egg. And this is the first triad of the intelligible Gods. But for the perfection of the second triad, they establish either a conceiving and a conceived egg as a God, or a white garment, or a cloud: because from them Phanes leap forth into light. For indeed they philosophize variously concerning the middle triad. But Phanes here represents intellect. But conceiving him over and above this, as father and power, contributes nothing to Orpheus. But they call the third triad Metis as *intellect*, Ericapaeus as *power*, and Phanes as *father*. But sometimes the middle triad is considered according to the three-shaped God, while conceived in the egg; for the middle always represents each of the extremes; as in this instance, where the egg and the three-shaped God subsist together. And here you may perceive that the egg is that which is united; but that the three-shaped and really multiform God is the separating and discriminating cause of that which is intelligible. Likewise the middle triad subsists according to the egg, as yet united; but the third according to the God who separates and distributes the whole intelligible order. And this is the common and familiar Orphic theology. But that delivered by Hieronymus and Hellanicus is as follows. According to them *water* and *matter* were the first productions, from which earth was secretly drawn forth: so that water and earth are established as the two first principles; the latter of these having a *dispersed* subsistence; but the former conglutinating and connecting the latter. But they are silent concerning the principle prior to these two, as being ineffable: for as there are no illuminations about him, his arcane and ineffable nature is from hence sufficiently evinced. But the third principle posterior to these two, *water* and *earth*, and which is generated from them, is a *dragon*, naturally endued with the heads of a bull and a lion, but in the middle having the countenance of the God himself. They add likewise that he has wings on his shoulders, and that he is called *undecaying Time*, and *Hercules*; that *Necessity* resides with him, which is the same as *Nature*, and incorporeal *Adrastia*, which is extended throughout the universe, whose limits she binds in amicable conjunction. But as it appears to me, they denominate this third principle as established according to essence; and assert, besides this, that it subsists as male and female, for the purpose of exhibiting the generative causes of all things.

But I likewise find in the Orphic rhapsodies, that neglecting the two first principles, together with the one principle who is delivered in silence, the third principle, posterior to the two, is established by the theology as the original; because this first of all possesses something effable and commensurate to human discourse. For in the former hypothesis, the highly reverenced and undecaying *Time*, the father of ether and chaos, was the principle: but in this *Time* is neglected, and the principle becomes a *dragon*. It likewise calls triple ether, moist; and Chaos, infinite; and Erebus, cloudy and dark; delivering this second triad analogous to the first; this being potential, as that was paternal. Hence the third procession of this triad is dark Erebus: its paternal and summit ether, not according to a simple but intellectual subsistence: but its middle infinite chaos, considered as a progeny or procession, and among these parturient, because from these the third intelligible triad proceeds. What then is the third intelligible triad? I answer, the egg; the duad of the natures of male and female which it contains, and the multitude of all-various seeds, residing in the middle of this triad. And the third among these is an incorporeal God, bearing golden wings on his shoulders; but in his inward parts naturally possessing the heads of bulls, upon which heads a mighty dragon appears, invested with the all-various forms of wild beasts. This last then must be considered as the *intellect* of the triad; but the middle progeny, which are *many* as well as *two*, correspond to *power*, and the egg itself is the *paternal principle* of the third triad: but the third God of this third triad, this theology celebrates as *Protogonus*, and calls him *Zeus*, the disposer of all things and of the whole world; and on this account denominates him *Pan*. And such is the information which this theology affords us, concerning the genealogy of the intelligible principles of things.

But in the writings of the Peripatetic Eudemus, containing the *Theology* of Orpheus, the whole intelligible order is passed over in silence, as being every way ineffable and unknown, and incapable of verbal enunciation. Eudemus therefore commences his genealogy from *Night*, from which also Homer begins: though Eudemus is far from making the Homeric genealogy consistent and connected, for he asserts that Homer begins from Ocean and Tethys. It is however apparent, that *Night is* according to Homer the greatest divinity, since she is reverenced even by Zeus himself. For the poet says of Zeus—"that he feared lest he should act in a manner displeasing to swift *Night.*" So that Homer begins his genealogy of the gods from *Night.* But it appears to me that Hesiod, when he asserts that Chaos was first generated, signifies by Chaos the incomprehensible and perfectly united nature of that which is intelligible: but that he produces earth the first from thence, as a certain principle of the whole procession of the Gods. Unless perhaps Chaos is the second of the two principles: but Earth, Tartarus, and Love, form the triple intelligible. So that *Love* is to be placed for the third monad of the intelligible order, considered according to its convertive nature; for it is thus denominated by Orpheus in his rhapsodies. But *Earth* for the first, as being first established in a certain firm and essential station. But *Tartarus* for the middle, as in a certain respect exciting and moving forms into distribution. But Acusilaus appears to me to establish *Chaos* for the first principle, as entirely unknown; and after this, two principles, *Erebus* as male, and *Night* as female; placing the latter for *infinity*, but the former for *bound*. But from the mixture of these, he says that *Ether*, *Love*, and *Counsel* are generated, forming three intelligible hypostases. And he places, *Ether* as the summit; but *Love* in the middle, according to its naturally middle subsistence; but *Metis* or *Counsel* as the third, and the same as highly-reverenced intellect. And, according to the history of Eudemus, from these he produces a great number of other Gods. But Epimenides establishes *Air* and *Night* as the two first principles; manifestly reverencing in silence the one principle prior to these two. But from air and night *Tartarus* is generated, forming as it appears to me the third principle, as a certain mixed temperature from the two. And thus mixture is called by some an intelligible medium, because it extends itself to both the summit and the end. But from the mixture of the extremes with each other, an egg is generated, which is truly an intelligible animal: and from this again another progeny proceeds. But according to Pherecydes Syrius, the three first principles are a *Perpetually-abiding Vital Nature, Time*, and an *Earthly Nature*: one of these subsisting, as I conceive, prior to the other two. But he asserts that *Time* generates from the progeny of itself, *Fire*, *Spirit*, and *Water*: which signify, as it appears to me, the triple nature of that which is intelligible. But from these, distributed into five profound recesses, a numerous progeny of Gods is constituted, which he calls *five-times animated* (*pantempsuchos*) and which is perhaps the same as if he had said (*pantekosmos*) or *a five-fold world*. But we may probably discourse on this subject at some other opportunity. And thus much may suffice at present concerning the hypotheses derived from the Grecian fables, which are both many and various.

But with respect to the theology of the Barbarians, the Babylonians[155] seem to pass over in silence the one principle of the universe. But they establish two principles, *Tauthe* and *Apasoon*. And they consider *Apasoon* as the husband of *Tauthe*, whom they denominate the mother of the Gods; from whom an only-begotten son *Mooumis* was produced: which, as it appears to me, is no other than the intelligible world deduced from two principles.[156] But from these another procession is derived, *Dache* and *Dachus*. And likewise a third from these, *Kissare* and *Assoorus*. And from these again three deities are produced, *Anus*, *Illinus*, and *Aus*. But from *Aus* and *Dache* a son called *Belus* is produced, who they say is the demiurgus of the world. But with respect to the Magi, and all the Arion race, as we are informed by Eudemus, some of them call all the intelligible and united world *Place*, and some of them *Time*: from which *a good divinity* and *an evil daemon* are distributed; *Light* and *Darkness* subsisting prior to these, according to the assertions of others. However, both the one and the other, after an undistributed nature, consider that nature as having a subsistence which distributes the two-fold co-ordination of better natures: one of which co-ordinations *Orosmades* presides over, and the other *Arimanius*. But the Sidonians, according to the same historian, place before all things, *Time*, *Desire*, and cloudy *Darkness*. And they assert that from the mingling of *Desire* and *Darkness* as two principles, *Air* and a *gentle Wind* were produced: *Air* evincing the summit of the intelligible triad; but the *gentle Wind* raised and proceeding from this, the vital prototype of the intelligible. And again that from both these the bird *Otus*, similar to a night raven, was produced; representing, as it appears to me, intelligible intellect. But as we find (without the assistance of Eudemus) the Phoenician mythology, according to Mochus, places *Ether* and *Air* as the two first principles, from which the intelligible god *Oulomus* was produced; who, as it appears to me, is the summit of the intelligible order. But from this god (yet proceeding together with him) they assert that *Chousorus* was produced, being the first unfolding pro-

---

155. A comparison between the cosmology of the Babylonians, as it is related by Damascius, the *Enuma elish*, and the Egyptian cosmology of Hermopolis is made by E.A. Wallis Budge in *The Gods of the Egyptians: Studies in Egyptian Mythology*, vol. 1 (New York: Dover Publications, 1969), pp.282–292.

156. That is, the Limit and the Unlimited.

cession. And after this an *egg* succeeds; which I think must be called intelligible intellect. But the unfolding *Chousorus* is intelligible power, because this is the first nature which distributes an undistributed subsistence; unless perhaps after the two principles *Ether* and *Air*, the summit is *One Wind*: but the middle *Two Winds*, the *south-west* and the *south*; for in a certain respect they place these prior to *Oulomus*. But *Oulomus* himself is intelligible intellect: and unfolding *Chousorus* the first order after the intelligible series. But the *egg* itself is heaven; from the bursting of which into two parts, the sections are said to have become heaven and earth. But with respect to the Egyptians, nothing accurately is related of them by Eudemus: we have, however, by means of some Egyptian philosophers resident among us, been instructed in the occult truth of their theological doctrine. According to these philosophers then, the Egyptians in certain discourses celebrate an *unknown Darkness* as the one principle of the universe, and this *thrice pronounced as such*: but for the two principles after the first they place *Water* and *Sand*, according to Heraiscus; but according to the more ancient writer Asclepiades, *Sand* and *Water*, from which and after which the first Kamephis is generated. But after this a *second*, and from this again a *third*; by all which, the whole intelligible distribution is accomplished. For thus Asclepiades determines. But the more modern Heraiscus says that the Egyptians, denominating the third Kamephis from his father and grandfather, assert that he is the *Sun*; which doubtless signifies in this case intelligible intellect. But a more accurate knowledge of these affairs must be received from the above-mentioned authors themselves. It must however be observed, that with the Egyptians there are many distributions of things according to union; because they unfold an intelligible nature into characteristics, or peculiarities of many gods, as may be learned from such as are desirous of consulting their writings on this subject.

GLOSSARY

Agalma—image, cult-statue, ornament, shrine, object of worship, something in which one takes delight; *theon agalmata* is the common phrase for "images of the gods" and "cult-statues" which may be "animated" by the theurgists; the word *agalma* contains no implication of likeness and is not a synonym of *eikon*; for Plato, the created cosmos is "a shrine brought into being for the everlasting gods" (*ton aidion theon gegonos agalma, Tim.* 37c); for the Emperor Julian, the visible Sun is "the living *agalma*, endowed with soul and intelligence and beneficent, of the noetic Father" (*Ep.* 51.434).

Aisthesis—sensation, perception, as an opposite of intellection (*noesis*), understanding, and pure thought; more loosely—any awareness; for Plato some *aistheseis* have names, such as sights, sounds, smells, cold and heat, distress, pleasures, fears, but nameless *aistheseis* are countless (*Theaet.* 156b); for Plotinus, perceptions in this world are dim intellections (*noeseis*), and intellections in the noetic world are vivid perceptions; Philo of Alexandria postulates an Idea of *aisthesis*, along with an Idea of *nous*, in the Intellect of God (*Leg. Alleg.* I.21–27).

Akh—the ancient Egyptian term for intelligence, spiritual light, illumination, irradiation; it may designate both a spiritual being (the winged soul, *ba*, divinized and raised above the Osiris state) and the entire spiritual dimension that corresponds to the Neoplatonic *kosmos noetos*; through a celestial ascent the pharaoh (prototype of the philosopher-mystic of later times) becomes a "shining one" (*akh*), a star irradiating light throughout the cosmos, and is united with Ra (the divine Intellect) as his "son."

Anagoge—ascent, elevation, bringing up; the approach to the divine realm by means of purifications (*katharmoi*), initiations (*teletai*), the Platonic dialectic and allegorical exegesis, contemplation (*theoria*), and the ineffable sacred rites employed in theurgy; it is prefigured by the sacred way which the initiates of mysteries (*mustai*) walk, the path to the mountain (*oreibasia*); typological analogies of the Neoplatonic ascent to the divine may be seen in the *Pyramid Texts* and the accounts of the *mi'raj* of the Prophet Muhammad in the later Islamic tradition.

Anamnesis—recollection, remembrance; in the Orphico-Pythagorean context, it is understood as a remembrance of one's true divine nature, revealed through sacred initiation; the idea of memory and the restoration of the soul's true identity is crucial for the Egyptian tradition as reflected in the *Book of the Dead* and later employed by Pythagoreans and by Plato, who explains *anamnesis* as recollection of things known before birth and forgotten (*Meno* 85d); thus Platonic learning is equated with remembering (*Phaed.* 72e).

Anthropos—man; in Gnosticism, the macrocosmic *anthropos* is regarded as the Platonic "ideal animal," *autozoon*, or a divine *pleroma*, which contains archetypes of creation and manifestation.

Apatheia—impassivity or freedom from emotions, understood as a philosophical virtue; *apatheia* means not being affected in any way and is applied both to the sages and transcendent entities by the Neoplatonists.

Apeiron (*apeiros, apeiria*)—lacking of limit, unlimited, as an opposite of *peras*, a bound; the even as an opposite to the odd; this is a fundamental Pythagorean term designating one of the main principles of manifested being; the Pythagorean Unlimited is indefinite and in need of Limit; it is infinite in a negative sense, as being infinitely divisible; in Neoplatonism, *peras* and *apeiron* constitute the primal archetypal duality located at a position between the ineffable One and the noetic cosmos.

Aporrhetos—secret, prohibited, unspeakable; the common designation of mysteries and sacred rites of initiation; in Neoplatonism the term is applied in metaphysics and negative theology, frequently understood as a characteristic of the First Principle.

Apotheosis—divinization; in the esoteric sense it is accomplished by the philosophical purification and theurgical *anagoge* which reveals one's primal and true identity with the divine principles; this is not a Homeric conception because Homer clearly separates the gods and men; however, following the ancient Egyptian spiritual patterns, the Orphic texts already promised *apotheosis* and immortality for the initiated soul who (like the Egyptian *ba* and the *psuche* in Plato's *Phaedrus*) restores her wings and raises up back to the divine homeland.

Arche—beginning, starting point, authority, government, heart, principle; *archai* are understood as the first principles by Neoplatonists; the term *archetupos*, archetype, is used already by Plotinus in the sense of a divine paradigm or noetic model of the manifested entity.

Arete—excellence, goodness, virtue; Plotinus makes a distinction between the civic virtues (*politikai aretai*) and the purificatory virtues (*kathartikai aretai*); Porphyry adds two other grades—the theoretic virtues (*theoretikai aretai*) and the paradigmatic virtues (*paradeigmatikai aretai*): the former being that of the soul which beholds *nous* within itself, and the latter being the virtue proper to the divine Intellect (*Nous*), itself; Iamblichus discerns seven grades of virtue which in an ascending order illustrate the anagogic path to the divine: natural, ethical, civic, purificatory, theoretic, and paradigmatic virtues are crowned by the hieratic virtues (*hieratikai aretai*) that are proper to the One—they make the soul godlike (*theoeides*) and unite it with the First Principle through theurgy.

Arithmos—number; for the Pythagoreans, number is the first principle (Aristotle, *Metaph.* 986a15); Iamblichus sometimes identifies the gods with *arithmoi*, regarding the first numbers from the monad to the decad as deities and archetypal models of manifestation; the numerical organization of the cosmos requires that the organizing principles of bodies be treated as physical numbers and distinguishes them from mathematical numbers, which are the paradigms of physical numbers; the ideal, noetic, or eidetic (*eidetikos*) numbers transcend even mathematical numbers.

Arrhetos—ineffable, unspeakable; this term is close to *aporrhetos* and is used to designate rites and visions of the mysteries, and the transcendent nature of the One in Neoplatonism.

Askesis—in ancient philosophy this term designates not an "asceticism," but spiritual exercises; thus *philosophia* is understood not as a theory of knowledge, but as a lived wisdom, a way of living according to intellect (*nous*); an *askesis* includes remembrance of God, the "watch of the heart," or vigilance (*nepsis*), and *prosoche*, or attention to the beauty of the soul, the examination of our conscience and knowledge of ourselves.

Autozoon—essential living Being, or noetic Animal, which contains within it Ideas of all the living creatures and Archetypes of the four elements (*Tim.* 30b); it is a completely coherent *archetypus mundus*, the timeless, ungenerated, immaterial, and perfect matrix of the psychic and physical cosmos; for Plotinus, it is a well-rounded whole, composed of individual intellects, or noetic lights; "a globe of faces radiant with faces all living" (*Enn.* VI.7.15).

Ba—an ancient Egyptian term which means "manifestation" of certain divine qualities, arranged in a descending and ascending hierarchy; in an eschatological and soteriological context, it may be understood as "soul" moving up and down (i.e., descending from above [the world of spiritual lights] and ascending again) as an individual in an out-of-body state which is attained through initiation or death, when the physical body (*khat*, Gr. *soma*) is experienced as a corpse; *ba* is the vehicle of ascent, pictured as a human-headed bird which flies into the spheres of light and finally becomes aware of itself as an *akh*; the concept of *ba* influenced the Pythagorean and Platonic concept of soul (*psuche*), who tries to restore her wings through *anamnesis*, initiation into philosophy, and then ascends to the divine realm.

Bios—life, or a way of life, analogous to the Hindu *darshana*; one thus speaks of the Pythagorean way of life, or the Orphic way of life; to be a philosopher implies a rupture with daily life (*bios*) and a purification of one's passions in order to experience the transcendence of the divine Intellect and the soul with respect to the mortal body.

Daimon—in the ancient Greek religion, *daimon* designates not a specific class of divine beings, but a peculiar mode of activity: it is an occult power that drives man forward or acts against him; since *daimon* is the veiled countenance of divine activity, every god can act as *daimon;* a special knowledge of *daimones* is claimed by Pythagoreans; for Plato, *daimon* is a spiritual being who watches over each individual, and is tantamount to his higher self, or an angel; whereas Plato is called "divine" by Neoplatonists, Aristotle is regarded as *daimonios,* meaning "an intermediary to god"—therefore Aristotle stands to Plato as an angel to a god; for Proclus, *daimones* are the intermediary beings located between the celestial objects and the terrestrial inhabitants.

Demiourgike seira—the vertical series of gods, irradiating in time from the Creator (*demiourgos*) in his timeless act of creation and crossing different levels of being, is called *demiourgike seira,* a demiurgic chain; similarly, a series of philosophers emanating in time from Orpheus, Pythagoras and Plato is called *chruse seira,* the golden chain; the appellation "golden" refers to the vertical rays of the divine light and the godlike nature of wisdom preserved by a "chosen race" (or "golden race") of philosophers.

Demiourgos—the Creator in Plato's *Timaeus,* literally "craftsman," who as the Father and King contains in one the perfection of all things; when these things are distributed to the particulated or manifested world, they become diversified and come under the power of different ruling principles; the Platonic Creator creates by appealing to a higher Paradigm, *autozoon,* which, for Neoplatonists, lies at the highest noetic level; for Proclus, *demiourgos* is the intellective Living-Being (*noeron zoon*), and the Forms in the Creator's Intellect are compared to the notions of public offices in the mind of a statesman; He is the efficient (*poietikos*), the formal (*eidetikos*), and the final (*telikos*) cause of the temporal, physical world; the Greek concept of the divine craftsman is related to the Egyptian god Ptah and the Ugaritian Kothar-wa-Hasis.

Diadochos—successor, the head of the Platonic Academy in the chain of transmission; however, the *diadoche* is hardly a matter of institutional continuity, and may be understood in the sense of the golden chain of philosophers which serves to transmit the sacred knowledge and principles of pure (*diakekatharmene*) philosophy.

Dialektike—dialectic; for Plato only those who philosophize purely and righteously bear the title of dialectician (*Soph.* 253e); sometimes the method of *sunagoge* (collection) and *diairesis* (division) is identified as dialectic; for Proclus, the Forms at the intelligible (*noetic*) and intellectual level cannot be defined, but they are definable at the level of soul and below; thus dialectic defines, by *diairesis*, these images of Forms, though the Forms themselves it can only contemplate; there are three processes of dialectic: (1) cathartic, used to purge ignorance; (2) recollective, which raises to the *anamnesis* of true reality; and (3) a mixture of the two; usually Proclus makes a sharp distinction between the so-called Parmenidean dialectic, which provides a path to the divine realities, and the dialectical method (*epicheirematike*) of the Peripatetics.

Dianoia—discursive reason, mind; discursive knowledge, located between immediate apprehension and fallible opinion (*Rep.* 511d); according to Proclus, the One, when we apprehend its presence in each of the Forms, "ought not to be viewed by the faculty of opinion, nor by discursive reason (*dianoia*), for these kinds of knowledge are not cognate with intellectual monads, which are neither objects of opinion nor of discursive reason, as we learn from the *Republic* (VI.511a). Rather it is proper to see by intuitive apprehension that simple and unitary existence of Forms" (*In Parm.* 880).

Dikaiosune—justice; its opposite is *adikia*, injustice; giving to each man his due is just, according to Plato (*Rep.* 331e); *dikaiosune* may be understood in a cosmic and divine sense, since to perform the task for which one is naturally equipped is to follow one's divine archetype, one's own *dharma*, to put it in Hindu terms, which is *lex aeterna*, the eternal law of creation.

Doxa—opinion; in Platonism, a sharp distinction is made between the eternal noetic world of Forms (Ideas, Archetypes) of which knowledge (*gnosis*) is possible, and the perceptible world of becoming which is only opiniable (*doxastos*); for Proclus, the perceptible entities are opiniable, but true being is an object of intellect (*Elements of Theology* 123); opinions may be true or false, knowledge only true.

Dunamis—power, capacity; Aristotle regards *dunamis* as one of the fundamental principles (*archai*); Plotinus describes the One as the seminal power of all things (*dunamis panton, Enn.* III.8.10.1); a net of divine powers in their descending and ascending order is a net of theophanies: in this respect *dunamis* is analogous to the ancient Egyptian *sekhem*; the powers of the divine Intellect and Soul appear to be present at every part of the cosmos, but the physical world (and the human body) is unable to receive the full power of incorporeal Reality; *dunameis* may sometimes be equated with the daimonic forces.

Eidolon—image, idol, double, apparition, phantom, ghost; in Homer, there are three kinds of supernatural apparitions that are called by the term *eidolon*: (1) the phantom (*phasma*), created by a god in semblance of a living person; (2) the dream-image, regarded as a ghostly double that is sent by the gods in the image of a real being; and (3) the *psuche* of the dead; the Homeric *psuche* is not a soul, but a phantom, a thin vapor that proves to be ungraspable; for Pythagoreans and Plato, *psuche* is no longer the *eidolon* of the body, but the immortal soul that constitutes one's real being; for Plotinus, the soul is the *eidolon nou*, a simulacrum of *nous*, an image that is already obscured; the conception of *eidolon* is partly related to the ancient Egyptian concept of *ka*.

Eidos—visible shape, form, the kind (or species) of a thing, the intelligible Form, or the noetic Idea, of Platonism; the word is etymologically connected with *video*, and the term *idea* also comes from the same root as the Greek verb *idein* and the Latin verb *videre*, both meaning "to see"; thus, *eidos* is closely connected with contemplation (*theoria*), transcendental or divine imagination, and mystical vision.

Eikon—image, icon; a mirror-image as a direct representation of its *paradeigma*; for Plotinus and other Neoplatonists, the sensible world is an image of the noetic world and time is an image of eternity (*Enn.* III.7.11), therefore the lower realities may be contemplated in ascending hierarchy as images, or traces, of the higher paradigms; Proclus makes a distinction between an *eikon* and a *sumbolon*; the Pythagoreans, before revealing directly the truths of their doctrine, present *eikones* of reality (*In Tim.* 1.29.31ff).

Ellampsis—irradiation, shining forth, manifestation, illumination, flowing from the principle as a cause; for Proclus, "only an illumination (*ellampsis*) from the intellective gods renders us capable of being connected to those intelligible-and-intellective Forms .... For this reason, indeed, Socrates in *Phaedrus* (249d) compares the contemplation to mystery rites (*teletais*), initiations (*muesesi*) and visions (*epopteias*), elevating our souls under the arch of Heaven, and to Heaven itself, and to the place above Heaven" (*In Parm.* 949).

Episteme—knowledge, scientific knowledge of that which is unchanging and necessary, e.g. the Platonic Forms; since *episteme* is regarded as a certain knowledge of reality, the objects of *doxa* (opinion) cannot be assigned to *episteme*; for Proclus, the task of science is the recognition (*gnosis*) of causes, and only when we recognize the causes of things do we say that we know them (*Elements of Theology* 11); science, or scientific knowledge (*epistemonike gnosis*), depends on the synthesizing power of mind, but "intellect (*nous*) is the proper spectator of the Forms, because it is the same nature as them" (*In Parm.* 924.32–37).

Epistrophe—reversion, return; in the Neoplatonic threefold scheme of manifestation, a thing, or rather an intelligible entity, proceeds from itself to multiplicity, and returns to itself, while its essential characteristic identity remains unchanged at the initial level; the three moments—remaining (*mone*), procession (*proodos*), and reversion (*epistrophe*)—are phases of a simple, continuous and dynamic process (sometimes regarded as simultaneous) that infuses unity-diversity, causation and predication; it is essentially a metaphysical and logical relationship.

Epopteia—the most important mystical vision; it has its culmination in the Eleusinian mysteries, a beholding of the secret symbols or epiphanies of the gods; *epopteia* is the highest stage of initiation; *epoptai* (beholders) are those who come back to watch the rituals again; in a similar way, philosophical purification and instruction culminates in *epoptika*—the direct revelation of truth and contemplation of the Forms, or divine realities.

Eros—love, sometimes personified as a deity, daimon, or cosmogonical, pedagogical and soteriological force, manifested in the process of demiurgy and within the domain of providence; for

Plato, philosophy is a sort of erotic madness (*mania*), because Eros, though implying need, can inspire us with the love of wisdom; in Plato's *Symposium*, Diotima describes education in erotics as an upward journey or ascent towards the perfect noetic Beauty; Plotinus uses the union of lovers as a symbol of the soul's union with the One (*Enn.* VI.7.34.14–16); Proclus distinguishes two forms of love: (1) ascending love which urges lower principles to aspire towards their superiors; and (2) descending or providential love (*eros pronoetikos*) which obligates the superiors to care for their products and transmit divine grace (*In Alcib.* 54-56); for Dionysius the Areopagite, who follows Proclus, the *eros ekstatikos* becomes the unifying factor of the cosmos.

Eusebeia—piety, meritorious piety; "to change nothing of what our forefathers have left behind"—this is *eusebeia* (*Isocr.* 7.30); for Platonists, piety means not simply bringing the sacrificial offerings and fulfilling the cultic duties, but also: humility, supported by philosophy, and combined with love (*eros*), faith (*pistis*), and knowledge (*gnosis*), which finally lead to assimilation to God.

Gnosis—knowledge; *gnosis* is contrasted with *doxa* (opinion) by Plato; the object of *gnosis* is *to on*, reality or being, and the fully real is the fully knowable (*Rep.* 477a); the Egyptian Hermetists made a distinction between two types of knowledge: (1) science (*episteme*), produced by reason (*logos*); and (2) *gnosis*, produced by understanding and faith (*Corpus Hermeticum* IX); thus, *gnosis* is regarded as the goal of *episteme* (*ibid.* X.9); the idea that one may "know God" (*gnosis theou*) is very rare in the classical Hellenic literature, which rather praises *episteme* and hieratic vision, *epopteia*, but is common in Hermetism, Gnosticism, and early Christianity; following the Platonic tradition (especially Plotinus and Porphyry), Augustine introduced a distinction between knowledge and wisdom, *scientia* and *sapientia*, claiming that the fallen soul knows only *scientia*, but before the Fall she knew *sapientia* (*De Trinitate* XII).

Goeteia—magic; a sharp distinction is made by Iamblichus (*De mysteriis*) between (1) sinister *goeteia*, and (2) *theourgia*, the sacramental divine work; however, magic is sometimes interpreted as *gnosis*, and *gnosis* pertains to the secret divine names as facilitating the power of magic; Hellenistic magic (frequently equated with the mysteries and labeled *musteria, musterion, musterion tou theou*) is related to the ancient mystery cult initiations and the Egyptian doctrine of *heka*—the miraculous power of creation, governed by the god Heka, who distributes *hekau*, the cultic words of power (cf. Hindu *mantras*) that perform divine liturgies and transformations of the soul; Hermes-Thoth, *Isidos pater*, regarded as the founder of the holy tradition (*paradosis*) of the magic arts and author of the secret names, "wrote in Heliopolis with hieroglyphic letters"; thus the magician is sometimes called the mystagogue (*mustagogos*).

Hairesis—taking, choice, course of action, election, decision; this term (pl. *haireseis*) refers to any group of people perceived to have a clear doctrinal identity; *hairesis* is a group with fairly coherent and distinctive theories, with an acknowledged founder (*hairesi-arches*) and leaders who articulate their rejection of rival theories through theoretically founded polemics; Diodorus of Sicily complains that the Hellenes, unlike the Orientals, always introduce doctrinal innovations in important matters, thus "founding new *haireseis*" (2.29.6); in the 2nd century C.E., *hairesis* had become a standard term for philosophical school; the early Christians used *hairesis* to refer to a body of false beliefs.

Hen (*to hen*)—the one, which can mean: (1) Unity or Oneness in general; (2) the unity of anything that has unity or is one thing; (3) that which has unity, anything that is one; and (4) the one thing we are speaking of, as opposed to "other ones" (see F.M. Cornford, *Plato and Parmenides* [London, 1969], p. 111); for Neoplatonists, the One is the ineffable source of Being, the Supreme Principle, explicitly regarded as God by Proclus; *to hen* transcends the demiurgic Intellect and constitutes the first divine *hupostasis* of Plotinus; it corresponds to Nun, the Father of the gods (*neteru*) in the ancient Egyptian theology.

Henas—henad, unit; the term is taken by Iamblichus, Syrianus and Proclus from Plato's *Philebus*, where it is used interchangeably with the term "monad"; since for every real being there is a unit, and for every unit a real being (Proclus, *Elements of Theology* 136), the henads are pure unities, the sources of being's identity, located between the pure One and the noetic One (or Being); more precisely, henad is the first principle (*arche*) and the measure (*metron*) of being; the One is imparticipable, but the henads are participable, and thus correlate with real beings; Proclus divides henads into (1) those that are transcendent or independent units, and (2) those that are immanent and belong to their participants and are irradiations of the first; in theurgy, henads constitute a set of theophanies, i.e. divinity in its many different forms at all different levels of reality; the divine henad thus stands for the god-entity as a whole; the difference between the One and the participable henads (which may be compared to the Egyptian *neteru*), opens the theurgic way of adoration, worship and ascent; according to Proclus, "the most divine thing in us is the 'one' in us, which Socrates called the illumination of the soul (*Rep.* 540a7), just as he called truth itself light" (*In Parm.* VII.48); since like is apprehensible by like, the "one of the soul" makes union with the ineffable One possible.

Henosis—unity; unity is the characteristic that everything has in common; everything depends on unity and only unity is the goal of all things; in Neoplatonism, the soul's purification, accomplished primarily through philosophy, culminates in noetic vision and finally in mystical union (Plotinus, *Enn.* VI.7.36); the divine truth is an indivisible *henosis* of real beings.

Hermaike seira—Hermaic chain (of transmission, or heavenly initiation); the Neoplatonists commonly associated themselves with the Hermaic chain, i.e. the vertical "golden" chain of noetic light and wisdom that emanates through Hermes Logios and other angelic powers from the divine Intellect (*nous*).

Hermeneus—interpreter; *hermeneus* owes his name to Hermes, the messenger of the gods; *hermeneus* is an interpreter of the hieratic rites and liturgies (in Egypt, such hermeneutical procedures, called "illuminations," were practiced at least from the times of the Middle Kingdom [c.2000–1785 B.C.E.]), divine omens, tokens, symbols, oracular utterances, and, in the case of Neoplatonists, the Homeric poems, Plato, Aristotle, and the *Chaldean Oracles*; the goal of *hermeneutike* is to reveal the inner meaning (*huponoia*) of the texts and indicate the highest truth that points beyond the discourses, thus elevating the soul to the first principles themselves; there is an ontological hierarchy of interpreters and interpretations; thus, each lower language of theophany functions as the *hermeneus* of the higher one and renders it comprehensible at a lower level at the expense of its coherence.

Hieratike techne—sacred art, hieratic art, namely the priestly art, or theurgy, accomplished by the gods themselves through different degrees of initiation, transformation, elevation (*anagoge*) and ineffable mystagogy; it represents the ascending path to the unification with the One through scientific training (*agoge epistemonike*) on certain henadic qualities, ontological symbols, sacred rites, divine names, and theurgic powers; according to Proclus, "the theurgists established their sacred knowledge after observing that all things were in all things from the sympathy that exists between all phenomena and between them and their invisible causes, and being amazed that they saw the lowest things in the highest and the highest in the lowest" (*Hier. Art* 148).

Hierophantes—hierophant, priest of Eleusis, he who shows sacred things; since the language of the mysteries was employed by Plato and the later Platonists, philosophy is often regarded in terms of a mystery initiation, and a true philosopher or a spiritual leader of *hairesis* is equated with the hierophant of the mysteries.

Hieros logos—sacred tale, sacred word or book (e.g. possessed by the initiation priests of Dionysus and by the Pythagoreans); there were *logoi* (accounts, explanations) within practical mysteries and additional *logoi* adduced from outside; they were both exoteric and esoteric, about the mysteries and within the mysteries, developed on three different hermeneutical levels: those of myth, allegory, and metaphysics.

Homoiosis theo—likeness to God; the phrase is derived from the famous passage of Plato's *Theaetetus* (176bc); it is understood as the end (*telos*) of life which is to be attained by knowledge (*gnosis*); for Iamblichus, "knowledge of the gods is virtue and wisdom and perfect happiness, and makes us like to the gods" (*Protrep.* 3).

Huparxis—the pure existence of a thing, an essential foundation; the term covers the level of pure unity (which is the foundation of all manifested realities) and the divine; for Proclus, being's pure essence is no actual being, but a unity (*henas*) with existence (*huparxis*), and this unity is the spark of divinity; the *huparxis* of henads is not existence of certain concrete subjects, but unqualified existence, unconditioned even by being.

Hupodoche—reception; the receptacle underlying all the world of becoming; for Plato—the material principle, the mother and receptacle of the whole visible cosmos (*Tim.* 51a); *hupodoche* is equivalent to space (*chora*) and nurse (*tithene*); according to Iamblichus, the pure and divine matter receives and reveals the gods in cosmogony (*De myster.* 232.17); each level on the Neoplatonic chain (*seira*) of theophany is regarded as the receptacle of its superior (which functions as a "form" in relation to "matter"); the embodied soul is a *hupodoche* of the god by virtue of the soul's capacity or theurgic suitability (*epitedeiotes*); in theurgy, minerals, plants, animals, divine statues and icons, temples and sacred landscapes, can be regarded as the receptacles of the descending divine light or power; this is the Egyptian doctrine of *descensio* and *translatio*: the gods and divine powers descend into their images (*akhemu*) and animate the material world, understood as an *imago caeli*.

Hupostasis—standing under, sediment, foundation; in Neoplatonism, *hupostasis* is a synonym of *ousia*, which means being, substance, existence; the three *hupostaseis* of Plotinus are three fundamental levels, or dimensions, of divine reality: the One, Intellect, and Soul.

Hupothesis—proposal, intention, argument, hypothesis, the premise of a syllogism; the nine hypotheses of dialectic in Plato's *Parmenides* are regarded by the Neoplatonists as the nine *hupostaseis*, or levels of reality, extending from the ineffable One to pure matter, or nonbeing.

Idea—in non-technical usage the term refers to the visual aspect of a thing; for Plato and Platonists, it is the highest noetic entity, the eternal unchanging Form, the archetype of the manifested material thing; in Plato, *idea* is a synonym of *eidos*, but in Neoplatonism these two terms have a slightly different meaning.

Katharsis—purification, purgation of passions; the term occurs in Aristotle's definition of tragedy (*Poetics* 1449b24) and seems to be borrowed from medicine, religious initiations, and magic.

Kosmos noetos—the intelligible cosmos of divine Forms and intellects, located between the One and the Soul; it embraces the hierarchy of different levels and orders (*taxeis*) of divine reality (such as Being, Life, and Intellect), filled with the various triads of the intelligible (noetic), intelligible-intellective (noetic-noeric), and intellective (noeric) gods; among the metaphysical categories and triads of *kosmos noetos* are: existence (*huparxis*) – power (*dunamis*) – activity (*energeia*); remaining (*mone*) – procession (*proodos*) – reversion (*epistrophe*); symmetry (*summetria*) – truth (*aletheia*) – beauty (*kallos*).

Logismos—numerical calculation, the power of reasoning, reason.

Logos—the basic meaning is "something said," "account"; the term is used in explanation and definition of some kind of thing, but also means: reason, measure, proportion, analogy, word, speech, discourse, discursive reasoning, and noetic apprehension of the first principles; the demiurgic *Logos* (like the Egyptian *Hu*, equated with Thoth, the tongue of Ra, who transforms the Thoughts of the Heart into spoken and written Language, thus creating and articulating the world as a script and icon of the gods) is the intermediary divine power: as an image of the noetic cosmos, the physical cosmos is regarded as a multiple *Logos* containing a plurality of individual *logoi* (*Enn.* IV.3.8.17-22); in Plotinus, *Logos* is not a separate *hupostasis*, but determines the relation of any *hupostasis* to its source and its products, serving as the formative principle from which the lower realities evolve; external speech (*logos prophorikos*) constitutes the external expression of internal thought (*logos endiathetos*).

Maat—the ancient Egyptian term for measure, harmony, canon, justice, and truth, shared by the gods and humans alike; *maat* is the essence of the sacred laws that keep and maintain a human community and the entire cosmic order; it establishes the link between above and below; "letting *maat* ascend" is a language offering during the hieratic rites and an interpretation of the cosmic process in terms of its mystic and salvational meaning; for Plato, who admired the Egyptian patterns, the well-ordered cosmos, truth, and justice are among the main objects of philosophical discourse.

Mania—madness, frenzy; the state of frenzy is connected with the psychic state called *entheos,* "within is a god"; being possessed by a god means a loss of one's understanding (*nous*); the god Dionysus is the Frenzied One, and thus some kind of enthusiasm, madness, and inspiration is related to prophecy and mystical experience; Plato distinguishes the prophetic *mania* of Apollo from the telestic *mania* of Dionysus, adding two other types of *mania*—the poetic, and erotic or philosophical enthusiasm (*Phaedr.* 244a–245a); the philosopher is the erotic madman, but the divine erotic madness and divine *sophrosune* (temperance, virtue, prudence) are to be united in the successful experience of love which elevates through *anamnesis* towards the divine realm.

Mathema—any study which a person may learn (*manthanein*); later confined to the mathematical sciences, harmonics, and astronomy.

Methexis—participation; for the Pythagoreans, things are imitations of numbers, but for Plato, the particulars participate in their Forms; Iamblichus extended "participation" into a general term for the informing of lower principles by higher ones and thus established the triad of transcendent Form, immanent universal, and material particular; this general scheme of unparticipated (*amethekton*), participated (*metechomenon*) and participant (*metechon*) terms may be applied to different levels of manifestation; the unparticipated terms operate on lower realities only indirectly, through the intermediary of the participated terms which they produce; thus the ontological levels are multiplied and divine transcendence is preserved.

Mimesis—imitation, representation; in his *Poetics* (1447ab), Aristotle includes all the fine arts under *mimesis,* among them epic, tragedy, comedy, painting, and sculpture; the images produced by *mimesis* are not at all like photographic images; according to A.H. Armstrong, the images of the classical Hellenic artists are mimetically closer to those of the traditional arts of the East than to those of nineteenth-century Europe: "if we establish in our imagination the figure of the masked singing actor as our image of *mimesis* we shall not do too bad" ("Platonic Mirrors," *Eranos 1986, Jahrbuch* 55 [Insel Verlag Frankfurt am Main, 1988], p. 151); however, in a vocabulary used by Proclus, the terms *mimesis* and *mimema* are usually reserved for art of an inferior type, though Proclus says that "the congenital vehicles (*ochemata*) imitate (*mimeitai*) the lives of the souls" (*Elements of Theology* 209) and "each of the souls perpetually attendant upon gods, imitating its divine soul, is sovereign over a number of particular souls" (*ibid.* 204).

Morphe—shape; e.g. *kata somatos morphen*: "in a bodily shape" (*Phaedr.* 271a); sometimes *morphe* is used as a synonym of *idea* and *eidos*.

Mustagogia—an initiation into a mystery; the leading and guidance of the initiate (*mustes*, pl., *mustai*) to the *telesterion* where initiations take place; a mystagogue is the introducer into the mysteries, the leading priest, instructor or spiritual guide; Proclus viewed the philosophy of Plato as a "mystagogy," an "initiation into the holy mysteries themselves" (*Plat. Theol.* I.1); for the Byzantine Christians, mystagogy means the liturgical contemplation of a mystery of the Church.

Musteria—mysteries; the proceedings of initiatory and sacred rites; the Eleusinian festival is known simply as *ta musteria* or *arrhetos teletai*; the initiates—*mustai* and *bacchoi*—walk a sacred way, the goal of which is inner transformation and eternal bliss: "happy and blessed one, god will you be instead of a mortal"; the Orphic mysteries have striking parallels in the Egyptian *Book of the Dead* and the *Coffin Texts*; the mysteries are characterized as esoteric, secret, forbidden (*aporrheton*) and unspeakable (*arrheton*); the special states, attained through initiation (*telete*), are claimed to be valid even beyond death; the mystery language is adopted by Plato and used by his followers; even the Stoic Seneca speaks of the initiatory rites of philosophy, "which open not some local shrine, but [the] vast temple of all the gods, the universe itself, whose true images and true likeness philosophy has brought before the mind's eye" (*Ep.* 90.28).

Muthos—myth, tale; *legomena*, "things recited," in the Eleusinian mysteries, i.e. the recitations of the *hieros logos* belong to the sphere of myth; the one-sided opposition between an irrational *muthos* and rational *logos* in Hellenic philosophy and culture, established by modern scholarship, is erroneous—even in Plato, myth constitutes

an essential part of philosophy; all true myths require a proper cosmological and metaphysical exegesis; according to Proclus, the hieratic myths have certain inner meanings (*huponoia*) and conceal
secret or unspoken (*apporrheton*) doctrines, sometimes inspired or
revealed by the gods themselves; Sallustius associates the highest
level of myth with the transcendent divine reality and the lowest
with the deceptive perceptions within the realm of the senses; thus
a Myth (like the Hindu *Maya*) is tantamount to the manifested cosmos itself, understood as the visible veil of the hidden invisible
truth.

Noesis—intellection, thought, intellectual intuition, pure intuitive
apprehension which transcends the discursive reason and is related
to *nous*; unified noetic intuition at different levels of reality; for
Proclus, intelligible and at the same time intellective (*noeton hama
kai noeron*) Life, which is characteristic of the self-substantiated
henads, exemplifies *noesis* as a process; at the highest ontological
level, *noesis* provides union with the intelligible (*noeton*) world
through the so-called "flower of intellect" (*anthos nou*); for
Iamblichus, the unifying power of the gods transcends all human
noesis (which appears to resemble Plotinian *dianoia*), but this
human *noesis* is a necessary part of ascent and co-operation with the
divine; the supreme *noesis* is attainable only through the working of
theurgy by the grace of god.

Nous—intelligence, immediate awareness, intuition, intuitive intellect; Plato distinguishes *nous* from *dianoia*—discursive reason; *Nous*
is the second *hupostasis* of Plotinus; every intelligence is its own
object, therefore the act of intellection always involves self-con-
sciousness: the substance of intelligence is its noetic content (*noeton*), its power of intellection (*nous*), and its activity—the act of
noesis; in a macrocosmic sense, *Nous* is the divine Intellect, the
Second God, who embraces and personifies the entire noetic cosmos (Being-Life-Intelligence), the Demiurge of the manifested universe; *Nous* may be compared to the Hindu *Ishvara* and solar gods
such as the Egyptian Ra; *nous* is independent of body and thus
immune from destruction—it is the unitary and divine element, or
the spark of divine light, which is present in men and through
which the ascent to the divine Sun is made possible.

Ochema—vehicle; a boat which conveys the souls of the dead; the soul's chariot in Plato's *Phaedrus*; Aristotle understands *ochema* as *pneuma*—the seat of imagination (*phantasia*), analogous to that element of which the stars are made; the *ochema-pneuma* as an astral body functions as a quasi-immaterial carrier of the irrational soul; daimons have a misty *pneuma* which alters its form in response to their imaginings and thus causes them to appear in ever-changing shapes; for Iamblichus, the ethereal and luminous vehicle (*aitherodes kai augoeides ochema*) is the recipient of divine *phantasiai*; *ochema* carries the soul down to the state of embodiment and is darkened until it becomes fully material and visible; the material or fleshly body is also a sort of *ochema*; Proclus distinguishes (1) the higher immaterial and luminous *ochema* into which Plato's Demiurge puts the soul (*Tim.* 41e), from (2) the lower, *pneumatikon ochema*, which is composite of the four elements and serves as a vehicle of the irrational soul—it survives bodily death, but is finally purged away.

Onoma—word, name; a noun as distinct from a verb; for Proclus, a name is an *eikon* of a *paradeigma*, a copy of a model; the words (*onomata*) are *agalmata*, the audible "icons" or "statues" of the higher divine realities; thus, true names are naturally appropriate, like images that reflect the form of the object, or like artistic icons that reflect the Platonic Forms rather that objects of the sensible world.

Ousia—being, substance, nature, essence; as Pierre Hadot has observed: "If we consider the series formed by *ousia* in Plato, *ousia* in Aristotle, *ousia* in the Stoics, *ousia* in the Neoplatonists, and the *substantia* and *essentia* in the church Fathers and the Scholastics, we shall find that the idea of *ousia* or essence is amongst the most confused and confusing notions" (*Philosophy as a Way of Life* [Oxford: Blackwell, 1995], p. 76); since the true being is permanent and intelligible, the substance (*ousia*) of beings is their *logos* and their essence, according to Plato (*Phaed.* 65d–66a); Proclus identifies pure Being (*on*) with the Essence and Substance itself (*autoousia*); for Neoplatonists, being, real existence, and essence are inseparable: beings exist insofar as they are accessible to intellect and have a fixed definition: in the intelligibles the essence is never distinguished from real being.

Paideia—education, culture; the program of traditional Hellenic education based on an imitation of the Homeric exemplars; Plato initiated a philosophically oriented *paideia* that challenged the traditional pattern of poetically sanctioned culture and shifted the emphasis from body to soul (see W. Jaeger, *Paideia: The Ideals of Greek Culture* [Oxford: Oxford University Press, 1943], 3 vols.).

Paradeigma—exemplar, paradigm, archetype, pattern, model; according to Plato, a paradigm of his perfect state is laid up in Heaven (*Rep.* 592b); the noetic Paradigm is regarded as the model for the creation: the visible world is a living creature made after the likeness of an eternal original, i.e. the ideal Living Animal in the world of Forms; the world is thus an image of the eternal paradigms (*paradeigmata*); the Demiurge makes the cosmos as an *agalma* (hieratic statue, cultic image, ornament) and sets up within it the *agalmata* of the individual gods.

Paradosis—transmission, tradition; e.g. *Orpheos paradosis*—the Orphic tradition.

Peras—limit, boundary; a fundamental cosmological principle of the Pythagoreans; the Unlimited (*apeiron*) is indefinite and in need of Limit which in the table of opposites is related to Odd, One, Right, Male, Rest, Straight, Light, Good, Square; the principles of the Limit and the Unlimited (discussed in Plato's *Philebus*) are the Pythagorean monad and dyad, which constitute the order of henads in Proclus and play a central role in the constitution of reality; limit and unlimited serve as two principles (*archai*) of mathematical reality (*ousia*).

Phantasia—imagination; for Plato, *phantasia* belongs to the realm of appearance and illusion; for Aristotle, *phantasia* is neither perception nor judgment, but a distinct capacity of the soul, the capacity which responds to appearances derived from memory, dreams and sense-perception; the 2nd century C.E. sophist Philostratus was the first to call the faculty of producing visual images *phantasia*, which is contrasted with *mimesis*: "For *mimesis* will produce only what she has seen, but *phantasia* even what she has not seen as well; and she will produce it by referring to the standard of the perfect reality" (*Life of Apollonius* 6.19); the Neoplatonists lack the concept of creative imagination, though the Neoplatonic *phantasia* can reproduce images of higher principles in mathematics and language; thus *phantasia*, as a mirror, is placed at the junction of two different levels of being: the mirror of imagination reflects not only images of phenomena, but also images of the noetic Forms, or Ideas, translating revelations and divine epiphanies into the visible icons and symbols of the higher realities; at the junction of *phantasia* (which is identified with *nous pathetikos* by Proclus) rational and irrational meet; the objects of *phantasia* are *tupos* (imprint), *schema* (figure), and *morphe* (shape).

Philosophia—love of wisdom; the intellectual and "erotic" path which leads to virtue and knowledge; the term itself was perhaps coined by Pythagoras; the Hellenic *philosophia* is a prolongation, modification, and "modernization" of the ancient Egyptian and Near Eastern sapiential ways of life; *philosophia* cannot be reduced to philosophical discourse; for Aristotle, metaphysics is *prote philosophia*, or *theologike*, but philosophy as *theoria* means dedication to the *bios theoretikos*, the life of contemplation—thus the philosophical life means participation in the divine and the actualization of the divine in the human through personal *askesis* and inner transformation; Plato defines philosophy as a training for death (*Phaed.* 67cd); the Platonic *philosophia* helps the soul to become aware of its own immateriality, it liberates it from passions and strips away everything that is not truly itself; for Plotinus, philosophy does not wish only "to be a discourse about objects, be they even the highest, but it wishes actually to lead the soul to a living, concrete union with the Intellect and the Good"; in late Neoplatonism, ineffable theurgy is regarded as the culmination of philosophy.

Phronesis—thought, understanding, practical wisdom, sagacity, prudence; according to some modern scholars, *phronesis* is closer to the English "wisdom" than *sophia*, because "wisdom" is, in standard English, applied to practical matters; but this is still a disputed issue, since for Aristotle, *sophia* covers bodily, aesthetic, political, theoretical, and religious or metaphysical areas of human activity (*On Philosophy*, fr.8).

Phusis (more usually transcribed as *physis*)—nature (of something), nature as opposed to the artificial; for Proclus, it is the last immaterial reality or power that exists immediately prior to the material world and is responsible for all the motion and change within it.

Pragmata—things; in Proclus *ta pragmata* also mean the transcendent realities, noetic entities, real beings.

Pronoia—providence; the well-ordered arrangement of things in the cosmos is based on a guiding and planning providence; the concept is developed before Socrates; according to Proclus, since all proceeding things in their essential aspect "remain" in their higher causes, or archetypes, the higher causes not only contain their lower effects but they know, or fore-know (*pro-noein*) these effects; foreknowledge is also a kind of love—the providential love (*eros pronoetikos*) by which the higher causes care for their effects.

Proodos—procession; a metaphysical term in the Neoplatonic scheme of *mone-proodos-epistrophe* (primarily a non-phenomenal process) that refers to the process of manifestation; the noetic Life covers multiplication, the unlimited, and potency or power (*dunamis*), that lead to *proodos*; for Proclus, remaining-procession-reversion apply to every form, property, or entity, except the One and matter.

Psuche (more usually transcribed as *psyche*): soul; breath of life, lifestuff; Homer distinguishes between free souls such as the souls of the dead, corresponding with *psuchai* (and still regarded as *eidola*), and body souls, corresponding with *thumos* (sometimes interpreted as the "blood-soul" contained in the diaphragm), *noos* (mind), and *menos* (power, desire); following the Egyptian theological patterns, the Pythagoreans considered the *psuche* as the reflection of the unchanging and immortal principles; from Plato onwards, *psuchai* are no longer regarded as *eidola*, phantoms or doubles of the body, but rather, the human body is viewed as the perishable simulacrum of an immaterial and immortal soul; there are different degrees of soul (or different souls), and thus anything that is alive has a soul (Aristotle, *De anima* 414b32); in *Phaedrus* (248b) the soul is regarded as something that is a separate, self-moving, and immortal entity (cf. Proclus, *Elements of Theology* 186); *Psuche* is the third *hupostasis* of Plotinus.

Seira—chain, series; the term, derived from Orphism and Homer, refers to a vertical series, consisting of a single principle, monad or henad, and repeated at different levels of reality; *seira* and *taxis* are both transverse and vertical series; each level of *seira* (which may be compared to a ray of light) reproduces those above it; thus the god's names refer not only to the henad as the source of each procession, but also to all the members of that procession: "For each chain bears the name of its monad and the partial spirits enjoy having the same names as their wholes. Thus there are many Apollos and Poseidons and Hephaestuses of all sorts" (Proclus, *In Remp.* I.92.2ff); the manifested reality is thus arranged as a hierarchy of chains that embrace divine, angelic, daimonic, heroic, human, and irrational levels (including animals, plants, and minerals), all dependent on their proper divine henad, in the sense of being in its *seira*; in some respect *seira* is tantamount to the Arabic Sufi term *silsilah* ("chain of transmission").

Skopos—aim, purpose, target; Iamblichus developed the doctrine that each philosophical source work, especially in the case of Plato's dialogues (since the dialogue is regarded as a microcosmic reflection of the divine macrocosm) must have one basic subject matter, or *skopos*, to which all parts of the text are related; consequently, the introductory portion of the dialogues assume an allegorical and metaphysical significance.

Sophia—wisdom; the term covers all spheres of human activity—all ingenious invention aimed at satisfying one's material, political, and religious needs; Hephaistos (like his prototypes, the Ugaritian Kothar-wa-Hasis and the Egyptian Ptah) is *poluphronos*, very wise, and *klutometis*, renowned in wisdom—here "wisdom" means not simply some divine quality, but wondrous skill, cleverness, technical ability, magic power; in Egypt all sacred wisdom (especially knowledge of the secret divine names and words of power, *hekau*, or demiurgic and theurgic *mantras*, which are able to restore one's true divine identity) was under the patronage of Thoth; in classical Greece, the inspired poet, the lawgiver, the politician, the magician, the natural philosopher, and sophist—all claimed to possess wisdom, and indeed "philosophy" is the love of wisdom, *philo-sophia*, i.e. a way of life with wisdom as its goal; the ideal of the *sophos* (sage) in the newly established Platonic *paideia* is exemplified by Socrates;

in Neoplatonism, theoretical wisdom (though the term *sophia* is rarely used) means the contemplation of the eternal Forms and becoming like *nous,* or a god; there are the characteristic properties which constitute the divine nature and which spread to all the divine classes: good (*agathotes*), wisdom (*sophia*), and beauty (*kallos*).

Sumbolon—symbol (*sumballein* means "to join"); a fragment of a whole object, such as a *tessera hospitalis,* which can be joined with the other half; *sumbolon* suggests both incompleteness and the hinting power of secret meaning; the so-called Pythagorean symbols are maxims (*akousmata,* "things heard") representing in an enigmatic and archaic form the basic teachings on the proper conduct of life; only in the allegorical tradition of Neoplatonic hermeneutics was the theory of metaphysical, cosmogonic, and theurgic symbolism elaborated, *sumbolon* then achieving the status of a major critical concept; in the *Chaldean Oracles,* the *sumbola* are sown throughout the cosmos by the Paternal Demiurge and serve as the essential means of ascent and return to the gods; every soul was created by the Demiurge with harmonic ratios (*logoi*) and divine symbols (*sumbola theia,* Proclus, *In Tim.* I.4.32–33); the *logoi* that constitute the soul's essence are *sumbola* and may be awakened through the theurgic rites; for Proclus, the inspired myths of Homer communicate their truth not by making images (*eikones*) and imitations (*mimemata*), but by making symbols (*sumbola* or *sunthemata*), because "symbols are not imitations of that which they symbolize" (*In Remp.* I.198.15–16).

Sunthema—token, passport, parole, symbol (in most cases having the same meaning as *sumbolon*); a plaited basket (*cista mystica*) of the Fleusinian mysteries is called the "watchword" (*to sunthema Eleusinion musterion,* Clement of Alexandria, *Protrep.* 2.21.2); the sunthemata of the *Chaldean Oracles* are considered as the "thoughts of the Father" and have a cosmogonic role similar to that of the Forms in Middle Platonism; they have an anagogic function: when the soul remembers the paternal *sunthema,* it returns to the paternal Intellect; according to Iamblichus, the gods create all things by means of images and signify all things through *sunthemata* (*De myster.* 136.6.ff); there are material *sunthemata* and immaterial *sunthemata* (among them: stones, shells, parts of animals, plants, flowers, sacred statues and icons, sounds, rhythms, melodies, incantations, lights, numbers, ineffable names of the gods); the material objects that preserve the power of the gods are regarded as *sunthemata* by the theurgists and function as receptacles for the gods; the *sunthema*, understood as the impression and power of the god (similar to the Hindu *yantra*), awakens the soul to the divinity which it presents or symbolizes.

Taxis—order, series; any level of reality, constituted by *seira* in which the distinctive property of a particular god or henad is successively mirrored; the chain of being proceeds from simplicity to complexity and subsequently from complexity to simplicity; the hierarchy of *taxeis* establish the planes of being or world-orders (*diakosmoi*).

Telestike—one of the Neoplatonic names for theurgy and hieratic rituals; the animation of statues; the *telestike mania* of *Phaedrus* (244e) employs purifications and rites; according to Hermeias (*In Phaedr.* 92.16–24), telestic madness is ranked above all the other forms of "madness" inasmuch as it gathers them all together and possesses them (i.e. theology, all philosophy and "erotic" *mania*); there are various kinds of *telestike*.

Telete—initiation, the rite of initiation; to initiate is *telein* or else *muein*; the initiate is called *mustes*, the ritual of initiation—*telete*, and the building where initiation takes place—*telesterion*; *telete* is also used to refer to religious celebration generally; the mysteries are called *teletai*; in Neoplatonism, souls follow the mystery rites (*teletai*) and prepare for the beholding of the realities of Being; according to Proclus, faith (*pistis*) is the cause of the ineffable initiation, "for on the whole the initiation does not happen through intellection and judgment, but through the silence which is unifying and is superior to every cognitive activity" (*Plat. Theol.* IV.31.8–16).

Theios aner—divine man, a god-like sage; the Neoplatonic ideal of "sainthood."

Theologia—divine science, theology, *logos* about the gods, considered to be the essence of *teletai*; for Aristotle, a synonym of metaphysics or first philosophy (*prote philosophia*) in contrast with physics (*Metaph.* 1026a18); however, physics (*phusiologia*) is sometimes called a kind of theology (Proclus, *In Tim.* I.217.25); for

Neoplatonists, considered among the ancient theologians (*theolo-goi*) are: Orpheus, Homer, Hesiod and other divinely inspired poets, the creators of theogonies, and the keepers of sacred rites.

Theoria—contemplation, theory; the contemplative virtue is called *theoretike*, like the beholding of festivals of the gods and their epiphanies, philosophy introduces the beholding of the well-ordered cosmos, still referred to by the same term, *theoria*; in Neoplatonism, the creative power of the cosmos is contemplation (*theoria*) and intellection (*noesis*); thus divine *praxis* is *theoria*; for Plotinus, on every level of reality creation is the result of the energy produced by contemplation (*Enn.* III.8.3–4); every intellect contemplates itself directly; contemplation may be compared to the mystery rites (*tele-tai*).

Theos—god; the term is sometimes used in a wide and loose sense; "everything is full of gods" (*panta plere theon*), according to Thales; the cosmos may be regarded as a theophany—the manifestation of the One (likened to the supreme transcendent Sun) and the divine *Nous*, which constitute the different levels of divine presence concealed by screens or veils (*parapetasmata*); in ancient Greece, when speaking of *theos* or *theoi*, one posited an absolute point of reference for everything that had impact, validity, and permanence; indistinct influences which affected men directly were referred to as *daimon*; for Plato and Plotinus, *nous*, the universal soul, the stars, and also the human soul are divine; there are thus invisible and visible gods, arranged in a hierarchy of henads which follow the arrangement of the nine hypotheses of Plato's *Parmenides*; *theoi* are the first principles, henads (as *protos theoi*), intellects and divine souls, but the supreme God is the ineffable One, or the Good; in some respects, *theos* is an equivalent of the Egyptian *neter*; *neteru* are the gods, the first principles, divine powers, manifestations—both transcendent and immanent.

Theourgia—theurgy; the rites understood as divine acts (*theia erga*) or the working of the gods (*theon erga*); theurgy is not an intellectual theorizing about God (*theologia*), but elevation to God; the term is coined by the editors of the *Chaldean Oracles*, but the ancient practice of contacting the gods and ascending to the divine goes back to the Mesopotamian and Egyptian hieratic traditions; Neoplatonic theurgy is based both on the Chaldean patterns and the exegesis of Plato's *Phaedrus, Timaeus, Symposium,* and other dialogues; it is thus regarded as an outgrowth of Platonic philosophy and Pythagorean negative theology; theurgical *praxis* does not contradict the dialectic of Plato; theurgy deifies the soul through the series of ontological symbols and *sunthemata* that cover the entire hierarchy of being and lead to a unification and ineffable unity with the gods; theurgy is based on the laws of cosmogony in their ritual expression and imitates the orders of the gods; for Iamblichus, it transcends all rational philosophy (or intellectual understanding) and transforms man into a divine being.

For a glossary of all key foreign words used in books published by World Wisdom, including metaphysical terms in English, consult:
www.DictionaryofSpiritualTerms.org.
This on-line Dictionary of Spiritual Terms provides extensive definitions, examples and related terms in other languages

SELECT BIBLIOGRAPHY FOR FURTHER READING

Armstrong, A.H. "Platonic Mirrors." *Eranos 1986, Jahrbuch* 55: 147-181. Insel Verlag Frankfurt am Main, 1988.

—— "Itineraries in Late Antiquity." *Eranos 1987, Jahrbuch* 56: 105-131. Insel Verlag Frankfurt am Main, 1989.

Athanasiadi, P. "Persecution and Response in Late Paganism: The Evidence of Damascius." *Journal of Hellenic Studies* 113 (1993): 1-29.

Blumenthal, H.J. *Aristotle and Neoplatonism in Late Antiquity: Interpretations of the De Anima.* London: Duckworth, 1996.

Brague, R. "The Body of the Speech: A New Hypothesis on the Compositional Structure of Timaeus' Monologue." In *Platonic Investigations*, edited by Dominic J. O'Meara, 53-83. Washington, D.C.: Catholic University of America Press, 1995.

Brown, P. *The World of Late Antiquity AD 150-750.* London: Thames and Hudson, 1997 (first ed. 1971).

Burkert, W. *Lore and Science in Ancient Pythagoreanism.* Cambridge, MA: Harvard University Press, 1972.

—— "Craft Versus Sect: The Problem of Orphics and Pythagoreans." In *Jewish and Christian Self-Definition, vol. III: Self-Definition in the Graeco-Roman World*, edited by Ben E. Meyer and E.P. Sanders, 1-22. London: SCM Press, 1982.

—— *Ancient Mystery Cults*, Carl Nuvell Jackson Lectures. Cambridge, MA and London: Harvard University Press, 1987.

Coulter, J.A. *The Literary Microcosm: Theories of Interpretation of the Later Neoplatonists.* Leiden: E.J. Brill, 1976.

Dillon, J.M. "Image, Symbol and Analogy: Three Basic Concepts of Neoplatonic Allegorical Exegesis." In *The Significance of Neoplatonism*, edited by R. Baine Harris, 247-262. Old Dominion University, 1976.

—— "Iamblichus of Chalcis." In *Aufstieg und Niedergang der Romischen Welt*, edited by Wolfgang Haase et al., 36, no. 2 (1987): 863-909. Berlin: Walter de Gruyter.

—— *The Middle Platonists: A Study of Platonism 80 B.C. to A.D. 220.* London: Duckworth, 1996 (rev. ed., first published 1977).

Edwards, M.J. "Two Images of Pythagoras: Iamblichus and Porphyry." In *The Divine Iamblichus: Philosopher and Man of Gods*, edited by H.J. Blumenthal and E.G. Clark, 159-172. Bristol, 1993.

Evangeliou, C.C. *The Hellenic Philosophy: Between Europe, Asia, and Africa.* Institute of Global Cultural Studies, Binghamton University: New York, 1997.

Finamore, J.F. *Iamblichus and the Theory of the Vehicle of the Soul.* Chico, California: Scholars Press, 1985.

Findlay, J.N. "The Neoplatonism of Plato." In *The Significance of Neoplatonism,* edited by R. Baine Harris, 23-40. Old Dominion University, 1976.

Fowden, G. "The Pagan Holy Man in Late Antique Society." *Journal of Hellenic Studies* 102 (1982): 33-59.

Griswold, C. "Plato's Metaphilosophy." In *Platonic Investigations,* edited by Dominic J. O'Meara, 1-33. Washington, D.C.: Catholic University of America Press, 1985.

—— *Self-Knowledge in Plato's Phaedrus.* New Haven and London: Yale University Press, 1986.

Hadot, P. *Philosophy as a Way of Life: Spiritual Exercises from Socrates to Foucault,* edited with an introduction by Arnold I. Davidson, translated by Michel Chase. Oxford: Blackwell, 1995.

Kingsley, P. *Ancient Philosophy, Mystery and Magic: Empedocles and Pythagorean Tradition.* Oxford: Clarendon Press, 1995.

—— *In the Dark Places of Wisdom.* Inverness, California: Golden Sufi Center, 1999.

Lewy, H. *Chaldean Oracles and Theurgy: Mysticism, Magic and Platonism in the Later Roman Empire,* Nouvell edition par Michel Tardieu. Paris: Études Augustiniennes, 1978.

Lloyd, A.C. *The Anatomy of Neoplatonism.* Oxford: Clarendon Press, 1991.

Merlan, P. *From Platonism to Neoplatonism.* 3rd. ed., revised. The Hague: Martinus Nijhoff, 1968.

Miller, M.H. *Plato's Parmenides: The Conversion of the Soul.* Pennsylvania State University Press, 1991 (first ed. 1986).

O'Meara, D.J. *Pythagoras Revived: Mathematics and Philosophy in Late Antiquity.* Oxford: Clarendon Press, 1997 (first ed. 1989).

Rappe, S. *Reading Neoplatonism: Non-discursive Thinking in the Texts of Plotinus, Proclus, and Damascius.* Cambridge University Press, 2000.

Rist, J.M. "Mysticism and Transcendence in Later Neoplatonism." In *Platonism and its Christian Heritage,* 213-225. London: Variorum, 1985.

Schuon, F. "Rationalism, Real and Apparent." In *Logic and Transcendence*, translated by Peter N. Townsend, 33-55. London: Perennial Books, 1975.

—— "Concerning Pythagorean Numbers." In *The Eye of the Heart: Metaphysics, Cosmology, Spiritual Life*, 19-26. Bloomington, IN.: World Wisdom Books, 1997.

Shaw, G. "The Geometry of Grace: A Pythagorean Approach to Theurgy." In *The Divine Iamblichus: Philosopher and Man of Gods*, edited by H.J. Blumenthal and E.G. Clark, 116-137. Bristol, 1993.

—— *Theurgy and the Soul: The Neoplatonism of Iamblichus.* Pennsylvania State University Press, 1995.

Sheppard, A. *Studies on the 5th and 6th Essays of Proclus' Commentary on the Republic.* Hypomnemata, Vanderhoeck and Ruprecht in Gottingen, 1980.

—— "Proclus' Attitude to Theurgy." *Classical Quarterly* 32, no. 1 (1982): 212-224.

Smith, A. *Porphyry's Place in the Neoplatonic Tradition: A Study in Post-Plotinian Neoplatonism.* The Hague: Martinus Nijhoff, 1974.

Steel, C. "Iamblichus and the Theological Interpretation of the Parmenides." *Syllecta Classica* 8 (1998): 15-30. University of Iowa Press.

Taylor, T. *Thomas Taylor the Platonist: Selected Writings*, edited with introductions by Kathleene Raine and George Mills Harper. Princeton University Press, 1969.

Uždavinys, A. "Putting on the Form of the Gods: Sacramental Theurgy in Neoplatonism." *Sacred Web: A Journal of Tradition and Modernity* 5 (2000): 107-120.

—— "Between Sameness and Otherness: The Rediscovery of Tradition." *Sophia: The Journal of Traditional Studies* 7, no. 1 (Summer 2001): 117-145.

Wallis, R.T. *Neoplatonism*, 2nd ed., with a foreword and bibliography by Lloyd P. Gerson. Bristol Classical Press, 1992 (first ed. 1972).

BIOGRAPHICAL NOTES

ALGIS UŽDAVINYS is a research fellow at the Institute of Culture, Philosophy, and Arts, and Associate Professor at the Academy of Arts in his native Lithuania. He is a published scholar in English, French, and Lithuanian. His three most recent books (in Lithuanian) are *Hermeneutical Philosophy and Mystagogy of Proclus* (2002), *Hellenic Philosophy from Numenius to Syrianus* (2003), and *The Egyptian Book of the Dead* (2003). His research includes work on Hellenic philosophy, especially Platonism and Neoplatonism, as well as traditional mythology and metaphysics, Sufism, and traditional art. In 1998 he was awarded an honorary fellowship to the British Academy and was voted Art Critic of the Year by the Lithuanian Association of Artists. Dr. Uždavinys has also translated the works of Frithjof Schuon, Ananda Coomaraswamy, and Plotinus into Russian and Lithuanian. His work is regularly featured in the traditionalist journals *Sophia* and *Sacred Web*.

JOHN F. FINAMORE is Professor and Chair, Department of Classics, University of Iowa. His areas of research interest include Neoplatonic philosophy from Plotinus to Philoponus, Greek and Roman philosophy, and Roman poetry. His most recent publication is *Iamblichus' De Anima: Text, Translation, and Commentary* (with J.M. Dillon). Dr. Finamore also serves as President of the U.S. Section of the International Society of Neoplatonic Studies and is Editor for book manuscripts in Neoplatonism, Brill Press Series.

INDEX

Titles in the Treasures of the World's Religions series by World Wisdom

The Essential Vedānta: A New Source Book of Advaita Vedānta, edited
by Eliot Deutsch and Rohit Dalvi, 2004

For God's Greater Glory: Gems of Jesuit Spirituality,
edited by Jean-Pierre Lafouge, 2005

*The Golden Chain: An Anthology of Pythagorean and Platonic
Philosophy,* selected and edited
by Algis Uždavinys, 2004

*In the Heart of the Desert: The Spirituality of the Desert Fathers and
Mothers* by John Chryssavgis, 2003

Not of This World: A Treasury of Christian Mysticism,
compiled and edited by James S. Cutsinger, 2003

Zen Buddhism: A History, Part I: India and China
by Heinrich Dumoulin, 2005

Zen Buddhism: A History, Part II: Japan
by Heinrich Dumoulin, 2005